Henry Tullidge

Triumphs of the Bible,

With the Testimony of Science to its Truth

Henry Tullidge

Triumphs of the Bible,
With the Testimony of Science to its Truth

ISBN/EAN: 9783337035181

Printed in Europe, USA, Canada, Australia, Japan

Cover: Foto ©Lupo / pixelio.de

More available books at **www.hansebooks.com**

TRIUMPHS OF THE BIBLE,

WITH THE

TESTIMONY OF SCIENCE

TO ITS TRUTH.

BY

REV. HENRY TULLIDGE, A.M.

— νικῶν, καὶ ἵνα νικήσῃ.—Rev. vi. 2.

"Science may scale new heights and explore new depths, but she shall bring back nothing from her daring and successful excursions which will not, when rightly understood, yield a fresh tribute of Testimony to the Bible."—Melville's *Sermons.*

NEW YORK:
CHARLES SCRIBNER, 124 GRAND STREET.
1863.

JOHN F. TROW,
PRINTER, STEREOTYPER, AND ELECTROTYPER,
46, 48, & 50 Greene St., New York.

PREFACE.

The following pages are the result of an effort to produce a book of Christian Evidences, adapted to the exigencies of the times. Upon a subject which has occupied so many illustrious minds, and given birth to monuments of sanctified genius and learning that rank among the foremost achievements of the human intellect, it might be supposed that nothing more was needed. Yet rich as English literature is in defences of our faith, most of them were written with distinct reference to some particular errors which they opposed in their own day. They are still, and will ever remain, invaluable to the student, as depositories and armories of research and argument, but they are not directly available against the peculiar difficulties with which Christianity is now called to contend. The objections which are brought against the religion of the Bible at the present day, are of a very different character from those which were so conclusively met by the profound and masterly reasonings of Butler, Campbell, Paley, Leland, and others. The adversary has returned to the assault with far deeper artifices and more plausible disguises. "Forms of error more subtile than ever Ebionite propounded or Marcionite devised, are now silently producing their influence on thousands and tens of thousands who bear on their foreheads the baptismal cross of Christ."[1] "Infidelity of late," said Dr. Croly, "has changed its tone; it is no longer contemptuous, insulting, and audacious. It now assumes the pretence of reluctant doubt, laborious learning, and conscientious investigation. Yet more desperate corruptions of the truth of God, more profligate attempts to unsettle the soul, or a more inveterate passion to throw

[1] Ellicott's Hulsean Lectures, p. 21, Am. ed.

man into the grasp of moral death, were never exhibited in the most ostentatious periods of hostility to the Gospel." This warning, uttered fifteen years ago, had special reference to the rationalistic developments in Germany, though there were not wanting indications that the errors which were there full blown, had already been transplanted, in their germ at least, to England. It may now be said, that in the latter country, as in Germany before, scepticism has penetrated even into the Sanctuary, donned surplice, gown, and cassock, and speaks from university chairs and parish pulpits. And there also the divine authority of Revelation is the main object of attack. "One period," says a German writer, "has fought for Christ's sepulchre; another for his body and blood; the present period contends for his word." By these preachers of a Gospel "adapted to the wants of the nineteenth century," the Bible is not avowedly rejected. Honeyed words are spoken by them in its praise, and they even profess to esteem it, "as a whole, far the noblest collection of sacred works in the world." But its claim to be received as an inspired and infallible record of divine truth—"the law and the testimony"—they utterly set aside, and accept its most positive statements only so far as they accord with the oracle within.[1] The Bible, they will admit, contains a revelation, but human reason is to determine what is the truth communicated. As a mathematician would cast out the irrelevant from a treatise on geometry, so do they claim the prerogative, in virtue of a "heaven-taught conscience" and the possession of a "verifying faculty," to separate the human from the divine—to sift the chaff from the wheat of inspiration. The Bible is thus in effect made a kaleidoscope, to be turned and shaken at the fancy of every man who handles it, presenting at each turn a new and fanciful combination of ever-varying truth. The existence of absolute, unchanging truth, at least as connected with religion, they do not, indeed, appear to recognise. In their system, the received facts of Christianity are sublimated into ideas, while its doctrines, ever as occasion requires, are to be moulded and conformed to the "new and higher forms of modern thought."

[1] "The Scriptural writers," says the Rev. Dr. Rowland Williams, "after all, were but men, and the condition of mankind is imperfect. They spoke of old, but all old times represent, as it were, the childhood of the human race, and therefore had childish things which we must put away."—*Rational Godliness*, p. 294.

This school of error is apparently on the advance. The famous "Essays and Reviews" in which two years ago the fundamental verities of Christianity were impugned by ordained ministers of the Church of England, are now followed by a book written by a prelate of the same church (Dr. Colenso), in which he undertakes to demolish the authority of the Pentateuch and the Book of Joshua, and it is intimated that, in his next effort, he may possibly essay to prove the Gospels to be "unhistorical!" Truly prophetic is the description which Spenser gives of Doubt, as being clad in "a coat of strange disguise," with "*sleeves* dependant." Unlike the first illustrious missionary bishop to the heathen, one of his successors in the apostolate thus seeks to destroy the faith he was commissioned to proclaim. For it is vain to say that these "new views" are reconcilable with holding to the essential verities of the faith. The enlightened mind, whose moral and intellectual perceptions have not been clouded by the mephitic vapors of transcendentalism and ideology, clearly sees that the foundation is thus attacked, and that vital interests are at stake. If the sacred vessel that holds the water of life be shattered, its precious contents, spilt upon the ground, can never be gathered up again. The "bewildered friends" of Christianity may be unaware of their position. "With numb and icy fingers they may feel around the cross which they do not grasp," but their Gospel is not that of Paul and of John. If they are not "breaking down the carved work of the sanctuary with axes and hammers," they are assiduously engaged in undermining it. And for what? That they may overturn the grand and stately temple which through so many ages "the goodly fellowship of the prophets" and "the glorious company of the apostles" were employed in rearing for us, and of which God himself is the Architect, and raise up in its room the "ever-toppling fabrics of scepticism"—

"Cloud towers by ghostly masons wrought
In shadowy thoroughfares of thought."

In view of such developments, it is no wonder that the old enemies of the truth are beside themselves with delight. Their interpretation of these "unwonted signs" is that they betoken "the advent of a great spiritual reformation." In its traditional and accepted forms, they already assume Christianity to be a thing of the past; but they console those who would regret its "dying out" with the assurance that "a purer and brighter light is about to dawn upon us." "The gallant ship" (of Christian truth), loosed from "the chains of a dogmatic theology," is now prosecuting "a voyage of discovery and adventure on the dark waters of unknown seas, and the bright light of the rising sun illumines her pathway to the haven where she would be." Already, it would seem, that her prow must have "grated the golden isles" of doubt—that the great "discovery" had been made which the "prophetic spirit" of Emerson, the "deep insight" of Carlyle, and the "spiritual earnestness" of the younger Newman, so long have waited for. At least such joy is theirs

> "As when to them who sail
> Beyond the cape of Hope, and now are past
> *Mozambic*, off at sea northeast winds blow
> Sabean odors from the spicy shore
> Of Arabie the blest."

The exulting champion of scepticism does not hesitate to claim that "the whole mental food of the day—science, history, morals, poetry, fiction, and essay—is prepared by men who have long ceased to believe."[1] It does not appear, however, what it is that has supplied the place of that "old belief" in which such men as Bacon, Newton, and Locke found rest to their souls. There is doubtless great exaggeration in the above statement, which rather expresses the wish of the writer than the condition of things as it actually exists. Still it also contains much truth. And there is not a little in the "signs of the times" to occasion serious apprehension to those who stand by "the faith once delivered to the saints."

The believer knows, indeed, that the hopes and aspirations of scepticism are doomed to disappointment—knows that the cause of Zion is in safe hands. The bands of error that are now gathered against her battlements, like "the midnight host of spectres pale" that once, according to the wild old legend, "beleaguered the walls of Prague," will be scattered by the light of the Morning Star. And even though the enemy succeed in effecting a lodgment within the citadel—

> 'Duci intra muros . . . et arce locari'—

[1] Westminster Review.

yet will not that device avail to overthrow the Christian Ilium. "God is in the midst of her, she shall not be moved." As from the earliest times the Church has been infested by "false teachers" within her walls, as well as assaulted by foes without, and has ever triumphed over both, so will it be again. Could the Bible be overthrown, then, indeed, would her Palladium be lost; but as Archbishop Whateley says, "Scripture is in itself invulnerable; and they who attack it, do but dash themselves to pieces against a rock." Yet, though the Church and the Bible are secure, it is requisite, as far as possible, to prevent error from multiplying its victims. The snares of the enemy must be laid bare and his artifices exposed. And this will not be done by alleging that the battle of Christianity has been already fought and won—that the vindications of its truth, bequeathed to us by the strong champions of old, are unanswered and unanswerable. It is doubtless true that the objections and theories of modern unbelief are, mainly, but reproductions in novel forms of speculations whose fallacies were long since exposed. Thus the pantheism of Spinosa is revived in the oracular utterances of Emerson, and the "absolute religion" of Theodore Parker is but a prosaic version of Pope's Universal Prayer. The "Colossal man" theory of Intellectual progression seems to have been anticipated in Lord Bolingbroke's dictum that there was an "intuitive knowledge" in man, which constituted "a perpetual standing revelation, always made, always making, to all the sons of Adam." And so also the "difficulties" of the Bishop of Natal's book are but a revival of the old objections of Von Bohlen and Bruno Bauer, long ago met and answered by Hengstenberg and other great German scholars. Still, as a safeguard to those who might otherwise be led astray, such attacks must not be suffered to pass unnoticed. The battle must be fought over again, though substantially with the same weapons that have proved their efficiency in so many former conflicts. If the old works of evidence will not now be read, then new ones should be written with corresponding adaptations to the new modes of attack adopted by the enemy. And especially should means be taken to convince the promising youth in our halls of learning, that Christianity is fully able to "stand the light of the age in which we live" —that there is no such "unbridged chasm," as scepticism insinuates, between Science and Revelation. And though we cannot doubt, that God's watchful care and grace will be over his Church to the end of time, so that the gates of hell shall not finally prevail against it, yet it should also be considered, that the necessity of human exertion, so long as second causes shall form part of the Divine economy, will not therefore be superseded. If the sceptic will occupy himself in the task of ransacking all ancient and modern learning, for the purpose of discovering some flaw, some inconsistency, in the charter of our salvation, it is at least incumbent upon the Christian scholar who is "set for the defence of the Gospel," to exercise a like zeal and industry in behalf of a trust so sacred and so tremendously important. Moreover, as there is the authority of Bishop Butler for the statement that "the evidences of Christianity are a long series of things, reaching from the beginning of the world to the present time, of great variety and compass, taking in the direct and also the collateral proofs, and making up all of them together but one argument,"—it is obvious, that as the materials for that "argument" accumulate, they should be wrought in, in order that its strength, impregnability, and grandeur may be duly apprehended.

It is not proposed in the present work to survey the whole field of Christian Evidence, nor have I taken more than a passing glance at the great pillars of argument for the truth, such as the prophecies and miracles of the Bible, which have already been elaborated with such surpassing skill. The special object at which I have aimed has been to vindicate the truth and authority of the Divine Word, and prove its harmony with the discoveries of Science, while incidentally, replies are given to some of the more prominent and plausible objections of modern unbelief. In following out the plan adopted, I have endeavored, first, to show that the "Triumphs of the Bible," *i. e.* the resistance it has overcome and the marvels it has accomplished in the world, demonstrate it to be from God. This is designed as an introduction to the main portion of the work, of which the three opening chapters are occupied with proofs of the harmony of Physical Science with Revelation, while in the remainder of the book, the most thorough investigations of what in distinction may be termed Historical Science, are shown to utter a like testimony. The wonderful attestations to the truth of Scripture, which have been obtained in recent years from the "lands of the Bible," and by which its Historic Reality is vindicated against the Mythical School of Scepticism, are brought out in the closing chapters.

CONTENTS.

PART I.

TRIUMPHS OF THE BIBLE.

PART II.

TESTIMONY OF SCIENCE TO THE BIBLE.

PRELIMINARY.

CHAPTER I.

ASTRONOMY.

CHAPTER II.

GEOLOGY.

CHAPTER III.

PHYSICAL SCIENCE CONTINUED.

CHAPTER IV.

THE UNITY OF THE HUMAN RACE.

CHAPTER V.

SACRED CHRONOLOGY.

CHAPTER VI.

PRIMITIVE HISTORIC TRADITIONS.

CHAPTER VII.

ANCIENT HISTORY.

CHAPTER VIII.

OBJECTIONS AND REPLIES.

CHAPTER IX.

SACRED GEOGRAPHY—TOPOGRAPHICAL ACCURACY OF THE BIBLE.

CHAPTER X.

TOPOGRAPHICAL ACCURACY OF THE BIBLE (*Continued.*)

CHAPTER XI.

ARCHÆOLOGICAL DISCOVERIES—OLD TESTAMENT.

CHAPTER XII.

ARCHÆOLOGICAL DISCOVERIES—NEW TESTAMENT.

PART I.

TRIUMPHS OF THE BIBLE.

Among the numerous evidences of the divine origin of the Bible, which the progress of time has accumulated, the persevering opposition it has resisted and overcome, is not, perhaps, the least considerable. So many and formidable are the assaults it has sustained, that its preservation to this day unimpaired, is an unanswerable proof that One mightier than man must have watched over its safety and integrity. No book has been so attacked and no book has so triumphed as the Bible. Many a volume that once bid fair for immortality has gone down to oblivion. Of the unnumbered thousands that have been written since the dawn of literature, how few, even of those that once filled the trump of fame and were ranked among the chief productions of human genius, have escaped the ravages of time and the forgetfulness of man! Though the shelves of mighty libraries groan with the learned labors of the past, yet of the vast majority of the works therein deposited, it may be said, that "like the bodies of Egyptian kings in their pyramids, they retain only a grim semblance of life, amidst neglect, darkness, and decay." Upon the sacred oracles alone, the lapse of ages has gathered no rust. Time has not outdated them. They are as fresh and living now, as when prophets and apostles first indited their burning words, and their power and influence were never before so great as they are to-day. Since they were first given to the world, mighty empires have risen and decayed; proud capitals have flourished and fallen into ruin; numerous generations have come and gone; change and revolution have again and again swept over the globe; yet this citadel of our faith has survived the desolations of ages, unmutilated and undecayed. During these revolving centuries, the Bible has encountered every form of peril. The great men and the mighty men, kings and nations, pagans and papists, have sought its extirpation. Popes and priests have sought to corrupt and deface it, or to substitute monkish legends for its words of life. All that learning could discover, all that eloquence could allege, all that wit, cunning, and sophistry could contrive, have been brought to bear against it. The bowels of the earth and the region of the stars have been alike explored to furnish means for its overthrow. Yet all has been in vain. Thousands of its friends have suffered martyrdom in its defence, yet, like the mystic bush which it chronicles, it has remained unconsumed. The malignant rage of Antiochus, Decius, and Diocletian, and the labored arguments of Celsus and Porphyry, have been equally powerless against the Word of the Lord. In modern times, the philosophy of Hobbes, the sceptic doubts of Bayle, the polished sarcasm of Bolingbroke, the subtlety of Hume, the learning of Gibbon, the mockery of Voltaire, and the vulgarity of Paine, have all proved unable to invalidate a single statement of the prophets of Israel or the fishermen of Galilee. Like the ark of Noah, upborne and protected by the invisible hand of the Almighty, the Bible has safely ridden "the resistless tide which has set in from the birth of Time," and which is continually overwhelming man and his works. Commenced in the Arabian desert ages before Homer sang, and finished fifteen hundred years afterward on an island in the Ægean Sea, it has come down to us from that remote antiquity unscathed and entire, like the fabled pillars of Seth, which are said to have bid defiance to the flood that swept all things else away. As Sir Thomas Browne has said, "The Bible is too hard for the tooth of time. It cannot perish, but in the general flames, when all things shall confess their ashes." "The grass withereth, and the flower thereof falleth away; but the word of the Lord endureth forever."

This wonderful preservation presents a twofold argument for the Bible. Its heavenly origin is vindicated by the intense and unremitting hostility it has encountered, and by its success in overcoming it. For it is impossible to assign that hostility to any other cause than the disclosures which it makes respecting the extreme deadliness of sin, and of the ineffable purity and justice of the Divine nature. These are the stumbling blocks which have in all ages elicited the enmity of the human heart and arrayed against it such powerful and numerous adversaries. Let it then be even supposed that the unaided genius of man could have produced such a volume as the Bible, displaying, as it confessedly does, in the judgment even of its enemies,[1] such sublimity of thought, such knowledge of the heart, and such amazing depth of wisdom; is it likely that writers of so extraordinary capacity would have given characteristics to their work which render it an object of such deep and widespread aversion? that they would have been so weak as to represent God and human nature in characters unpalatable to the natural man, and most of

[1] The infidel Rousseau was constrained to utter such an eulogium as the following: "The majesty of the Scriptures strikes me with astonishment. Look at the volumes of all the philosophers, with all their pomp, how contemptible do they appear in comparison with this! Is it possible that a book at once so simple and sublime can be the work of man?"

all, on the supposition that they were impostors, unpalatable to themselves? Such a mixture of weakness and wisdom, we must at once see to be incongruous and impossible.

And the fact of the Bible's preservation in the midst of all this hostility; that it should stand unto this day, amid the wreck of all that is human, substantially entire in every part, is an argument for its divinity which no sophistry of infidelity can explain or overthrow. "The resistance of ages is its crowning legitimation. It is felt and feared by all the rulers of the darkness of this world. It is the visible battle-field of invisible forces, showing in the radiant faces of the martyrs who have died for it, and the unearthly struggles of those who have hunted it from the earth, what mysterious interests are suspended on its safety or destruction." "For could we but see a volume bearing marks of all that these holy oracles have passed through, what should we behold but an ancient volume exhibiting signs of having been at one time trampled on by rage, at another moth-eaten by neglect; now interpolated by error, then erased by pride; here, scorched by the fires of bigotry; there, stained with the venom of infidelity; in every page, sprinkled with the blood of its martyred defenders; and yet so substantially entire in every part as to show that it has always been in the keeping of Omnipotence—in the hollow of His hand."

There are yet other considerations germane to the above argument, which yield a testimony, perhaps little less convincing, of the divine origin of the Bible. "The Scripture itself," says Dean Trench, "is full of remembrances of its own power. He who, tolerably well acquainted with the history of the Church, with the struggles which accompanied the unfolding, fixing, and vindicating of her dogma,—he who, furnished with this knowledge, passes over Scripture, may in some moods of his mind pass over it as a succession of battle-fields. He may be likened to a traveller journeying through some land which, by the importance of its position or the greatness of its attractions, has drawn contending hosts to its soil, and been a battle ground for innumerable generations. Besides, in all those pages which speak more directly to himself, they are eloquent to him with a thousand stirring recollections. For at every step which he advances, he recognizes that which has been the motive of some mighty and long-drawn conflict, in which the keenest and brightest intellects, the kingliest spirits, the Bernards and the Abelards of their day, were engaged. Here, there, and everywhere, be it that he wanders among the extinguished volcanoes of controversies which have now burned themselves out, or among those which are flaming still, he meets with that, to maintain their conviction about which, men have been content to spend their lives, to make shipwreck of their worldly hopes, have dwelt in deserts, in caves, and in dungeons, yea, gladly have encountered all from which nature most, and most naturally shrinks. And whatever there may have been of earthly and of carnal mingling in the motives of the combatants, however in some of them he can recognize only the champions of error, yet in these mighty and passionate strivings, in these conflicts which generation has bequeathed to generation, he reads the confession which all past ages have borne, that this Word was worth contending for,—being felt by those worthiest to judge, dearer than life itself, and such that things else were cheap by comparison with it."

It would, however, convey a very imperfect view of the triumphs of the Bible, if we confined our attention to its having survived the ordeal of all-conquering Time, and escaped uninjured the hostility of its numerous and persevering enemies, together with the undying interest it has excited in the noblest intellects of successive generations. The Bible is the document of Christianity, and is indeed identified with it; for we need not repel the imputation of the infidel, though intended as a sneer, that ours is a "Book revelation." The wonderful results that Book has achieved, and is still achieving in the world, regarding it as the armory of the Church's weapons, or rather as the conductor of those holy influences through which the Church has won all her triumphs, afford a sufficient reply, as well as additional and unanswerable demonstration of its heavenly origin.

First among these is *the propagation of Christianity.* We cannot imagine an instrumentality in itself more utterly inadequate to the effect, than when the first preachers of the Gospel, "with no diadem but the crown of thorns, no sword but the sword of the Spirit," went forth to subdue the nations to the obedience of Christ. A little company of poor, friendless fishermen, what were they, to contend against all the prejudices, sins, and follies of mankind, the weight of learned authority, the advantages of birth, the edicts of the civil power,—in a word, against the combined hostility of the world? The Gospel was a stumbling block to the Jew, and to the Greek foolishness. How could the haughty Pharisee and the worldly minded Sadducee welcome a religion which destroyed their hopes and humbled their pride? which required them to recognize the promised Son of David in the lowly Nazarene, and renouncing their delusive expectations of earthly conquest and dominion under the banner of Messiah, to embrace a life of poverty, self-denial, and persecution? No wonder they turned from it with scorn and loathing. Nor were less difficulties to be encountered in the Gentile world. There a cruel and licentious idolatry reigned supreme. It has been said, indeed, that the spirit of Polytheism was "mild and tolerant;" which being granted, it might be inferred that in it Christianity would find no obstacle. The tolerance of the heathen, however, as in the case of the Romans, only extended to the occasional adoption, from motives of imagined interest, of the gods of the countries which they conquered, recognising them as the tutelary deities of their particular districts. The prevailing sentiment of antiquity was that which is depicted by the caustic pen of Juvenal:

> "Summus utrinque
> Inde furor vulgo, quod numina vicinorum
> Odit uterque locus, quum solus credat habendos
> Esse deos, quos ipse colit."[1]—*Sat.* xv.

The crime for which Socrates suffered martyrdom in refined and polished Athens, was the promulgation of purer doctrines concerning God and Providence. Cicero but uttered the voice of Roman opinion when he pronounced it "among the most necessary laws of every wise state, that no one, not excepting strangers, should be allowed to offer worship to any gods excepting such as had received a public recognition." If the religion of Jesus could have admitted of a compromise—could have consented on the same terms with the worshippers of Isis and Mithras, to share the empty honors of a statue or an altar, the obstacles in the way of its acknowledgment might have been overcome. But, at the bidding of a few unlettered men, to displace the Jupiter of the Capitol for the Crucified of Judea—yea, to hurl from their seats all the deities of the Pantheon, and account their whole religious system, though sanctioned by tradition, hallowed by patriotism, and radiant with unrivalled attractions of poetry and art, as a tissue of fraud and fable, this was a requirement which

[1] Between two neighboring towns, a deadly hate,
Sprung from a sacred grudge of ancient date,
Yet flames; a hate no lenience can assuage,
No time subdue, a rooted, rancorous rage!
Blind bigotry, at first, the evil wrought,
For each despis'd the other's gods, each thought
Its own the true, the genuine, in a word,
The only deities to be adored."—GIFFORD'S *Trans.*

excited the astonishment and hatred of the heathen world, and especially incensed the pride and arrogance of Rome. In the schools of philosophy also, fresh difficulties were to be met. Those schools were at this time more frequented than ever, and the Portico and the Grove at Athens were the acknowledged thrones of the intellectual world. Beneath the spell of the subtile and dazzling theories which were there elaborated, all the cultivated minds of heathendom cringed in willing thraldom. How vain then, apparently, to expect that the disciples of Plato and Aristotle would exchange their lofty speculations, reaching "beyond the utmost bounds of human thought," for the humbling tenets of a religion which taught that "the wisdom of this world is foolishness with God!" Another element of opposition to the pure and uncompromising Gospel, was found in the vices of an age which, according to all the pictures that have been drawn of it, seems to have exceeded the usual measure of corruption. Amid much exterior refinement, morality was unknown, and the most detestable vices everywhere prevailed. The world was one great temple of pollution. "Darkness covered the earth and gross darkness the people." They did not "like to retain God in their knowledge," and He had given them up to a "reprobate mind." Statesmen, philosophers, and priests, not less than the great body of the people, were shamelessly depraved. Their very amusements, the gladiatorial shows, eagerly attended by women as well as men, in which hundreds and thousands of human victims were

"Butchered to make a Roman holiday!"

sufficiently prove the brutality of their manners and the hardness of their hearts. These human victims, be it also noted, were fed on a succulent diet for some weeks previous to the exhibition, in order that their veins, being full, might bleed more freely, for the greater gratification of the spectators! The other leading nation of antiquity was not, indeed, stained with the cruelty which, it has been said, asserted the presence of the wolf's milk in the moral constitution of the masters of the world; but Greeks as well as Romans, not only practised, but gloried in abominations which we cannot even execrate by name. Such was the character of nations among whom the arts and literature flourished; and facts confirm what might reasonably be inferred, that nothing could be found in barbarian lands to relieve the sombre shades of the picture. If without the vices of a corrupt civilization, other nations were under the spell of idolatries far more revolting—

> "Things worse
> Than fables yet have feigned or fear conceived—
> Gorgons and hydras, and chimeras dire."

Where science and literature had shed their light, there was a point of approach, something to which the teachers of the new faith could appeal. But here "a darkness that might be felt," apparently rendered access hopeless.

When we consider that such were the obstacles to be overcome, and contrast with them the intrinsic feebleness of the instrumentality employed, nothing would appear more hopeless than the success of the Gospel. Yet in the face of all this complicated opposition, the heralds of the Cross went forward undaunted and undismayed. They allowed of no compromise with sin, but proclaimed the wrath of God against all "ungodliness and unrighteousness of men." Mahomet could allure followers to his standard by the promise of a paradise of sensuality;[1] but

[1] "The progress of Mahometanism is in full contrast," says Bishop Wilson, "in all its causes and characteristics, with that of the Christian faith. It arose in the seventh century among a warlike people, in an age of gross darkness; was founded by a person of one of the best families of his country; it was composed of Jewish legends, and the popular superstitions of Arabia, mingled with sentiments and doctrines gathered from the Christian Scrip-

they required their disciples to "crucify the flesh with the affections and lusts," and to "follow holiness." They enforced upon all, without distinction, upon Greek and barbarian, bond and free, learned and unlearned, the same necessity of seeking pardon through a crucified Saviour and the relinquishment of every other ground of hope toward God. And what was the result? Mighty as were the obstructions, and seemingly weak and inadequate as were the instruments, yet those weak instruments triumphed, and those obstructions gave way. The plant which grew out of a dry place became beautiful and glorious; and the stone which the builders rejected was made the head of the corner. Ere the apostles were all of them gathered to their rest, "their line had gone out through all the earth and their words to the ends of the world." Before a century had elapsed, Pliny, writing to

tures; and proposing a code of morals comparatively lax, together with sensual and voluptuous recompenses—in other words, it was a religion adapted to the corrupt taste, indulgent to the passions, and modelled to the ignorance of the times. In all these respects it illustrates, by the contrast, the purity and beneficence and sublimity of the Christian doctrine. Mahomet, further, was entirely destitute of credentials—no miracles were even alleged—he pretended to no prophecies—no seal, therefore, of divine authority was appended to his claims. Whatever success then may have attended a debased and vicious religion, resting on no one attestation of a divine original, but simply courting the passions of an age of ignorance and depravity, can never be placed in competition with the doctrine of Christianity. But Mahometanism, be it noted, had, after all, no success, so long as the peaceful means of persuasion and argument were alone employed; whereas Christianity converted the whole world by meek instruction and patient suffering. Mahometanism failed of making any progress, till it renounced the arts of peace, and unsheathed the sword. The design of the Koran was, as we have observed, not to propagate a religion but to form soldiers, and inspire martial courage; and it was in this way that it obtained prevalence and prosperity. It followed in the train of armies and was propagated at the edge of the scimitar. Such a contrast displays in yet brighter lustre the mild glory of that doctrine which, unaided by human power, and in the midst of sufferings and contempt, surpassed, in the extent and splendor of its conquests, all the sanguinary conversions of the false prophet."—*Evidences of Christianity*, vol. i, p. 225.

the emperor Trajan, reports, that "the contagion of the superstition had seized, not cities only, but the lesser towns also, and the open country; so that the heathen temples were almost forsaken; few victims were purchased for sacrifice, and a long intermission of the sacred rites had taken place." The most refined and remorseless cruelty was employed by the Roman tyrants to stay the progress of the "superstition," but in vain. Fifty years after Pliny wrote, Tertullian, addressing the rulers of the empire, could affirm: "We were but of yesterday, and have filled your cities, islands, towns, and boroughs, the camp, the senate, and the forum. They (the heathen adversaries of Christianity) lament that every sex, age, and condition, and persons of every rank also, are converts to that name." Torture and death were employed with redoubled zeal, but "the blood of the martyrs was still the seed of the Church," until at length the hard-fought field was won. Within three centuries from the death of Christ, the triumphant banner of the Cross was erected on the ruins of the Capitol, and the fanes of heathenism, purified from their idolatries, became temples of the Christian's God. And not only were the oracles hushed, and Jupiter and Apollo with their Olympian compeers driven from their shrines,—now

—"Domos Ditis vacuas et inania regna."—*Æn.* vi, 269.

but philosophy yielded her proud pretensions to that "light divine," which alone can guide the pilgrim of earth on his dim and perilous way. Not only the outcast, the poor, and the ignorant, but the learned and the gifted, the men of intellectual might, surrendered their most cherished convictions, and renounced all hopes of worldly advancement, to embrace a faith whose rewards are beyond the tomb. "Spain heard the Gospel voice; far-off Britain, and those northward and inclement Scandinavian shores, which the lordly Roman shivered when he named, listened to its call; Egypt, Ethiopia, and North Africa had apostolic missionaries; Gaul bowed to the Cross; the inhuman superstitions of the Druids faded before its gentle lessons; the bloody war-gods of the Goths were given up for the rule of the Prince of Peace; wild Arab tribes and fierce men of Parthia and Bactria were among the converts; India was not so distant, but some gleams of that primitive light reached her coral strand; many a strange tongue swelled the Church's anthems; and the noble army of martyrs bore the blood-sprinkled banner farther than imperial legions had ever carried the victorious standards of Rome."

Yet the infidel would account for this wide-extended spiritual conquest by the operation of merely human means. The historian Gibbon has exhausted his learning and ability in endeavoring to assign causes, which, apart from supernatural agency accompanying the preaching of the Word, would explain so mighty a revolution. But they are manifestly inadequate. Not "the intolerant zeal of the Christians," or "the clear development of the doctrine of another life," or "the miraculous powers ascribed to the primitive Church," or "the pure and austere morals of its members," or even "the new discipline of the Christian Community," can account for the fact that a religion which entered the world at a most inauspicious period, supposing it to be an imposture—which had not one principle in common with the religions which then obtained—propagated by a few obscure persons, universally despised and hated, opposed from the very first by Jew and Gentile, and especially by those who held the seats of power and influence—a religion hostile to human opinion, human prejudice, human interest, and human nature, should have triumphed over all opposition, and, after the lapse of eighteen centuries, still have maintained its ground. Surely we are warranted by every sound principle of reason in inferring, that such an effect must be due to supernatural power. "A flame living on the very bosom of the deep, opposed by all the winds of heaven, often obscured, nearly extinguished, always resisted, yet rising from apparent exhaustion and decay into new brightness, enlarging the circle on which it shines age after age, and smiling on the elements which are battling against its existence, must be sustained by ethereal fires."

Had the great work gone on according to its glorious commencement, the world would have been won, long ages since, to the faith of Christ. Long since would He who "tasted death for every man" have been acknowledged and adored by all. But too soon the Gospel's triumphant career was checked. Though there were in every age zealous witnesses for the truth—for never has the lamp of God gone out in the temple of the Lord—yet as a whole, the Church became unfaithful to her trust, ceased to make war on the territories of sin and death, and a night of a thousand years overshadowed the earth.

That long night passed away, and Zion has risen from the dust. Her slumbering energies have been again aroused to grapple with the mighty work committed to her by her ascended Lord. With the dawn of the present century, she again set forth on her errand of mercy, and has pledged herself to rest no more, until the world has been leavened with the truth and won for Christ. And gladdening results have shown that the Gospel is still mighty through God to the pulling down the strongholds of sin and Satan. Wherever the Cross has been lifted up, it has still proved a "conquering sign," and from the region and shadow of death, among the dark places of the earth and the habitations of cruelty, has won its triumphs and its trophies as of old. Look in what direction we may, the horizon of hope enlarges and brightens. The ancient systems of idolatry and superstition have become effete, Mahometanism wanes and "the Cross alone is crescent." Much land indeed remaineth to be possessed, and to a merely human view, the obstacles which still impede the universal triumph of the Gospel would even now seem insuperable. So arduous are the difficulties yet to be overcome, so numerous are the strongholds yet to be overthrown, that the enterprise which aims at such a result must appear to a worldly mind more than all others romantic, chimerical, and absurd. But the Christian is encouraged to believe that the same Power which of old wrought such wonders through feeble instrumentalities, is now, in like manner, preparing to achieve a triumph vastly more glorious. It has been said that "the Old Book, the Book of our Redeemer's gift and our fathers' faith, ... has been gradually ascending; taking to it new tongues, spreading open its page in every land, printed in Chinese camps, pondered in the Red man's wigwam, sought after in Benares, a school book in Feejee, eagerly bought in Constantinople, loved in the kloofs of Kaffir land; while the voices of the dead from Assyria to Egypt have been lifted up to bear it witness." What earthly or infernal might can arrest its progress or hinder its predicted triumph? "It shall come—that long-expected hour—when Christianity is to attain universal dominion. The march around Jericho shall have an end; the mystic seven shall all have been reckoned; and then shall God specially inspire the Church with a spirit of expectation and prayer, so that a loud shout shall be raised, as though, in ceasing to weary earth with their tread, the thousands had resolved to invade heaven with their voices. And God will answer the cry of His people. He will recompense that patient trust which has been displayed, century after century, in the encompassing the city, and assailing it with no carnal weapons. On a sudden shall there be a mighty interference; the temples of idols shall crumble into dust; every form and feature of falsehood shall vanish away; every household and every heart shall be a shrine for Christian truth; and when the vast revolution is surveyed, and its producing cause demanded by those who would understand the dealings of God, the answer—the triumphant answer will be: "By faith the walls of Jericho fell down, when they were compassed about seven days."

"The powers of darkness on the hills afar
Watch for the sun, and bend the listening ear
To catch the rumbling of the distant car,
And ever and anon start up in fear,
As echo whispers of his coming near.
Hark! how they wail their tottering shrines around,
Warning the slumbering idols as they go.
See, pale and trembling at the distant sound,
Baal boweth down, and Nebo stoopeth low,
And haughty Dagon wails his final overthrow."

An argument akin to the foregoing, yet distinct from it, is found in the *temporal benefits* which Christianity has already conferred upon the world. These still further illustrate the triumphs and vindicate the divinity of the Bible. Facts innumerable can be adduced to prove that, in whatever place and under whatever circumstances man's lot may be cast, he needs the Gospel, even that he may participate in the comforts and blessings of the present life.

In order that the strength of this argument may be adequately demonstrated, it will be necessary to take a fuller and more comprehensive view of a subject already briefly glanced at, in enumerating the active elements of opposition to the propagation of the Gospel. We have only to compare the two most polished and refined of ancient nations with modern and Christian, in order to perceive what the religion of the Bible can accomplish even for the present welfare of man.

The materials for the comparison are derived from the valuable Boyle lectures of Mr. Harkness, in which every particular statement is verified by references to standard classical authorities.

"Athens," says Mr. H., "was acknowledged to have been the most lenient government of antiquity. Yet the mind that is refined to gentleness and pity by the spirit of the Gospel, can scarcely bear to dwell on the ruthless exercise of dominion, which is exhibited in the pages of its history. The tyranny exercised by the Athenian people over those who were subject to their control, surpasses description or belief. No accumulations of reproachful epithet, or opprobrious metaphor, could compass their savage abuses of authority. The despotism of one is bad: but the despotism of many is incalculably worse. Not to mention their wanton acts of cruelty, of caprice, of aggression, and of injustice, which were as familiar with them—perhaps more familiar—than with any of the most sanguinary tyrants, whose names are infamous in the annals of mankind; but to confine myself strictly to the enormities, which originated in their political morals, we shall find by looking at the conduct of that brilliant people, that the vaunted democracy of Athens was animated by all the selfish passions, was directed by all the narrow principles, was supported by all the ignominious arts and iniquitous precautions, which characterize the dominion of the despot. No Dionysius or Agathocles ever exhibited a more timid and ungenerous suspicion of his subjects, or followed up his suspicions with more of the oppressive vigilance of terror. Riches were objects of jealousy: they might be made the means of obtaining too commanding an influence in the republic; and the wealthy existed, therefore, in a state of constant persecution and alarm. 'While I had riches,' says Charmides, 'I was obliged to caress every informer. Some imposition was continually laid upon me; and I was never allowed to travel or be absent from the city. Now I am poor, I look big, and threaten others; the rich are afraid of me; I am become a kind of tyrant in the city.'[1] Fame was an object of jealousy: nothing of excellence, or wealth, or reputation, might, with impunity, overtop the level of the democracy. The unrelenting people proscribed every superiority as a thing of dangerous consequence. The same cautious politics produced the Ostracism of Athens, and the Petaleum of Syracuse, and expelled every citizen whose fame or power overtopped the rest. Virtue was an object of jealousy; and so susceptible was the prudence of their tyranny, that it instigated them to attack even the honorable distinctions which recompense superior integrity and purity of life; and Aristides was banished for the celebrity of his justice."

Hume, in his Essays, gives the following account of an accomplished Athenian: "I think I have fairly made it appear, that an Athenian man of merit might be such a one as with us would pass for incestuous, a parricide, an assassin, an ungrateful perjured traitor, and something else too abominable to be named; not to mention his rusticity and ill manners. And, having lived in this manner, his death might be entirely suitable; he might conclude the scene by a desperate act of self-murder, and die with the most absurd blasphemies in his mouth. And, notwithstanding all this, he shall have statues, if not altars, erected to his memory; poems and orations shall be composed in his praise; great sects shall be proud of calling themselves by his name; and the most distant posterity shall blindly continue their admiration. Though, were such a one to

[1] Xenophon, Banquet of Socrates.

arise among themselves, they would justly regard him with horror and execration."

To exhibit a corresponding picture of Roman manners, Mr. H. presents his readers with the observations of a Christian stranger, who might have visited Rome in the first century after our Saviour's ministry on earth:

"The door of the house in which he is received, to the distress of every Christian sentiment, is opened by a chained slave. He is conducted to the master of the house, who is at supper, and is invited to take a place at the banquet. Instead of that liberal equality which has been introduced by the general prevalence of the Christian dispensation, and which has smoothed the irregularities of society, and rendered persons of a more distinguished opulence and rank attentive to the sensibilities of the poorer and more humble classes of society, he finds the inferior guests studiously reminded of their subordinate condition, removed to a distance from the luxurious table of the master of the feast, aud insulted by the offensive coarseness of their entertainment. During a scene of the greatest gluttony and intemperance, he is opprest, as the spirits of the party become elevated, by the most appalling licentiousness of conversation. A father speaks of the difficulty he had found in persuading his wife to the murder of their new born infant. The young men boast of their successful rapes, their perilous adulteries, or their unnatural attachments. Disgusted with these appalling circumstances, the Christian visitor might omit remarking on the unbridled sensuality with which his new companions surrender themselves to the protracted pleasures of the table, as if to eat were the first privileges of existence, and they had artificially increased their appetites, that they might lengthen their capacity of indulgence. Wearied of such society, he retires to his chamber, but not to rest; for his repose is broken by the noise of whips and lashes, and the cries of the chastised slaves, whom the master of some neighboring mansion is rigorously correcting. In the morning he prepares to accompany his host to the exhibitions of the Circus. As they are departing from the house, an aged and half-starved slave timidly endeavors to elude their observation; he is detected; his master notices his infirmities, and orders that he should no longer be retained as an unprofitable expense and incumbrance to his household, but should be exposed to die of starvation, in recompense for the labors of his youth. The Christian remonstrates against this act of cruelty; he assures his host that not a single individual of his own religion would be guilty of such barbarity, even to one of the inferior creatures—to the aged hound, or the drooping war horse—if it had been serviceable to his interests or his amusements. The heathen cannot comprehend his sentiments. He informs his guest that this is the usual method of disposing of all superannuated domestics; that some masters suffer them to starve to death about their houses; that others leave them to perish on an island in the Tiber; that others cast them alive into their preserves to fatten their fish; that, in short, the practice was universal among his countrymen, and adopted without remorse, sanctioned by the example of the illustrious Cato, and one from which, as it was extremely convenient, he could see no reason for departing. The Christian is silenced; they proceed to the theatre. On their way, they pass a company of Patrician youths, one of whom is on the point of exhibiting his dexterity in the use of the broad-sword. A poor wretch, suffering from the deep afflictions of domestic misery, has been bribed, by the offer of a few minæ, to devote himself as the victim of the barbarous experiment, on condition that the necessities of his family should be relieved by the stipulated purchase-money of his murder. They arrive at the Coliseum. There is great difficulty in securing situations. Nearly forty thousand persons are already impatiently assembled. It is a day of extraordinary expectation. Many celebrated gladiators are to be brought on the arena. It is anticipated that some hundreds will be slaughtered in the various conflicts which are appointed to succeed each other in the progress of the entertainment; but a more than usual curiosity and interest is excited for those contests, in which the ill-fated wretches are to be exposed in opposition to the wild beasts of the desert or the forest, as on this occasion the lions and the panthers have been fed on human flesh, for the purpose of sharpening their thirst of blood, and stimulating the keenness of their ferocity. Unable to sustain the sight—while the first victim is expiring, unpitied and unregarded, amid the thunders of acclamation that reward the exertions of his competitor—the Christian visitor of the heathen capital hastily withdraws himself from the scene of sanguinary festival. He is immediately followed by his host, who ridicules his compassion on the authority of the most approved philosophers, and interrupts his eloquent lamentations over the departure of the ancient virtue and simplicity of the Roman character, by assurances, that the people have not degenerated; that vice may have varied in its form, but not increased in magnitude; that its ratio has been permanent and equal; and that, whatever enormities may have been engendered of power and luxury and refinement, at all events, those ruder ages could never be deserving of regret, during which a supposed pestilence, that appeared to be depopulating the city, was discovered to be effected by the prevalency of the art of poisoning; a practice which was so accordant to the morals and sentiments of the people, that the prætor in a single province, after having capitally punished three thousand persons for the offence, still complained of the increasing number of the accusations.

"In the above sketch of the private morals of the ancient Romans, I have studiously cast a veil over that horrible and undisguised impurity which saturated the whole body of society; which haunted the precincts of their temples; which mingled with their religious rites and festivals; which so frequently made the subject of their conversation and their poetry; which addressed the grossness of the public mind in the signs exhibited in their streets, and in the monuments that defiled their gardens, and of which the images were constantly before the eyes, to pollute and debase the soul, engraved on the common utensils of daily existence, on their lamps and their vases and their drinking vessels."

Such was the social condition of those celebrated nations, ere the Gospel had put forth among them its renovating power and purified the fountains of domestic life. In the monuments of sanctified benevolence alone with which Christian lands are studded, we have abundant evidence of the tendency of Christianity to confer blessings upon man.

"Her coming found the heathen world without a single house of mercy. Search the Byzantine Chronicles and the pages of Publius Victor; and though the one describes all the public edifices of ancient Constantinople, and the other of ancient Rome, not a word is to be found in either of a charitable institution. Search the ancient marbles in your museums; descend and ransack the graves of Herculaneum and Pompeii; and question the many travellers who have visited the ruined cities of Greece and Rome; and see, if amid all the splendid remains of statues and amphitheatres, baths and granaries, temples, aqueducts and palaces, mausoleums, columns and triumphal arches, a single fragment or inscription can be found, telling us that it belonged to a refuge for human want, or for the alleviation of human misery."[1] All the asylums on earth for poverty, decrepi-

[1] Dr. Harris's "Great Commission." The progress of the moral triumph which Christianity ultimately achieved in Rome is thus finely delineated in the great work of Dean Milman: "Rome must be imagined in the vastness and uniformity of its social condition, the mingling and confusion of races,

tude and disease, are to be traced to the influence of the Bible. Yet this is but a small part of the benefits it has conferred on all those countries where it has been received and according to the degree in which it has prevailed. What but the religion of the Bible has banished vices and abominations of classic Paganism, practised and avowed by the great and the respected, to hide themselves from public scorn, if they still exist upon earth? What else has abolished serfdom in modern Europe, and is bringing on the time, slowly it may be, but surely, when whatever inequalities of condition may still exist, man shall universally recognize a brother in man?[1] And though it has not yet made wars to cease, what else has softened war's horrors and rendered comparatively unheard of the barbarities of

languages, conditions, in order to conceive the slow, imperceptible, yet continuous progress of Christianity. Amid the affairs of the universal empire, the perpetual revolutions which were constantly calling up new dynasties, or new masters over the world, the pomp and state of the imperial palace, the commerce, the business flowing in from all parts of the world, the bustle of the Basilicas, or courts of law, the ordinary religious ceremonies, or the more splendid rites on signal occasions, which still went on, if with diminishing concourse of worshippers, with their old sumptuousness, magnificence and frequency, the public games, the theatres, the gladiatorial shows, the Lucullan or Apician banquets, Christianity was gradually withdrawing from the heterogeneous mass some of all orders, even slaves, out of the vices, the ignorance, the misery of that corrupted social system. It was instilling humanity, yet unknown, or coldly commended by an impotent philosophy, among men and women whose infant ears had been habituated to the shrieks of dying gladiators; it was giving dignity to minds prostrated by years, almost centuries, of degrading despotism; it was nurturing purity and modesty of manners in an unspeakable state of deprivation; it was enshrining the marriage-bed in a sanctity long almost entirely lost, and rekindling to a steady warmth the domestic affections; it was substituting a simple, calm and rational faith and worship for the worn-out superstitions of heathenism; gently establishing in the soul of man the sense of immortality, till it became a natural and inextinguishable part of his moral being." Latin Christianity, vol. i, p. 26.

[1] "Christianity," the profound De Tocqueville has remarked, "is the companion of liberty in all its conflicts—the cradle of its infancy, and the divine source of its claims."

former conflicts? What has raised the female sex from the degraded position which they still occupy in lands unblessed with the light of revelation? What has united liberty and law, and thrown a sanction and security around the rights and possessions of the weak and the defenceless, the widow and the orphan, which did not formerly exist? What has shed such benign efficacy on the social relationships of life, on the ties which bind together husband and wife, parent and child, and thus made "home" a sacred electric word? The only answer that can be given is, that it is the religion of the Bible which has scattered such countless blessings in its path. Nothing else will explain these beneficent changes but the cause which the eminent Chancellor Kent thus assigns: "The influence of Christianity has been very efficient toward the introduction of a better and more enlightened sense of right and justice among the several governments of Europe. It taught the duty of benevolence to strangers, of humanity to the vanquished, of the obligation of good faith,—of the sin of murder, revenge, and rapacity. The history of Europe, during the earlier periods of modern history, abounds with interesting and strong cases, to show the authority of the Church over turbulent princes and fierce warriors, and the effect of that authority in meliorating manners, checking violence, and introducing a system of morals which inculcated peace, moderation, and justice."[1] Where the Bible is unknown, man is still sunk in debasing ignorance, idolatry and superstition, "without God and without hope in the world." Where it is unknown, woman is still degraded and enslaved, and infanticide and other crimes against nature, are tolerated if not enjoined. Wherever it has come, like the healing gale of spring changing the scene of wintry desolation into one of life and loveliness, it has caused the moral desert to rejoice and blossom as the rose. It has renovated the character of individuals, fami-

[1] Kent's Commentaries, vol. i, p. 9.

lies, and nations; and in the proportion in which its influence has been felt, it has banished sin and misery from the abodes of men. "Give me," said the old Christian father Lactantius, "a man who is choleric, abusive in his language, headstrong and unruly; with a very few words,—the words of God,—I will render him as gentle as a lamb. Give me a greedy, covetous, parsimonious man, and I will presently return him you a generous creature, freely bestowing his money by handfuls. Give me a cruel and bloodthirsty man; instantly his ferocity shall be transformed into a truly mild and merciful disposition. Give me an unjust man, a foolish man, a sinful man; and on a sudden he shall become honest, wise, and virtuous. So great is the efficacy of divine wisdom when once admitted into the human heart." In what innumerable instances has that pledge been redeemed! Bringing with it "the promise of the life that now is," as well as "of that which is to come," Christianity diffuses order and happiness over the whole surface of human society, and even adds features of additional loveliness to the scenery of nature. "The swamp and the morass disappear before the labors of industry and the habitations of men. The pride of cities and the monuments of art now dazzle and surprise, where nothing was once beheld but the rude cairn, piled in loneliness and silence to mark the scene consecrated to infernal offerings, and rights of pollution and death. Temples and palaces glitter amidst the waste, and commerce gladdens with her ships, her harbors and her merchandise, shores once abandoned to solitude and desolation. Ferocity gives place to gentleness, sterility to beauty; and while it changes the desert into fruitfulness, it elevates the savage into a man." And all this is even now being exemplified. In lands which but a few years since lay in heathen darkness—where devils were worshipped and crime was hallowed—where men roved untamed as the beasts of their forests, and revelled in deeds of cruelty and bloodshed,—under the auspices of Christian missionaries, this blessed transformation may even now be seen. Thousands of once wretched beings, emerging from their moral degradation, at this moment are ascribing their enfranchisement to that benign interposition. The rude Bushman of South Africa, the painted savage of Polynesia, advanced to the privileges and blessings of civilized life, are living witnesses of what the religion of the Bible can accomplish even for man's temporal welfare. And if a tree is known by its fruits, may we not confidently point to such effects as a proof which can not be controverted, of the divinity of its origin? "Men do not gather grapes of thorns or figs of thistles."

It is true that compared with the vastness of the field for which it is designed, the beneficial effects of Christianity are as yet but limited, and there is much in the present aspect and condition of the world to counterbalance the auspicious signs of progress. "Contrary to rash expectations, gleams of light and hope, alternating with massive clouds and shadows, have passed over the stage of the civilized world like dissolving views, one melting into another, fleeting by while we are gazing, and that so swiftly, that we are kept in breathless uncertainty what will come next." When, indeed, we consider the unrest and turbulence which during the present age have characterized the most civilized nations —the outbreakings of human passion and lawlessness that have threatened the demolition of the social fabric—"the winds and the waves roaring and men's hearts failing them for fear,"—it would at times even seem that we were receding from rather than approaching a brighter day. But seen in the light of prophecy, these apparently disastrous omens indicate that the long deferred hope of ages is hastening to its fulfilment. The groan and travail of the world will yet have a glorious consummation! Through all the seething fermentation which society exhibits, and which is a consequence of the emancipation of the general mind from blind unreasoning acquiescence in whatever wore the semblance of authority, under the ever present agency and control of that Divine Spirit who of old brooded over Chaos, the process still goes on, which is to bring it to its destined form and law. The mission of the Bible will be accomplished—its ideal be realized. "The chemist has his solution that requires but one added drop to bring out its crystals, yet that solution may grow purer and purer, and so at the moment of completion may form a finer gem than had it come before. So also year by year one error after another is precipitated and the world's thought grows clearer, though it cannot rest, until at length the magic moment of the Bible's spiritual alchemy will arrive, when its hand shall drop the living truth, and the waiting world shall flash into solid order and crystalline beauty."[1] The last vestiges of sin and misery shall then disappear, and throughout a regenerated earth shall arise "scenes surpassing fable" to bear witness that its work is done. "For as the rain cometh down and the snow from heaven, and returneth not thither, but watereth the earth, and maketh it bring forth and bud . . . . so shall My word be that goeth forth out of My mouth; it shall not return unto Me void . . . . instead of the thorn shall come up the fir tree, and instead of the brier shall come up the myrtle tree."

"Methought there were long ages come and gone,
Pale worlds were crumbling to their last decay.
Far in the East a coming glory shone,
And morning broke, the morning of that day
Never again to set; a slanted ray
Bridged earth and heaven with its quivering flame,
Thereon an angel trod his rushing way,

[1] For the above beautiful illustration, I am indebted to a speech of remarkable power delivered before the Am. Bible Society, by the late Rev. A. D. R. Mercein, a gifted minister of the Methodist Communion.

And folding a white wing and flashing came,
Sounded a golden blast, and hastened to proclaim,-

"Glory to God, salvation and release!
Tell it among the nations, tell it wide,
'Glory to God on high, on earth be peace.'
So shouted he, so sang; from side to side,
'Amen! Amen!' the morning stars replied;
The winds were heralds of their minstrelsy,
The clouds upbore it till the echoes died,
Answered the billowy voices of the sea,
And utmost earth's acclaim formed meet antistrophe."

Cambridge Prize Poem.
By J. S. Gibson.

But we also claim for the Bible, that not only is it the great almoner of temporal blessings to mankind, alleviating the lot of the afflicted, the destitute and the oppressed, not only is it the civilizer of manners and elevator of morals, but it has been the great agent of man's *intellectual advancement.* Inquire where intelligence is most diffused among the people, where the arts and sciences have made the greatest advancement, where literature is most cultivated and progress the most realized, and it will be found that the favored lands are those in which the Bible is circulated and has most obtained sway.

It is true that long previous to the Christian era, and among nations upon whom the light of revelation had not dawned, a high state of civilization had been attained. There were in the old classic world, poets of undying fame, philosophers of wonderful subtilty and profundity of thought, orators whose eloquence still transmits its thrilling echoes down "the corridors of time;" there were magnificent works of art and stately palaces and temples,

——— "Skill of noblest architects,
With gilded battlements conspicuous far,
Turrets and terraces, and glitt'ring spires.

Many a fair edifice besides, more like
Houses of gods, * * * * * pillars and roofs,
Carv'd work, the hand of fam'd artificers
In cedar, marble, ivory, or gold."—*Paradise Regained.*

No brighter eras of intellectual achievement have since appeared than the ages of Pericles and Augustus. The lays of Homer and Virgil—the orations of Demosthenes and Cicero—the histories of Thucydides and Tacitus—the Parthenon, the Venus de Medici and the Apollo Belvidere, are still types of ideal excellençe in Literature and in Art. "The poetic legend, the gleaming marble, the pillared temple, the speaking statue,—the graceful robe, the mystic fillet, the tragic cothurnus, the symbolic procession, the bearded pontiff, the mighty orator, the crowned monarch, the visioned sage,—the charm of the scenery, the clearness of the atmosphere, the beauty of the climate, the imagination of the multitude,—dome bending itself to the azure concave above it, pediment sculptured with the dreams of the classic antiquity,—the intermixture of all with the institutions of education and policy,—its ever present recollection in gymnasium as well as sanctuary,—the romance and pageant,—the exhaustion of taste, genius, and splendor upon its fables and ceremonies,—even to our times, constitute the ancient Paganism a marvel of all that was attractive and magnificent."[1] But in all that refined culture and

[1] Prize Essay on Christian Missions by Dr. Hamilton, of Leeds. In this connection, a very remarkable but undeniable historical fact may be stated, which certainly claims a place among the "difficulties of Infidelity:" "Whilst all the surrounding world lay immersed in the profoundest moral darkness; whilst Egypt, which has been celebrated as the instructress of mankind, lay grovelling before her oxen, her birds, her reptiles, and her potherbs; whilst Grecian and Roman altars, even at a moment when heathen refinement was at its highest, were smoking before the emblems of the grossest appetites and of the rankest intemperance;—there in an obscure corner of the globe, overlooked and despised by the surrounding nations, was to be seen the astonishing spectacle of one small people, with no literature but their own sacred books, no arts but those derived from a most limited and

splendid civilization, there was a worm at the core,—a vital, irremediable defect. As unconsciously but significantly expressed in the Athenian symbol of the golden grasshopper, it was of the earth earthy. This world and its regalements for the life of sense, were its all. The beautiful was there in an unequalled development, but it lacked the good and the true. "There was no provision for the wants of the inner man. Heathenism had no line to reach the depths of human depravity, and no power to raise up man from his degradation, to break the spell by which he was bound to sensual objects, and to set his spirit free. It had no object of religious worship fitted to call forth love, veneration, gratitude; and no body of truth that could be instrumental in purifying and ennobling man's mental powers, in connecting him with the higher world, and renewing him after the image of God." Some portion of primitive truth and traditional morality it had indeed possessed, and while this was retained, it was the salt which kept it from corruption, the cement which held it from dissolution. But when, by the increase of luxury and vice, these had become obliterated, then literature, philosophy and art, all hastened to decay. The fire went out upon its altars. Destitute of those higher influences which Christian faith alone can supply, it was like a magnificent structure built upon the sand, and when the barbarian torrent came, it was already tottering to its fall.

But from the first, the religion of the Bible proved itself to be the true element, both of intellectual progress and conservation. Even amid the decaying embers of the ancient civilization, it kindled a flame which gave evidence

unwilling intercourse with their neighbors, celebrating as they had done for ages the praises of the great unseen immaterial Creator of the universe, in sentiments the justness and sublimity of which poetry in her highest flights has never to this day been able to equal, nor philosophy in her utmost pride of discovery to improve."—Bishop Shuttleworth.

of its heavenly descent. Dispelling the gloom which had rested on the future, it supplied fresh motives for the exercise of the mental powers, roused faculties which had long lain dormant, and gave vitality to reason and thought. The master spirits of the world soon ranged themselves on its side, and after the second century of the Christian era, with few exceptions, the literature of Greece and Rome is to be looked for in the pages of the Christian fathers alone.

With the introduction of Christianity among the various nations of Europe, knowledge was its inseparable attendant. The most assiduous cultivators of learning in those early ages were the pioneers and advocates of the Gospel. In the fourth century Ulphilas, bishop of the Mœsian Goths, introduced a written language as well as translated the Scriptures into the vulgar tongue for his illiterate countrymen. And so great was their improvement under his instructions, that some of the Goths soon made such attainments as to be able to compare their version with the Latin, the Greek, and the Hebrew originals. Before the Gospel was brought to its shores in the fifth century, Ireland was almost utterly uncivilized. Its natives were without an alphabet, and rude ballads committed to memory were the only vehicles to preserve any knowledge of their history and antiquities, the genealogies of their kings and the exploits of their heroes. The ability to recite a number of these verses was considered as a high accomplishment, and the bard who made any addition to them was certain of fame and reward. The coming of Christian missionaries, however, redeemed them from ignorance, and so rapid was their progress that in the next age Ireland was called the country of saints and of learned men. During the eighth and the early part of the ninth centuries, when learning had been driven from her ancient seats, Ireland was, as Aldhelm, Bede, and Camden inform us, "the sacred mart of letters," whither "troops of scholars were daily transported to be initiated by her learned masters in the treasures of the Greek and Roman classics and of divine knowledge." And with Ireland, let Iona also be mentioned, designated by Johnson as "that illustrious island, which was once the luminary of the Caledonian regions, where savage clans and roving barbarians derived the benefits of knowledge and the blessings of religion." Nor was England reclaimed from barbarism until the conversion of her Saxon conquerors in the sixth century to Christianity. When, by the preaching of the Word, the fierce tribes of Hengist and Horsa were persuaded to exchange "dark idol prayer and hoarse battle-cry" for the "hallelujahs" of Christian worship; then, and not till then, did the "sceptred isle" enter upon the career, to be made so illustrious by the masters of science and of song.[1] The Danes, Swedes, and Cimbri of the North, were still in heathen ignorance, when, in the ninth century, Ansgarius, the chief apostle of the Scandinavians, came to bring them the Gospel and to establish schools for the instruction of their youth. During the same century, two Greek monks, Cyril and Methodius, sons of Leo, a Greek nobleman, were the instruments not only of Christianizing, but of civilizing the Bulgarians, Moravians, and Bohemians. To the zeal of these missionaries, were those nations indebted for an alphabet as well as for the knowledge of revealed truth. So late as the latter part of the ninth century, the people of Russia were

[1] The civilization of the Roman conquerors of ancient Britain in the course of four centuries had made so little impression on its inhabitants that in the reign of Constantine that famous island was regarded, says Macaulay, in the polished East "with mysterious horror—a region inhabited by the ghosts of the departed, where the ground was covered by serpents, and the air was such that no man could inhale it and live."

The successors of the Romans were the savage worshippers of Woden, and until the Gospel of Christ came to them, "England knew no church within the limits of their sway, but the temple of an idol; no priesthood but that of Paganism; no god but the sun, the moon, or some hideous image." Sermon preached before the University of Cambridge, A. D. 1573.

still in savage barbarism, nor were they rescued from it until the teachers of Christianity brought with them, at the same time, the Gospel and letters, the rudiments of the arts, of law and of order. And thus with all the once barbarous nations of Europe; their introduction to letters was simultaneous with their conversion to Christianity.

When it is considered that these intellectual triumphs accompanying the propagation of the Gospel were achieved during those centuries, when a night of ignorance, deep as Egyptian darkness, had settled over the dismembered fragments of the Roman Empire, we must feel that the great historian only utters the voice of truth when he says: "The Church has many times been compared by divines to the ark of which we read in the book of Genesis; but never was the resemblance more perfect than during that evil time when she alone rode, amidst darkness and tempest, on the deluge beneath which all the great works of ancient power and wisdom lay entombed, bearing within her that feeble germ from which a second and more glorious civilization was to spring."[1] As the barbarian flood receded, the seeds proceeding from that "feeble germ" were scattered over the new and virgin soil which it left. Gradually, with whatever perversions and admixtures, the truths and principles of the Bible were diffused among the rising nations, and thus was a foundation laid for social and civil advancement. By a necessary consequence, intelligence was quickened and learning revived; this effect reacted upon Christianity, and we know from History that the daybreak of letters was coeval with the dawn of the Reformation. When the long night was passed, the sun of righteousness and the sun of science rose together, and to that blending and interfusing of moral and spiritual with intellectual light, the marvellous career of the human mind which was then inaugurated, and the triumphs of research and discovery

[1] Macaulay's History of England.

which have made illustrious the ages since, must be ascribed. For the greatest boon of the Reformation was to remove the Papal Interdict from the Bible and bring it within the reach of the people. And what was the effect of this upon literature? It is indisputable that "the study of the Scriptures in the vulgar tongue by the mass of the people, and by scholars in the original Hebrew and Greek, was the initiatory step to various other departments of knowledge, and led to investigations in History, Laws, Geography, and Antiquities, not less than in Theology. Amid the intellectual excitement thus occasioned, principles were evolved, destined to change the face of society,—to lead society forward to the great discoveries of modern times, and to impart to literature a degree of vigor, originality, and influence on the progress of society hitherto unexampled." And how could it be otherwise? There are a power and majesty breathing from the sacred page which must needs have expanded and ennobled the mind once emancipated from the errors of superstition. Its sublime doctrines, its pure and lofty precepts, imposing as they then were from their novelty as well as from their grandeur, could not fail to have taken the strongest hold upon the intellect, the imagination and the heart, upon every faculty and every affection of our nature. The surpassing literary attractions of the Bible, moreover, were well fitted to strengthen and deepen the impression. "The Scriptures contain," says Sir William Jones (whose competency to pronounce such a judgment cannot be impugned), "independently of a divine origin, more true sublimity, more exquisite beauty, purer morality, more important history, and finer strains of poetry, than could be collected within the same compass, from all other books that were composed in any age, or in any idiom." Here was opened a poetic fountain more inspiring far than any at which the Grecian Muse[1] ever drank.

[1] There is a fine passage in the preface to Cowley's Davideis on the unrivalled superiority of the sacred oracles, which may here be cited: "What

Another accomplished scholar[1] says,—"In lyric flow and fire, in crushing force, in majesty that seems still to echo the awful sounds once heard beneath the thunder-clouds of Sinai, the poetry of the ancient Scriptures is the most superb that ever burned within the breast of man. The picturesque simplicity of their narration gives an equal charm to the historical books. Vigor, beauty, sententiousness, variety, enrich and adorn the ethical parts of the collection." "What is there equal in romantic interest to the story of Joseph and his brethren; of Rachel and Laban, of Jacob's dream, of Ruth and Boaz, the descriptions in the book of Job, the deliverance of the Jews out of Egypt, or the account of their captivity and return from Babylon? There is in all these parts of Scripture, and numberless more of the same kind, to pass over the Orphic hymns of David, the prophetic denunciations of Isaiah, or the gorgeous visions of Ezekiel, an originality, a vastness of conception, a depth and tenderness of feeling, a touching simplicity in the mode of narration,"[2] unmatched and unapproachable even by classical antiquity. The whole story of redeeming love, the Son of God incarnate, the cradle and the manger, the cross and the crown in heaven, the spiritual warfare and

can we imagine more proper for the ornaments of wit and learning, in the story of Deucalion, than in that of Noah? Why will not the actions of Samson afford as plentiful matter as the labors of Hercules? Why is not Jephthah's daughter as good a woman as Iphigenia? and the friendship of David and Jonathan more worthy celebration than that of Theseus and Pirithous? Does not the passage of Moses and the Israelites into the Holy Land yield incomparably more poetic variety than the voyages of Ulysses or Æneas? Are the obsolete, threadbare tales of Thebes and Troy half so stored with great, heroical, and supernatural actions (since verse will needs find or make such), as the wars of Joshua, of the Judges, of David, and divers others? Can all the transformations of the gods give such copious hints to flourish and expatiate upon, as the true miracles of Christ, or of his prophets and apostles? What do I instance in these few particulars? All the books of the Bible are either already most admirable and exalted pieces of poesy, or are the best materials in the world for it."

[1] Sir Daniel K. Sandford. [2] Hazlitt.

the final triumph, when his people shall reign with Christ, are fraught with deeper wonder and sublimer romance, than ever thought of man conceived. They are replete with poetic as well as with evangelic inspiration. "Indited under the influence of Him, to whom all hearts are known, and all events foreknown, they suit mankind in all situations, grateful as the manna which descended from above and conformed itself to every palate. The fairest productions of human wit, after a few perusals, like gathered flowers wither in our hands, and lose their fragrancy; but these unfading flowers of Paradise become, as we are accustomed to them, still more and more beautiful; their bloom appears to be daily heightened, fresh odors are emitted, and new sweets extracted from them." Here at Siloa's brook and not at the Pierian spring, Dante and Milton drank their copious draughts of unearthly sublimity, and were animated for their noblest flights. Here Michael Angelo and Raphael filled their golden urns, and by their labors, Art emancipated from the sensualism of Pagan dreams, vindicated her heavenly origin.

That was indeed a timely vindication, and the result was a triumph of Scripture truth deserving of special commemoration. For although the revival of art and literature in Europe was under Christian auspices, yet at the era of the Reformation, the classical school had become the ruling power in both, and no themes but those of Greek and Roman story were thought worthy to employ the powers of genius. This reaction is thus accounted for by Henry Heine in his work on German literature: "The arts are nothing but the mirrors of life, and as Catholicism was extinguished in life, so also did it grow faint and die away in art . . . . A contemporary Protestantism at that time was stirring in art equally as in life . . . . It was then as if men felt themselves suddenly freed from an oppression of a thousand years; the artists above all breathed freely again, as the Alp of Catholicism seemed rolled from the breast; they plunged enthusiastically into the sea of Greek gladness, out of whose foam the Goddess of Beauty again emerged for them; the painters painted again the ambrosial joy of Olympus, the sculptors chiselled again, with the same pleasure as of old, the ancient heroes out of the marble block; the poets celebrated again the house of Atreus and Laïus; the period of the new classical poetry arose."

Yet vain was the endeavor to impart spirit and life to the faded forms and shadows of antiquity. "Phœbus' chariot course was run," Pan was dead, the sacred fire of Vesta could not be rekindled. But the unequalled productions of the mighty masters who sleep in Santa Croce and the Pantheon, proved that the true Promethean spark was in the Bible, and that art lost nothing by becoming Christian, even though all the mythic fancies which "live no longer in the faith of reason," should vanish into the mists of the past.

> "*Then* sculpture and her sister arts revive,
> Stones leaped to form and rocks began to live;
> With *sweeter* notes each rising temple rung,
> A Raphael painted and a Vida sung."—POPE.

Thus was the returning wave of classicism arrested, and now what Homer was in the ancient world, that has the Bible become in the modern, in relation to poetry and all the imitative arts—the inspiring source of beauty and sublimity—the model and archetype of expression. Under its influence modern art has developed a power to minister to the desire of the elevated and the beautiful, which the boasted productions of the classic school, and even such of the chef-d'œuvres of antiquity as have come down to us, cannot approach. "Look," says an eloquent writer, "at the sepulchral monuments of Grecian art—the frigid mysteries, the abhorrent ghosts, yet too corporeal, shrinking from Lethe, and the dismal boat—the unpromising, unpitying Charon: then turn to some of the sublime Christian monuments of art that speak so differently of that death—the coronation of the virgin, the ascension of saints. The dismal and the doleful earth has vanished—choirs of angels rush to welcome and support the beatified, the released: death is no more, but life breathing no atmosphere of earth, but all freshness, all joy, and all music; the now changed body glowing, like an increasing light, into its spirituality of form and beauty, and thrilling with

> "That undisturbed song of pure consent,
> Aye sung before the sapphire-color'd throne
> To him that sits thereon,"—

Then shall we doubt, and not dare to pronounce the superior capabilities of Christian art, arising out of its subject-poetry? We prefer, as a great poetic conception, Raphael's Archangel, Michael, with his victorious foot upon his prostrate adversary, to the far-famed Apollo Belvidere, who has slain his Python; and his St. Margaret, in her sweet, her innocent, and clothed grace, to that perfect model of woman's form, the Venus de Medici. Not that we venture a careless or misgiving thought of the perfectness of those great antique works: their perfectness was according to their purpose. Higher purposes make a higher perfectness. Nor would we have them viewed irreverently; for even in them, and the genius that produced them, the Creator, as in "times past, left not Himself without witness." In showing forth the glory of the human form, they show forth the glory of Him who made it, who is thus glorified in the witnesses; and so we accept and love them. But to a certain degree they must stand dethroned, their influence faded. Graces and Muses in their perfectness of marbled beauty, what are they to faith, hope, and charity, and the veiled virtues that like our angels shroud themselves? These virtues of the soul, far greater in their humility, in the sacred poetry of our

Christian faith, shine like stars, even in their smallness on the dark night of our humanity; and they are to take place in the celestial of art; and we feel that it is His will, who, as the hymn of the blessed Virgin—that type of all these united virtues—declares, "hath put down the mighty from their seat, and hath exalted the humble and the meek."[1]

The triumphs which Christianity has achieved in Literature and Art, were, in the beginning of her career, the least to have been expected. In the felicitous words of Dean Trench: "How many things Christianity might, at first sight, have threatened to leave out, to take no note of, or indeed utterly to suppress, which, so far from really warring against, it has raised to higher perfection than ever in the old world they had attained. With what despair, for example, a lover of art, one who at Athens or at Rome fondly had dwelt among the beautiful creations of poet and of painter, would have contemplated the rise of the new religion, and the authority which its doctrines were acquiring over the hearts and spirits of men. What a death-knell must he have heard in this to all in which his soul so greatly delighted. He might have been ready, perhaps, to acknowledge that our human life, under this new teaching, would be more rigorously earnest, more severe, more pure; but all its grace and its beauty, all which it borrowed of these from the outward world, he would have concluded, had been laid under a ban, and must now vanish forever . . . . Little, indeed, could friend or foe of the nascent faith, have forecast that out of it,—that nourished by the Christian books, by the great thoughts which Christ set stirring in humanity, and of which these books kept a lasting record, there should unfold itself a poetry infinitely greater, an art infinitely higher, than any which the old world had seen; that this faith, which looked so rigid, so austere, even so forbidding, should clothe itself in forms of

[1] Blackwood's Magazine.

grace and loveliness, such as men had never dreamt of before; that poetry should not be henceforward the play of the spirit, but its holiest earnest; and those skilless Christian hymns to Christ as to God," of which Pliny speaks, so rude probably in regard of form, should yet be the preludes of strains higher than the world had listened to yet. Or, who would have supposed that those artless paintings of the catacombs had the prophecy in them of more wondrous compositions than men's eyes had ever seen—or that a day should arrive when above many a dark vault and narrow crypt, where now the Christian worshippers gathered in secret, should arise domes and cathedrals, embodying loftier ideas, because ideas relating to the eternal and the infinite, than all those Grecian temples, which now stood so fair and so strong, but which aimed not to lift men's minds from the earth which they adorned?

"How little would the one or other, would Christian or heathen have presaged such a future as this—that art was not to perish, but only to be purified and redeemed from the service of the flesh, and from whatever was clinging to and hindering it from realizing its true glory,—and that this book, which does not talk about such matters, which does not make beauty but holiness, its end and aim—should yet be the truest nourisher of all out of which any genuine art has ever proceeded; the truest fosterer of beauty, in that it is the nourisher of the affections, the sustainer of the relations between God and man; which affections and which relations are indeed the only root out of which any poetry or art worthy the name, ever have sprung. For these affections being laid waste, those relations being broken, art is first stricken with barrenness, and then, in a little while, withers and pines and dies—as that ancient art, which had been so fertile while faith survived, was, when the Church was born, already withering and dying under the influence of the scepticism, the profligacy, the decay of family and national life, the extinction of religious faith, which so eminently marked the time; only having a name to live, resting merely on the traditions of an earlier age, and on the eve of utter dissolution. Such was its condition when Christ came, and cast in his Word, as that which maketh all things new, into the midst of an old and decrepit and wornout world."[1]

The late professor Wilson has also written eloquently on this theme. Comparing the Christian with the old classic world, he says in his "Recreations:" "We seem to feel more profoundly than they—to see, as it were, into a new world. . . . . Since the revelation of Christianity, all moral thought has been sanctified by religion. Religion has given to it a purity, a solemnity, a sublimity which, even amongst the noblest of the heathen, we shall look for in vain. The knowledge that shone by fits and dimly on the eyes of Socrates and Plato, 'that rolled in vain to find the light,' has descended over many lands into the 'huts where poor men lie;' and thoughts are familiar there, beneath the low and smoking roofs, higher far than ever flowed from Grecian sage meditating among the magnificence of his pillared temples."

"Christ hath sent us down the angels;
And the whole earth and the skies
Are illumed by altar candles
Lit for blessed mysteries;
And a Priest's hand, through creation,
Waveth calm and consecration—
And Pan is dead."—Mrs. Browning.

The triumphs of modern science, also, are due to the Bible. Not only did it communicate the intellectual impulse which led to their achievement, but the true method of investigation, without which all or most of them would have remained in impenetrable darkness, is to be ascribed to its influence. In all ages of the world, heathen and

[1] Hulsean Lectures, Am. ed., pp. 132–3.

Christian, down to the revival of letters, when the Bible first reached the intellectual ascendency it has ever since maintained, the only test and standard of truth which men knew and recognized was human reason. The profoundest thinkers confounded physics with metaphysics, and without troubling themselves to observe the processes of nature as carried on in the mighty laboratory of the universe, proposed to possess themselves of her secrets, by using the rules of syllogistic art.

"Previous to the publication of the Novum Organon of Bacon," says Sir John Herschel, "natural philosophy, in any legitimate and extensive use of the word, could hardly be said to exist. Among the Greek philosophers, of whose attainments in science alone we have any positive knowledge, and that but a very limited one, we are struck with the remarkable contrast between their powers of acute and subtile disputation, their extraordinary success in abstract reasoning, and their intimate familiarity with subjects purely intellectual, on the one hand; and, on the other, with their loose and careless consideration of external nature, their grossly illogical deductions of sweeping generality from few and ill-observed facts, in some cases; and their reckless assumption of abstract principles having no foundation but in their own imaginations, in others; mere forms of words with nothing corresponding to them in nature, from which, as from mathematical definitions, postulates, and axioms, they imagined that all phenomena could be derived, all the laws of nature deduced." Thus

"Sages after sages strove
In vain to filter off the crystal draught
Pure from the lees, which often more enhanced
The thirst than slaked it, and not seldom bred
Intoxication and delirium wild."

But from the time that the reign of the Bible began, the dominion of false principles of inquiry and research in the realms of physical science began to pass away. In the light of revelation men learned that reason was but a blind guide in such high matters as the laws and order of the universe. They had found and recognized in the Bible an unimpeachable standard for moral duty, and thus was the desire awakened to obtain a basis of equal certainty for the facts of the physical world. In the progress of human thought, the true province of reason with respect to revelation had at length been defined, and it was now understood that man's convictions of what is divine truth must be consequents upon and not antecedents to his examination of the divine word. It was perceived that man might be able to understand and interpret such statements and disclosures as the wisdom of God might see fit to make known to him; but that, without that aid, to discover what should be the principles and laws of the divine order and government, is beyond his power. This lesson applied with equal directness and force to the moral and to the physical government of God. It furnished the lever[1] by which Lord Bacon overthrew the long-established scholastic philosophy, and "substituted induction for syllogism, fact for theory, practical experiment for abstract speculation." Utterly discarding the idea that the human mind could determine on purely theoretic and à priori grounds, what facts of nature are to be allowed or disallowed, he showed the office of man in search of truth to be that of servant or interpreter,—by patient observation and comparison to decipher what God has written in the great book of nature, and thus climb truth's ever-ascending pathway, which, if it be steep, is yet open and accessible. Armed with this principle, the mighty genius of Bacon, like the magic wand of Prospero, dislimned

[1] "The road to true philosophy is precisely the same with that which leads to true religion; and from both one and the other, unless we would enter in as little children, we must expect to be totally excluded."—*Nov. Org.*, lib. i, aph. 68.

the "airy charms and unsubstantial pageants" of abstract conceptions and subtile distinctions, among which man had so long been lost and bewildered, and brought him forth into a world of real existences. Finely and truly has Cowley said:

> "From these and all long errors of the way,
> In which our wandering predecessors went,
> And like th' old Hebrews, many years did stray
> In deserts of but small extent,
> Bacon, like Moses, led us forth at last;
> The barren wilderness he past
> Did on the very border stand
> Of the blest promis'd land,
> And from the mountain's top of his exalted wit
> Saw it himself, and show'd us it."

The Bible, therefore, is the great intellectual elevator of mankind. Its influence has enlightened and schooled philosophy, stimulated science, ennobled poetry and art, and at the same time has touched all things, human life most of all, with sublimity and grandeur. Coeval with the infancy of Time, it still remains and widens in the circle of its intelligence. "It adapts itself with facility to the revolutions of thought and feeling which shake to pieces all things else, —and flexibly accommodates itself to the progress of society and the changes of civilization. Even conquests,—the disorganization of old nations,—the formation of new,—do not affect the continuity of its empire. It lays hold of the new as of the old, and transmigrates with the spirit of humanity; attracting to itself, by its own moral power, in all the communities it enters, a ceaseless intensity of effort for its propagation, illustration, and defence." "King and noble, peasant and pauper are delighted students of its pages. Philosophers have humbly gleaned from it, and legislation has been thankfully indebted. Its stories charm the child, its hopes inspirit the aged, and its promises soothe the bed of death. The maiden is wedded under its sanction, and the grave is closed under its comforting assurances. Its lessons are the essence of religion, the seminal truths of theology, the first principles of morals, and the guiding axioms of political economy. It is the theme of universal appeal. In the entire range of literature, no book is so frequently quoted or referred to. The majority of all the books ever published have been in connection with it. The Fathers commented upon it, and the subtile diviners of the middle ages refined upon its doctrines. It sustained Origen's scholarship and Chrysostom's rhetoric. It whetted the penetration of Abelard, and exercised the keen ingenuity of Aquinas. It gave life to the revival of letters, and Dante and Petrarch revelled in its imagery. It augmented the erudition of Erasmus, and roused and blessed the intrepidity of Luther. Its temples are the finest specimens of architecture, and the brightest triumphs of music are associated with its poetry. The text of no ancient author has summoned into operation such an amount of labor and learning, and it has furnished occasion for the most masterly examples of criticism and comment, grammatical investigation, and logical analysis. It has also inspired the English muse with her loftiest strains. Its beams gladdened Milton in his darkness, and cheered the song of Cowper in his sadness. It was the star which guided Columbus to the discovery of the New World. It furnished the panoply of that Puritan valor which shivered tyranny in days gone by. It is the magna charta of the world's regeneration and liberties. The records of false religion, from the Koran to the Book of Mormon, have owned its superiority, and surreptitiously purloined its jewels. Among the Christian classics it loaded the treasures of Owen, charged the fulness of Hooker, barbed the point of Baxter, gave colors to the palette and sweep to the pencil of Bunyan, enriched the fragrant fancy of Taylor, sustained the loftiness of Howe, and strung the plummet of

Edwards. In short, this collection of artless lives and letters has changed the face of the world, and ennobled myriads of its population."[1] Not only do we owe to it our social and moral advantages, but the brilliant achievements of modern science, the miracles of modern art, and the master works of modern literature, are to be reckoned among its trophies.

To these claims for the Bible, infidelity would, however, object, that the mighty change which has been wrought in man's moral condition, and also his intellectual advancement, are due, not to the influence of Revelation, but to the unfolding of our nature from its own inherent vigor and natural growth in its progress toward perfection. The philosophers of the modern "positive" school argue that, as an individual passes through the different stages of infancy, childhood, and manhood, so society, under the influence of natural law, progresses from one generation to another. The whole human race is to be viewed as "a colossal man, whose life reaches from the creation to the day of judgment,"[2] and to whose education, "in the economy of Providence, the poetical and legendary mythology of Greece and Rome, the animal worship of Egypt, the sun worship of the East, with their various systems of law and civil government," have as truly contributed as the religion of the Bible. Under all these means and agencies, man has been gradually approximating toward that goal and consummation which Creative wisdom designed he should attain.

There is a mixture of truth with the error of this hypothesis, that lends it plausibility. For it is undeniable that man is a creature of progress and expansion, and there is a sense in which the philosophic poet truly says:

> "I doubt not through the ages one increasing purpose runs,
> And the thoughts of men are widened with the process of the suns."
>
> TENNYSON.

[1] Dr. Eadie. [2] Dr. Temple in the Essays and Reviews.

There are bounds of limitation for the inferior creation. The bee constructs its cell, the eagle builds its eyrie, the nautilus hoists its membrane sail, as they did in the early morning of the world, without change or improvement. They, and all others of every species, soon reach the full maturity of their being, and can rise no higher in the scale. But the faculties of man are not thus hopelessly circumscribed. He is capable in himself of boundless improvement, and of appropriating "the long result of time," the accumulated treasures of knowledge and thought, which the ages have transmitted—

> "Augescunt aliæ gentes, aliæ minuuntur,
> Inque brevi spatio mutantur sæcla animantum,
> Et quasi cursores vitai lampada tradunt."—LUCRETIUS.

> "Nations by turns increase, by turns decay:
> Like Racers, bear the Lamp of life and live,
> And their Race done, their Lamp to others give."

Individuals and nations perish, but the progress of humanity is continued. Or, to use another illustration than that supplied by Lucretius: "The whole gigantic growth of human knowledge and science may be compared to those deposits which geologists describe, full of the remains of vegetable and animal life,—beautiful once and beneficial still. The luxuriant foliage and huge forest growth of science and literature which now overshadow us, are themselves rooted in strata of decaying or decayed mind, and derive their nourishment from them; the very soil we turn is the loose *detritus* of thought, washed down to us through the long ages." The great increase in knowledge of the physical globe, the greater acquaintance with the powers and forces of the created universe, the marvellous progress in the inventive arts, that characterize the present age, have doubtless, in part at least, sprung from this accumulation. But this admission by no means implies the progress of the race in such a sense as the school of writers referred to contend for. Their hypothesis entirely ignores the necessity of such a remedial process for the restoration and development of man as Christianity contemplates and designs. And when we examine history, we find that that hypothesis completely fails as it respects the vast majority of our race. Where there has been progression, it can be shown that it has always been due, not to the operation of a blind inherent law, but to agencies and impulses acting upon it from without, and in accordance with the development of that "increasing purpose" or divine plan recognized by the poet. "God," it has been said, "is in history," and in the mighty scheme which under the superintendence of his ever-present agency is continually evolving, all events are included. The rise and fall of states and empires are but among the subordinate means and instrumentalities for promoting "the unhasting yet unresting progress of a kingdom, ordained ere time began, to be completed when time shall be no more."[1] If there were such a "natural law of historic progress," as writers like Hegel, Comte, and Buckle contend for, it ought, like all the laws of nature, to be constant in its tendencies and uniform in its results. But how is this reconcilable with the fact that many of the countries most civilized in the days of Augustus are now in a state of hopeless barbarism? It is certain that the only true law and the only direct line of the world's sure and stable progress, which can be traced in all the annals of the past, have been coincident with the advancement and prevalence of Bible truth and knowledge. If this be denied, how shall we solve the problem presented by such countries as China and Hindostan, where letters and philosophy flourished in those remote ages, when the cruel rites of Druidism were practised in Britain, and the savage tribes who then inhabited Germany, worshipped Odin and Thor,

[1] Prof. H. B. Smith.

if we contrast them as they now are, with what Christendom has become? To what can we refer the difference, but to the influence of Bible truth in the latter, and its absence in the former? Where that has been wanting, after a certain point has been reached, the progress has ever been in the direction indicated in the well-known lines of the Roman poet:

"Damnosa quid non imminuit dies?
Ætas parentum, pejor avis, tulit
Nos nequiores, mox daturos
Progeniem vitiosiorem."—Hor., Od. iii, 6.

"Our fathers' race,
More deeply versed in ill
Than were their sires, hath borne us yet
More wicked, duly to beget
A race more wicked still."—Martin's Trans.

"The downward tendencies of human nature, which constitute the substance of Secular, as distinguished from Sacred History; the acknowledged deterioration of languages, literatures, religions, arts, sciences, and civilizations; the slow and sure decay of national vigor, and return to barbarism; the unvarying decline from public virtue to public voluptuousness; in short, the entire history of man,"[1] so far as he is or has been left to his natural development, all utter the same testimony. In the teeming vices of the great cities of Europe and America, there is abundant proof that man is the same now as when Horace wrote. And if modern communities have not sunk into the very lowest depths of that almost incredible profligacy that marked the declining years of Roman greatness, it is to no growing perfectibility of human nature that we owe it, but to that Gospel which modern scepticism affects to despise. It is the moulding, modifying influence of the precepts and

[1] Professor Shedd's Philosophy of History.

truths of the Bible, wrought into all our institutions, like the name of Phidias in the shield of Minerva, that has produced the superiority of modern to ancient civilization. In the presence of that element, we have a safe assurance that the world's progress henceforth shall be onward—that humanity is being restored to the heights whence it fell—that the light of improvement now kindled, shall never expire.

Were such confirmation needful, the position above taken might be fortified by numerous testimonies of great and illustrious men. On such a point, who so qualified to utter an opinion as England's "scholar, metaphysician, bard," Samuel Taylor Coleridge? It is the recorded judgment of that imperial mind, that "for more than a thousand years the Bible, collectively taken, has gone hand in hand with civilization, science, law—in short, with the moral and intellectual cultivation of the species—always supporting, and often leading the way. Its very presence, as a believed Book, has rendered the nations emphatically a chosen race, and this, too, in exact proportion as it is more or less generally known and studied. Of those nations which in the highest degree enjoy its influences, it is not too much to affirm, that the differences, public and private, physical, moral, and intellectual, are only less than what might have been expected from a diversity of species. Good and holy men, and the best and wisest of mankind, the kingly spirits of history, enthroned in the hearts of mighty nations, have borne witness to its influences, have declared it to be beyond compare the most perfect instrument of Humanity."

To this eloquent utterance, may be added a similar testimony from America's accomplished orator and statesman, the Hon. Edward Everett. He says, "The highest historical probability can be adduced in support of the proposition, that, if it were possible to annihilate the Bible, and with it all its influences, we should destroy with it the whole spiritual system of the moral world—all our great moral ideas—refinement of manners—constitutional government—equitable administration and security of property—our schools, hospitals, and benevolent associations—the press—the fine arts—the equality of the sexes, and the blessings of the fireside; in a word, all that distinguishes Europe and America from Turkey and Hindostan."

But the greatest triumph of the Bible is the power which its truth imparts to fortify the believer against *the ills of life and the fear of death.* It is an affecting and impressive incident that is related of the closing hours of the most eminent and popular author of the present century. A few days before his death, during an interval of comparative ease from his malady, turning to his son-in-law, he expressed a wish that he should read to him. "From what book shall I read?" said he. "Can you ask?" the dying Scott replied; "there is but One." No page of his own matchless romances or enchanting poetry could minister comfort to him then. And to all of living men, there is coming a time, when they will be shut up to a like necessity. Life may now appear like a fairy scene, all nature wear a smile of gladness, and the heart be filled with joy,

"Youth on the prow and pleasure at the helm;"

but the spell will be broken and the enchantment disappear. For there is a reverse to the picture. "Though a man live many years and rejoice in them all, yet let him remember the days of darkness, for they shall be many." There is a train of inevitable evils from which the most favored lot is not exempt. In the garden there is a sepulchre. Sickness and sorrow, weariness and pain, disappointment and separation from those we love, and "death the end of earth," who shall escape these? Unto these troubles man is born as the sparks fly upward. The last of them has been expressively termed "the king of terrors." Apart from the hope which Revelation proffers, he is and ever has been, since the entrance of sin marred our inheritance, a skeleton at life's richest banquet,—in its sunniest path, a serpent among the flowers,—in its clearest sky, an ever-threatening cloud. What though the votary of ambition achieve the glittering prize of "youth's dreaming hope, and labor's midnight oil," yet the inevitable hour will come to close the scene and extinguish his fairest prospects. For what is human life?

> "A flower that does with opening dawn arise,
> And flourishing the day, at evening dies;
> A winged eastern blast, just skimming o'er
> The ocean's brow, and sinking on the shore;
> A fire, whose flames through crackling stubble fly;
> A meteor, shooting from the summer sky;
> A bowl, adown the bending mountain rolled;
> A bubble breaking,—and a fable told:
> A noontide shadow, and a midnight dream;
> Are emblems, which, with semblance apt, proclaim
> Our earthly course."—PRIOR'S *Solomon*.

Viewed in this aspect alone, life seems an undesirable possession. When we consider only its trials and vicissitudes, its pains, sorrows, and disappointments—that man's greatness ripens but to fall, and "the paths of glory lead but to the grave," we are ready to say with the afflicted patriarch, "I loathe it, I would not live alway," or with the world's despairing votary—

> "Known were the bill of fare before we taste,
> Who would not spurn the banquet and the board?
> Prefer th' eternal but oblivious fast
> To life's frail fretted thread, and death's suspended sword?"

These lines are from a poem written by the gifted author of "Lacon," just before with his own hand he terminated his miserable life. To them may be appended the melancholy confession of that great but perverted genius

Rousseau, as he approached the shores of eternity: "I now found myself," says he, "in the decline of life, a prey to tormenting maladies, and believing myself at the close of my career without having once tasted the sublime pleasures after which my heart panted. Why was it that, with a soul naturally expansive, whose very existence was benevolence, I have never found one single friend with feelings like my own? A prey to the cravings of a heart which have never been satisfied, I perceived myself arrived at the confines of old age, and dying ere I had begun to live. I considered destiny as in my debt, for promises which she had never realized. Why was I created with faculties so refined, yet which were never intended to be adequately employed? I felt my own value, and revenged myself of my fate, by recollecting and shedding tears for its injustice."[1]

Is then this life wholly a labyrinth of confusion and disorder? a flat, and stale, and unprofitable scene of guilt and misery? of power exerted without an object? of energies, of hopes, of sympathies, terminating in nothing? Can it be that the benevolent Author of our being has left us with no provision for our deepest necessities—no balm for our sufferings—no medicine to soothe our griefs? No; God has not left his work unfinished. He has provided a remedy for all these ills. There is that which if cast into these bitter waters, they will become healthful and pleasant. There is that which, when all earthly hopes vanish, can replace them with visions of secure and everlasting joys. Let a man truly believe the Bible, let him receive it as an authoritative revelation from God, and bow his mind and heart in willing submission to its blessed teachings and he will find that life's gloom will soon disperse and "all things become new." The fairest boons that earth can offer, like the Dead Sea fruit, may turn to ashes on the lips, but the

[1] Rousseau's Confessions. Part ii, book 9.

talisman hence obtained will cause the water of this world to become wine of heaven, and the common bread of this life to prove angels' food. For here is abundant provision, exquisitely adapted, as light to the eye and music to the ear, to all the necessities and exigencies of our condition, in whatever aspect it may be viewed. "Here is authority in which the feebleness of the soul may rest, yet tempered with such an exquisite sympathy for every human weakness as the experience of a God incarnate could alone supply. Not a doubt that is not solved; not a fear that is not removed; not a want that is not satisfied; not a sorrow incident to life that is not cheered by its appropriate comfort, till even life's darkest passages become beautiful in that flood of heavenly light and love that streams from the cross of Christ. Here we find pardon for sin; reconciliation with God; a new life in the soul divinely implanted, and that beats pulse to pulse with the heart of God himself; sonship with the Almighty, with those privileges of free intercourse, constant protection, and future inheritance that belong to sonship; a new charm thrown over life; all fear taken from death; the veil of the further world uplifted, and such a glimpse given of unutterable bliss that human language has no words to utter it, human hearts as yet no experience by which to measure it. All this blessed revelation is not an outward communication dependent for its effect on the vigor of the human understanding, but is instinct with a Divine Spirit that sustains with almighty strength the feebleness of the human will, and directs the waywardness of the human affections."

"Of all the boons which God has bestowed on this apostate and orphaned creation, we are bound to say that the Bible is the noblest and most precious. We bring not into comparison with this illustrious donation the glorious sunlight, nor the rich sustenance which is poured forth from the storehouses of the earth, nor that existence itself which allows us, though dust, to soar into companionship with angels. The Bible is the development of man's immortality; the guide which informs him how he may move off triumphantly from a contracted and temporary sphere, and grasp destinies of unbounded splendor, eternity his lifetime, and infinity his home. It is the record which tells us that this rebellious section of God's unlimited empire is not excluded from our Maker's compassion; but that the creatures who move upon its surface, though they have basely sepulchred in sinfulness and corruption the magnificence of their nature, are yet so dear in their ruin to Him who first formed them, that He hath bowed the heavens in order to open their graves." "It is this that has nerved the faith which has overcome the world; this has strengthened the martyr's heart till he has gone to death as to a victory, and made the valley of the shadow of death glorious with hallelujahs; this has bound up the mourner's bleeding wounds, and made the tongue of the dumb to sing; this has rendered the tender woman and the feeble child more than conquerors over all at which unassisted human nature shudders; this has brightened life and sweetened death, till the pallid brow of the dead saint has become glorious as a conqueror's, and the coffin and the winding-sheet have been the investiture of a blessed immortality. These are the triumphs of the Bible." [1]

"Most wondrous book! bright candle of the Lord!
Star of eternity! the only star
By which the bark of man could navigate
The sea of life, and gain the coast of bliss
Securely; only star which rose on Time,
And, on its dark and troubled billows, still,
As generation, drifting swiftly by,
Succeeded generation, threw a ray
Of heaven's own light; and to the hills of God,
The everlasting hills, pointed the sinner's eye."—POLLOK.

[1] Garbett's Boyle Lectures.

But great as have been the triumphs and achievements of the Bible; though through so many centuries its adversaries have assailed it in vain; though its victories have been far more wonderful than those of Cæsar or Alexander; though it has moulded anew the life of nations, and wherever its mission has been welcomed and its influence has had "free course," has renewed the face of the earth; though it is man's guide in the morning and noon of life, and both his staff and telescope when its evening shadows fall; though in that dread hour when man's flesh and heart fail and all earthly things recede, it has so oft exhibited its power to light up death's glazing eye with immortal hope, and arm the departing believer to meet the "king of terrors" unappalled, yet let us not suppose that its earthly warfare has ceased. Its pure uncompromising doctrines still call forth the enmity of the carnal mind and corrupt heart of man. "The religion which imposes self-restraint upon the wilful, humility upon the arrogant, mercy upon the cruel; which would bend the knees of the self-righteous philosophers before the cross of a crucified Redeemer, and which would quell all the tumultuous desires which attach us to this world, that it may plant the sublime hopes and aspirations of eternity in their room;—that religion can never hope to command the willing deference of an unconverted world. So long as a single sophism can be found to justify disobedience to its dictates; so long as man will continue to argue from the suggestions of passion rather than of cool and impartial reflection; so long as the scanty area of man's knowledge will be too narrow for the difficulties with which it is beset, and the bad passions of mankind shall be ready to take advantage of those difficulties; so long as any one branch of science shall remain uninvestigated, and the obscurities of ancient literature afford the slightest ground for plausible speculation;—so long, we may confidently assert, will Christianity see, not only the proud, the violent, and the sensualist, but even scholars and philosophers drawn up in array against her." Infidelity, so often repulsed, still keeps the field, and if she intermit her efforts, it is only to recruit her forces for a new campaign and to assault positions hitherto unattempted. "There is," says an able writer, "there is coming upon the Church a current of doubt, deeper far and darker than ever swelled against her before—a current strong in learning, crested with genius, strenuous yet calm in progress. It seems the last grand trial of the truth of our faith. Against the battlements of Zion, a motley throng have gathered themselves together. Socinians, atheists, doubters, open foes and bewildered friends are in the field, although no trumpet has openly been blown, and no charge publicly sounded. There are the old desperadoes of infidelity—the last followers of Paine and Voltaire; there is the stolid, scanty and sleepy troop of the followers of Owen; there follow the Communists of France, a fierce, disorderly crew; the commentators of Germany come, too, with pick-axes in their hands, crying, 'Raze it, raze it to the foundations.' There you see the garde-mobile, the vicious and vain youth of Europe. On the outskirts of the fight hangs, cloudy and uncertain, a small but select band, whose wavering surge is surmounted by the dark and lofty crest of Carlyle and Emerson. 'Their swords are a thousand'—their purposes are various; in this, however, all agree, that Christianity and the Bible ought to go down before advancing civilization."[1] Since this graphic description was penned, indications have multiplied that "the last conflict of great principles, the final contest between truth and error, the mystic Armageddon, it may be, of the Apocalypse has, indeed, commenced. As never, since the Apostolic age, have the triumphs of the Bible been greater nor its friends more sanguine; so never have its enemies

[1] British Quarterly Review.

been more numerous and determined. To the old open warfare, have been added weapons of attack far more subtile and dangerous. These have been skilfully adapted to the refinement and intelligence of the age; and with a great show of learning and science, and not seldom under the garb of reverence for the Bible and adherence to Christianity, modern sceptics and unbelievers have aimed the most deadly blows against the records of our faith, and no conceivable appliance has been left untried for the purpose of uprooting that tree whose leaves are for the healing of the nations. But as the storm which beats upon the oak only causes it to strike its roots and fibres deeper in the soil, so shall these assaults continue to prove innocuous and unavailing. The tree which a Divine hand hath planted, shall still flourish in undecaying vigor and immortal beauty, when the last dagon of infidelity shall have fallen. The prophet of scepticism may talk contemptuously of "old Jew-stars gone out;"[1] but the Bible yet lives. "Every age has more than one Erostratus; but while they are quarrelling for preëminence, the temple stands and their torches expire. Strauss abolishes Paulus: and Ewald declares that in Strauss there is absolutely nothing new. The giants, sprung from the dragon-teeth of scepticism, slay each other, while the Bible, like the immortal letters of Cadmus (which are indeed its own), passes on to mingle with the thought and speech of all lands and all centuries."

But while the experience of the past and the Almighty care which unceasingly watches over it, assure us of the ultimate triumph of the Bible over all its enemies, it is the manifest duty of every Christian, especially in view of the craft and subtilty of modern unbelief, to be armed in its behalf; not only to be himself convinced of "the certainty of those things which are most surely believed among us,"

[1] Carlyle.

but to be able to answer the cavils of the gainsayer, and to show that his faith rests not upon "cunningly devised fables." It is essential to our happiness and security, that we should steadfastly believe the sublime doctrines and undoubtingly rest on the consoling promises of the Bible; but it is also requisite that we have an intelligent persuasion of the firmness and stability of the foundation on which they rest. We are not to sit idly and at ease, in unquestioning reliance upon lessons of custom and authority; but we must "walk about Zion, and go round about her, and tell the towers thereof; we must mark well her bulwarks and consider her palaces, that we may tell to generations following, this God is our God forever and ever."

As an humble aid to the performance of this duty, and in view of the peculiar exigencies of the Christian at the present time, the following pages have been written. It is proposed to confront the "oppositions of science falsely so called," and the doubts and difficulties of modern scepticism, and to establish the Harmony of the Bible with the facts of Physical Science, and also the Historical Accuracy and Reality of its statements and narratives. Against these positions, the utmost efforts of infidelity have been directed. As the wonders of modern science have been unfolded, each new discovery, it was hoped by the enemies of Christianity, would convict the sacred writers of ignorance and error. As antiquarian research has brought to light new and unexpected facts from long-buried monuments of the past, each fresh accession has been eagerly pounced upon with the view of extracting from it some contradiction of the inspired records. And if at any time, some apparent discrepancy could, for a moment, be sustained, the cry of the enemies of the Bible then was, 'Falsus in uno, falsus in omnibus,'—false in one respect, false in all. How can a book which is thus proved erroneous, claim our confidence? How can it be the word of the infallible God? But it will here be shown that those pæans of triumph were premature, and that there is no cause for apprehension in the Christian camp,—that the Bible is able to resist every assault, from whatever quarter it may come—that it is prepared for every scrutiny of philosophy or of history, and that every fresh discovery which has the remotest bearing upon its authority and veracity, but adds to the "cloud of witnesses" which attest that "the words of the Lord are pure words; as silver tried in a furnace of earth, purified seven times."

PART II.

TESTIMONY OF SCIENCE TO THE BIBLE.

PRELIMINARY.

In undertaking to demonstrate the harmony existing between the statements of Revelation and the discoveries of Science, it seems proper that their difference in aim and object should first be distinctly recognized. It has been said by one of the oracles of human wisdom[1] that "the scope or purpose of the Spirit of God is not to express matters of nature in Scripture otherwise than in passage, for application to man's capacity, and to matters moral and divine." Had this indisputable maxim been borne in mind, many of the unhappy controversies which have occurred between the votaries of Science and the friends of the Bible would have been avoided. For it enunciates a principle which is the true key to the relations of Scripture and Science. It was no part of the design of the sacred writers to communicate scientific truth. The mission with which they were charged was of a far higher character. It was to announce the claims and declare the will of God as the moral Governor of the universe, and to prepare a chart whereby man might be guided in reference to his eternal destiny. It was to unfold the mysteries, not of the kingdom of nature, but of grace. Hence, when they have occa-

[1] Lord Bacon.

sion to refer to "matters of nature in passage," they simply mention a fact as it appears, without any regard to scientific accuracy of expression. They never use the dialect of the schools, but speak of all the appearances and phenomena of nature in popular and optical language, "not as they would be seen by us were we placed in the sun; but as they are represented by our human senses in our present relative position."[1] It is thus they tell us that "the sun stood still over against Gibeon, and the moon in the valley of Ajalon." For it was only such an expression that would be understood by those for whom it was intended. It is the common language which mankind have used in all ages, and will continue to use. And if the most profound astronomers of the present day had occasion to speak of such phenomena as the rising and the setting sun, they would doubtless ignore the true theory of the solar system. Moreover, it should also be considered that for the inspired writers to have done otherwise,—to have taught the truths or corrected the errors of science, and thus have thrown light upon the paths of physical research, would have counteracted the divine plan for the disciplining and training of man, and the gradual and timely development of the activities of his intellect.

The divine wisdom is manifested, therefore, in ordering that the references in the Bible to the facts and phenomena of the natural world should be, as the nature of the case demanded, conventional, not scientific, expressed in the universal language of appearances, and therefore capable of being understood by the unlettered, and in ages wholly ignorant of science. The absence of scientific accuracy by no means involves any real discrepancy or contradiction. There may be a seeming variance between the glowing allusions of the sacred writers to the beautiful phenomenon of the dew and the true theory of its formation, but it is

[1] Coleridge's Aids to Reflection.

seeming only. While, however, there are passages of this sort, in which strictly philosophical language, until comparatively recent times, would have made Scripture a stumbling block both to the learned and unlearned, there are also numerous others containing statements which exhibit a remarkable agreement with modern discovery. The laws and processes of nature are unfolded nowhere in its pages, so as to render human inquiry and toil unnecessary; but by the light of modern science we are now enabled to perceive that in the pregnant expressions uttered ages ago by the inspired writers, truths lay concealed, the discovery of which by slow and laborious processes of investigation, has immortalized not a few of the world's master minds. The secrets which they have won from the domain of the material universe were already in the sacred word, "not indeed in all the minute particulars which the wants and wishes and growth of human society should age by age develop, but there in evidence to show that the hundred gates of Science, as applied to nature, were opened by a divine and gracious hand, that man might enter in, and walk its golden streets, or reap its wide-spread fields." [1]

It is proposed, therefore, in the three following chapters of the present work, to vindicate the Bible against the objections which have been drawn from the discoveries of Physical Science, not merely by showing that seeming contradictions may be explained by referring to the use of optical and conventional language, but that many of those discoveries have been anticipated in its statements, in a manner which unmistakably indicates the presence of an Omniscient Mind. As Astronomy and Geology have been supposed to be especially antagonistic to Revelation, the testimony of those sciences will be separately examined; after which another chapter will be occupied with a setting

[1] Lecture on Religion and Science by Rev. H. M. Mason, D.D.

forth of the contrast which the Bible exhibits, viewed in its scientific relations, to the religious books of the heathen and ancient systems of philosophy,—additional allusions to physical phenomena,—and its recognition of those great primary and leading principles which are the ultimate results of Science.

CHAPTER I.

ASTRONOMY.

The Heavens, which "declare the glory of God," have been invoked by the infidel to disparage the authority of His word, and the unenlightened zeal of not a few of its advocates for a time favored the idea that a real hostility did exist between that sublime science which seeks an intelligent acquaintance with the hieroglyphics of the sky, and the sacred oracles. The progress of scientific discovery and the establishment of the true principles of interpretation have, however, as will be shown, removed the apparent contradictions and demonstrated their entire harmony.

A seeming collision between the Bible and Astronomical Science was found in the use of the word which in our translation is rendered "firmament." It is well known that according to the philosophy of the ancients, the heavens are a mighty and vaulted arch of transparent solid matter in which the fixed stars are firmly riveted, and which with them performs a daily revolution round the earth as a centre. The planets which move in an opposite direction were supposed to belong to a lower and nearer region. In accordance with this view, the Latin Vulgate renders the original Hebrew word "firmamentum," which is an exact synonym of the word "stereoma" used in the Greek Septuagint, and both signify something firm and solid. Josephus also (Antiquities, Book I, c. i, § 1) evidently understood the Scriptures to teach that at the creation the earth was surrounded with a "crystalline firmament" or vault. While the true system of the universe remained unknown, the language of the Bible on this point seemed to accord with what was then known of science. But when, in the light of advancing discovery, the figment of a crystalline vault above us vanishes like a dream of the night, a seeming contradiction is disclosed between the Word and the Works of God. How is it to be met? The usual explanation has been that Moses here used the language of appearances, and that he accommodated the expression to the notions current in the time in which he lived. This has generally been acquiesced in as satisfactory. Recently, however, Mr. Goodwin, one of the contributors to the celebrated "Essays and Reviews," apparently supposing that the word admitted of no other interpretation, has taken pains to show that it is "irreconcilable with the discoveries of modern Astronomy." This is an instance, however, of misdirected zeal, for upon turning to the Hebrew Bible, we find that the word originally used by the inspired writer, does not necessarily mean a solid mass, but should be translated "expanse." "And God said, Let there be an expanse in the midst of the waters, and let it divide the waters from the waters. And God made the expanse. . . . And God called the expanse heaven." We thus find that the sacred historian of the Creation has been misunderstood, and that the word he employs is the best possible that could have been selected to express both the appearance and the actual celestial arrangement. Instead of contradicting, the Bible has here anticipated science.

A like result has attended the once famous controversy respecting the motion of the earth. Three centuries ago, another principle of the scientific creed of the ancients—that the earth was the immovable centre of the celestial mechanism, and that all the heavenly bodies were created for its use—remained undisturbed. Under the influence of Aristotle, it had become an indisputable axiom in the human mind, and his dogma was supposed to be the doctrine of the Bible. When, therefore, the discoveries of Copernicus, Kepler, and Galileo overturned the error of the Stagirite, and demonstrated the motion of our planet round the sun, the innovation upon the established opinions of mankind was denounced as inconsistent with the Christian faith. The Bible was held to be committed to the Aristotelian dogma, by such passages as that in which David has sung that "God hath established the earth upon its foundations; it shall not be moved forever and ever. The going forth of the sun is from end of the heaven, and his circuit unto the ends of it." Solomon also had said: "One generation passeth away, and another generation cometh; but the earth abideth forever." The promulgation of the supposed heresy elicited the thunders of the Vatican, and "the illustrious Galileo was sent to the dungeons of the Inquisition for thinking," as Milton says, "in Astronomy otherwise than the Franciscan and Dominican licensers thought." And among Protestants, divines of such ability, learning, and piety as Calvin and Turretin, held it to be antiscriptural to disbelieve the immobility of the earth. Yet out of this supposed conflict with what is now universally regarded as a true Astronomy, the Bible has come unscathed. It is now seen that there is no real collision. The solution is, that in this case as in others, the sacred writers avoided scientific phraseology and used the language of appearances. They were guided to speak intelligibly to learned and unlearned.

But more than this can be claimed. In one of the very passages above cited, which was supposed to contain a contradiction to science, one of the greatest discoveries of science is plainly recognized, or at least implied. In order to make this appear, it should be stated that the sacred writers elsewhere teach the globular form of the earth, and that it is suspended upon nothing, or on a bottomless space. When, therefore, the Psalmist says that God hath laid the foundations of the earth that it should not be removed forever, what is this but a recognition of the mighty law of gravitation, demonstrated by Newton, whereby the planets are held in their orbits?

> "All intellectual eye, our solar round
> First gazing through, he by the blended power
> Of gravitation and projection saw
> The whole in *silent* harmony revolve."—THOMSON.

This view finds further corroboration in the sublime interrogatory addressed by the Deity to the patriarch in the 38th chapter of the book of Job: "Who shut up the sea with doors when it rushed forth and came out of the womb? When I made the cloud its garment, and the *haraphel* or thickest darkness its swathing band? When I brake upon it my decree, and put bars and doors, and said, Hitherto shalt thou come and no farther, and here shalt thou stop in the proud swelling of thy waves." What is this but the same universal law impressed by the Almighty upon matter at the Creation, by which the relation between land and sea is permanently established, and without which the waters would toss and overspread the earth, so as to render it uninhabitable. This exquisite adjustment thus sublimely set forth in the world's oldest poem, it has been one of the greatest triumphs of modern science to demonstrate and establish.

In the following interrogatory in the same chapter, we find another anticipation of one of the remarkable achievements of modern discovery: "Hast thou commanded the morning and made the day-spring to know his place?" The reference here is to two facts which modern science has ascertained, but which could have been known then only to an Omniscient Mind—the stability of the earth's axis and the uniformity of the earth's rotation. The meaning of the question may be thus expressed: "Hast thou so constituted the earth that it should revolve on its axis, and made it to move with such wonderful precision?" It is now known that the earth preserves a perfect uniformity in its rotation on its axis. And but for this it is evident that the morning would not know its place, nor would there be any regularity in the rising or setting of the stars, which depended on the above conditions. But with such unerring exactness has this uniformity been preserved, that calculation has shown that for two thousand years it could not have varied the one hundredth part of a second of time. And God's covenant of the day and night is elsewhere brought forward in Scripture as the peculiar emblem of God's faithfulness to his promises. "If ye can break my covenant of the day and my covenant of the night, and that there should not be day and night in their season, then may also my covenant be broken with David my servant." Change is written on all the other phenomena of the universe; this is the only ordinance of fixed, immutable stability. But certainly in the times of the patriarch Job, that fact could have been known only to God.[1]

When the Scriptures speak of the stars in the aggregate, the same supernatural knowledge is revealed. It compares their number to the sand. "As the hosts of Heaven cannot be numbered nor the sands of the sea measured."[1] (Jeremiah xxxiii, 22.) But this is a fact which has only been known since the discoveries of modern science have made us aware how vast the scale on which the universe is built. The ancient astronomer Hipparchus fixed the number of stars at 1022, which was increased by the later observations of Ptolemy to 1026. It is now ascertained that in our latitude, during the clearest night, only 1160 stars are visible to the naked eye, while

[1] Prof. Mitchell's Lectures on Astronomy.

an observer watching all night at the equator, may be able to number about three thousand. But the discoveries of the telescope, still recent, have enabled us to realize that the declaration of Holy Scripture uttered so many ages back, is more than a figure of speech. It is calculated that the mighty disc of Lord Rosse's instrument has augmented the magnitude of the stellar universe 125,000,000 times. "God," says Sir John Herschel, after a telescopic survey of the groups of stars and nebulæ in the vast fields of space, "has scattered them like glittering dust on the black ground of the general heavens."

"—— Depth, height, breadth,
Are lost in their extremes, and where to count
The thick sown glories in these fields of fire
Perhaps a seraph's computation fails."

From this wondrous disclosure of science, infidelity has drawn, however, what has been considered as one of the most formidable objections against Revelation, requiring, therefore, a somewhat extended examination.

When from the improvements in the telescope and the discoveries of Galileo and his successors, the illimitable extent and marvellous grandeur of the physical universe had dawned upon human conception, the sceptical objection was soon advanced that it was extravagant and incredible to suppose that amid the millions of globes which are scattered through the vast domains of space, one of the least considerable should be singled out as a special scene of the Creator's care and kindness. Is it probable, the sceptic argued, that the infinite Ruler of such a multiplicity of worlds and systems, many of them far grander than our own, is it probable, that He would send his coequal Son to die for a single rebellious race, the entire loss of which would no more be missed, than the fall of a withered leaf impairs the honors of the forest or the removal of a single grain would diminish the sand of the sea shore? "Is it not as absurd to maintain this, as it would be to hold at the present day the old Ptolemaic hypothesis, according to which the earth is the centre of the vast mechanism of the universe, instead of the newer Copernican doctrine, which teaches that the earth revolves round the sun? And is not the book in which so incredible an assumption is to be found, thereby necessarily disproved?"

To the answering of this objection, Dr. Chalmers addressed himself in his celebrated discourses on "the Modern Astronomy." A brief abstract of his course of argument may serve to show how conclusively he demonstrated its fallacy.

After a brilliant sketch of the wonders of the heavens, he enters upon his reply by showing that the objection is utterly alien to "the modesty of true science," that it indeed violates the first rule of the now universally accepted inductive philosophy, since it must necessarily rest upon an unproved assertion. How does the infidel *know* that Christianity was designed for this world only? If he cannot demonstrate this primary fact, all his reasoning falls to the ground. Who is authorized by the possession of superhuman information, to tell us that in any of the bright worlds that stud the firmament above us, the name and religion of Jesus are unknown? On the contrary, it is probable, that the *moral* influence of the wondrous plan of Redemption is felt and was designed to be felt, to the remotest bounds of Creation. We are justified in believing that the Cross of Christ not merely secures a glorious salvation to perishing sinners of earth, but attracts the wondering gaze of other worlds, and may, by the lessons which it teaches, be the means of confirming myriads of unfallen, sinless beings in their allegiance to God. In the divine moral government of the universe a problem had been presented, to the solution of which the highest created intelligence was unequal. Man created perfect and in the image of God, had transgressed. How shall he be restored? Infinite justice demanded the death of the offender. Yet the misery of his creature appealed to the mercy of God. How shall these jarring claims be reconciled? "A medium is required; it is found. The Word, the Revealer and the Glorifier of the Father, is made flesh; he lives on earth, he suffers, he dies; but in dying, as his bleeding head falls on his quivering breast, the divine harp is struck; and while the curtain is darkly descending on Nature and her dying Lord, the chords of justice and of mercy roll forth their blended notes that echo through every circling sphere, to the most distant regions of the peopled universe." Those glorious and happy intelligences, who, safe in their original purity, had beheld with transport the wonders of Creation and Providence, were now called to see the still greater wonders of Grace and salvation. The unfolding of such a mystery might well employ their eager and delighted contemplation. Were it possible for a planet by some convulsion to be driven from its orbit, and then restored by Omnipotence to its allotted pathway in the heavens, such a phenomenon would be observed with the deepest interest and regarded by men of science as worthy of the most profound investigation. But as far as mind is superior to matter, such an event shrinks into insignificance when compared with the restoration of an alienated, rebel race of accountable beings, wandered far from holiness and God, to the one, harmonious, unchanging system of love and righteousness.[1] The poet only echoes the common voice of mankind when he says:

> "Behold this midnight splendor, worlds on worlds;
> Ten thousand add, and twice ten thousand more,

[1] The thought contained in the above illustration has been thus impressively presented by an eminent living preacher, the Rev. Newman Hall of London: "God is the grand centre of attraction, the only fountain of life and love to all holy souls. Toward Him they adoringly look—round Him they

> Then weigh the whole: one soul outweighs them all,
> And call the seeming vast magnificence
> Of unintelligent creation poor."

Moreover, we are expressly informed in the inspired word, that "the angels" do "desire to look into" the mysteries of Redemption, and that among the ends contemplated by the mighty plan of Grace, it was designed, "that now unto the principalities and powers in heavenly places might be known by the Church the manifold wisdom of God."

If these considerations are thought insufficient to meet the difficulty, it is also to be remembered that "God's ways and thoughts are not ours," and we shall greatly err, if we suppose that our estimate of what is small or great,

reverently revolve—in His radiance alone they shine. Obeying his laws they move in harmony with the great universe—they roll on without rub in the grand mechanism of the divine purposes; and with voices more real and jubilant than the music of the spheres, they evermore, in rapturous hallelujahs, express their own gladness and their Creator's praise. But should any of these, in wilful disobedience, break loose from that spiritual gravitation, which, being voluntary, is capable of being resisted—should any soul turn away from the Central Sun to gaze on other objects in regions beyond its orbit—should the lust after forbidden objects, wilfully and wickedly encouraged, engender an anomalous centrifugal force, causing it to break loose from that gravitation toward the Deity on which the order and happiness of the moral universe depend,—could such a soul expect to enjoy the same privileges and security as before? Rushing from the light, must it not now roam on in gloom—one degree of darkness ever leading to another more deep? The golden chain of love which hitherto bound it to the Eternal Throne being broken, instead of circulating around that throne radiant in its glories, must it not now pursue its solitary, ignominious course; and having forsaken the happy path of obedience, plunge wildly on in its own self-chosen career, destruction its final and inevitable doom?

"If a planet under such circumstances could not be brought back; yet, thanks be to God, a wandering sinner can. For the Sun of Righteousness comes after the wanderer to draw him once more into his true orbit—the attracting centre pursues the guilty fugitive as he rushes away from light and joy. Jesus came to seek and to save the lost. Yield to the attractions of His cross, and He will replace you in your true orbit."—*Exeter Hall Lectures*, 1859.

can be entertained by a Being who is infinite in all perfections. To us, indeed, the cedars of Libanus may seem more striking and majestic than the little hyssop which springeth out of the wall; and the Leviathan which "maketh the deep to boil like a pot," more than the conies which are a "feeble folk and make their dwelling among the rocks." But let us not imagine that He who made them all, is influenced in his care and attention to all, by the respective magnitude of each. The inconceivable extent of his dominions does not necessarily lessen the interest which he feels in particular portions. He can at the same moment watch over the revolutions of worlds and the fall of a sparrow; and it is in keeping with what we elsewhere see of the glory of God in the minute as well as in the vast, not only in the sublimities of Alps and Andes, but also in the lustre of an insect's wing, and in the curious aqueducts by which a leaf is nourished,—that He should thus lavish the treasures of his wisdom and his grace, to rescue from a ruin, otherwise irretrievable, even this humble province of his universal empire. As the largest telescope is insufficient to carry the power of human vision to the remotest bounds of creation, but leaves it where mighty systems dwindle to a faint nebulous speck of light, so have we reason to believe that the most powerful microscope that ever has been or will be constructed, will be altogether unable to guide our views to the utmost limits in the *descendiny* scale of creation. If the one has brought into view worlds as numerous as the drops of water which make up the ocean; the other has brought into view a world in almost every drop of water.[1] And in the mechanism of that little world

[1] "Professor Ehrenberg," says Mrs. Somerville, "has discovered a new world of creatures in the infusoria, so minute that they are invisible to the naked eye. He found them in fog, rain, and snow, in the ocean and stagnant water, in animal and vegetable juices, in volcanic ashes and pumice, in opal, in the dusty air that sometimes falls upon the ocean; and he detected eighteen species twenty feet below the surface of the ground in peat earth,

and its myriads of inhabitants, we behold the same display of wisdom and benevolence, the same elaborate skill and contrivance, which are shown in the construction of the elephant or the whale, or in those mighty globes that float around us in the sky. If the telescope has more fully unfolded to us the meaning of the inspired declaration, "He telleth the number of the stars and calleth them all by their names;" the microscope enables to perceive a deeper sense in the answering utterance, "Even the very hairs of your head are all numbered." And the combined lesson of both is that "we are in the midst of being, whose amount, perhaps, we cannot estimate, but which is yet all so exquisitely related, that the perfection of its parts has no dependence upon their magnitude; of being within whose august bosom the little ant has its home, secure as the path of the most splendid star; and whose mightiest intervals—if Infinite Power has built up its framework—Infinite Mercy and Infinite Love glowingly fill, and give all things warmth, and lustre, and life—the sense of the presence of God, to whom an atom is a world, and a world an atom." There would certainly be force in the objection we are considering, if man were to rest his claim to such an astonishing display of mercy and love as the scheme of Redemption unfolds, upon any excellency of his own or upon the importance of the position which he holds in the scale of creation. But his claim, if so it can be called, is of a far different kind and derived from a different principle, and becomes so much the stronger as science extends its empire. His title is

which was full of microscopic live animals; they exist in ice, and are not killed by boiling water. This lowest order of animal life is much more abundant than any other, and new species are found every day. Magnified, some of them seem to consist of a transparent vesicle, and some have a tail; they move with great alacrity, and show intelligence by avoiding obstacles in their course; others have silicious shells. Language, and even imagination, fails in the attempt to describe the inconceivable myriads of these invisible inhabitants of the ocean, the air, and the earth."—*Physical Geography.*

derived from his own necessity on the one hand, and on the other from the infinite love and compassion of Him who came from Heaven to save. If that love could be measured by a human standard, if the goings forth of its tenderness and mercy could be elicited only by the high qualities of the being in whose behalf it is exercised, it might be in harmony with man's conceptions and estimates, but it would not be the mercy of God. It would not be that mercy of which man knoweth not the height nor depth, nor length nor breadth, a mercy which left the angels to perish while it redeemed man, and which is so touchingly illustrated by our Lord's parables concerning the "lost piece of silver," and the "one lost sheep," to seek and to save which, the shepherd left "the ninety and nine which went not astray." The lower the place assigned man in the scale of the Creator's works, and the more Science expands that creation in widening circles around him, the more his redemption becomes in harmony with the Creator's attributes, and the deeper and more profound the meaning we can recognize in the language with which the Psalmist expresses his astonishment at the Divine Condescension: "When I consider thy heavens, the work of thy fingers, the moon and the stars which Thou hast ordained; what is man that Thou art mindful of him? and the son of man that Thou visitest him?" "As is His majesty, so is His mercy."

The infidel objection from the vastness of the material universe has been thus conclusively met and answered by considerations drawn from science itself. Yet another argument, perhaps, not less convincing, may be deduced from the analogies of the word of God. The stupendous humiliation of the Incarnation is in entire harmony with all the other facts which marked the early life of Immanuel. It was wholly destitute of human pomp and grandeur. No unearthly palace was let down from the skies to be his dwelling place. No monarch was driven from his throne for him to occupy it. A stable was his first habitation and his first couch was spread among the beasts of the stall. The far greater portion of his life was spent in obscurity, and all in poverty. A few poor fishermen were his attendants; his only crown, a crown of thorns; a reed given him in derision was his sceptre; a cross of ignominy was his throne. If then the mystery of godliness is great, it is so throughout. From the manger to the cross and the grave, it is one harmonious whole. But from all these scenes of wondrous humiliation a divine glory streams, conveying to the mind of every earnest seeker after truth irresistible conviction that in that lowly suffering form, God tabernacled with men. Let it be then that our earth is but a little world—that, like its own Bethlehem Ephratah, it shrinks from comparison with thousands of its sister spheres —that "it does not swell so largely to the eye, or shine so brightly to the night," yet since it has been ennobled by the events of Gethsemane and Calvary, not the less may we feel assured that as an object of interest it eclipses them all. Since it received the visit of the Son of God, in the eye of the universe, the entire globe is a Holy Land.

But not only have the discoveries of Astronomy been urged as inconsistent with the revealed plan of Redemption, modern infidelity has sought to find in the same sublime science proofs and arguments wherewith to assail the Bible doctrine of creation. The great Lord Bacon "would rather believe all the fables in the Legend, and Talmud and Alcoran, than that this universal frame is without a mind;" but philosophers of the present age have sought to demonstrate and establish an hypothesis, whereby the system of the universe with all its varied phenomena might be explained and accounted for by the operation of physical laws to the exclusion of divine, creative agency. "By the aid of the so-called 'Nebular Theory,' unnumbered assaults have been made upon the Old Testament; and we were assured, a quarter of a century ago, that it would soon be exploded altogether. Feeling himself impregnable while standing upon that theory for his basis, 'the inductive Philosopher' very confidently asserted 'that there never had been such a thing as *creation*, in the generally received sense of the term;' and transferred us from the dominion of Jehovah to that of some unintelligent and inexorable 'law,' or of some Oriental boodha, who, having called the principles of nature into existence, and set them a-going, retired into quiescence forever."[1]

As the doctrine of an all-wise and almighty God, the Creator of all things visible and invisible, is the fundamental truth of all religion, natural and revealed, it will be pertinent to the design of the present work to examine this theory, and also to bring forward some of the evidences of creative design which Astronomy presents.

The idea that nebulæ or loose masses of fiery vapor, which seemed to be floating in the depths of remote space, might form the materials out of which were gradually elaborated suns and planets, was an original conception of the illustrious discoverer, Sir William Herschel, though without any thought by him of the use to which it could be applied. It was caught at and adopted by the great French Astronomer Laplace, and having been by his labors brought into definite and tangible form, as a theory it is associated with his name. It supposes that loose masses of nebulous vapor, at first without definite form or movement, gradually assumed by virtue of gravitation, a regular spheroidal and rotating form, lightest at the circumference and gradally increasing in density toward the centre, at which point the greatest density is attained. This was the nucleus from which suns were gradually evolved, around which by the combined processes of rotation and further condensation, successive and concentric rings were formed on the outer

1 Christian Observer.

limits of the nebulous disks, of which, it is supposed, we have a faint illustration in the rings of Saturn. These rings, according to the theory, subsequently became broken up and detached, when the matter composing them naturally agglomerated into spheres, which by an analogous process of condensation and evolution of rings, produced planets and their satellites.

Such is the celebrated Nebular Hypothesis, which has enjoyed a great popularity, and, for a time, threw the Mosaic Cosmogony into the shade. Infidel philosophy seemed to have achieved the triumph of showing how the universe could be formed without a God. Physical law was alleged to have unfolded that wondrous magnificence and beauty which we behold in the Heavens and in the earth, instead of Him who liveth forever.

With the advancement of discovery, however, this brilliant theory has been losing ground. The searching ken of Sir John Herschel's powerful telescope at the Cape of Good Hope, disclosed the fact that some of the nebulæ were resolvable. Faint patches of light as seen through feebler instruments, now assumed a grandeur beyond the dreams of science. The giant telescopic eye framed by Lord Rosse has made discoveries even more remarkable. The nebulous light in the northern region of the milky way was at once resolved into "distinct stars and star dust," and the white fleecy cloud of Orion which had hitherto baffled all attempts to disclose its texture, was shown to be "a gorgeous bed of stars." And many other dim, faint, misty spots put off their nebulous features, and assumed the glories of sidereal bodies. Thus has the idea been gradually matured in the scientific mind, that all those hieroglyphics in the sky betoken inconceivably distant and "countless myriads of firmamental star-clusters, which are themselves, severally, what the cluster is that is seen by the naked eye to spangle the surrounding heavens at night; that there are families of firmaments, as there are groups and associated clusters of stars or suns." This magnificent conception cannot be numbered among the fixed results of science, and is not, therefore, to be urged as a direct argument in disproof of the Nebular Hypothesis. But from what has already been discovered, it is now conceded, that could another instrument of considerably greater power than that of Lord Rosse, be constructed, that ingenious theory already so much damaged, might be completely destroyed. "As advanced by Laplace," says Professor Whewell, "it was a mere conjecture. It is a mere conjecture still. Hitherto it has lost ground in the progress of Astronomical researches." And says Dr. Lardner, "Such an hypothesis" (as that of diffuse luminous matter) "is not needed to explain appearances which are so much more obviously and simply explicable by the admission of a gradation of distances."

But even if, for argument's sake, we grant the hypothesis to be correct, that out of a "diffused luminosity" were gradually evolved suns and planets, it does not prove, or even necessarily suppose that anything has been done without the intervention of intelligence and design. Its only effect is to transfer our view of the skill exercised and the means employed to another part of the work. It is related of Epicurus that when, as a boy, he was reading with his preceptor the verses of Hesiod, which tell us that—

> "Eldest of beings, Chaos first arose,
> Thence earth-wide stretched the steadfast seat of all
> The immortals—"

the young scholar first betrayed his inquisitive genius by putting the inquiry, "And Chaos whence?" And thus is it in the case before us. The attempt to erect a physical system which shall explain how the beauty and grandeur of the universe were gradually produced, only places the necessity of divine interposition and creative agency farther back. Unless *that* be granted, innumerable questions and difficulties will still arise, for which an answer will be sought in vain. "Why," it may be asked, "must the primeval condition be one of change at all? Why should not the nebulous matter be equally diffused through space, and continue forever in its state of equable diffusion, as it must do, from the absence of all cause to determine the time and manner of its separation? Why should this nebulous matter grow cooler and cooler? Why should it not retain forever the same degree of heat, whatever heat be? If heat be a fluid—if to cool be to part with this fluid, as many philosophers suppose—what becomes of the fluid heat of the nebulous matter, as the matter cools down? Into what unoccupied region does it find its way?" These and numerous similar questions can only be met by admitting that the nebulous mass diffused throughout space, supposing such to have existed, came not there without the fiat of the Almighty; and suns and planets were not formed out of that mass without the intervention of infinite wisdom. "Let it be supposed," says Professor Whewell, "that the point to which the hypothesis leads us is the ultimate point of physical science; that the farthest glimpse we can obtain of the material universe by our natural faculties, shows it to us as occupied by a boundless abyss of luminous matter; still we ask how space came to be thus occupied, how matter came to be thus luminous? If we establish by physical proofs, that the first fact which can be traced in the history of the world is that 'there was light;' we shall still be led even by natural reason, to suppose that before this could occur, 'God said, Let there be light.'"

But whatever method the Divine Architect may have chosen whereby to frame and build up this magnificent universe, and make it a temple to his praise, the wonderful provision He has made for its stability and permanence, which it has been one of the most brilliant triumphs of modern science to unfold and demonstrate, bears so unmistakably the impress of his infinite wisdom, that none but those who are incapable of reasoning from effect to cause, or by some anomaly in the laws of intellect, are insensible to the clearest evidence, can resist the conviction, that here is the finger of God ![1]

Since the laws which govern the movements of the heavenly bodies have been understood, certain irregularities and disturbances have been perceived in the planetary orbits, arising from the mutual attraction of the different planets upon each other, which suggest the arrival of an epoch in the course of revolving ages, when the effects of these irregularities, now minute, shall have accumulated sufficiently to derange the whole order of nature and reduce our system, now harmonious, to chaos and confusion. Actual observation, moreover, of the state of the Heavens at different periods, has established the fact, that in conse-

[1] The validity of the argument that the evidence of design demonstrates the existence of God, has, indeed, been called in question by the recklessness of modern scepticism. It is, says the infidel, the "petitio principii of dialectics," and he denies that there is any such evidence. To this it may be replied that the greatest intellects whom the world has known have acquiesced in it as an axiom or self-evident proposition, which requires no demonstration. The noble passage which Baron Humboldt has quoted in his Cosmos from Aristotle (a passage from a lost work, preserved by Cicero), expresses, in a heathen form, the inextinguishable conviction of every intelligent mind, in which "the light" has not become "darkness." It runs thus: "If there were beings who lived in the depths of the earth, in dwellings adorned with statues and paintings, and everything which is possessed in rich abundance by those whom men esteem fortunate; and if these beings could receive tidings of the might and majesty of the gods, and could then emerge from their hidden dwellings through the open fissures of the earth to the places which we inhabit; if they could suddenly behold the earth, and the sea and the vault of heaven; could recognize the expanse of the cloudy firmament, and the might of the winds of heaven, and admire the sun in its majesty, beauty, and radiant effulgence; and lastly, when night veiled the earth in darkness, they could behold the starry heavens, the changing moon, and the stars rising and setting in the unvarying course ordained from eternity, they would surely exclaim, There are gods, and such great things must be the work of their hands.' "—*Cosmos*, Amer. ed., vol. ii, p. 29.

quence of these perturbations great changes in the relative position of the heavenly bodies have taken place, rendering the conclusion irresistible, that we are apparently gradually approaching such a catastrophe.

It becomes, therefore, a question of deep interest, whether, in the mechanism of the universe, this contingency has been provided for and any adjustment prepared whereby to avert its consequences. This is a problem which could not be solved when the difficulty was first perceived. Its decision required such progress in the invention and improvement of mathematical methods, as occupied the best mathematicians of Europe the greater part of the last century. Even Sir Isaac Newton could devise no other solution than the special interference of the Almighty to arrest the ruin of his work. The combined researches of Lagrange, Laplace and others have, however, by means of a refined analysis, demonstrated the wondrous fact that the solar system itself contains an element of self-conservation—that this contingency has been provided for, and that at the very moment when these perturbations shall have reached their maximum, and the crash of worlds appear inevitable, a series of compensations will commence which will precisely bring back the system to the state in which it existed before. Like the oscillations of a pendulum, "each orbit undergoes deviations on this side, and on that of its average state; but these deviations are never very great, and it finally recovers from them, so that the average is preserved. The planets produce perpetual perturbations in each other's motions, but these perturbations are not infinitely progressive, they are periodical; they reach a maximum and then diminish. The periods which this restoration requires are for the most part enormous; not less than thousands, and in some instances millions of years; and hence it is that some of these apparent derangements have been going on in the same direction since the beginning of the history of the world. But the restoration is in the sequel as complete as the derangement; and in the mean time the disturbance never attains a sufficient amount seriously to alter the adaptations of the system."

"Thus," says Professor Mitchell, "do we find that God has built the heavens in wisdom, to declare his glory, and to show forth his handy-work. There are no iron tracks with bars and bolts, to hold the planets in their orbits. Freely in space they move, ever changing but never changed; poised and balancing, swaying and swayed, disturbing and disturbed, onward they fly, fulfilling with unerring certainty their mighty cycles. The entire system forms one grand, complicated piece of celestial machinery; circle within circle, wheel within wheel, cycle within cycle; revolutions so swift, as to be completed in a few hours; movements so slow, that their mighty periods are only to be counted by millions of years. Are we to believe that the Divine Architect constructed this admirably adjusted system to wear out, and to fall into ruin, even before one single revolution of its complex scheme of wheels have been performed? No! I see the mighty orbits of the planets rocking to and fro, their figure expanding and contracting, their axes revolving in their vast periods; but stability is there. Every change shall wear away, and after sweeping through the grand cycle of cycles, the whole system shall return to the primitive condition of perfection and beauty."

And can this exquisitely contrived plan of compensation and adjustment be the effect of chance, or produced by a process of natural laws working in them and by them? Surely, the contemplation of so amazing a contrivance must compel us to declare with Newton, that "this beautiful system could have its origin no other way than by the purpose and command of an intelligent and powerful Being, who governs all things, not as the soul of the world, but as the Lord of the universe; who is not only God, but Lord and Governor;" or, in the still more expressive language of the inspired Hebrew historian: "In the beginning God created the heavens and the earth."

There is another admirable arrangement, equally suggestive of divine wisdom, whether we adopt or reject the hypothesis of Laplace. In the annual motion of the earth round the sun, its axis is inclined from the perpendicular to its orbit at an angle of twenty-three degrees, and remains constantly parallel to this direction. By this arrangement the changes of temperature on the earth's surface, and of the seasons are produced. Had the axis of the earth, instead of being so inclined, been perpendicular to the plane of its orbit, as is the case in Jupiter, the sun would always have been vertical to the same line of places, the equatorial regions would have been parched by the heat, while the regions, called temperate in the present arrangement, would have been consigned to utter desolation. By the existing disposition, the various parts of the earth are brought more fully under the solar influence, and we have all the delightful and beneficent effects which flow from the variety of climates.

"Again, the earth is nearer the sun at one season than at another, and without some counteracting influence there would be an inconvenient increase both of the cold of winter and the heat of summer in the southern hemisphere, and the climate of the two hemispheres would be rendered altogether unlike each other. But any injury which might arise from this cause is made to disappear, chiefly by means of the circumstance that the point of the earth's orbit which is nearest the sun is that over which it moves with the greatest speed. It is ascertained that the quantity of heat which is conveyed by the sun to the earth, is the same during the passage from the vernal to the autumnal equinox, as in returning from the latter to the former. The much longer time which the sun takes in the first part of his course is exactly compensated by its proportionably greater distance, and the quantities of heat which is conveyed to the earth are the same, whether in the one hemisphere or the other, north or south."[1]

Surely, the denial of divine wisdom in such exquisite adjustment, can only be accounted for by wilful blindness. That mind must be closed to conviction which does not respond to the declaration of the apostle, that "the invisible things of Him from the creation of the world are clearly seen, being understood by the things which are made, even his eternal power and Godhead."

But with all the evidences of design that are manifested in the construction of the material system, and the provision which Infinite Wisdom has made for its stability, there are not wanting indications that it is still of a temporary nature, and that a period is destined to arrive in the cycles of the universe, when it shall come to an end.

Among the agencies which may be considered as pointing to such a result, is the resisting medium whose existence throughout the boundless space traversed by the heavenly bodies, is now generally recognized among astronomers as the cause of the long observed acceleration in the motions of the comet of Encke. The excessive tenuity of such bodies fitting them to be readily affected by its action, evidently, can afford us no clue as to the period which must elapse, ere its effects could derange the mechanism of the solar system. Still, granting the existence of a resisting medium, it necessarily follows that there must be such a period. "It may be millions of millions of years," says Professor Whewell, "before the earth's retardation may perceptibly affect the apparent motion of the sun; but still the day will come (if the same Providence which formed the system, should permit it to continue so long), when this cause will entirely change the length of

[1] McCosh on Typical Forms and Special Ends in Creation.

the year, and the course of our seasons, and finally stop the earth's motion round the sun altogether. The smallness of the resistance, however small we choose to suppose it, does not allow us to escape the certainty. There is a resisting medium; and, therefore, the movements of the solar system cannot go on forever. The moment such a fluid is known to exist, the eternity of the movements of the planets becomes as impossible as a perpetual motion on the earth."

Not in the least, however, does this oppose or weaken the evidence of a Supreme, Creative Intelligence exhibited by the arrangements of the universe. For does it not furnish an unanswerable proof that the present order of things which must have an end, must also have had a beginning? "There must have been a period in which the impulse now proceeding originated. A period of commencement implies a cause; the order and regularity of the system imply an Intelligent Cause; and thus the idea of Creator is forced upon us; and instead of an eternal operation of mechanical powers, and an eternal succession of organized existences, which is the dream of the atheist, we see a system, glorious with the impress of a Divine hand, and rejoicing in the smile of a present Deity."

For the permanence of that system during the period which Almighty Wisdom intended it should occupy, as we have seen, an exquisite arrangement has been made. So long as the heavenly bodies continue to revolve, this provision will rectify the irregularities of their orbits and counteract the tendencies to derangement; nor will this result be affected by the action of the resisting medium, the action of which does not tend to increase or diminish the eccentricities of the celestial motions. Still its ultimate effect must be to arrest those motions and bring this mighty universe to an end. And in addition to this cause, "the constant radiation of heat from the sun into space, and the absorption of vital power by the mutual action of the moon and the tide wave, together with the fragments of broken planets, the descent of meteoric stones upon our globe, the wheeling comets welding their loose materials at the solar surface, the volcanic eruptions of our own satellite, the appearance of new stars and the disappearance of others," all seem to foreshadow the approaching termination of our present system.

And is not this catastrophe in harmony with what appears to be creation's universal law? Absolute permanence is written nowhere on the face of nature. The oak of the forest wears for centuries its leafy honors and then decays; the stupendous mountains crumble and wear away; "where the long street roars, hath been" (so Geology teaches us), "the stillness of the central sea;" and it now appears that the law of change reaches even to the firmament, and the unwearied circuits of the planets have an end.

> "What does not fade? The tower that long had stood
> The crush of thunder, and the warring winds,
> Shook by the slow but sure destroyer Time,
> Now hangs in doubtful ruins o'er its base;
> And flinty pyramids and walls of brass
> Descend; the Babylonian spires are sunk;
> Achaia, Rome, and Egypt moulder down.
> Time shakes the stable tyranny of thrones;
> And tottering empires rush by their own weight.
> This huge rotundity we tread grows old,
> And all those worlds that roll around the sun.
> The sun himself shall die, and ancient night
> Again involve the desolate abyss."—AKENSIDE.

"But after all," says Professor Nichol, "why should such an anticipation be painful? The fact of change merely intimates that, in the exhaustless womb of the Future, unevolved wonders are in store. The phenomena referred to would simply point to the close of one mighty cycle in the history of the solar orb—the passing away of arrangements which have fulfilled their objects, that they might be changed into new. Thus is the periodic death of a planet, perhaps, the essential of its prolonged life; and when the individual dies and disappears, fresh and vigorous forms spring from the elements which composed it. Mark the chrysalis! It is the grave of the worm, but the cradle of the sun-born insect. The broken bowl will yet be healed and beautified by the potter, and a voice of joyful note will awaken one day even the silence of the urn."

"Nay, what though all should pass? What, though the close of this epoch in the history of the solar orb should be accompanied, as some by a strange fondness have imagined, by the dissolution and disappearing of all these shining spheres? Then would our universe not have failed in its functions, but only have been gathered up and rolled away, these functions being complete. That gorgeous material framework, wherewith the Eternal hath adorned and varied the abysses of space, is only an instrument by which the myriads of spirits borne upon its orbs may be told of their origin, and educated for more exalted being; and the time may come when the veil can be drawn aside—when spirit shall converse *directly* with spirit, and the creature gaze without hindrance on the effulgent face of the Creator."

The final catastrophe of the present system of things (using a limited acceptation of that phrase) to which Science points, is in perfect harmony with the teachings of the Bible, while the anticipations of what is to follow, so glowingly expressed in the brilliant words of Professor Nichol, are but the echo of the far sublimer descriptions of the future inheritance prepared for the righteous, to be found in the inspired Word. Long ago had the royal bard of Judah sung: "The Heavens are the work of thy hands. They shall perish, but Thou shalt endure; yea, all of them shall *wax old* like a garment, as a vesture shalt Thou change them and they shall be changed." And long ago from the rocky shores of Patmos, the beloved apostle had seen, in prophetic vision, the new heavens and the new earth which are to succeed the dissolution and passing away of the heavens and the earth that now are. By that awful and tremendous catastrophe, though it is to be accomplished by the agency of fire, whose materials, as Science tells us, are laid up in the composition of the atmosphere, of the waters, and of the earth itself, we are not authorized to suppose that the glorious works of God shall literally be destroyed. But, as the records of the rocks reveal that our planet has already undergone mighty transformations, so shall it be at the predicted period of "the restitution of all things." And when the fires of purification shall have swept over its surface, and the memorials of man's art and man's iniquity have alike been destroyed in the avenging flame, the earth shall emerge from the conflagration, not consumed, but emancipated from the thraldom of the curse, and, as we cannot doubt, arrayed in a garb of loveliness, far more glorious than it wore, even in that hour when God first pronounced His work to be "good," and "the morning stars sang together and all the sons of God shouted for joy." This is a result which the statements of Holy Scripture lead us to anticipate, and which the discoveries of Science, as to past changes of the earth, confirm. It does not follow, however, from this, that the renovated earth is to be the exclusive seat or boundary of the future heaven of the righteous; though it is far from improbable, that, associated as it is and ever must be, with such imperishable recollections, it may be one among the "many mansions," which they shall be permitted from time to time to visit and occupy. Neither the Bible nor Science indicates to us the locality of the special home of the sanctified family of God, the "place" which the Redeemer went "to prepare;" but through the discoveries of the marvellous grandeur of the universe opened up by Modern Astronomy, faith may be assisted to descry, what now the material eye cannot see, the spires and turrets of that celestial city, in which "there shall be no night, and they need no candle nor light of the sun." They can give us no positive information whatever, yet the views of the inexhaustible resources of the Creator which those discoveries suggest, are in harmony with the scattered intimations of Scripture on this deeply interesting subject. These are necessarily indefinite, yet their careful consideration will, perhaps, lead us to adopt the conclusion, thus eloquently expressed by Bishop Pearson: "This first aerial heaven, where God setteth up his pavilion, where 'he maketh the clouds his chariot, and walketh upon the wings of the wind,' is not so far inferior in place as it is in glory to the next, the seat of the sun and moon, the two great lights, and stars innumerable, far greater than the one of them. And yet that second heaven is not so far above the first as beneath the third into which St. Paul was caught. The brightness of the sun doth not so far surpass the blackness of a wandering cloud, as the glory of that heaven of presence surmounts the fading beauty of the starry firmament. For in this great temple of the world, in which the Son of God is the High Priest, the heaven which we see is but the veil, and that which is above, the holy of holies. This veil indeed is rich and glorious, but one day to be rent, and then to admit us into a far greater glory, even to the mercy seat and cherubim. For this third heaven is the proper habitation of the blessed angels, who constantly attend upon the throne."

One of the grandest achievements of modern science has been the discovery of the new planet Neptune, in October, 1846—a discovery not by accident, but to which the observers were led by scientific theory and deduction alone. Some time previous to the verification of Leverrier's analysis, Sir John Herschel predicted with undoubting confidence the great astronomical triumph in the following beautiful language addressed to the meeting of the British Association: "Among the remarkable events of the last twelvemonth, it has added a new planet to our list.[1] It has done more—it has given us the probable prospect of the discovery of another. We see it, as Columbus saw America from the shores of Spain. Its movements have been felt, trembling along the far reaching line of our analysis, with a certainty hardly inferior to ocular demonstration." This anticipation has been realized, and by the aid of the telescope, the eye of the astronomer has actually descried a new and mighty planet of our system, so remote in the depths of space as to include within its orbit the farthest range of the comet of Halley, which requires seventy-five years for its period of revolution. The faith which is "the evidence of things unseen," can, however, far surpass this wondrous achievement and realize to the spiritual vision a world far more remote and inconceivably more glorious. True, our knowledge of its existence is derived from different sources than was the persuasion of the Genoese mariner, who saw in the floating trees and plants borne by the gulf stream of the tropics to the shores of Europe, tangible evidence of the western continent. Nor can we hope to verify our belief by our material vision, even though aided by "the philosophic tube, that brings the planets home into the eye of observation." Yet with an assurance more firmly grounded than that of the great navigator, or the astronomer, we may know and believe, that beyond the azure canopy above us, there is "a better—an heavenly country." It is remarkable, that the progress of astronomical discovery seems now to be tending toward the recognition of a grand centre of the universe, around which suns and planets, stars and constellations, in one mighty system, harmoniously revolve. Should this

[1] Astrea, discovered by Mr. Drencke of Dreisen, Dec. 8, 1845.

sublime theory, which, indeed, already appears to rest upon a scientific basis far above mere conjecture,[1] be certainly demonstrated, perhaps, it were not absurd to imagine, that there in its great and awful reality might be the Throne of God, and that there might be the spot where abides the ascended Redeemer in his glorified humanity, the centre of unity at once to the physical and moral creation. And although the most costly and gigantic telescope of science cannot avail to give us the faintest glimpse of "that land very far off, where dwelleth the King in his beauty;" where stands his throne of glory, more radiant than the sun, and his shining palace brighter than the light; and where his shining peers and princely subjects are ever to live with him and behold his glory; yet even here there are "delectable mountains," known to Christian experience, as favored pilgrims have assured us, whence the far off city of God with its gates of pearl and its streets of gold may almost be descried through the mists of earth, and "sweet echoes of unearthly melodies" dimly fall upon the ear. As he approached the confines of the eternal world, the dying Payson said: "The eternal city is full in my view. Its glories beam upon me, its breezes fan me, its odors are wafted to me, its sounds strike upon my ears, and its spirit is breathed into my heart." A view so strong and clear as

[1] "The two great laws of gravitation and inertia, by which our own system is regulated and maintained, have been proved to exist with precisely the same powers, at least in some of the fixed stars. The probability, therefore, is, that all these are universal qualities inherent in all material objects. This being granted, seems to imply the necessity of a balanced rotatory motion in every system of worlds, for preserving the general equilibrium of the whole; because the universal attraction must prevent any body from remaining stationary. Now, the same principle appears to apply to groups of systems which applies to systems themselves. Hence we may infer a complication of movements of the most wonderful and extensive kind, combining not merely worlds with worlds, and systems with systems, but nebulæ with nebulæ, embracing the whole material creation and extending to infinity."—*Eclectic Magazine.*

this, few can hope to attain from these mortal shores. Yet the glass of Scripture is open to all, and from the "glorious things" it reveals to our faith of the "city of God," every believer may form and cherish an ideal of the future home awaiting him at the close of his pilgrimage, to which the Pagan dreams of Elysian fields, Hesperian gardens, and Islands of the Blest, are as tapers to the sun.

"About the holy city rolls a flood
Of molten chrystal, like a sea of glass,
On which weak stream, a strong foundation stood;
Of living diamonds the building was,
That all things else, besides itself, did pass;
Her streets, instead of stones, the stars did pave,
And little pearls, for dust, it seem'd to have,
On which soft-streaming manna, like pure snow, did wave.

"In midst of this city celestial,
Where the Eternal Temple should have rose,
Lightened the Idea Beatifical—
End and beginning of each thing that grows;
Whose self no end nor yet beginning knows,
That hath no eyes to see, nor ears to hear,
Yet sees and hears, and is all eye, all ear;
That nowhere is contained, and yet is every where.

"A heavenly feast, no hunger can consume;
A light unseen, yet shines in every place;
A sound no time can steal; a sweet perfume
No winds can scatter; an entire embrace
That no satiety can e'er unlace:
Ingraced into so high a favor, there
The saints, with their beau peers, whole worlds outwear,
And things unseen do see, and things unheard do hear.

"No sorrow now hangs clouding on their brow,
No bloodless malady empales their face,
No age drops on their hairs his silver snow,
No poverty themselves and theirs disgrace,
No fear of death the joy of life devours,
No loss, no grief, no change wait on their winged hours."

REV. GILES FLETCHER.

CHAPTER II.

GEOLOGY.

FROM that sublime science which traverses the fields of immensity and presents to our contemplation the glories of the firmament, and which claims an antiquity coeval with the infancy of society, we will now turn to another hardly less attractive, but of comparatively recent origin, which calls our attention to evidences of Creative power, wisdom, and goodness, hidden in the deep recesses of the earth. "In the magnitude and sublimity of the objects of which it treats, Geology," says Sir John Herschel, "undoubtedly ranks, in the scale of the sciences, next to Astronomy." "If the discoveries of Astronomy are vast, the discoveries of Geology are no less vast: they extend through time, as those of Astronomy do through space. They carry us through millions of years, that is, of the earth's revolutions, as those of Astronomy do through millions of the earth's diameters, or of diameters of the earth's orbit. Geology fills the regions of duration with events, as Astronomy fills the regions of the universe with objects."[1] Let us interrogate its discoveries respecting their harmony with revelation.

Until near the commencement of the present century, it was, perhaps, the generally received opinion, sanctioned, it was supposed, by Holy Scripture, that the earth, if not the whole universe, dated from an epoch of about six thousand

[1] Plurality of Worlds.

years ago, and that previous to that period, the matter of which it is composed, was not in existence, much less was it the home of animal or vegetable life. It was supposed also, that previous to the fall of man, decay and death were unknown in the creation, and that the beasts of the field were partakers of our immortality. But modern science has contradicted these suppositions; and innumerable wrecks of a former state of nature, wonderfully preserved ("like ancient medals and inscriptions in the ruins of an empire") have been brought from the deepest caverns of the earth and the bottoms of the mountains, "from scarped cliff and quarried stone," to prove the immeasurable antiquity of our globe, and that death was a law among its animal tribes, ages before man had made his appearance upon its surface.

From a careful study of some fossil organic remains found in the gypsum quarries near Paris, the celebrated French naturalist Cuvier was the first to establish an order of facts pointing to the above conclusion. Since his time, the various strata of the earth and their embedded contents, which had been for centuries the occasion of wonder and perplexity, have been laboriously investigated by the ablest scientific minds, and with great and surprising results. And, contrary to a too prevalent notion respecting the science of geology, those results cannot be impugned on the ground that the principles of the science are unsettled and constantly changing. If there were cause for the imputation, while it was yet in a state of immaturity, the case is different now. Geology is still a youthful science, but is no longer immature. Its principles are as clearly ascertained and "as well settled as the theory of the earth's diurnal and annual motions in astronomy, or the doctrine of definite proportions in chemistry."

"The most important of these principles are the following: The whole accessible crust of the globe has undergone entire, and oftentimes repeated metamorphoses, since the rocks were created; enormous erosions have taken place upon the earth since it was consolidated; existing continents, by slow vertical movements, have been below the ocean several times; processes are now going on around us, capable of producing nearly all the known varieties of rock, with the aid of water and heat; water and heat have been the grand agents of all geological changes; the whole globe has once been in a state of igneous fusion; there was a time when no animals or plants existed on the earth; several distinct economies of life, or groups of animals and plants, have occupied the surface, each adapted to the altered condition of things; these ancient races have been unlike one another, and, with a few exceptions in the highest formations, unlike those alive, the resemblance between the living and the fossil types becoming more unlike as we descend; some ten or twelve miles in thickness of fossiliferous rocks were deposited previous to the creation of man, who was among the last of the animals that have appeared upon the globe; and finally, amid all the diversities of organic structure, and change of species, genera, and families, in different formations, the feature of one grand system can be seen running through the whole series, linking all past minor systems together, and to the existing races, and showing the one grand plan of creation, as it lay originally in the Divine Mind."[1]

The most important geological fact in the above enumeration in its bearings upon Revelation, is the existence of organic remains embedded in the rocks. These are subdivided into several strata, and each of the strata is a vast catacomb in which lie buried innumerable generations of creatures that have lived and died during the period of its deposition. "The quantity of fossil remains is so great," says Mrs. Somerville, "that probably not a particle of matter exists on the surface of the earth, that has not at some time

[1] Bibliotheca Sacra.

formed part of a living creature. Since the commencement of animated existence, zoophytes have built coral reefs extending hundreds of miles, and mountains of limestone are full of their remains all over the globe. Mines of shells are worked to make lime; ranges of hill and rock, many hundred feet thick, are almost entirely composed of them, and they abound in every mountain chain throughout the earth. The prodigious quantity of microscopic shells discovered by Ehrenberg, is still more astonishing; shells not larger than a grain of sand form entire mountains; a great portion of the hills of Casciano, in Tuscany, consists of chambered shells, so minute, that Saldani collected 10,454 of them from one ounce of stone. Chalk is often almost entirely composed of shells; the polishing portion of tripoli is owing to their silicious coats; and there are even hills of great extent consisting of this substance, the debris of an infinite variety of microscopic insects."[1] For such vast accumulations, the geologist claims it as unquestionable that incalculable periods of time must have been required, compared with which the antiquity of man upon the earth dwindles to an insignificant point.

The inductive process which has led to the conclusions of Geology is thus forcibly stated by Hugh Miller: "All nature is a vast tablet, inscribed with signs, each of which has its own significancy; and Geology is simply the key by which myriads of these signs, hitherto undecypherable, can be unlocked and perused. We are told by travellers, that the rocks of the wilderness of Sinai are lettered over with strange characters inscribed during the forty years' wanderings of Israel. They testify in their very existence, of a remote past, when the cloud-o'ershadowed tabernacle rose amid the tents of the desert; and who shall dare say whether, to the scholar who could dive into their hidden meanings, they might not be found charged with the very

[1] Physical Geography.

song sung of old by Moses and by Miriam, when the sea rolled over the pride of Egypt? To the geologist every rock bears its inscription engraved in ancient hieroglyphic characters, that tell of the Creator's journeyings of old, of the laws which He gave, the tabernacles which He reared, and the marvels which He wrought,—of the mute prophecies wrapped up in type and symbols,—of the earth gulfs that opened and of reptiles that flew,—of fiery plagues that devastated on the land, and of hosts more numerous than that of Pharoah, that 'sunk like lead in the mighty waters.'"

It must be granted that there is an *apparent* discrepancy between the teachings of Geology and the statements of the Bible, and it is not surprising that apprehension was excited in religious minds when they were first advanced. Cowper no doubt expressed the general sentiment of serious Christians of his day, when he wrote:

"Some drill and bore
The solid earth, and from the strata there
Extract a register, by which we learn,
That He who made it, and revealed its date
To Moses, was mistaken in its age."

Inspired by the supposed necessity of vindicating the truth of Scripture, numerous attempts have been made to overthrow the interpretations which Geology has given to the records found in the stone book of nature. The favorite counter-explanation has been the effect produced by the deluge of Noah. That mighty catastrophe, anti-geologists have maintained, is sufficient to account for all the deposits of fossil remains in the rocks, without resorting to such incalculable periods of time as necessary to their production. This hypothesis, however, is readily overthrown by the application of scientific tests and the ordinary laws of nature. Unless that awful event is to be viewed as in every respect removed from the sphere of natural law, it is evident that whatever marks of physical action, if any, it may have left upon our globe, must have been confined to its surface, or at farthest to its upper strata. No ordinary laws of natural agency will identify its effects with those organic remains which are buried more than a thousand feet deep in the hardest rocks, and which in many instances are covered by overlying strata of a flinty hardness, which no passing flood of waters could possibly penetrate, and particularly a flood of such short duration as that of Noah. Evidently its effects must have been mechanical, not chemical, but in a very small degree. It might disturb the relative position of rocks or denude their surface, but it could not make them. It might deposit a bank of sand or gravel, but we can not conceive of its power being sufficient to dissolve or disturb or affect to any considerable degree, a bed of rock thousands of miles in geographical extent, and thousands of yards in thickness. Moreover, if in the face of these objections, we still refer the fossil remains of organic life in the various primary and secondary rocks to such a cause, how can we account for their orderly and regular distribution? They are not found in any part of the earth in that confused and disorderly mass to which they would be reduced by such a violent mechanical agitation. They are almost as scientifically arranged, according to their genera and species, throughout the different formations, as they would be in the museum of a naturalist—the most ancient and the extinct species in the lower, the recent and existing species in the upper strata of the earth. Such an arrangement, it is evident, can not be attributed to a *disturbing* agency. "Rushing waters were not the scene for calm deposits, where all the bones and spines of the most delicate structures, and the forms of leaves and plants in endless variety, could be laid and kept unhurt. A deluge, and that, too, of only one hundred and fifty days' duration, was not the workshop in which strata ten miles thick could be formed and packed with their teeming population; neither had it time to do the work, nor had it room to hold the materials."[1] Yet to this, as well as other absurd conclusions, we are driven, if we maintain that all the mighty changes which the records of the rocks reveal, took place in the short period which the Noachian deluge lasted.

Another class of writers have sought to remove the difficulty, by arguing that since it is possible for God to do all things, it was possible for Him by a single fiat to create all those skeleton structures that have been supposed to indicate creatures of

> "Monstrous shapes that one time walk'd the earth,
> Of which ours is the wreck."

According to this theory, the myriads of sea shells, the impressions and fossil specimens of plants, and skeletons of the higher animals, which we find in their progressive order of super-position in the rocks, were but accompaniments of the creative act, mere illusions and shadows, "deceptive *simulacra*," which never had any answering realities in the vegetable or animal world! All the wonders of intelligence which great scientific minds have recognized in the stratified rocks of the earth, are thus held to reveal (says the eminent Professor Owen) "an elaborate design to deceive and not to instruct." The only argument which is used to support this attempt to "untie the Geological knot," must indeed be conceded. The Divine Power is certainly competent to such a creation. But infinite wisdom being an attribute of the Deity as truly as his omnipotence, how can we conceive of such a creation as forming a part of his glorious plan? Where can be found the *intelligible purpose* in the production of forms which, in such a case, would have been to human conceptions so *evidently useless?* It is equally undeniable that God *could*

[1] Archdeacon Pratt's "Scripture and Science."

have created Herculaneum and Pompeii under their volcanic beds of lava and ashes, and the Egyptian mummies in their tombs and sarcophagi, just as we now find *them;* but reason at once turns from the supposition as to the last degree improbable. And the same reason compels us to place a theory of equal if not greater improbability, resorted to in order to defend the authority of the Bible against the supposed hostility of Geological discoveries, on a par with the folly of the Bramin, who dashed the microscope in pieces when it crossed his superstitious practices by the wonders it revealed.

Such absurd resorts to explain undeniable phenomena have proved as unnecessary as the alarm occasioned in the Vatican by the discoveries of Galileo. They have only served to wound religion in the house of its friends. Here again, the discrepancy is only apparent, and the true and consistent exposition of the inspired record of Moses has established its perfect harmony with the disclosures of geology. The difficulty in effecting their reconcilement has been not with Scripture itself, but with misconceptions of its meaning. "It should be recollected," says Dr. Buckland in his Bridgewater Treatise, "that the question is not respecting the Mosaic narrative, but of our interpretation of it; and still further, it should be borne in mind that the object of this account was, not to state *in what manner*, but *by whom*, the world was made. As the prevailing tendency of men in those early days was to worship the most glorious objects of nature, namely, the sun, moon and stars, it should seem to have been one important point in the Mosaic account of creation to guard the Israelites against the polytheism and idolatry of the nations around them, by announcing that all these magnificent celestial bodies were no gods, but the works of the Almighty Creator, to whom alone the worship of mankind is due." Had he done this in the language of science, it is obvious that he must have used that language in its farthest development, which would have rendered his sublime disclosures a hopeless enigma to all but a comparative few of our race. It not being his object to teach science, he has entirely avoided its terms and phraseology, yet has he so written as to stand the test of science. His simple yet lofty and majestic narrative is so worded as to be intelligible to all generations of men from the beginning to the end of time, and yet the utmost scrutiny of modern discovery can find in it nothing to impugn.

But as in the instances already given under the head of Astronomy, much more than this can be justly claimed for the Mosaic record of Creation. Not only is it free from scientific error, not only does the most searching investigation fail to discover any discrepancy or contradiction between its statements and the discoveries of Geology; there are also to be found remarkable coincidences between the language of that narrative and those discoveries. By accurately following the very words of Moses, without wresting them in the least degree beyond their plain and obvious import, we obtain, as it respects the *order* of creation, an exact parallelism with the language which geologists, many of them sceptics, indifferent to Moses and hostile to Revelation, have laboriously decyphered from the rocks and strata of the earth. They have found the fossil remains of animal and vegetable life deposited beneath the surface of the globe in the very succession in which the lawgiver of Israel declared them to have been created. It has been said, that if one should try to give a sketch in the very fewest words of the Celestial Mechanism of Laplace, the Cosmos of Humboldt, and the geology of the latest and best authorities, he would do so in the very language of Moses. A brief comparison of his statements with the "testimony of the rocks" will show that this statement is not unfounded.

Thus from Scripture we learn, that "in the beginning God created the heavens and the earth, and that the earth was without form and void (invisible and unfurnished), and darkness was upon the face of the deep." From Geology we know, that there was a period in the ceaseless flow of time, when the earth, which is now clothed with verdure and throbs with animated nature, was a watery waste, devoid of physical life, and enveloped with muddy vapors and dense clouds of mist and fog which effectually shut out the rays of the sun from its surface.

From Scripture we learn, that while darkness was yet upon the face of the deep, the creative Spirit of God brooded upon the waters, and life preceded light. By Geology we are taught that the Spirit of the Creator terminated the lifeless state of our planet in the next succeeding period of time, by pouring submarine life into the expanse of the primæval ocean, and the earliest created specimens of animal life, anemones, zoophytes and coral animalculæ, from the combination of whose tiny labors the vast beds of limestone have proceeded which are found in every part of the world, first made their appearance, but all of them had this peculiarity that they were devoid of organs adapted to the perception of light; thus leading to the conclusion, that according to the Mosaic narrative, light did not dawn upon the globe when life first stirred in the waters.

From Scripture we learn, that on the second day the Atmosphere was formed, and that a canopy of clouds was suspended above the firmament, veiling the heavenly host of sun, moon and stars, from the face of the globe; that afterwards, on the third day, dry land and vegetation appeared; and finally, on the fourth day, the canopy of clouds being dissolved, the heavenly bodies were for the first time discerned, to be from thenceforth 'for signs and for seasons, and for days and for years.' From Geology we know that at the close of the Silurian submarine creation vast mountains were upheaved by volcanic forces from the deep, and land vegetation made its first appearance, attesting the previous existence of an atmosphere; and from the same source disclosing to us the mineral contents of the great coal measures, we know that the nature, quantity and quality of the vegetation which then sprang up, were such as demonstrate the growth to have taken place under circumstances of *long continued shade*, which must at last have been dispelled by the dispersion of the superincumbent clouds, and the admission of the direct rays of the sun to the earth's surface. *The plants of the great carboniferous epoch are such as never have been touched by a sun beam.* They are such precisely as would have grown in a humid atmosphere; their wood is not hardened, as that of plants on which the pure sun-light falls. Thus, both the Mosaic and Geological records concur in testifying that the order of creation was—a clouded atmosphere, a dry land and its vegetation, succeeded by the direct and unimpeded radiance of the sun, moon and stars.

From Scripture we learn, that the next display of creative power was an abundance of great sea monsters, terrestrial reptiles and winged creatures; and Geology exposes to our view in the next succeeding strata, the organic remains of the then existing tyrants of the ocean, the land and the air; and we behold profuse swarms of the gigantic Saurians which peopled the earth in "the age of Reptiles. Elaniosauria, tyrants of the deep; Dinosauria, tenants of the land; and Ptero-dactyles and feathered birds, the flying of wing through the firmament above the earth.

"From Scripture we learn, that the next step was the creation of cattle and creeping things, and beasts of the earth (the Mammalia). From Geology we know, that the race of quadruped Mammals did not come into existence until after the age of Reptiles; that the Saurian monsters, with the other oviparous reptiles and birds, had been tenants of our globe for ages before we find any traces of a quadruped Mammal.

"Lastly, from Scripture we learn, that the closing and completing work of the Creation was Man; and Geology trumphantly confirms the revealed fact, that submarine animals, land vegetation, Reptiles, Birds and quadruped Mammals, were all of them in existence successively and collectively, ages before the first of the human race. It is only in the latest diluvial deposits of the tertiary period and which are the newest on the earth's crust, that the remains of man are to be found."[1] Yet had the human race existed in the primæval ages of our planet, unquestionably their remains would have been found intermingled with the countless fossils of extinct plants and animals which the rocks have preserved. Our bones, composed of the same elements as those of the animal races, are equally capable of being kept from destruction.

But in the absence of these or any traces of man in any save the most superficial deposits, we are compelled to acknowledge that Science confirms what Revelation had previously declared—that the palace was prepared ere the king appeared; that the empire was put in order ere the sovereign was appointed. "For him volcanic fires had fused and crystallized the granite, and piled it up into lofty table lands. For him the never wearied water had worn and washed it down into extensive vallies and plains of vegetable soil. For him the earth had often vibrated with electrical shocks, and had become interlaced with rich metallic veins. Ages of quiet had succeeded each revolution of nature, during which the long accumulating vegetables of preceding periods were, for him, transmuted into stores of fuel—some of the deposits of primæval waters were becoming iron—and successive races of destroyed animals

[1] This comparison of the two records, Mosaic and Geological, is mostly derived from McCausland's "Sermons in Stones."

were changed into masses of useful material." Thus through all these varied operations, ordered and arranged by Creative power, wisdom and benevolence, the earth was gradually framed and furnished as a habitation for man. When the foundations of the house had been fixed, and its walls reared, and its star-spangled canopy overhung, and its floor carpeted with soft green, and fuel and water laid up in store-houses, then, and not till then, did man appear,

——— "the master work, the end
Of all yet done, a creature who not prone
And brute as other creatures, but endued
With sanctity of reason, might erect
His stature, and upright with front serene
Govern the rest, self-knowing; and from thence
Magnanimous to correspond with heaven,
But grateful to acknowledge whence his good
Descends, thither with heart, and voice, and eyes
Directed in devotion, to adore
And worship God supreme, who made him chief
Of all his works."—MILTON.

Thus the Record of Moses and Nature's Record bear each other witness in every particular. The same narrative told by the ruler of Israel four thousand years ago, is also told in its own expressive and intelligible language by the very earth on which we tread, as it were "graven with an iron pen and lead in the rock forever." "To a sincere and unsophisticated mind, it must be evident," says Professor Guyot, "that the grand outlines sketched by Moses are the same as those which modern science enables us to trace; however imperfect and unsettled the details furnished by scientific inquiries may appear on many points. Whatever changes we may expect to be introduced by new discoveries, in our present view of the universe and the globe, the prominent traits of this vast picture will remain. And these only are traced out in this admirable account of Genesis. These outlines were sufficient for the moral purposes of the book; the scientific details are for us patiently to investigate. They were no doubt unknown to Moses, as the details of the life and of the work of the Saviour were unknown to the great prophets who announced his coming, and traced out with master hand his character and objects centuries before his appearance on earth. But the same Divine hand which lifted up before the eyes of Daniel and of Isaiah the veil which covered the tableau of the time to come, unveiled before the eyes of the author of Genesis the earliest ages of the creation. And Moses was the prophet of the past, as Daniel and Isaiah and many others were the prophets of the future."

As it regards the supposed difficulty of death's being in the world previous to the sin of Adam, it should be considered that the Bible is nowhere committed to the statement that the death of the animal creation is a consequence of the Fall of man. The assertion of the apostle that "by one man sin entered into the world and death by sin," does not necessarily mean that the sin of Adam brought death upon the irrational tribes as well as upon the human race. While the facts which the Book of Nature reveals were unknown, such a conclusion from the Apostle's words was not, perhaps, unreasonable; yet long before the discoveries of Geology, Jeremy Taylor considered man to have been *created mortal.* "They are injurious to Christ," he writes, "who think that from Adam we might have inherited immortality. Christ was the giver and preacher of it; he brought life and immortality to light through the Gospel." By the aid of science we now learn that the Apostle's true meaning is, not that Death had never appeared in the irrational world before the fall of man, but that in that fearful event sin had degraded God's intellectual creature to the level of the brutes in his animal nature, and in his spiritual to that of a lost fallen being. If the fact of death's being already in the world seem to us inconsistent with its being the happy abode of innocence, the difficulty will be removed when we reflect that Infinite Wisdom foresaw what man would become, and therefore may have adapted the world to his permanent rather than his temporary condition. It is certain that carnivorous instincts were implanted in the animal tribes from the very first, and perpetual destruction has been followed by continual renovation. The wise benevolence of this divine arrangement is thus conclusively vindicated by Dr. Buckland: "The law of universal mortality being the established condition on which it has pleased the Creator to give being to every creature upon earth, it is a dispensation of kindness to make the end of life to each individual as easy as possible. The most easy death is, proverbially, that which is least expected; and though, for moral reasons peculiar to our own species, we deprecate the *sudden* termination of our mortal life, yet, in the case of every inferior animal, such a termination of existence is obviously the most desirable. The pains of sickness and decrepitude of age, are the usual precursors of death, resulting from gradual decay; these, in the human race alone, are susceptible of alleviation from internal sources of hope and consolation, and give exercise to some of the highest charities and most tender sympathies of humanity. But, throughout the whole creation of inferior animals, no such sympathies exist; there is no affection or regard for the feeble and the aged; no alleviating care to relieve the sick; and the extension of life through lingering stages of decay and of old age, would to each individual be a scene of protracted misery. Under such a system, the natural world would present a mass of daily suffering bearing a large proportion to the total amount of animal enjoyment. By the existing dispensations of sudden destruction and rapid succession, the feeble and disabled are speedily relieved from suffering, and the world is at all times crowded with myriads of sentient and happy beings; and though to many individuals their allotted share of life be often short, it is usually a period of uninterrupted gratification; whilst the momentary pain of sudden and unexpected death is an evil infinitely small, in comparison with the enjoyments of which it is the termination."

The Biblical objection which has been supposed to conflict with this divine arrangement, is thus conclusively met by Professor Hitchcock: "Physiology teaches us that death is a general law of organic natures, from which law, as we infer from Revelation, man was exempt so long as he obeyed the law of God. As a special favor he was to remain unaffected by the decay and dissolution to which other beings were subjected. The penalty of disobedience was, that he would forfeit this enviable distinction, and be subjected to a death more revolting than the brutes. The reward of obedience was a continued immunity from evil, and a final translation, without suffering, to a more exalted condition. A presumptive argument in favor of this view is, that if Adam had not seen death in the animal tribes, it is difficult to perceive, how he could have any idea of the nature of the threatening. And we may be sure that God never promulgates a penalty without affording his subjects a means of comprehending it." [1]

But there still remains the difficulty of reconciling the *vast antiquity* of the globe which the various geological phenomena have unanswerably demonstrated, with the chronology of the Mosaic record, which has been supposed to teach that the earth is nearly coeval with the appearance of man. There are two schemes by which this objection is met and obviated, each of which has had the advocacy of learned and able writers, and which are equally admissible, without resorting to any forced construction, by the language of Scripture.

The first supposes that the opening verse of the first

[1] Hitchcock's Religion of Geology, p. 92.

chapter of Genesis refers to the original *fiat* which called the material universe into existence,—after which an undefined and enormous interval of time took place; and that the globe was then cast into the chaotic state of emptiness and waste described in the second verse as preceding the six days, each of twenty-four hours' duration, in which it was fitted and arranged as a habitation for man.

It is claimed for this hypothesis, that there is nothing in it which is not entirely consistent with the discoveries of geology. "Here, (say its advocates,) we find a beginning, old enough for all that geology can require. These opening sentences, separated off from the rest of Genesis, imply no date whatever; they do not "fix the antiquity of the globe." Between them and the subsequent narrative, there is ample duration for the discoveries of Geology to intervene. All the pre-Adamite formations may be allowed to follow this first opening statement. The earth may have been brought into shape, replenished with living creatures, and again reduced into chaos, as often as the needs of science demand. Periods of whatever duration it requires, may have elapsed in those successive creations, *before* that at which the inspired historian takes up the narrative to relate how, at a time when the earth was again "without form and void," the Spirit of God again moved upon the face of the waters, to inaugurate the creation of which man is the distinguishing feature. And here, it is claimed, we have all the facts concerning the origin of man and the habitation in which he is placed, which the wisdom of God saw it fitting to communicate, or which it was needful for man to know. It was a matter of deep and vital interest to man to know how he came upon this earth and who was the Author of his being. It did not concern him to know the number of the planets, or the nature of the laws of the solar system, and upon these points Scripture is silent. Nor was it needful for him to know how many revolutions this our globe had gone through before he himself was created, or what strange beings had walked its surface, before the last great convulsion; and accordingly no allusion was made to his long past history. And surely this silence as to other worlds and other states of this world, matters which had no bearing on man's own interests, ought to be ranked as one among many internal evidences of the Mosaic narrative. An impostor would have sought to minister to the cravings of the human intellect for "things hidden and marvellous" and spoken upon many points concerning which the oracles of God are dumb; but the inspired writer gives us only the simple record of the progressive work of creation. Saying nothing of the intermediate condition in which the earth may have lain and the changes it may have undergone, during a long series of ages, he takes up its history where Geology leaves it, after the great convulsion which closed the Tertiary period, and shows us how in six days Almighty wisdom and benevolence fitted the globe as a residence for man. Thus, without encroaching in the least degree upon the literalities of the Mosaic narrative, we may yet allow the widest scope to the geologist, and at the same time believe that the globe was in existence for immeasurable ages before man appeared, that it underwent a long series of revolutions, was tenanted by animals and clothed with vegetation, until at length a stop was put to these changes by the ushering in the birth-day of a higher and more glorious creation.

It must be allowed that these are forcible and weighty considerations, and the theory which they are brought to support, was for a long time thought to meet all the requirements of Geology. It has numbered among its advocates by far the greater number of those who have sought to harmonize the language of Scripture with the discoveries of science, and is still, probably, that which is most generally received. But it is now contended by eminent geologists, many of whom are the earnest friends of Revelation, that this scheme of reconciliation is no longer adequate. It requires, in order to maintain its ground, that there should be a "break" or chaotic period, at the end of the Tertiary period and just previous to the creation of man. But it is asserted that all the facts of Geology go to show that there was no such universal catastrophe at that epoch, but that all the different tribes and species of animals and plants have been gradually introduced, and that one unbroken chain of organic existence connects the modern world with those pre-Adamite worlds that have passed away. If these alleged facts have an established scientific basis,[1] the theory in question must be relinquished, unless it is maintained that vast numbers of the animal and vegetable races now existing were exterminated just previous to the appearance of man, and then recreated; but in such a procedure, it is forcibly urged that we can not recognize the signature of infinite wisdom. It becomes, therefore, of the highest importance to ascertain if there be not another hypothesis, which will at once harmonize with the statements of Revelation and meet the requirements of Geology. Such a one has been brought forward by the late Hugh Miller, and sustained by him with great power of argument and illustration in his "Testimony of the Rocks," though it was held by some previous to his day, and even dates back to the age of St. Augustine, being found in his celebrated treatise on "the City of God." The support of Origen is also claimed for it, and that of the venerable Bede. This scheme of reconciliation agrees with the former in prefixing the opening sentence of Genesis to the geologic periods; but instead of

[1] It should here be stated, that some of the present advocates of the first hypothesis maintain that the required "catastrophe" has been found. In his "Science and Scripture," Archdeacon Pratt cites the authority of the "Podrome de Palæontologie" of. M. d'Orbigny, for the statement, that "between the termination of the Tertiary period and the commencement of the Human or Recent period, there is a complete break."

imagining those periods to be *omitted* from the subsequent narrative, it supposes them to be *successively indicated* in the work of the several days recorded by Moses. According to its interpretation of the sacred text, those days were periods of great and indefinite extent, instead of being natural days of twenty-four hours each. By this theory, sufficient time is afforded for any duration which the necessities of Geology require, while it has the advantage of presenting to us the works of creation in precisely the same *order* in which, as we have seen, they are disclosed to us by the succession of strata and the development of organic life. The only obstacle to its admission seems to be the generally limited acceptation of the word "day" and the difficulty of deviating so far from its ordinary meaning. But for this interpretation, it is able to quote the authority of Scripture itself, which in texts innumerable, uses the word "day" to indicate some appointed period of indefinite length appropriate to a particular purpose; hence "the day of salvation," "the day of Jerusalem," "the day of Christ," "the day of visitation," and many others. This use of the word is indeed so well established, that we find St. Peter guarding his disciples against the unbelief of their times by the consideration that "one day is with the Lord as a thousand years, and a thousand years as one day;" a proverb so directly connected with the received Jewish belief concerning the first chapter of Genesis, that we are told the Rabbis regarded each of the six days there mentioned to be (at least) emblematic of a thousand years. Nor can it be said that the word is limited to the duration of a solar day by the words "morning and evening," with which it has been supposed to be synonymous. For there could be no apparent rising and setting of the sun, so as to afford a periodic measure of time, before his beams were made to penetrate the clouds and vapors that enveloped the earth, which was not until the fourth day. It is remarkable, moreover, that whereas at the end of each of the six working days of creation we find an evening, the morning of the seventh, which is mentioned at the close of the sixth, is not followed by such a sequel, leading to the inference that it is still open. There is, therefore, no absolute and insurmountable difficulty in our interpreting the word "day" to mean a period of time, which was occupied in the production of certain events upon the earth, and which is commensurate with the rise and decline of a definite order of existence upon its surface. And if there are no other reasons to forbid the interpretation, it appears to render the reconciliation of the facts of Geology with the Mosaic narrative at once simple and complete.

There is, however, a Scriptural difficulty in the way of this hypothesis, which to some minds appears insurmountable. This is found in the reason given in the book of Genesis and repeated in Exodus (xx. 11) for the institution of the Sabbath. We are commanded to work for six days, and rest on the seventh, because in six days God created the universe, and rested on the seventh. The days of the first part of the commandment are obviously those which compose the natural week. Then similar, it is argued, must be the days in the latter part; otherwise the same word is used in two different significations in one passage of Scripture. And if the meaning is not the same, how could the analogy hold good or where could be the legality of the inference?

To this objection Hugh Miller makes the following reply: "Is there any real difficulty," he asks, "in conceiving that the smaller divisions of human time are to be ordered after the larger ones employed by the Creator? Work for six days and rest on the seventh, is the law which God has prescribed to himself and to us. But must his days and ours necessarily be of the same duration? Must He be held to have crowded all the diversified phenomena of nature, past, present, and to come, into an hundred and forty-four hours, because that is the measure of a man's weekly labor? As a vast continent or the huge earth itself is very great, and a map or geographical globe very small; but if, in the map or globe, the proportions be faithfully maintained, and the scale, though a minute one, be true in all its parts and applications, we pronounce the map or globe, notwithstanding the smallness of its size, a faithful copy; so may it be in regard to the divine and human periods. The vastness of the one does not contradict the smallness of the other."

In addition to this, "it may be maintained," says Mr. Bayne, "that the Age theory alone exhibits, in all their Scriptural and scientific breadth, the grounds of the Sabbatic rest. The scheme of the geologic periods points to the resting of God as a *fact*. Since the appearance of man in the world, the work of creation has ceased. No species is known to have come into existence since the procession of being was closed by its king. Here, then, is direct confirmation of Scripture. And if the redemption of man is God's Sabbath day's work, and the reasoning head of this lower creation is permitted, on each recurrent Sabbath in the natural year, to praise and magnify His greatness in that work, shall we say that the sanctions attached to the Sabbath day have become, on account of the light cast by science on God's word, less binding or less sacred?"

In support of the same hypothesis, Professor Silliman says,—"The allusion in the commandments and in other parts of the Scriptures to the six days would of course be made in conformity with the language adopted in the narrative, which being for the masses of mankind was necessarily a popular history, although of divine origin; and the historian adopted a division of time that was in general use, although as to half the time at least, it was inconsistent with astronomical laws. Extension of the time so as to cover the events by the operation of physical laws, removes every difficulty, and interferes with no doctrine of religion."[1]

Each of these hypotheses, let it be observed, is perfectly consistent with the letter of Scripture, and if in consequence of the advancement of discovery, the former is rendered untenable, the latter will remove the difficulty, satisfactorily meet all the discoveries of the Geologist, and at the same time, sustain the Mosaic account of the Creation.[2] Either of them will harmonize with the indefinite periods of duration, through which, as science has shown, our planet must have passed anterior to the appearance of man. There is, therefore, no ground for the objection of the infidel that

[1] Lecture on Geology before the Smithsonian Institute.

[2] Another scheme of reconciliation has been proposed by a learned dissenting divine of England, Dr. J. Pye Smith, in his "Relations of Scripture to Geology." He agrees with the first hypothesis in holding that the Mosaic days were natural days, and that a vast undefined interval elapsed between the commencement of these days and the original universal creation announced in the first verse of Genesis, during which an almost unlimited series of changes in the structure and products of the earth may have taken place. After this, at a comparatively recent epoch, a *small* portion of the earth's surface was brought into a state of disorder, ruin and obscuration; out of which the creation of the existing species of things, with the recall of light, and the restored presence of the heavenly bodies, took place literally, according to the Mosaic narrative, in six natural days. Outside the area of that limited creation, and during the period of its evolution, many of our present lands and seas may have enjoyed the light of the sun, and been tenanted by animals, and occupied by plants, the descendants of which still continue to exist.

This theory, though supported by its author with great learning and ingenuity, has failed to win wide acceptance, and has now, probably, few, if any supporters, which may be accounted for by the fact that it is open to objections fully as grave as those which it removes. We find it hard to believe that the majestic sentences of the inspired historian require so great a diminution of the meaning we have been accustomed to attach to them. Moreover, as Hugh Miller has observed, "although creation can not take place without a miracle; it would be a strange reversal of all our previous conclusions on the subject, should we have to hold that the dead, dark blank out of which creation arose was miraculous also."

the results of science contradict the cosmogony of Moses. It is for him to show that their reconciliation is impossible. If there is one mode of reconcilement, the authority of Scripture is sustained.

Another point of contact between Geology and Scripture, is the deluge of Noah. Until the discoveries of recent years, it was supposed that the inspired account of that awful judgment of God, was sufficiently vindicated by the organic remains which are found alike on the mountain summits and in torrent worn valleys of the earth. In this view geologists formerly acquiesced, and one of the most learned and able of their number, the author of the Bridgewater Treatise on Geology, wrote a book on the subject, describing a cave at Kirkdale, in Yorkshire, where bones of numerous animals had been accumulated, it was supposed, by the waters of the Noachian deluge. This view he afterwards retracted, and it is now held by all geologists that such conclusions were premature. A more rigid scrutiny of the supposed diluvial evidences has assigned them to a far remoter epoch than the flood of Noah, and it is now considered as an established result of scientific research that no traces of a comparatively recent and temporary deluge are now to be found on the earth's surface. The embedded shells and other fossils which are found on different tracts of the earth's surface, and which are probably to be ascribed to *diluvial* action of some kind, can not be, it is said, the results of *one universal* simultaneous submergence, but of *many distinct* local aqueous forces, for the most part continued in action for long periods, and of a kind precisely analogous to those now at work. This final result of geological research has been eagerly seized upon by the enemies of Revelation, and because there are no *physical* evidences of such a catastrophe as the flood whose history Moses has transmitted, they would impugn its credibility as an historical fact. "But is it not unreasonable to expect to find any traces of such an event at the present day so many ages after its occurrence? Any marks it left, must have been long since obliterated, or so mixed up with the effects of subsequent gradual changes as to be undecipherable, even if they ever possessed any characteristic features peculiar to themselves." The really strong objections are those which are urged against the deluge being in the widest sense *universal;* and it must be conceded that some of these have considerable weight. The submersion of the entire globe would have been, it is said, an event for which there was no adequate reason; and moreover, all the resources of nature would not have been sufficient to produce it, and miracles are never resorted to unless demanded by some special exigency. The entire atmosphere condensed into rain, and the depths of the ocean utterly exhausted, would not have been sufficient, it is asserted, to envelop the globe with water to the height of fifteen cubits (twenty or more feet) above the summits of the loftiest mountains. The inmates of the ark raised above the earth to the elevation of five miles, would have found an atmosphere, from its extreme tenuity or intense cold, fatal to animal life. If the omnipotence of Him to whom "all things are possible," be presented as a sufficient answer to such objections, yet there are certain facts (it has been urged), which go to prove that Almighty power was not on this occasion put forth to the extent supposed. These are found in the appearance of various volcanic regions in different countries, especially in the province of Auvergne in the south of France. Here are to be seen the craters of volcanoes, extinct long before the period when History commences, surrounded by beds of scoriæ and cinders, which it must have taken ages to accumulate, but which if the waters of Noah's deluge overflowed them, must have been entirely swept away. Difficulties are also started about the capacity of the ark to contain pairs of all the different species of animals, including the peculiar and unique zoology of Australia and New Zealand,—about the possibility of nourishing them with appropriate food, and of their being dispersed from one point, the mountains of Ararat, across seas and oceans over the whole face of the earth. In view of these grave objections, it becomes important to ascertain whether the commonly received interpretation of the Mosaic account of the deluge is necessarily the correct one. Does the sacred writer intend to say that the entire globe, with its continents and islands, its hills and mountains, was all buried beneath the waters of the flood? Certainly, he speaks of the purpose of God to "destroy the earth." He says, "All the high hills under the whole heaven were covered. But the dove found no rest for the sole of her foot, *for the waters were on the face of the whole earth.* And I will establish my covenant with you; neither shall all flesh be cut off any more by the waters of a flood, neither shall there be any more a flood to *destroy the earth.*" But similar terms are employed in other passages of Scripture in an evidently restricted sense. In another place in which it is evident that only Palestine and the countries in its immediate neighborhood can be meant, the language used by the inspired writer is,—"This day will I begin to put the dread of thee and the fear of thee upon the nations that are *under the whole Heaven*, who shall hear report of thee, and shall tremble, and be in anguish because of thee." (Deut. ii. 25.) And in other passages we read: "And the famine *was over all the face of the earth.* And *all countries* came into Egypt to Joseph to buy corn; because that the famine was so sore in *all lands.*" (Gen. xli. 56, 57.) Obadiah declares to Elijah, "As the Lord thy God liveth, there is *no nation or kingdom* whither my lord hath not sent to seek thee." In these instances universal terms have most clearly a limited signification. By what principle are we, then, to determine the extent of the signification of universal terms?

Where are we to look for the key of the interpretation? Most clearly we must seek it in the general scope and purpose of the writer. What then are that scope and purpose in the case in question? Are they to teach physical or moral truth—to write the natural history of the earth or the moral history of man? The same writer who says: "In the beginning God created the heavens and the earth," says, "And behold I will destroy them with the earth." Would it not seem that the language in the latter case is of as wide a signification as in the former? If we regard the *words*, we must answer in the affirmative; if the *spirit* in the negative. In the history of the creation, the great purpose of the author was to teach the existence of one God, the Creator of all things, as a *moral*, however, rather than as a *natural* truth. Were there no moral relations between man and his Creator, were we not bound to worship, love, serve, and obey Him as the source of all things, the doctrine would have found no place in a book whose object is to communicate to man religious knowledge. But the terms, the heavens and the earth, must here be taken in their widest sense. If not, the writer has failed of expressing the idea of a one Creator. The earth, without any doubt, signifies the entire earth. Whatever be its form and dimensions, whether it be the earth of the Hebrews,

> "Founded upon the seas,
> And established upon the floods,"

a stationary plain, or the revolving globe of modern science, it matters not; it was all made in the beginning, by one God the Creator. Let us apply the same rule of interpretation to the history of the deluge. What in this history was the great object of the writer? Obviously, to record a most important era in the dealings of God with mankind. It was to exhibit, as a moral example, the destruction of the human race by the hand of the Creator, repenting that

He had made man upon the earth, so great had become his violence and corruption. The destruction of the earth and of the brute creation was incidental to the major purpose. It would not have been mentioned, had it not been connected with the destruction of man. Aside from its moral bearings, it was as unimportant for the writer's great purpose, as the history of Sirius, or the changes which may have occurred on the planet Jupiter. What was the earth, which was corrupt,—the earth which was filled with violence? Was it the entire terrestrial surface of the globe, inhabited or uninhabited, or was it rather that earth which was the abode of man—the theatre of human life? Plainly the latter. Now this was the earth God announced his purpose to destroy. If the human race had become diffused co-extensively with the *antediluvian* earth, which might have been the fact; then, without doubt, the entire surface of the dry land was comprehended in the threatened destruction of the earth. But if this was not the fact, then we can not fairly extend the sense of the sacred writers to include every portion of the terrestrial surface of the globe, inhabited or uninhabited, unless such a destruction was incidentally necessary for the accomplishment of the great object.[1]

Most probably, however, the occupation of the earth's surface at that time was very limited, and the late Hugh Miller, in his "Testimony of the Rocks," has shown how all the phenomena of the Deluge might have been produced by the gradual submergence and rising again of the country comprised within a radius of a few hundred miles around the dwelling place of Noah, so as to include the portion of the globe then inhabited. This phenomenon of the change of level of large portions of the earth's surface, by depression or elevation, is not unknown to geologists; though the periods in which these vast oscillations occur are of immeasurably longer duration than that of the Deluge. He

[1] Fellowe's History of the Deluge.

shows that the depression during the first forty days might, nevertheless, have been so gradual as to be almost imperceptible, except from the effects—the pouring in of the mighty waters from the neighboring seas into the growing hollow, and the disappearance of the mountain tops. And when, after a hundred and fifty days had elapsed, the depressed hollow began slowly to rise again, the boundless sea around the ark would flow outwards again towards the distant ocean, and Noah would see that "the fountains of the deep were stopped, and the waters were returning from off the earth continually."

The above hypothesis, which was supported in former times by such eminent authorities as Bishop Stillingfleet and Matthew Poole,[1] furnishes a complete answer to all the ob-

[1] Said Bishop Stillingfleet, "I can not see any urgent necessity from the Scripture to assert that the flood did spread over all the surface of the earth. That *all mankind*, those in the ark excepted, were destroyed by it, is most certain, according to the Scriptures. The flood was universal as to mankind; but from thence follows no necessity at all of asserting the universality of it as to the globe of the earth, unless it be sufficiently proved that the whole earth was peopled before the flood, which I despair of ever seeing proved."—*Origines Sacræ*, B. 3, c. 4.

The eminent commentator, Matthew Poole, in his Synopsis on Gen. 7:19, has the following observations: "It is not to be supposed that the entire globe of the earth was covered with water. Where was the need of overwhelming those regions in which there were no human beings? It would be highly unreasonable to suppose that mankind had so increased before the deluge, as to have penetrated to all the corners of the earth. Absurd it would be to affirm that the effects of the punishment inflicted upon men alone, applied to places in which there were no men. If then we should entertain the belief that not so much as the hundredth part of the globe was overspread with water, still the deluge would be universal, because the extirpation took effect upon all the part of the world which was then inhabited."

To the above may be added the following remarks by Dr. King of Glasgow, in his "Principles of Geology Explained." "If we adopt," he says, (p. 61,) "the principle which the Scripture itself so unequivocally sanctions—that general terms may be used with a limited sense—the whole account is simple and consistent. A deluge of great extent inundated the dry land. In respect to men, whom it was designed to punish for their wickedness, it was

jections which were supposed to lie against the Mosaic history of the Deluge, and derives from Geology a presumption in its favor, inasmuch as that science demonstrates that our globe at various periods must have been subjected to the operation of similar agencies. It is said that a recent examination of a large tract of Asia; comprising Armenia, Georgia, and part of Persia, and of certain marine deposits which are found therein, is strongly corroborative of the same view. Not impossibly, we may be approaching the era of a more interesting discovery than that which has called forth ancient Nineveh from her long entombment. Truth is sometimes stranger than fiction, and it may be, says an able writer in the North British Review, that "the first city—the city of Enoch, may yet be surveyed in stone or in dust, beneath some nameless heap where the Armenian shepherd now feeds his flocks; and the brass and iron utensils of Tubal Cain may yet exhibit to us the infant ingenuity of our race. The planks of Gopher wood which floated Noah over the universe of waters may yet rise from the flanks or the base of Ararat in lignite or in coal; and the first altar—that which Noah builded to his Maker and Preserver, may yet be thrown up from its burying place by the mighty earthquakes that shake the plain of the Araxes."

Whether these brilliant conjectures shall ever be realized or not, it is certain, that with the advancement of discovery, the opposition which had been supposed to exist between Revelation and Geology has disappeared, and of the eighty theories which the French Institute counted in 1806, as hostile to the Bible, not one now stands. "The minute philosphers, to borrow an epithet of the great Berkeley, may

universal, excepting only Noah and his family, whom it pleased God to spare alive. Along with them were preserved such animals as were most useful to them, and such as were fitted to fulfil the purposes of Providence after the waters should have retired."

think for a time, that their boasted discoveries are irreconcileable with revelation. They may raise the sand hills of their systems, and think from them to demolish the fortress of the divine word. Vain and impotent the attempt! Some fortunate discovery, as science advances, demolishes the whole by a single roll of its mighty waters, and the next wave dashes it into oblivion." "Shall it any longer be said, that a science which unfolds such abundant evidence of the being and attributes of God, can reasonably be viewed in any other light than as the efficient auxiliary and handmaid of religion? Some there still may be, whom timidity, or prejudice, or want of opportunity, allow not to examine its evidence; who are alarmed by the novelty, or surprised by the magnitude and extent of the views which geology forces on their attention; and who would rather have kept closed the volume of witness which has been sealed up for ages beneath the surface of the earth than to impose on the student in natural theology the duty of studying its contents —a duty in which for lack of experience they may anticipate a hazardous or laborious task, but which, by those engaged in it, is found to be a rational, and righteous, and delightful exercise of the highest faculties in multiplying the evidence of the existence, and attributes, and Providence of God. The alarm, however, which was excited by its first discoveries, has well nigh passed away; and those to whom it has been permitted to be the humble instruments of their promulgation, and who have steadily persevered, under the firm conviction that "truth can never be opposed to truth," and that the works of God when rightly understood, and viewed in their true relations, and from a right position, would at length be found to be in perfect accordance with his word, are now receiving their high reward in finding difficulties vanish, objections gradually withdrawn, and in seeing the evidences of geology admitted into the list of witnesses to the truth of the great fundamental doctrines of Christianity." Bridgewater Treatise on Geology, vol. i. p. 593.

The claim which Dr. Buckland here asserts in behalf of his favorite science, finds still farther vindication in the important services rendered by the discoveries of Geology to the cause of Revelation, in the unanswerable refutation they have furnished to the development hypothesis of Lamarck, Oken and others, and the once boasted argument of Hume against the miracles of the Bible. Akin to the nebular theory by which suns and planets are supposed to be gradually evolved by the condensation of a widely diffused vapor or fire-mist, a system has been devised and elaborated by a certain school of modern philosophers, supported by ingenious arguments and an imposing show of science, by which in place of the Almighty fiat calling them into existence, all vegetable and animal forms of organic life are accounted for by the agency of natural laws. Man has not been created but developed. "We call in question," says the author of the "Vestiges of Creation," "not merely the simple idea of the unenlightened mind, that God fashioned all in the manner of an artificer seeking by special means to produce special effects, but even the doctrine in vogue among men of science, that 'creative fiats' were required for each new class, order, family, and species of organic beings, as they successively took their places upon the globe, or as the globe became gradually fitted for their reception." According to the Bible, "God said, Let us make man in our image, after our likeness. So God created man in his own image, in the image of God created He him." But according to this theory, a "primary cause," which philosophy does not venture to define, created at first only microscopic monads or embryonic points, and from these, by a process of natural development extending through vast, indefinite periods of duration, arose all the various tribes of animated being. Creatures of "the simplest and most primitive type gave birth to a type superior to it in compositeness of organization and endowment of faculties; this again produced the next higher, and so on to the highest; the advance being in all cases, small, but not of any determinate extent." Thus one unbroken chain connects the animalcule with man! Such is the theory by which "science falsely so called" would remove the Creator from his throne to be replaced by a blind necessity called the law of development. But how does it agree with the stubborn facts of inductive science? Ask the geologist what witnesses he has found in the primitive records of the rocks, and he will tell you that "he has gone down in his search to the foundations of the earth, where the igneous rocks have warned him that he had reached primæval creation; and in his upward journey he has met with mosses and ferns and palms, and higher vegetable productions; each of which, as standing at the head of a species, he is bound to regard as having been brought into existence separately and independently.[1] Ascending

[1] The following valuable observations on this point are from a recent scientific work of the highest authority. "There are no doubt differences in the individuals of a species, depending on soil, and on different conditions of heat, light and moisture. But these differences are not incompatible with the idea of a common origin; and, moreover, we find that there is always a tendency to return to type. What is called a *variety*, is an individual of a species exhibiting variations which are not in general of a permanent character, and which can not be kept up in the natural state, or, in ordinary circumstances, by seed. By means of buds or slips such varieties may be continued; but if their seeds are sown in ordinary soil, and left to grow wild, the plants tend to return to the specific type. In certain plants, such as cereal crops and culinary vegetables, varieties have been perpetuated from seed by the art of cultivation; and thus races are kept up by artificial means. But when the seeds of such plants are sown in ordinary circumstances, and the plants are allowed to grow wild, we then see that there is a return to the parent type. In illustration of this statement, we may refer to ordinary vegetables, such as cabbage, cauliflower, broccoli, etc. (Brassica Oleracea.) This plant grows wild on our sea shores in certain places, and when cultivated it assumes peculiar forms. Thus it forms a heart, as in ordinary cabbage; its flower stalks become thickened or shortened, as in cauliflower or

higher still, he has discovered various forms of animal life, higher and lower; and he confesses that he knew no other or scientific way of accounting for their existence, than that of a *new creation*—the action of a power above nature bringing them into nature. Ask him if "development" is not equal to the production of those forms? and he will tell you, that in all his scientific observations he has never known the occurrence of the transition of one of these forms of life to another,—he has never witnessed the operation, and the earth has disclosed to him no case in which it was progressing or performed. But, as Cuvier asks, "why, if such transformations have occurred, do not the bowels of the earth preserve the records of such a curious genealogy?" That they are wholly unknown to the realms of nature is a point upon which the most distinguished geologists and anatomists are unanimous. At each arrangement of organic life after the creation, says Professor Sedgwick, "tribes of sentient beings were created and lived their time upon the earth. At succeeding epochs, new tribes of beings were called into existence, not merely as the progeny of those that had appeared before them, but as new and living proofs of creative interference,—and though formed on the same plan and bearing the same marks of wise contrivance, often as unlike those that pre-

broccoli; or its cellular tissue is largely developed, so as to give rise to the curled appearance of greens. These varieties are continued by cultivation; and after a series of generations, the seeds of the varieties propagate, more or less completely, plants of a similar nature. But if they are allowed to grow wild, then in the progress of time the variations disappear, and the original type of the species is reverted to. The varieties of apples and pears are continued by the art of horticulture and the process of grafting; but the seeds of these plants, when allowed to grow wild, produce the original stock, viz., the crab apple or crab pear, whence all the varieties have been produced. All these facts show the permanency of species in nature, and contradict the crude ideas of those so-called naturalists, who state that one species can be transmuted into another in the course of generations."—*Botany and Religion, by* Prof. Balfour.

ceded them, as if they had been matured in a different portion of the universe, and cast upon the earth by the collision of another planet." "For myself," says Agassiz, "I have the conviction that species have been created successively at distant intervals, and that the changes which they have undergone during a geological epoch are very secondary, relating only to their fecundity, and to migrations dependent on epochal influences." Lyell gives it as the result of careful inquiry, "that species have a real existence in nature, and that each was endowed at the time of its creation with the attributes and organs by which it is now distinguished." "Everything," says Sir Charles Bell, in his Bridgewater Treatise, "declares the species to have its origin in a distinct creation, not in a gradual variation from some original type; and any other hypothesis than that of a new creation of animals suited to the successive changes in the inorganic matter of the globe—the condition of the water, atmosphere, and temperature—brings with it only an accumulation of difficulties."[1] That new species of living creatures were introduced at various periods in the history of the ancient earth, is one of the most certain of the discoveries of geology, and as no cause can be found among natural agents fitted to produce the effect, we are compelled to recognize the only known cause capable of producing it—the fiat of the Creator. "Nature is but the name for an effect whose cause is God."[2]

[1] Pearson on Infidelity.

[2] In a recent inaugural address at Edinburgh University, Sir David Brewster thus scatters the air-woven speculations of Mr. Darwin: "As Mr. Darwin has appealed to facts and principles in support of his theory, we must appeal to facts and principles for its refutation. He maintains: 1. That variations in species actually arise in the course of descents from a common progenitor. 2. That many of these variations are an improvement on the original stock. 3. That, by a continued natural selection, from among these improved specimens, occasioned by a struggle for life, the most vigorous individuals become the progenitors of the next generation. 4. That there is a power in nature everywhere affecting this selection. Naturalists of high

The same geological discoveries strike also at the root of every sceptical argument against *miracles*. As these constitute a main pillar of Christian evidences, the enemies of the Bible have taxed all their resources of wit and sophistry to break down their testimony. Hume argued against their probability on account of their being opposed to what he calls "the uniform experience of mankind," and his followers in the school of doubt, at the present day, deny the possibility of supernatural interposition in any case whatever. Because a certain order and arrangement have been impressed upon the face of nature, in accordance with which, as by an inevitable necessity, fire will burn and a body will sink in water, and other physical causes produce their customary effects, therefore, the sceptic argues, "the antecedent improbability of a miracle or a deviation from the laws of nature is so great, that no testimony in its behalf can ever possibly amount to a probability, much less to a proof." By various learned pens, the fallacy of this

authority have followed Mr. Darwin through all his arguments, and have shown in the clearest manner that his theory is inconsistent with the very facts upon which he has rested it. It is out of my sphere, and yours also, to discuss this question as one of natural history; but even in this aspect of it, we may allow that species do admit of great variations, and may, by new methods of feeding and culture, rise to a higher scale, and yet deny that there is any evidence even of one species of the same genus having passed into another, and still less that fish have passed into fowl, or birds into beasts, or quadrupeds into men. We have absolute proof, indeed, of this immutability of species, whether we search for it in historic or geological times. The cat and dog embalmed in Egypt four thousand years ago, are the same as the cat and dog of the present day; and in the fossil remains of the pre-Adamite ages, there is not the slightest proof of any variations in the successive inhabitants of the earth. Mr. Darwin himself admits, to use his own words, 'that this is the most obvious and grave objection to his theory;' but yet he conjectures that rocks still undiscovered, and myriads of years older than the Cambrian or azoic strata, may still bear testimony to his views. *When* such strata with such indications are discovered, when the instinct of the elephant shall have expanded into reason, and the chatter of the parrot have its climax in speech, we may then claim kindred with the brutes that perish."

reasoning has been most thoroughly and ably exposed. It has been shown that the objection confounds *general* with *universal* experience, and that nothing can be more unfounded and irrational than to assume that all things which are or can be, must fall within the measure of the finite understanding of man. As well might a blind man assume that, through the senses he possesses, he gains all possible knowledge of creation. Miracles are not a breaking in upon the order of nature "in any other sense than that in which the will of man, in every moment of man's conscious existence, is a breaking in upon the order of nature. In this sense all the world is a scene of perpetual confusion—it is a chaos of 'violences;' for wherever man comes in upon the material world, he comes in to turn aside its course, or to interrupt, or to give a new direction to, its order. The order of nature allows the bird to wing itself from East to West, or from tree to tree; but the shaft of the savage, or the gun of the sportsman, brings its plumage to the dust." But apart from reasoning, here is "testimony" from "the rocks" which cannot be gainsayed or eluded. Geology furnishes evidences, in the changes both of the globe itself and of its successive living creatures, that the course of nature has not always been what it is now. It is certain that the whole globe has once been in a state of igneous fusion; that there was a time when no animals or plants existed on the earth; that several distinct economies of life, or groups of animals and plants, have occupied the surface, each adapted to the altered condition of things; that these ancient races have been unlike one another, and with a few exceptions in the highest formations, unlike those alive, the resemblance between the living and fossil types becoming more unlike as we descend; and that man's appearance on the globe has been comparatively recent. Thus through the measureless ages before the appearance of man, the history of the creation had been the history of the miraculous. And is it philosophical to conclude, that on the creation of man everything of this nature abruptly and forever ceased? May we not more rationally infer that if God has so frequently interposed by special acts in the ages preceding the present state of the globe, it forms a strong presumption that He has done so at that most wondrous epoch of the world's history—the introduction of Christianity? The miracles of the Bible are in themselves worthy of His infinite wisdom, majesty and grace,—they are authenticated by the clearest and most commanding evidence, and Geology has now shown that there is no antecedent improbability which should forbid their reception.

CHAPTER III.

PHYSICAL SCIENCE CONTINUED.

We have thus far seen that there is no real discrepancy or contradiction between the teachings of Astronomy and Geology and the statements of the Bible, and that as those sciences have advanced, previous difficulties have vanished, and the closer has the harmony been manifested that exists between the records of revelation and the operations of the Creator in the material world. Our object in the present chapter will be to show that this harmony is capable of yet wider illustration, and that the more thoroughly we investigate the relations of the Sacred Scriptures with Physical Science, the clearer and more convincing will be the evidence that the Author of nature and of revelation is the same.

How can the sceptic account for the undeniable fact that no errors or absurdities connected with science, are to be found in the Bible? The Mosaic records date back to the infancy of our race, and the entire sacred canon was closed ages before the wondrous march of scientific discovery can be said to have commenced; yet in the numerous references and allusions which the inspired writers make to physical facts, though expressed in language suited to all time, and capable of being understood in ages wholly ignorant of science, not all the light which, in the present and preceding centuries, has been thrown upon the secrets of nature, has been able to detect a single blunder or discrepancy.

This is a test which the Zendavesta, the Koran and the Shaster, with all the oracles held sacred by the heathen, cannot stand. As soon as they touch upon the domains of science, their statements reveal the grossest ignorance, so that it has been said that the spread of scientific knowledge ensures the overthrow of all the religions of heathendom. The slightest examination of the sacred books of the heathen, and even of the systems of their most renowned philosophers, will show that their science was no less absurd than their theology.

Thus in Greek and Latin philosophy, the heavens were a solid vault over the earth, a sphere studded with stars, as Aristotle called them. The sages of Egypt held that the world was formed by the motion of the air and the upward course of flame; Plato that it was an intelligent being; Xenophanes that God and the world were the same thing. Empedocles maintained that there were two suns; Leucippus that the stars were kindled by their motions, and that they nourished the sun with their fires.

Some of the followers of Pythagoras supposed the milky way to be an old disused path of the sun, out of which, some said, he was frightened by the banquet of Thyestes. Anaxagoras is said to have thought it was the shadow of the earth; Aristotle believed it to be sublunary, and to consist of exhalations of the same matter as comets. Posidonius took it for a band of fire; Theophrastus for a solid and luminous band, joining together the two hemispheres; while Diodorus thought it was a celestial fire shining through the cliffs of the solid heavens.

Another class of Greek philosophers conjectured that matter is eternal, and that all the beauty, order, and grandeur of the universe, are the result of chance or a fortuitous concourse of atoms!

All Eastern nations believed that the heavenly bodies exercised powerful influence over human affairs, often of a disastrous kind, and that all nature was composed of four elements, viz., fire, air, earth and water,—substances certainly not elementary.

In the Hindoo Philosophy, the globe is represented as flat and triangular, composed of several stories, the whole mass being sustained upon the heads of elephants, who in turn were supported by a huge tortoise. Their shaking of themselves was supposed to be the cause of earthquakes. Mahomet taught that the mountains were created to prevent the earth from moving and to hold it as by anchors and chains. The Fathers of the Church themselves teach doctrines scarcely less absurd. "The rotundity of the earth is a theory," says Lactantius, "which no one is ignorant enough to believe." And even the great Kepler, who made some of the most important discoveries ever achieved in science, was not freed from those strange and to us childish imaginings, which were current in former times as explanations of difficult problems in the phenomena of nature. In 1619 he published a work in which he affirmed that the earth was a living animal, for that "when a stone was thrown into the deep clefts of a high mountain, a sound was returned from them; and when it was thrown into one of the mountain lakes, which, without doubt, were bottomless, a storm immediately arose; just as a ticklish animal would shake its head, or run shuddering away, when a straw was thrust into his ear or nose." This was the extravagant conception of one of the world's master minds, the observer for whom (according to his own famous boast) the universe so long had waited. Yet the same work contains a defence of the view that the orbs of heaven are engaged in performing a concert of music, in which Jupiter and Saturn take the bass; Mars, the Earth, and Venus, the tenor; and Mercury the treble.

In their observation of those positive facts which are the basis of natural science, we find the same credulity and extravagance. "If the theologians of pagan antiquity were poets, as Bacon observes, their naturalists were even worse. Animals that crowded about their steps, and which they could not move their eyes without seeing, are the heroes of the most extravagant legends. The whole world is metamorphosed by superstition. Truth is ignominiously swept out, and dreams substituted for reality. Writers stride forward from prodigy to prodigy, with the arrogance and self-esteem of authors who scorn to be observers.

"According to the doctrine of the Metempsychosis, introduced into Greece by Pythagoras and Timæus, the brute animals are human beings in altered forms. In their new shape, they preserve a recollection of their former condition. They were believed by some philosophers to possess three souls—the sensitive, rational, and vegetative soul—corresponding to what, in recent times, has been termed intellectual, organic, and animal *life*. A book was written by Plutarch, to prove that animals possess reason, inasmuch as the operations of our boasted understanding are more liable to error than the mysterious operations of instinct. Poets, and even philosophers, regarded them as our earliest teachers of the useful arts.

"According to Pliny, fishes with horses' heads were often seen in the Arabian Sea, out of which they crawled at night to graze in the fields. The same learned writer testifies to having seen a centaur, embalmed in honey, exhibited in Rome in the reign of Claudius, while the earliest Christian writers, Justin, Cyprian and Jerome, admit their existence, and believed them to be fallen angels, condemned to wander through dismal solitudes and uninhabited forests, until the day of judgment.

"The existence of the phœnix also was an object of the firmest belief in the ancient world, and is attested by the very gravest historians. The appearance of a phœnix in the consulship of Paulus Fabius, and Vitellius, or the thirty-fourth year of our era, is described by Tacitus as an event of the first importance, and worthy of transmission to the remotest posterity. "Every five hundred years the phœnix," says Tacitus, "comes into existence, though it is true," he adds, "some assign four hundred and sixty-one years as the true period. The first phœnix appeared in the reign of Sesostris; the second was seen in the reign of Amasis; and the last under Ptolemy III. This last phœnix, surrounded by a crowd of feathered attendants whom it far outshone in splendor of plumage, took its flight to Heliopolis, the city of the sun."

Pliny also gravely informs us that "it is not generally known, what has been discovered by men eminent for their learning, in consequence of their assiduous observations of the heavens, that the fires which fall upon the earth, and which receive the name of thunderbolts, proceed from the three superior stars, but principally from the one (Jupiter) that is placed in the middle."

To this list of absurdities which the most gifted and cultivated minds once mistook for science, a list which might be indefinitely extended, we will only add that Virgil has anticipated the famous "discovery" of Mr. Crosse. In his fourth Georgic, he gives a recipe for the production of bees where the hive may have lost its usual colony, whereby a brood of the ingenious insects may be "spontaneously generated" from the blood of a slaughtered heifer.[1]

How striking a contrast to this mass of error and absurdity, is presented in the pages of the Bible! Though composed long before the dawn of science, and though few of its writers could lay claim even to the learning and culture that were attainable in the times in which they lived, they have yet so written as to stand the test of science. No crude theories or exploded principles of Astronomy, Geology, or any of the sciences, no story of the four

[1] Georgics, iv, 308.

elements, no legend of such terrestrial supporters as the tortoise and the elephant, are to be found within its compass. While the stars are frequently introduced in Scripture language in magnificent comparisons, there is no mention of their benign or malign aspects; we have none of the nonsense of Astrology, which pervaded all reference to the heavenly bodies in the writings of learned men until two centuries ago. There is not a shadow of this in the Bible; star-gazers and prognosticators are mentioned there only to be derided. And of such monstrous absurdities respecting the facts of the kingdom of nature, as those which, as we have seen, received the undoubting credence of the best minds of antiquity, there is not the slightest trace. "And to what can this immeasurable superiority of the sacred writers be ascribed, but to the direct influence and control of an Omniscient Mind, whose instruments they were? Must we not be compelled to perceive the infinite wisdom of God overruling their thoughts and guiding their expressions; guarding their ignorance against intruding into a domain foreign to their subject? so that, whether they pursue the course of sober narrative, or pour forth the outbursts of prophetic song, they never imperil or degrade the truth of God by entwining around it the foreign growth of human prejudices and misconceptions in science. In their writings, the tree of life shoots up like the palm tree in the desert, with straight tapering stem, free from every meaner undergrowth and parasitical appendages, waving its verdant crown in the pure air and calm light of Heaven." [1]

And not only is the Bible free from every shade of error;—its language possesses another remarkable characteristic, which has already received partial illustration. Though it is the language of appearances and carefully avoids scientifical technicalities, it can yet be readily adjusted to every new scientific discovery, and harmonized

[1] Thompson's Lectures on Inspiration.

with every successive stage of human advancement. "As each new world of wonders has risen upon our view, and each grand discovery has added its light to the firmament of our science, the language of the Bible has opened to receive it, as if endued with the power of an endless life, and the expansive power of an infinite intelligence. In a multitude of passages, its pregnant oracular words, enigmatical and dark at first, have become luminous with the lapse of time."[1] As obscure prophecies have been made plain by the events which fulfilled them, so the progress of science enables us now to see that its brilliant discoveries were already anticipated in the sacred word.

A striking example of the Bible's entire avoidance of error in its allusions to the grand phenomena of nature is found in the 104th Psalm. This magnificent composition, than which, says Bishop Lowth, "nothing can be conceived more perfect of its kind," demonstrates the glory of the Creator from the wisdom, beauty, and variety of his works. It may be considered as a poetical version of the narrative of creation in Genesis. Like Moses, the inspired Psalmist begins with God, the Almighty King of kings, whose raiment is the light, whose palace is in the heavens, whose chariots are the clouds, and whose retinue are angelic spirits, who hasten like the wind and the lightning to fulfil his pleasure. He then glances to the earth and tells us who "laid its foundations that they should not be moved forever." "From the inanimate creation he makes a transition by the springs and streams of water to the living creatures which quench their thirst and rejoice in their Creator's bounty. He speaks of the provision made for such creatures as the wild asses of the desert, and the fowls of heaven which sing among the branches of the trees. And then he speaks of man, of the provision made for man, and of the adaptation of all things to man, the chief of all these lower

[1] Literary Attractions of the Bible, by Dr. Halsey.

works of God." The whole psalm is written in the highest style of poetry, and yet in all this wide range of topics, the keenest eye of science cannot discern the slightest error, while the phenomenal language respecting the earth's immovability, as has already been shown, contains an implied recognition of a great scientific truth. How remarkable a testimony to the Bible this accuracy is, will be felt when it is remembered that Milton, who wrote his immortal poem hardly two hundred years ago, speaks of the "five other wandering fires," supposing that to be the number of the planets which with the earth and sun make up our system. No such charge of ignorance can be fixed upon David or any other of the sacred writers. Baron Humboldt, who cannot be accused of any undue partiality for the Bible, thus speaks of this sacred hymn: "We are astonished to find in a lyrical poem of such a limited compass, the whole universe—the heavens and the earth—sketched with a few bold touches. The calm and toilsome life of man, from the rising of the sun to the setting of the same when his daily work is done, is here contrasted with the moving life of the elements of nature. This contrast and generalization in the conception of natural phenomena, and the retrospection of an omnipresent invisible Power, which can renew the earth or crumble it to dust, constitute a solemn and exalted form of poetic creation."

Surely a sketch of the "Cosmos" which was written when science, at least what is now recognized as such, can hardly be said to have existed, and which yet elicited the admiration of a mind like Humboldt's, familiar with the whole range of science, must have been penned under the guidance of Omniscience.

But there are also other instances in the Bible of what we can now perceive to be anticipations of the brilliant discoveries of science.

Thus the Bible has anticipated science in the distinction

which Moses makes between the primitive light and that whose benefits we derive from the sun. He has represented it to us as an element independent of that luminary, having been called forth by the Almighty fiat on the first day, whereas he seems to ascribe the creation of the sun and moon to the fourth day. This statement was long regarded by believers in Revelation as a great difficulty, and was pointed to by the sceptic as a palpable contradiction to physical facts. It was thought impossible that light could have existed apart from that great luminary which presides over the day. But the advance of science has dispelled the difficulty and established the accuracy of the Mosaic narrative. The exhumed remains of animals belonging to ages long preceding man's appearance on earth, had eyes, which by a necessary inference argued the co-existence of light. It is now known also, that the gigantic vegetation which produced the coal deposits could not have grown under the blaze of *solar* light. This conclusion is a result of botanical considerations. Moreover, the fossils of plants and animals which are found in the rocks of the carboniferous period in *all latitudes*, being analogous only to those which *now* flourish between the tropics, reveal a state of climate which could not have been governed in any great degree by the rays of the sun. Late discoveries also of certain peculiarities in the nature of light have given additional strength and probability to the *theory of vibrations*, according to which there is an ethereal fluid diffused throughout the universe of inconceivable rarity and elasticity, and that light and heat are phenomena evolved from it by the action of the sun. In harmony with this hypothesis, a more critical examination of the original language of the Scriptures, has shown that it is not said that light was *created* or *made*, but it was *called forth*, i. e., commanded to shine out of the darkness which was upon the face of the deep; and the sun and moon are styled, not lights, but "light bearers," intimating that they were but reflectors of light to the earth, and that it existed independently of them.

In the twenty-eighth chapter of Job, which has already been quoted, we find also a remarkable anticipation of modern discovery in relation to the laws which govern light. "The day spring" is there said "to take hold of the ends of the earth," and "it is turned as clay to the seal, and they stand as a garment." In this beautiful figure there is an allusion to the cylindrical seals that were used in ancient Babylon. Just as such a seal rolls over the blank and formless clay, and there instantly starts up in relief a fine group of objects, so the day spring revolves over the space which the darkness made empty and void; and as if created by the movement, all things stand forth in brilliant attire.

But there is evidently here a reference to that adaptation of light to the earth's atmosphere and to that property of light by which it is refracted, bends down, and takes hold of us by slow degrees. The action of the atmosphere upon the course and direction of the sun's rays, is the cause of the day's breaking upon us with such delicacy and gentleness. If there were no atmosphere, the sun would burst upon us suddenly, and we should pass in an instant from the darkness of night to the full blaze of day; but now the air waits for his coming, and "takes hold" of his rays, and bending and refracting them, gradually spreads them over the horizon, thus gently drawing aside the curtain of night, and revealing the radiance of the sky, the verdure of the fields, the tints of flowers, the lovely diversity of the landscape, all clad in

> "Nature's resplendent robe![1]
> Without whose vesting beauty all were wrapped
> In unessential gloom."

[1] A remarkable illustration of the fundamental doctrine of the Holy Trinity, which has been developed by modern researches into the laws and prop-

In like manner, Scripture first informed us that God "gave to the air its weight, and to the waters their just measure."[1] The property which is here assigned to the invisible but potent fluid which surrounds the earth, remained unknown, even to such students of nature as Aristotle and Bacon, until the experiments of Galileo and Toricelli demonstrated a truth which had lain uncomprehended in the Bible for ages. The "measure of the waters" expresses that existing proportion of land and sea which the advancement of physical knowledge now enables us to per-

erties of light, claims an insertion here. "Light is easily separated into its component colors, by transmitting it through a glass prism, where it is resolved into red, orange, yellow, green, blue, indigo and violet, which constitute, when combined, white or ordinary light. This band of colors is called spectrum. Now it will be perceived that red, yellow and blue are its primary or essential colors, the others being merely produced by the admixture or overlapping of two adjoining primary colors; thus, orange is found between the red and yellow, green between the yellow and blue; so that, in fact, we have only the three primary colors to deal with, each of which has its peculiar properties and attributes distinct from the others; thus, the red is the calorific or heating principle; the yellow is the luminous or light-giving principle; while it is in the blue ray that the power of actinism, or chemical action is found. Now, it is this trinity of red, yellow and blue, which constitutes, when combined, the unity of ordinary or white light. When separated, this unity of light is divided into the trinity of colors. Although one and the same, neither can exist without the other. The three are one, the one is three. Thus we have a unity in trinity, and a trinity in unity exemplified in light itself; and "God is light." Plants will live and grow luxuriantly under the influence of the red and yellow rays; but however promising the appearance, the blossom dies, and no fruit can be produced without the enlivening power of the blue rays. When this invisible action is wanting, the trinity and unity is incomplete. Life is unproductive until the three, united in one, bring all things to perfection. Thus each member of the trinity in unity of light has its especial duty to perform, and is in constant operation visibly or invisibly, although one power. Even far beyond the visible violet ray of the prismatic spectrum, the spirit of actinism prevails. Its chemical influence can be proved to extend beyond the limits of our vision. Thus there is in light an invisible agency always in action; and the more the subject is investigated, the more striking is the illustration between the Holy Spirit of God made manifest, and the wonderful properties of light which have been gradually unfolded by the researches of man."—*Temple Bar Magazine.*

[1] Job xxviii, 25. "Ruach" in this passage evidently means air.

ceive to be just that which is essential to the maintenance of both animal and vegetable life.

The superior weight of the atmosphere is the intermediate cause by which "vapors ascend from the ends of the earth," enumerated by David in the 135th Psalm, among the special reasons for thankfulness to God. Yet it is only by the aid of modern science that we are enabled to understand the importance of this arrangement. We now perceive that if this wonderful and extensive process of nature were to cease, there would be no rains or dews to fertilize our fields, and the consequence would be, the earth would be parched, and the vegetable productions which afford us subsistence would wither and decay, the whole system of terrestrial nature would be deranged, and man, and all the other tribes of animated nature deprived of those comforts which are essential to their existence, would in a short time perish from the earth.

Science has of late endeavored to investigate the laws which govern the winds and rule the sea, and has arrived at some interesting conclusions; but in a few words, the royal Solomon has expressed truths which volumes have been written to illustrate. He tells us that "the wind goeth toward the south, and turneth about unto the north; it whirleth about continually, and the wind returneth again according to his circuits." That is, various and capricious as their movements may appear, they are yet governed by laws as fixed and certain as those which regulate the tides of the ocean or the orbits of the planets. The same All-wise and Almighty Ruler who hath set bounds to the waters of the deep, and said to them, "Hitherto shalt thou come, and no further," hath assigned "their circuits" to the winds of heaven, from which they cannot deviate, and within which they are perpetually confined. Again he says, "all the rivers run into the sea; yet the sea is not full; unto the place from whence the rivers come, thither they return again." What is this but a setting forth of that wonderful and beautiful economy of nature, according to which the thirsty air is continually drinking up the sea—sucking up the waters of the deep in spongy clouds, and bearing them away upon the wings of the wind, and dashing them against the lofty ridges of the land, and thus filling the far off lakes and far up fountain heads whence the rivers come; and thereby maintaining, undisturbed and unaltered from age to age, that ceaseless circulation of the watery element, by virtue of which the rivers continually flow, while yet no increase is ever made to the volume of the deep—a perfect balance being thus preserved between them. Science is beginning to unfold the wisdom and harmony of cosmical arrangements, but it is evident that some at least of her discoveries had been "searched out" by Solomon long ago.

An interesting example of the correctness of Scripture allusion to physical facts has been recently pointed out by one of the most distinguished of living geologists. It has been found that the distribution of gold in its original vein-stone, or parent rock, differs from that of every other metal in the superficial range of its particles or threads. Lodes of iron, copper, and argentiferous lead ores, when followed downward, generally become more and more productive—the reverse being the case with gold. "The indisputable fact is, that the *chief quantities of gold*, including all the considerable lumps and pepitas, having been originally embedded in the upper parts of the vein-stones, have been broken up and transported with the debris of the mountain tops into slopes and adjacent valleys. . . . Modern science, instead of contradicting, only confirms the truth of the aphorism of the patriarch Job, which thus shadowed forth the downward persistence of the one and the superficial distribution of the other: "Surely there is *a vein* for the silver. . . . The earth hath dust of gold." (Job xxviii, 1, 6.) Murchison's Siluria, p. 457.

A very remarkable expression occurs in the Apocalypse (xvi, 18), bearing on the work of preparing the earth for man before man was made: "And there was a great earthquake, such as was not since men were upon the earth, so mighty an earthquake and so great." There the advent of man as an inhabitant of this earth, is formally given as the epoch after which great earthquakes did not occur. It is well known now that earthquakes must have rent this globe before the birth of man, which make all that have occurred since sink into insignificance; but how was John the fisherman led to employ, eighteen hundred years ago, a phraseology which the researches of our own day have now for the first time shown to be philosophically exact? Speaking of this verse and quoting it freely, John Bunyan (Reign of Antichrist) says, "For the earthquake, it is said to be such as *never was*, so mighty an earthquake and so great." He thought the phrase "since men were upon the earth," was equivalent to "never," and was thus led into what we now see to be an error. What but the superintendence of the Omniscient Spirit preserved John the Apostle from the mistake into which John Bunyan fell?

Still other facts of Physical science that are indicated in the Bible might be enumerated. But enough have been given to justify the remark of the illustrious Sir John Herschel, "that all human discoveries seem to be made only for the purpose of confirming more strongly the truths come from on high, and contained in the sacred writings."

This does not, however, exhaust the testimony of Physical science to the Bible. Not only are the primary facts of the kingdom of nature accurately delineated in the pages of Scripture, but those great principles which are the ultimate results of science, and which have been obtained by long and laborious processes of induction, are there recognized and frequently and plainly asserted.

Thus, it has been one of the great achievements of

modern science to demonstrate the universal prevalence of law—that it extends where the uninstructed mind sees only caprice or supernatural agency—that it regulates not only the motions of the planets, the succession of the seasons, and the tidal vibrations of the ocean, but every fitful breeze, every forming cloud, and every falling shower. Yea, even

> "The very law that moulds a tear,
> And makes it trickle from its source,
> That law preserves the globe a sphere,
> And guides the planets in their course."

This is also the doctrine of the Bible. It knows nothing of fortuitous occurrences, but everywhere asserts the dominion of invariable, natural law, extending to things animate and inanimate, the heavens and the earth. It teaches us that according to the ordinances which God has established, there is a decree for the rain and a way for the thunder flash—the sea "passeth not" its bounds and the earth abideth forever—the sun serveth for a light by day, and the moon and the stars for a light by night. Seed time and harvest, and cold and heat, and summer and winter, and day and night, do not cease. The hawk is said to "fly by his wisdom; the eagle mounteth up at his command, and maketh her nest on high, from whence she seeketh her prey, and her eyes behold it afar off." "The stork in the heavens knoweth her appointed times; and the turtle, the crane and the swallow observe the times of their coming." "Forever, O Lord, thy word is settled in heaven. Thou hast established the earth and it abideth. They continue this day according to thine ordinance; for all are thy servants." While, however, atheistic philosophers have endeavored to deduce an argument from the uniform processes of nature against the possibility of supernatural interference, as if "the laws of nature" were an inexorable chain of adamant (an inference, which, as we have seen, both Astronomy and Geology disprove), the Bible accords with the discoveries of science in ascribing immutability to the Mind of Him who constituted the natural order of things and not to that order itself. "God," says Sir Isaac Newton, "acteth in what is called nature according to accurate and uniform laws, except when it be good for Him to act otherwise." And the Bible teaches us: "He doeth whatsoever pleaseth him in heaven and in earth, in the sea and in all deep places." It was not by the blind operation of mere lifeless laws that this glorious universe sprang into being, nor is it by them alone that it is still upheld. There is a wise and beauteous order of cause and effect, a law whose "voice is the harmony of the world, and to which all things in heaven and earth do homage," but "her seat is the bosom of God." The highest link of the golden chain is in his hand. "Tell me not," says an eloquent writer,[1] "of forces centripetal and forces centrifugal—tell me not of gravitation holding the invisible reins by which the unresting steeds of the sky are by strong curb restrained within appointed bounds, and compelled to keep their path; will these forces account for the first propulsion? Who at the beginning launched forth those stupendous orbs? Who impressed on them that primeval force? Who gave them their first direction? Who weighed them in scales, regulating their orbit and their speed? And who ordained these relationships between the various forces of nature, so that the tendency to rush to the centre might be so counterpoised by the impulse to rush from the circumference, that a steady motion along the same path is the result? By whose arrangement and upholding power is it that we never dread the moon dashing against the earth, the earth hastening to terrible collision with the sun, the planets rushing madly through space, and the sky becoming thus a vast battle field, strewn with the fragments of stars and satellites?

1. Rev. Newman Hall.

"Have ye not known—hath it not been told you from the beginning—have ye not understood from the foundation of the earth? It is He who sitteth upon the circle of the earth, and the inhabitants of the earth are as grasshoppers; that stretcheth out the heavens as a curtain, and spreadeth them out as a tent to dwell in. Lift up your eyes on high, and behold who hath created all these things, that bringeth out their host by number? It is He who meted out the heavens with a span, and comprehended the dust of the earth in a measure, and weighed the mountains in scales and the hills in a balance. It is He who stretcheth out the North over the empty place, and hangeth the earth upon nothing. By His Spirit He hath garnished the heavens. He telleth the number of the stars, He calleth them all by their names. He commandeth the sun, and it riseth not, and sealeth up the stars. He bindeth the sweet influences of Pleiades, and looseth the bands of Orion. He bringeth forth Mazzaroth in his season, and guideth Arcturus with his sons. Lo! these are but a part of His ways, but the thunder of His power who can understand?"

By the aid of geologic discovery, Science has proved that in addition to those unvarying physical laws, by which in accordance with a wise and benevolent arrangement uniformity is preserved in the present system of things, there is also a higher law of progress and development. The "testimony of the rocks" has taught us that through the unmeasured ages of the past, the mineral, vegetable, and animal kingdoms of nature have exhibited continually fresh manifestations of creative power, wisdom, and goodness. "From the lowly seaweeds of the silurian strata and marsh plants of the old red sandstone, we rise (speaking in general terms) to the prolific club mosses, reeds, ferns, and gigantic endogens of the coal measures; from these to the exagons or true timber trees of the tertiary and current eras. So also in the animal kingdom; the graptolites and trilobites of the silurian seas are succeeded by the higher crustacea and bone-clad fishes of the coal measures; the sauroid fishes by the gigantic saurians and reptiles of the oolite; the reptiles of the oolite by the huge mammalia of the tertiary epoch; and these in time give place to existing species, with man as the crowning form of created existence." [1]

At the very commencement of the Bible (as has in effect been already shown) we have this identical principle embodied in the gradual elaboration ot all things in the six creative days or periods, rising from the formless void of the beginning, through successive stages of inorganic or organic being up to man. This culmination reached, however, the process was arrested by that fatal act which broke the harmony of creation—when

> "Earth felt the wound, and Nature from her seat
> Sighing through all her works gave signs of woe,
> That all was lost."

The golden link was then broken which bound man and all the lower creatures with Him to the throne of God. Here Science fails us, and unaided by revelation is unable even to read the traces which the moral ruin of our race has stamped upon the face of nature. And of the developments of the Creator's boundless and inexhaustible resources to be unfolded in the future, she can tell us nothing. The uniform confession of her votaries is that, respecting these, it were vain to offer the wildest conjecture.

> "Reason's spell might not disclose
> The gracious birth to come."

But here Revelation comes to our aid and teaches us that "the whole creation groaneth and travaileth" in hope of a glorious regeneration. It teaches us that the broken link has been restored and the unending progression is to

[1] Advanced Text Book of Geology, by David Page, F.G.S.

be resumed. This is finely shown in the Hulsean Lectures of Dean Trench: "The Heaven which had disappeared from the earth since the third chapter of Genesis, reappears again in visible manifestation, in the latest chapters of the Revelation. The tree of life, whereof there were but faint reminiscences in all the intermediate time, again stands by the river of the water of life, and again there is no more curse. Even the very differences of the forms under which the heavenly kingdom reappears are deeply characteristic, marking as they do, not merely all that is won back, but won back in a more glorious shape than that in which it was lost, because won back in the Son. It is no longer Paradise, but the New Jerusalem—no longer the *garden*, but now the *city* of God, which is on earth. The change is full of meaning; no longer the garden, free, spontaneous and unlabored, even as man's blessedness in the state of a first innocence would have been; but the city, costlier indeed, more stately, more glorious, but at the same time, the result of toil, of labor, of pains—reared into a nobler and more abiding habitation, yet with stones which, after the pattern of the "elect corner stone," were each in its time laboriously hewn and painfully squared for the places which they fill." Such the prospect to which the eye of faith looks forward,

—"At return of Him, the Woman's Seed,
Last in the clouds, from heaven to be revealed
In glory of the Father, to dissolve
Satan with his perverted world, then raise
From the conflagrant mass, purged and refined,
New heavens, new earth, ages of endless date,
Founded in righteousness, and peace, and love,
To bring forth fruits, joy, and eternal bliss."

Modern science has delighted to unfold the wonderful *adaptation* of natural laws and objects to each other, to the happiness of the animal creation and to the use and service of man. Everything, it has been shown, serves an end.

Throughout the animal and vegetable kingdoms, there is a wonderful series of special adjustments irresistibly suggestive of a designing, infinite Intelligence. Thus the atmosphere is essential to the respiration, without which no individual of either kingdom can prolong its life. It furnishes oxygen to animals, carbon to vegetables. Had it been constituted of other gases, neither kingdom could have existed. It is also the vehicle for the conveyance of water from the ocean to the land. For the earth to receive its supply of rain, it is necessary that the water rise in vapor from the ocean as well as from the land, be diffused over the surface of the continents, and again descend from the atmosphere in its liquid condition. The tendency of water to constant evaporation supplies the air with moisture. The variations of temperature and of electrical condition again condense the vapor and precipitate it in the form of rain or dew. These and numberless other arrangements and adaptations are not only exquisitely contrived in themselves, but serve to make the earth a fitting habitation for man. This deduction of science is a principle entirely familiar to the inspired writers. While they recognize God as the great end of all things, by whom and for whose pleasure they are and were created, they fail not to point out the subordinate purposes of wisdom and benevolence which they subserve. They tell us that the tempest is ordered and the clouds arranged by wisdom, to give water to the wilderness where no man is, to cause the bud of the tender herb to shoot forth. They tell us how perfectly God has fitted the various animal tribes to their several localities. And finally they represent man as the chief created being for whom this earth has been prepared and designed. To "replenish the earth and subdue it" was the commission with which he was invested in the hour of his creation. In these words we have another instance of the expansive power of the language of the Bible which has already been illustrated. Their full import could not be understood, until the facts respecting man and nature to which they refer were brought to light. "What the earth is, and what man is—that the one is a compact globe under the dominion of uniform laws, and that the other, by his powers, mental and physical, his capacity of knowledge, invention, construction and execution, is equal to the task of exploring and understanding the material world, and of mastering and transforming its various substances and forces from their natural employments to the service of his own superior nature—are facts that could not even be thought of till they were brought before our eyes. Now, however, man's conquests have been carried so far, that society has become aware of the end to which all the separate lines of progress are steadily tending. The prophecy of Moses is fulfilling; man is subduing the earth; the earth is placing herself under the feet of man. What the great Hebrew saw afar off, from that mount of God to which he was lifted up three thousand years ago, is present with us and plain to our senses. Restored by the second Adam to the powers lost and the rights forfeited by the first, the human race is taking possession of the dominion given to it by God in Paradise. This is the end to which all science and all art, all the labor and all the thought of men in all ages and in all places, have been, and are still steadily and unconsciously contributing; the predicted end, toward the achievement of which not the least efficient laborers have been some of those very sons of science, who have laughed to scorn both the prophet and his inspirer."[1]

Another principle, the truth and importance of which have but recently been distinctly recognized by the philosophic student of nature, though in all ages it has more or less dimly dawned upon the minds of profound thinkers, is the law of type or pattern. It is now understood that as

[1] "Nuggets from the Oldest Diggings." Edinburgh. Constable & Co.

in the production of human works of design, the skilful artist keeps in view some pattern, style or order, according to which the whole is arranged, and the mutual relation of the parts adjusted, so is it in the works of the Almighty. In the kingdoms of vegetable and animal nature, we find the same idea exhibited and carried out. Numerous as are their orders and varieties, there are a few leading types of structure, under which they may all be arranged. Thus in respect to the vertebrate skeleton, or the bony framework of all that class of animal forms that have a backbone, as distinguished from shell fish and the other creatures where the hard skeleton surrounds the fleshy and soft parts, it has been shown that all these animals, from the fish and reptile up to man, are made on one pattern, varied to suit their different peculiarities; and that a fundamental or general skeleton can be assigned as a point of departure for the whole. Man, the highest of the vertebrates, is thus the archetype representing and including all the lower and earlier members of the vertebrate type. "All his parts and organs," says Professor Owen, "had been already sketched out in anticipation in the inferior animals," a philosophic deduction which strikingly illustrates the declaration of the inspired Psalmist: "In thy book were all my members written, which in continuance were fashioned, when, as yet, there were none of them." This great principle is, moreover, plainly implied and illustrated in the whole order of creation, as set forth in the first chapter of Genesis, where we have specific type in the production of plants and animals after their kinds or species, each rising step a prophecy of something nobler yet to come. As thence deduced, it has been thus expressed by Coleridge, and embellished with the felicitous touches of genius: "Let us carry ourselves back in spirit to the mysterious week, to the teeming work-days of the Creator; as they rose in vision before the eye of the inspired historian of 'the generations of the heavens and the earth, in the days that the Lord God made the earth and the heavens.' And who that hath watched their ways with an understanding heart, could contemplate the filial and loyal bee: the home-building, wedded and divorceless swallow; and above all, the manifoldly intelligent ant tribes, with their commonwealths and confederacies, their warriors and miners, the husband-folk that fold in their tiny flocks on the honeyed leaf, and the virgin sisters with the holy instincts of maternal love, detached, and in selfless purity, and not say to himself, Behold the shadow of approaching humanity, the sun arising from behind, in the kindling morn of the creation!"[1] As the glories of that morn unfold, there arises from under the Divine hand, and stands erect, a being formed in the very image of the Creator, in whom all those mute prophecies that had gone before found a wondrous fulfilment.

> "From harmony to harmony,
> Through all the compass of the notes it ran,
> The diapason closing full in Man."—DRYDEN.

But when man being in honor abode not in it—when the image of God was defaced and broken, and creation's crown fallen dishonored to the dust, what then can Science teach us? Here, again the Bible comes to our aid and directs our thoughts to a far more glorious ideal of humanity. Not only does it harmonize with the teaching of Science, that before the creation of the first man, all nature was preconfigured to him and a mute prophecy of what he would be, but where Science can teach us nothing, it introduces us into a new world of wonders. It teaches us how "from the time of the Fall everything symbolized and supposed the coming of the second man. Everything assumed a position pointing, preconfigured to him. The first sinner himself; why is he not destroyed? why kept in being? Another Adam is coming to expiate the guilt

[1] Coleridge's Aids to Reflection. Aph. xxxvi.

and remedy the evil. His sinful posterity—I see them rapidly increase in numbers, but more rapidly in guilt; why, when punishment overtakes them, is it always arrested in its course, always partial in its infliction? A second man is on the way to endure and exhaust it for them. Sinai is kindled and the law proclaimed; but why is this, when man has made himself notorious chiefly as its transgressor? Another is expected to fulfil it. I pass into the land of Canaan and find it cleared of its ancient heathenism, and planted over with types and symbols; who is to be the anti-type of all these figures, the substance of all these shadows? I pass into the temple, but everything I see is pointing to the future; here is an altar, but where is the sacrifice? for 'the blood of bulls and goats cannot take away sin;' here is a sanctuary, but the entrance is closed, the veil is down; and worshippers, but they are all in the attitude of unsatisfied expectation. And here on Zion is an empty throne. Everything appears unfinished and waiting."[1] "Far off His coming shone" through a long processional train of objects and events and typical persons like Moses and David and the high priests of Israel, until in the fulness of time, "God sent forth his Son," in the form of God and equal with God, and yet "found in fashion as a man," in the "body which had been prepared for him," the glorious Archetype of redeemed humanity. "The first man is of the earth earthy; the second man is the Lord from heaven." And have we not here more than an intimation that the unity of the Divine plan which Science teaches us has been preserved through the remote ages past, will remain unbroken in the future, though carried out to a more glorious ideal? "The advent of man, simply as such, was the great event prefigured during the old geologic ages. The advent of that divine man, 'who hath abolished death, and brought life and immortality to light,'

[1] "The Second Adam," by Dr. John Harris.

was the great event prefigured during the historic ages. It is these two grand events, equally portions of one sublime scheme, originated when God took counsel with himself in the depths of eternity, that bind together past, present, and future—the geologic with the Patriarchal, the Mosaic, and the Christian ages, and altogether with that new heavens and new earth, the last of many creations, in which there shall be no more death nor curse, but the throne of God and the Lamb shall be in it, and His servants shall serve Him."[1]

"But still in One, whose soul, aloof from wrong,
Was fill'd with earnest unpolluted good,
Resounds thy voice an undiscordant song,
And tells Thy will as at the first it stood.

"Thy word fulfill'd was He, forever shown,
To man the living Archetype of Life,
In whose embodied light our spirits own
A certain hope—a rest secure from strife."—STERLING.

The examination we have thus given has, we trust, made it clear that, as it respects physical science, Revelation has no reason to fear the light; but that, on the contrary, the brilliant trophies which the human mind in these recent ages has won from the outward world, have been triumphs for the Bible. Has Astronomy been invoked to aid in its overthrow? The very stars in their courses have fought against the infidel attempt. Has Geology been summoned to enter the field against it? The earth has literally "disclosed her dead" to attest the truth of Moses, and to silence the cavil of the rationalist who would banish the Creator from his works. In every instance where they have come in contact, God's works have verified his word.

Apart from the hopes with which that Word inspires the believing heart, of what permanent value are the splendid achievements of science to man? Viewed in the

[1] Testimony of the Rocks, p. 216.

light of his threescore years and ten, are they not almost as evanescent as the palace of the Arabian enchanter? And how utterly do they fail to meet the yearning wants of the soul! They cannot soothe a troubled conscience, or lift the burden of remorse from an aching heart. Truly has the world's favorite poet said that

> "Knowledge is not happiness; and science
> But an exchange of ignorance for that
> Which is another kind of ignorance."—MANFRED.

"Thousands of years ago, as one of the most ancient of the holy writings tells us, the question was asked: 'Where shall wisdom be found? and where is the place of understanding?' and in many works that have been written since, men have tried in one way or another to answer it. The thoughtful patriarch who proposed it, sought in vain from all the wisdom and knowledge of his time a reply that would give peace to his restless spirit. And if we turn to the more mature science of our own day, and repeat the question: Whence then cometh wisdom, and where is the place of understanding? what is the answer? Even as it was ages ago. The geologist drills and bores through stratum after stratum, and digs and delves far 'deeper than plummet ever sounded,' only to return and tell that 'the Depth saith, It is not in me.' The voyager covers the sea with ships. With sail, and paddle-wheel, and Archimedes' screw, they speed north and south, and east and west, and round about the pendent globe. Many run to and fro, and knowledge increases. What the foam-crested waves will not tell, the abyss may reveal; and with net, and dredge, and diving-bell, the 'dark unfathomed caves of ocean' are searched through, and gazed into, and 'gems of purest ray,' and monsters who never saw the sun, are brought into the 'light of common day.' But, above all the stir and strife of man's endeavor, the murmuring billows lift their voices, and 'the Sea saith, It is not with me.' The chemist gathers together every object which has shape, or weight, or volume, living or dead, and with fire, and furnace, and potent agent, and electric battery, tests and assays it. But when 'victorious analysis' has done its best, he replies, 'It cannot be valued with the gold of Ophir, with the precious onyx or the sapphire. The gold and the crystal cannot equal it. The price of wisdom is above rubies.' The naturalist wanders through the pathless forests of far distant lands, and with pain and toil grows familiar with the habits of everything that lives; but after he has gone the round of all creation in search of wisdom, he answers with mournful aspect, 'It is hid from the eyes of all living, and kept secret from the fowls of the air.' The anatomist makes the writhing animal agonize under his torturing hand, and slays it, that perchance in the page of death the mystery of life and of wisdom may be found written; but he will venture in reply to say no more than that 'Destruction and Death say, We have heard the sound thereof with our ears.'

"But while all the oracles of science are silent on this great question, lo! through the thick darkness a ray of light descends, and a voice, solemn but benignant, proclaims to us as it did to the first anxious seeker after Truth, 'The fear of the Lord, that is wisdom; and to depart from evil is understanding.'[1]

"To have my understanding opened to my own nature, origin, and destiny; to know that I am alien from perfect good; to tremble before the consequences of such an alienation; but at the same time to have arrived at a clear conviction of the immortal properties of that accursed and self-accusing spirit—this is knowledge, this is truth. To have brought home to my understanding and more to my heart, that this perfect good which alone is God, has been

[1] British Quarterly Review.

reconciled in the mysterious process of assuming and sacrificing itself for the imperfect and spotted nature that is within me,—this is love; finite indeed, but responding to infinite love; and what is truth and love together, but the religion of the cross? The lowliest of the sons of men is capable of this; the burning seraph of no more. All other science—the science of this earth—must pale before it, because all else may die; this never. Those brilliant fires which light up yonder sky, and utter mystic music revolving in their spheres, as day unto day uttereth speech and night unto night showeth knowledge, shall, in the progress of ages vanish and be stricken from the creation of God. With them this globe, and all that is material, must one day be dissolved. Where then shall live the science born of matter and of earth? That only portion will remain, which has so operated on the immortal mind in this portion of its existence, as to prepare and fit it for a better, happier, and endless state beyond the grave."[1]

"Welcome, dear book, soul's Joy and food! The feast
Of Spirits; Heav'n extracted lyes in thee,
Thou art life's Charter, the Dove's spotless nest
Where souls are hatch'd unto Eternitie.

"In thee the hidden stone, the Manna lies;
Thou art the great Elixir rare and Choice;
The Key that opens to all Mysteries,
The Word in Characters, God in the Voice."

HENRY VAUGHAN.

[1] Lecture on Science and Religion, by Rev. H. M. Mason, D.D.

CHAPTER IV.

THE UNITY OF THE HUMAN RACE.

In passing from the Physical to the Historical sciences, our attention is naturally first arrested by a subject which is related perhaps equally to both, and which has of late years been the source of the most persistent assaults against the Bible.

The peculiarities of form and color which are now found among the different human races, are irreconcilable, it has been alleged, with the identity of ancestral origin claimed by Moses for all the tribes and families of men. Instead of a common descent from a single pair, it has been argued from scientific considerations, that several pairs of human creatures were either created by Almighty power, or came up into humanity from some lower order of being; and that from these, occupying different localities from one another on the earth's surface, must the diverse races of mankind have descended. "The negro at least" (we are told) "is a distinct race, and must have had a separate origin. Negroes cannot have sprung from the same stock as the white man!" A celebrated Professor of Natural History remarks: "Men were primitively located in the various parts of the world they inhabit, and they arose everywhere in those harmonious proportions with other living beings, which would at once secure their preservation, and contribute to their welfare." He also affirms that the Bible professes to give "the history of the Jews;" and by a strange oversight, ventures to assert that "nowhere the colored races, as such, are even alluded to;" while he challenges those who maintain that mankind originated from a single pair, to "quote a single passage in the whole Scriptures, pointing at those physical differences, which may be adduced as evidence that the sacred writers regarded them as descended from a common stock."

Could these startling assertions be substantiated, a fatal blow would be struck at the authority of the Scriptures. If they are true, the whole of the Bible history must be surrendered. They would destroy the brotherhood of man, and thereby render worthless the inspired account of his ruin and remedy. They would falsify the Bible explanation of the entrance of sin and death and deny the universality of that atonement, which proclaims that "as in Adam all die, so in Christ shall all be made alive."

But, fortunately, the greater weight of scientific authority is still on the side of the Bible, while, from unexpected sources, strongly corroborative testimony has been obtained.

We know from an investigation of the laws of nature, and from the anatomy and physiology of the human frame, that all the varieties of the race, numerous as they are, possess the same physical properties. In the structure of his body, and in the physical organization which distinguish him from every other species of animals, man is the same being in China and South America, on the shores of the Polar Sea, and on the burning sands of Africa. "Change his condition; transplant him from his natural soil and climate; take him in the wilds of the forest, or under the culture of civilized and polished life; and he has everywhere the characteristics which designate the same species. These characteristics are obvious, striking and permanent, even to the number of teeth and bones, the number and arrangement of the muscles, and the digestive, circulatory, secretory, and respiratory organs. There is no difference in these particulars which has as yet been detected among the different races; there is the same uniformity in the white and the black, the Mongolian, the Malay, and the American. They are all omnivorous, and capable of living on all kinds of food, and of inhabiting all climates; while all have the same period of gestation, the same slow growth, are subject to the same diseases, possess the same average longevity, and in every shade of amalgamation, produce a fertile offspring."

And not only is there this physical identity; but the moral and intellectual constitution of the different races is everywhere the same. Whether we search the page of history sacred or profane, back to the remotest times, or traverse countries savage or civilized, heathen or Christian, to the ends of the earth; though in different degrees of development and cultivation, we ever find the same wondrous capacities, the same universal lineaments of the human soul, which distinguish man from the beasts that perish.

By collection of numerous interesting facts illustrating this remarkable uniformity in the conditions of species which is to be found in all the tribes and races of mankind, under all the peculiarities and varieties of form and color, Dr. Prichard, in his great work on the Natural History of Man, has constructed a powerful and conclusive argument for the derivation of the whole human species from one stock. If the unity of the race is not to be made out genealogically, because profane history does not ascend so high as to meet the historical narrative of Moses, in reference to Gentile nations, he demonstrates that unity by the fact that it is essential to the nature of man. Agreeing with Buffon and Cuvier, to define species as "a constant succession of individuals capable of reproducing each other," he goes on to prove that there is a law, prevailing alike in the vegetable and animal creation, which renders the perpetuation of hybrids, so as to produce new and intermediate species, impossible. The facts adduced lead, with the strongest force of analogical reasoning, to the conclusion that, as the various tribes of men may, by intermarriage, perpetuate their race, they belong to the same species. Additional light is thrown on the subject by his careful analysis of collected evidence on the nature and origin of varieties. In answer to the great question, How could such various nations and tribes as are now existing among men, have all sprung from the same stock, he proves by an inductive appeal to facts, that sporadic or accidental varieties may arise in one race, tending to produce in it the characteristics of another; that these varieties may be perpetuated; and that food, climate, employment and other secondary causes, account for the existing varieties of the human race and for the perpetuation of those varieties. And he comes to the conclusion, that there are no permanent lines of demarcation separating the different tribes or nations; that there is scarcely an instance in which the actual transition cannot be proven to have taken place; and that there is every reason to infer, quite irrespectively of the Scripture testimony, that all the families of the earth are descended from common parents, and that at no very distant period.

No fact of science can, indeed, be considered as more certain, than that man, and not only man, but the inferior animals, acquire certain changes of color, hair and form, when removed from one climate or locality to another, or when subjected to any great change in manner or habits of life. "Whether," says another writer, "the external condition of these changes be the chemical solar rays; the altitude or depression of the general level; the difference of geological formations; the varying agencies of magnetism and electricity; atmospheric peculiarities; miasmatic exhalations from vegetable or mineral matter; difference of soils; proximity to the ocean; variety of food, habits of life and exposure—all of which perhaps at times come in play—or other causes yet more occult; there can be no question about the fact that such causes are at work. The general fact is, that when the other physical conditions are the same, tribes living nearest the equator, and level of the sea, are marked with the darkest skin and the crispest hair. Thus, we make a gradual ascent from the jetty negro of the line to the olive-colored Arab, the brown Moor, the swarthy Italian, the dusky Spaniard, the dark-skinned Frenchman, the ruddy Englishman, and the pallid Scandinavian." In regard to the duration or permanence of these varieties, it appears to be a general fact that when once acquired, they are transmitted through successive generations, "under the influence of the law of assimilation between parent and offspring, even though the causes which originally determined the variation from the original type should have ceased to operate."[1]

The following decisive Historical testimony as to the effects of climatic and geographical changes, after a long continued period, upon the physical constitution of man, is given by an eminent writer on Physiology, Dr. W. B. Carpenter, as the result of the researches of Prichard, Latham and others. He says that "the Magyar race in Hungary, which is not now inferior in mental or physical characters to any in Europe, is proved by historical and philological evidence to have been a branch of the great northern Asiatic stock, which was expelled about ten centuries since from the country it then inhabited (bordering on the Uralian mountains), and in its turn expelled Slavonian nations from the fertile parts of Hungary, which it has occupied ever since. Having thus exchanged their abode, in the most rigorous climate of the old continent—a wilderness in which the Ostiaks and Samoiedes pursue the chase during only the mildest season—for one in the South of Europe, amid fertile plains abounding in rich harvests, the Magyars grad-

[1] Professor Cabell's "Unity of the Human Race."

ually laid aside the rude and savage habits which they are recorded to have brought with them, and adopted a more settled mode of life. In the course of a thousand years, their type of cranial formation has been changed from the pyramidal (or Mongol) to the elliptical (or Caucasian); and they have become a handsome people, with fine stature and regular European features, with just enough of the Tartar cast of countenance, in some instances, to recall their origin to mind. Here it may be said that the intermixture of the conquering with the conquered race has had a great share in bringing about this change; but the Magyars pride themselves greatly on the purity of their descent; and the small infusion of Slavonic blood which may have taken place from time to time, is by no means sufficient to account for the complete change of type which now manifests itself. The women of pure Magyar race are said by good judges to be singularly beautiful, far surpassing either German or Slavonian females. A similar modification, but less in degree, appears to have taken place among the Finnish tribes of Scandinavia. These may be almost certainly affirmed to have had the same origin with the Lapps; but whilst the latter retain (although inhabiting Europe) the nomadic habits of their Mongolian ancestors, the former have adopted a much more settled mode of life, and have made considerable advances in civilization. And thus we have in the Lapps, Finns and Magyars, three nations or tribes, of whose descent from a common stock no reasonable doubt can be entertained, and which yet exhibit the most marked differences in cranial characters, and also in general conformation, the Magyars being tall and well made, as the Lapps are short and uncouth."

The observations of Bishop Heber in India, are in harmony with the above conclusions. That country, he says, "has been always, and long before the Europeans came hither, a favorite theatre for adventurers from Persia,

Greece, Tartary, Turkey and Arabia, all white men, and all in their turn possessing themselves of wealth and power. These circumstances must have greatly contributed to make a fair complexion fashionable. It is remarkable, however, to observe how surely all these classes of men in a few generations, even without any intermarriage with the Hindoos, assume the deep olive tint, little less dark than a Negro, which seems natural to the climate. The Portuguese natives form unions among themselves alone, or if they can, with Europeans. Yet the Portuguese have, during a three hundred years' residence in India, become as black as Kaffirs. Surely this goes far to disprove the assertion, which is sometimes made, that climate alone is insufficient to account for the difference between the Negro and the European. It is true that in the Negro are other peculiarities which the Indian has not, and to which the Portuguese colonist shows no symptom of approximation, and which undoubtedly do not appear to follow so naturally from the climate, as that swarthiness of complexion which is the sole distinction between the Hindoo and the European. But if heat produces one change, other peculiarities of climate may produce other and additional changes, and when such peculiarities have 3,000 or 4,000 years to operate in, it is not easy to fix any limits to their power. . . . Thus, while hardships, additional exposure, a greater degree of heat, and other circumstances with which we are unacquainted, may have deteriorated the Hindoo into a Negro, opposite causes may have changed him into the progressively lighter tints of the Chinese, the Persian, the Turk, the Russian, and the Englishman."

The researches of travellers in Africa corroborate the same view. The Rev. John Campbell, who some years ago travelled on a missionary exploring tour several hundred miles north of the Cape of Good Hope, remarks that the complexion of the inhabitants assumed a deeper hue—

uniformly becoming darker, till it became quite black as he approached the equator. It is also a well ascertained fact that there is a colony of Jews at Cochin, upon the coast of Malabar, who are now as black as the other Malabarians, who are hardly a shade lighter than the people of Guinea, Benin, or Angola.

That the legitimate deductions of science tend to corroborate the Scripture doctrine of the unity of the human race, we have the distinguished authority of Baron Humboldt. "Whilst attention was exclusively directed to the extremes of color and form," says that profound student of nature, "the result of the first vivid impressions derived from the senses, was a tendency to view these differences as characteristics, not of mere varieties, but of originally distinct species. The permanence of certain types, in the midst of the most opposite influences, especially of climate, appeared to favor this view, notwithstanding the shortness of the time to which the historical evidence applied; but, in my opinion, more powerful reasons lend their weight to the other side of the question, and corroborate the unity of the human race. I refer to the many intermediate gradations of the tint of the skin and the form of the skull, which have been made known to us by the rapid progress of geographical discoveries in modern times; to the analogies derived from the history of varieties in animals, both domesticated and wild; and to the positive observations collected respecting the limits of fertility in hybrids. The greater part of the supposed contrasts to which so much weight was formerly assigned, have disappeared before the laborious investigations of Tiedemann on the brain of negroes and of Europeans, and the anatomical researches of Vrolik and Weber on the form of the pelvis. When we take a general view of the dark-colored African nations, on which the work of Prichard has thrown so much light, and when we compare them with the natives of the Australian Islands, and with the Papuans and Alfourans, we see that a black tint of skin, woolly hair and negro features are by no means associated." . . . "Mankind are therefore distributed in varieties, which we are often accustomed to designate by the somewhat vague appellation of races."[1]

Thus it appears that according to the principles admitted by the most eminent physiologists and naturalists, whether friendly or not to Christianity and the Bible, there is nothing in the natural differences observable between different parts of the human race distributed over the globe, which is incompatible with the Scripture statement which claims for all these parts a common origin. Simple diversity within limits hitherto reached cannot be claimed as proving an original diversity of races.

An attempt has been made, however, to evade this conclusion. The objectors, under the pressure of the facts and arguments brought against their theory, now generally admit that notwithstanding the varieties at present existing among the several tribes and nations of the earth, all races may have sprung from an original stock, if we allow a sufficient duration to have elapsed for the causes of change in operation to produce such results. But they contend that the time in which the earth was repeopled after the flood, according to the reckoning of the Bible Chronology, falls very far short of meeting the requirements of the case. It is claimed that on the monuments

[1] Humboldt's Cosmos, vol. i, p. 351. As to the value of Dr. Morton's observations in support of the theory of original diversity of races, the eminent philosopher, Sir William Hamilton, makes this observation: "What first strikes me in Dr. Morton's Tables, completely invalidates his conclusions—he has not distinguished male from female crania. Now, as the female encephalos is, on an average, some four ounces Troy less than the male, it is impossible to compare national skulls with national skulls, in respect of their capacity, unless we compare male with male, female with female heads, or at least, know how many of either sex go to make up the national complement." Extract from Sir W. Hamilton's Lectures on Metaphysics.—*Appendix* ii. (c).

of Egypt there are pictorial delineations of the Negro, Egyptian and Asiatic, executed as far back as the age of Thothmes III, fifteen centuries before the Christian era, in which the peculiarities of race in form, color and hair, are as perfectly distinct as they are now. Such marked national diversities could not, say the objectors, have been produced in so short an interval of time as the 850 years which had elapsed between the Deluge and the reign of that monarch, supposed to synchronize with the Exodus of the Israelites, if all the races had their origin from one man—the patriarch Noah. Nothing short of a miracle, it is urged, could, during that time, have effected such a commutation, which the subsequent experience of thirty centuries has proven to be a physical impossibility.

This objection has at first sight a formidable appearance; but upon examination, the difficulty soon loses its dimensions. Let it be granted that a miracle was necessary to effect the change into different races from one, yet who can affirm that the required miracle was not wrought? In the brief record of the earliest times given in Genesis, there is a statement by which this very difficulty is met and amply provided for. We are there informed that when the descendants of Noah had become sufficiently numerous to commence the occupation of the different portions of the earth, there *was* a direct intervention of the Almighty to "confound the language" of men, and hence necessitate that result. When by supernatural power this change was wrought, may not the same agency have been employed to effect such diversity in the appearance and structure of the different branches of one human family, as to adapt them to the diversified localities, climates and conditions they were destined to occupy? This is an hypothesis which can be regarded as untenable, only by those who reject the possibility of a miracle, an objection which has already been answered. To a believer in Revelation and the Divine Omnipotence, it satisfactorily accounts for all the phenomena presented in the varying races of mankind without doing violence to a single passage or a solitary word of Holy Writ.

Yet apart from a Divine intervention to produce this result, there are other considerations which will go far to obviate, if they do not entirely remove the difficulty. The objection is based upon the presumption that the rate of change in man's physical condition, is the same now that it was in those early patriarchal ages. But instances are not wanting even now of remarkable peculiarities of form and structure which have been propagated for several generations. It is said that certain reigning families of Europe can readily be distinguished by singularities of feature which have marked them for centuries. And it is quite conceivable that in those primitive times, physiological changes might take place much more rapidly than they have done since. It must be granted that there is a striking contrast in those early paintings appealed to by the objectors, between the portraiture of the red Egyptian and that of the jet-black Negro,—yet let this be taken with the fact that on the borders of the Red Sea tribes are to be found constituting a series of links between the two, and therefore pointing to a common origin. And if the negro be regarded as a wide departure from the Caucasian or primitive type of man, it appears to be a law of human nature that deterioration should take place much more rapidly than restoration or improvement. Moreover, it has been ascertained that color is an uncertain mark of origin and descent. The offspring of European and Hindoo parents may be either white or colored; and if the children be white, the grandchildren may be colored, showing that as it respects the transmission of color, there is an apparent want of all law. And although the earth was repeopled by the descendants of one man, there were three fathers of the race, and they or their wives may have possessed some of those marked features which distinguish their descendants —Ham of the African, Japhet of the European, Shem of the Asiatic. Noah is not, therefore, the only starting point of the renovated world, and national characteristics of form and feature may be traced back to the centuries antecedent to the deluge.

But there is an attempt to justify this anti-scriptural theory by an appeal to Scripture itself, which demands a passing notice. In the fourth chapter of Genesis we read, "And Cain went out from the presence of the Lord and dwelt in the land of Nod . . . . . and he builded a city and called the name of the city after his son Enoch." Hence it has been inferred that there must have been men to form this city; whereas now that Abel was dead, Cain and his son, as far as Scripture acquaints us, were the sole descendants of Adam. Upon this flimsy basis, it has been sought to people the land of Nod with descendants of another race distinct from Adam, in the face of the plain and decisive declarations of the Bible that "Eve was the mother of all living," and that "God hath made of one blood all nations of men for to dwell on all the face of the earth." Yet the slightest acquaintance with Scripture should be sufficient to teach us that all the children of Adam are not mentioned by name, any more than of the patriarchs after him. In Genesis v. 4, we are expressly told that Adam "begat sons and daughters;" but no daughters are anywhere named. Between Cain's birth and Abel's death, 127 years elapsed, during which interval several sons and daughters must have been born to our first parents, who in all probability ere its expiration, became the parents of many children also. In the "Dissertations" of the learned Saurin, there is a calculation which makes it out that at the time of the death of Abel (which the writer supposes to have been in the year of the world 128), there might have been 32,768 persons, descended from eight children of Cain and Abel, born before the year 25; and that, adding other subsequent children of Cain and Abel, their children and children's children, there might have been 421,164 men descended from them, without reckoning women and children. Yet without implicitly adopting such calculations, or in the least transcending the limits of probability, it is certain that Cain and Abel may have had a considerable number of children and grandchildren at the time indicated; and allowing for other possible children of Adam and Eve, there must have been at the time a considerable number of persons in the world—quite sufficient to account for Cain's dread of being slain for the murder of Abel; and also for his building a city so soon after his migration from the paternal roof.

An apparently more formidable objection than any of the foregoing to the unity of mankind, is presented by the vast inequality of mental endowment and capacity which is found in the different human races. It would, perhaps, be difficult to place this in a stronger light than has been done by Dr. Prichard. He says: "Let us imagine for a moment, a stranger from another planet to visit our globe, and to contemplate and compare the manners of its inhabitants, and let him first witness some brilliant spectacle in one of the highly civilized nations of Europe,—the coronation of a monarch, the installation of St. Louis on the throne of his ancestors, surrounded by an august assembly of peers and barons, and mitred abbots, anointed by the cruse of sacred oil, brought by an angel to ratify the divine privilege of kings; let the same person be carried into a hamlet of Negro land, in the hour when the sable race recreate themselves with dancing and barbarous music; let him then be transported to the saline plains, over which bold and tawny Mongols roam, differing but little in hue from the yellow soil of their steppes, brightened by the saffron flowers of the tulip and the iris; let him be placed near the solitary den of the Bushman, where the lean and hungry savage crouches in silence like the beast of prey, watching with fixed eyes the creatures which enter his pitfall, or the insects and reptiles which chance brings within his grasp; let the traveller be carried into the midst of an Australian forest, where the squalid companions of kangaroos may be seen crawling in procession, in imitation of quadrupeds; can it be supposed that such a person would conclude the various groups of beings whom he had surveyed to be of one nature, one tribe, or the offspring of the same original stock? It is much more probable that he would arrive at an opposite conclusion."

The contrasts, however, which are apparently so irreconcilable with unity of origin, lie no deeper than the surface. The learned author proceeds to show at length how much more cogent and convincing is the proof, that "the mind is the same in different countries and in different races of men."

The result of his examination is thus expressed: "We contemplate among all the diversified tribes, who are endowed with reason and speech, the same internal feelings, appetencies, aversions; the same inward convictions, the same sentiments of subjection to invisible powers, and, more or less fully developed, of accountableness or responsibility to unseen avengers of wrong and agents of retributive justice, from whose tribunal men can not even by death escape. We find everywhere the same susceptibility, though not always in the same degree of forwardness or ripeness of improvement, of admitting the cultivation of these universal endowments, of opening the eyes of the mind to the same clear and luminous views which Christianity unfolds, of becoming moulded to the institutions of religion, and of civilized life; in a word, the same inward and mental nature is to be recognized in all the races of men." "In the busy cities of Europe, with all their restless competitions; then across the Atlantic, where the haunts of wandering Indians have grown, with a rapidity that startles the mind, into busy towns and far-spreading villages of peaceful industry; amid the sunny isles of the Pacific, where the beauty of the Creator's works has stood in strange contrast with the ferocity of man; in the throbbing heart of populous Africa; in the hold of yonder slaveship, and in the breasts of the unhappy beings which it bears ruthlessly away from liberty and home,—in each and all, is there not the same wondrous constitution,—the same sensitive frame,—the same feeling soul? Savage or civilized, heathen or Christian, the universal lineaments are not to be mistaken; it still is—man!" When we compare this fact with the established identity of specific instincts and physical endowments of all the distinct tribes of mankind, how can we resist the conclusion, that all human races are of one species and of one family?

Another argument for the unity of the human race is to be found in a source of evidence, which was formerly claimed by the sceptic as militating strongly against it—viz., the great diversities of language which prevail among the different nations of the globe. The opponents of revelation have asserted that the variety of languages is so great, and their differences of character so wide, and history is so far from furnishing any example of even one new language, that it is inconceivable that mankind could ever have spoken only one tongue; and they deny that "the fable" (as they term it) of the dispersion on the plains of Shinar is sufficient to explain the endless and wide variations which at present prevail. The problem here presented was far more difficult of solution than any questions pertaining to Ethnology proper or descriptive. At first sight it would seem impossible, out of the apparent chaos, to bring anything to rebut the objection. The subject has, however, received the attention of the most eminent philologists, and the result of their labors has been a new science, Comparative Philology, the principles of which are in every respect accordant with the statements of the Bible. The discoveries made in this direction have, indeed, been among the most remarkable of the present age. It was soon found, to the surprise of those who had entered upon the investigation, that languages grouped themselves into families, and that there were so many affinities and resemblances among all of them, that there was a strong possibility at least of a common origin. Referring to the conclusions of Humboldt, Klaproth, Schlegel, Niebuhr, Balbi, Pott, Adelung and Vater, Dr. Wiseman observes: "It was found that the Teutonic dialects received considerable light from the language of Persia; that Latin had remarkable points of contact with Russian and the other Sclavonic idioms; and that the theory of the Greek verbs in *mi* could not be well understood without recourse to their parallels in Sanscrit or Hindoo Grammar. It was demonstrated that one great speech, essentially so called, pervaded a considerable portion of Europe and Asia, and stretching across in a broad sweep from Ceylon to Iceland, united in a bond of language nations possessing the most dissimilar institutions, and bearing but a slight resemblance in physiognomy and color. This family has received the name of Indo Germanic, or Indo European. Its great members are the Sanscrit and Persian, ancient and modern; Teutonic with its various dialects; Sclavonian, Greek and Latin, accompanied by numerous derivatives; and to these must now be added the Celtic dialects." Further researches have not only confirmed these conclusions, but have disclosed wider coincidences. And the crowning result has been that the learned Klaproth, one of the greatest of modern philologists, says, with a confidence which his vast attainments will excuse and justify, that he flatters himself that "in his works, the universal affinity of languages is placed in so strong a light, that it must be considered as completely demonstrated." "This," he adds, "does not appear explicable on any other hypothesis than that of admitting *fragments of a primary language yet to exist.*" "It is only out of the tombs of dead languages that new languages arise, like new towns, built on the ruins of ancient cities. The bricks with which the modern city of Baghdad is built on the borders of the Tigris, bear all, as Colonel Rawlinson tells us, the cuneiform legend of Nebuchadnezzar, stamped upon them, for they had been taken from the ruins of ancient cities built by this Assyrian monarch. In the same way, if we examine the structure of modern dialects, we shall find that each word bears still the unmistakable stamp of an older language whose decayed fragments have furnished the materials for a new structure."

The result to which the discoveries of Comparative Philology point, is thus forcibly stated by one of its most eminent and successful investigators, Dr. Max Muller: "The evidence of language is irrefragable, and it is the only evidence worth listening to, with regard to ante-historical periods. It would have been next to impossible to discover any traces of relationship between the swarthy nations of India and their conquerors, whether Alexander or Clive, but for the testimony borne by language. What authority would have been strong enough to persuade the Grecian army that their gods and hero ancestors were the same as those of King Porus, or to convince the English soldier that the same dark blood was running in his veins and in those of the dark Bengalee? And yet there is not an English jury nowadays which, after examining the hoary documents of language, would reject the claim of a common descent and a legitimate relationship between Hindu, Greek and Teuton. Many words still live in India and in England that have witnessed the first separation of the northern and southern members of the Arian family; and these are witnesses not to be shaken by any cross-examination. The terms for God, for house, for father, mother, son, daughter, for dog and cow, for heart and tears, for axe and tree—*identical in all the European idioms*—are like the watch-words of soldiers. We challenge the seeming stranger; and whether he answer with the lips of a Greek, a German, or an Indian, we recognize him as one of ourselves. Though the historian may shake his head, though the physiologist may doubt, and the poet scorn the idea, all must yield before the fact furnished by language."

Thus as the "testimony of the rocks" has verified the statements of revelation, so have the "fossil remains" of the different languages of the earth been found to bear witness to the common origin of the nations speaking them. For when it is considered that according to the laws of combination, millions of chances lie against the application of a few similar unexceptionable words in different languages to the same objects, we may be said to possess mathematical evidence of the common origin of all languages, and consequently of the original unity of all mankind. Thus by the investigations of the learned, without in the least intending it, the philological result is in exact accordance with the teachings of Moses, who says, that while the descendants of Noah dwelt in the plains of Shinar and were planning the erection of the tower of Babel, "the whole earth was of one language and of one speech."

The following admirable summary of the arguments which assert the common origin of mankind, is from the able pen of the Rev. Dr. R. J. Breckinridge. In his "discourse on the Black Race," he says: "The unity of the human race must be considered a fundamental and an accepted truth. Every department of knowledge has been searched for evidence, and all respond with a uniform testimony. The physical structure, constitution, and habits of the race—the mode in which it is produced, in which it exists, in which it perishes—everything which touches its mere animal existence, demonstrates the absolute certainty of its unity—so that no other generalization of physiology is more clear and more sure. Rising one step, to the highest manifestation of man's physical organization—his use of language and the power of connected speech—the most profound survey of this most complex and tedious part of knowledge, conducts the inquirer to no conclusion more indubitable than that there is a common origin, a common organization, a common nature, underlying and running through this endless variety of a common power, peculiar to the race and to it alone. Thus a second science—philology—has borne its marvellous testimony. Rising one more step, and passing more completely to a higher region, we find the rational and moral nature of men of every age and kindred, absolutely the same—those great faculties by which man alone—and yet by which every man—perceives that there is in things that distinction which we call true and false, and that other distinction which we call good and evil; upon which distinctions and upon which faculties rests at last the moral and intellectual destiny of the entire race; belonging to us as men, without which we are not men, with which we are the head of the visible creation of God. So has a third science—a science which treats of the whole moral constitution of man, embracing in its wide scope many subordinate sciences—delivered its testimony. If we rise another step, and survey man as he is gathered into families, and tribes and nations, with an endless variety of development, we still behold the broad foundations of a common nature reposing under all—the grand principles of a common being ruling in the midst of all. So a fourth, and the youngest of the sciences—ethnology—brings her tribute. And now, from this lofty summit, survey the whole track of ages. In their length and in their breadth, scrutinize the recorded annals of mankind. There is not one page on which one fact is written—which favors the historical idea of a diversity of nature or origin—while the whole scope of human story involves, assumes and proclaims, as the first and grandest historic truth, the absolute unity of the race. And then mounting from earth to heaven, ask God—the God of truth, and he will tell you, that the foundation truth of all his work of creation and of providence is the sublime certainty that our race was created in his own image, and of one blood; and thereupon, when they had fallen, he offered to them a common salvation, through his only begotten Son, made manifest in their common nature.

"A bond of common brotherhood unites every portion of the race; it is felt the most keenly by those who are most exalted; and even in the most abject its weak pulsations will still live to attest the depth of the truth, that our race is one. It is in the life and doctrine of Jesus Christ that this profound instinct of human nature finds itself exalted into one of the grandest truths of religion, and invested with the sanction of heaven. In Him, the conception of this universal brotherhood,—which nature teaches, and all knowledge fortifies,—becomes a precious, living truth."

CHAPTER V.

SACRED CHRONOLOGY.

ALTHOUGH, compared with the antiquity of the globe itself, the whole period of man's existence upon it is of brief duration, yet to fix the exact epochs of his early history is a matter of great, if not insuperable difficulty. The learned Scaliger complained that no two systems of ancient Chronology could be found to agree, and that he arose from the study more doubtful than ever. And though the profound genius of Sir Isaac Newton was occupied with investigations of this subject during the greater part of the last thirty years of his life, he did not succeed in settling the disputed points in such a manner as to obtain general acquiescence.

The system of Chronology adopted by the English translators of the Sacred Scriptures, and placed in the margin of our Bibles, is derived from the Hebrew text. According to it, the deluge was 1,656 years from the creation, from thence to the birth of Abraham 292 years, to his leaving Haran 134 years more, and the whole period between the flood and the birth of our Lord was 2,348 years. This system is considered as open to grave objections, and it is especially urged against it that it allows of too short a period for so advanced a state of political civilization as appears to have been attained in the days of Abraham. This difficulty is not, however, so great as has been supposed. For "there is nothing surprising in a high civilization, even within a very short time from the deluge; for the arts of life, which flourished in the antediluvian world, would have been preserved by those who survived the catastrophe, and might rapidly revive among their descendants. Rather, it is surprising that, except in Egypt, there should be so few traces of an early civilization."[1] But we are not restricted to the chronology of the Hebrew text. There are valid reasons for preferring the Septuagint chronology, which fixes the date of the deluge at B. C. 3,159, and the birth of Abraham at 1,002 years afterward. It is now, perhaps, the general opinion of Biblical scholars, that the modern Hebrew text has been greatly vitiated in the department of chronology, and more especially in the genealogical tables which respect the antediluvian patriarchs, as well as of the generations after the flood. "The Septuagint version," says Mr. Rawlinson, "was regarded as of primary authority during the first ages of the Christian Church; it is the version commonly quoted in the New Testament; and thus, when it differs from the Hebrew, it is at least entitled to equal attention. The larger chronology of the Septuagint would, therefore, even if it stood alone, have as good a claim as the shorter one of the Hebrew text, to be considered as the chronology of Scripture. It does not, however, stand alone. For the period between the flood and Abraham, the Septuagint has the support of another ancient and independent version—the Samaritan. The identity of the numbers in these two versions, it is difficult to account for but on the supposition that they are the real numbers of the original." And these numbers deprive the sceptical objections which have been raised on this point of all their force. If perfect certainty here were essentially important, doubtless He who has so unceasingly watched over His Word, would have provided ample means

[1] Rawlinson's Essay on the Pentateuch.

for our attaining it. But the Bible was not given to teach all things that man might desire to know with certainty, and as the literary value of the Iliad is not lessened because scholars have always disagreed as to the time when Homer flourished, so neither does it touch the authority of Revelation, because the learned have not as yet been able to construct from it an unchallenged system of chronology.

Still the antiquity of the human race and important epochs of early history must be regarded as approximately fixed by the Bible within certain limits of time, and its authority may be considered as in some degree committed to their correctness. Fifty years ago, this was thought to be a vulnerable point, and even Christian men trembled lest some discovery in the ruins of dead empires, should evoke a past, the length of whose bygone ages would disprove the sacred record. Says an eloquent writer: "The infidel boasted his assurance that every unwound papyrus would furnish refutation. He regretted that the sibyl's books were lost, or they would have been unanswerable. But the Egyptian Hieroglyphics were his favorite resource. Here was a store to be opened up of arguments against our religion, a quiver full of shafts. The Pyramid was to be the monument of Deism; the Mummy from its cerements should start up as its advocate; ancient Zodiacs would glow anew to illustrate it; and a sepulchral blast, scattering the hope of ages, must sweep from the cities of the dead. 'Memphis' should bury it. When the Rosetta stone was found, the free thinkers were thrown into a tumult of delight. They could now extort the secret,—Silence should speak, and Death confess! The heart of the mystery once more beat! The long-imprisoned voice essayed its earliest articulations! The first ray had been touched, after a lingering night; Memnon's statue, and its lyre awoke! Compare the researches of a Belzoni and the readings of a Champollion, and what is their result? The chronology of Moses is there figured. Though the dynasty of the Pharaohs has perished and the line of the Ptolemies is consumed, yet out of these relics there is deciphered a demonstration of an authentic tale and date, to which the scrolls of Herculaneum are but as letters of yesterday, and the cycles of Benares and Ujjayani, the almanacs of a few bygone years. 'The reproach of Christ' lives through all these 'treasures of Egypt.'"[1]

The story of the attacks which were made on the Bible in this quarter, and their entire discomfiture, forms an interesting chapter of Christian Evidences.

Toward the close of the last century, the Astronomical works and tables of the Hindoos furnished materials for assault. These tables professed to record observations conducted through many thousands of years. Attempts were made to verify this remote chronology, and to show that there was internal proof that the observations must have been made at the time specified. One table in particular was adduced, the epoch of which was the commencement of the Cali-yuga or iron age of the Hindoo Mythology, 3,102 years before the Christian era and more than 700 years before the Deluge! A conjunction of the sun, moon, and planets is recorded in the Hindoo books, as having then occurred, and is mentioned in such a manner as to imply that the matter was one of direct observation.

These claims were conceded by several philosophers of note in Europe and in Britain; they were advocated by some of the leading journals, and for a time infidelity seemed to have gained a victory. Its triumph, however, was short. By Bentley, Delambre, Laplace and others, these tables to which the Bramins had assigned so high an antiquity, were subjected to more exact and scientific scrutiny. It was then ascertained that the Hindoos had, ages ago, made respectable attainments in Astronomy, and

[1] Hamilton's Prize Essay on Missions.

that the rules which they followed in their calculations were approximately true, but that they were approximately true only. By observations of the sun, moon, and planets, they had discovered cycles, in which, after a long period of seeming irregularities, the heavenly bodies returned to the same relative positions. This enabled them to predict beforehand the occurrence of eclipses and certain configurations of the planets; and by the same method they could also retrace the past and determine what similar astronomical phenomena had occurred thousands of years ago. They could thus, if disposed, falsify their history, and confirm the falsification by Astronomical evidence, and as long as the laws which govern the sidereal motions, were imperfectly understood, there was no means of detecting the fabrication. But since these have been ascertained, the test of rigid calculation disclosed the fact that the Hindoo cycles having been calculated backward on insufficient data, though nearly exact, were not quite so. They contained an error which made the cycle at every revolution of its period when it was applied to past ages more and more wrong; so that, through the accurate methods of modern Astronomy, it has now been shown that the phenomena of such a conjunction, as is pretended to have been observed, could not have taken place at the date assigned, nor at any period near it. It has also been demonstrated on scientific grounds, upon internal evidence drawn from the Table itself, that higher antiquity cannot be claimed for it than the 12th century of our era. Upon this point it is sufficient to cite the explicit testimony of the eminent astronomer Laplace, who cannot be accused of any special veneration for the Bible. "The origin of Astronomy," he says, "in Persia and India, is lost, as among all other nations, in the darkness of their ancient history. The Indian tables suppose a very advanced state of Astronomy; but there is every reason to believe that they can claim no very high antiquity." He adds, as the result of his own examination, that "they were not grounded on any true observation." It has also been proved that "the Surya Siddhanta," which the Hindoos consider as their most ancient Astronomical treatise, and pretend to have been revealed to their nation more than two millions of years ago, must have been composed within the 750 years last past. It is, indeed, considered by scholars as more than probable that the Astronomy of the Hindoos was wholly derived from the Greeks who were colonized in Bactria by the conquests of Alexander. The coincidence between it and the Greek Astronomy is, at all events, both remarkable and suspicious. Thus, the days of the week are seven in number, and named after the seven planets; while they follow in the same order as they do in the Greek. The ecliptic is divided as among the Greeks into twelve signs, with the same names, emblems, and arrangement; and the signs are also divided into thirty degrees. As these matters are purely arbitrary, they cannot but have had the same source. The confirmation, therefore, which the Astronomical labors of the Hindoos were supposed to lend to the fabulous national antiquity claimed by the Bramins, and the objection to the Chronology of the Bible from that source, are shown to be baseless and void.

Simultaneously with the foregoing objection, a similar difficulty was discovered by French infidel writers in the historical records of China and India. Long lists of kings were produced, with dynasty upon dynasty of reigning families, extending back, it was claimed, for ages beyond the period which the Scriptures assign for the creation of man. The authenticity of these lists being assumed; here, it was thought, an objection had at length been found against the credibility of the Scriptures, which could not be overcome. For a time Infidelity triumphed and the friends of the Bible were alarmed. But the result showed that the triumph was premature and the alarm groundless. Subsequent researches of the learned into the history and literature of China, have clearly shown that such pretensions to incalculable antiquity are as unfounded as they are extravagant. The eminent missionary Gutzlaff, who had probably better opportunities than any other foreigner has possessed for obtaining the truth on the subject, says, in his "Sketch of Chinese History": "Not only is the fabulous part of Chinese History very uncertain, but even the first two dynasties, Hea and Shang, labor under great difficulties, which have never been entirely removed. We must in fact date the authentic history of China from Confucius, 550 years B. C., and consider the duration of the preceding period as uncertain. Chinese ancient astronomy has been celebrated by many; but if we suppose their calculations to have been correct, the ancient Chinese, who lived, according to their historians, four thousand years ago, greatly surpassed their posterity of the present day, who, after so much instruction from foreigners, still betray a childish ignorance on many essential points of this difficult science. Confucius evidently labors to refer the origin of his doctrines (which either originated with himself or were transmitted to him by tradition) to the remotest antiquity, for the purpose of inspiring his countrymen with veneration for them. In order to effect this, he had to create for his nation an authentic history out of the materials furnished by tradition. As there were no regular annals, or any celebrated historiographer who flourished before his era, he was not able, notwithstanding the most laborious researches, to avoid error. The destruction of the greater part of Chinese books by Che-hwang-te, the first universal monarch of China (whose reign commenced 246 years B. C.), who hoped by this means to transmit his name to posterity as the founder of the empire, doubtless contributed likewise to render the chronology more erroneous." It is remarkable that, as in the case of the Hindoos just considered, the record of a similar Astronomical phenomenon has been found among what has been preserved of ancient Chinese annals, which helps us to fix the limits of their antiquity. The Chinese have ever had a custom of inserting in their calendars remarkable eclipses or conjunctions of the planets, together with the name of the emperor in whose reign they were observed. To these events they have also affixed *their own dates.* A singular conjunction of the sun, moon and several planets, is recorded in their annals as having taken place nearly at the very commencement of their history. The celebrated Cassini, to ascertain the fact, calculated back, and decisively proved that such an extraordinary conjunction actually did take place at China on the 26th of February, 2,012 years before Christ. This would take them back to something like three centuries after the Deluge, or 150 years after the confusion of tongues at Babel, in which event the primitive pictorial language of the Chinese has not improbably been supposed to have originated. There is nothing in the independent testimony of their historians irreconcilable with the sacred history, but rather corroborative of its statements. China refuses to contradict the Bible. As it respects the Hindoos it is now fully admitted that they have no history. Among an incalculable number of books of mystical theology and abstruse metaphysics, they do not possess a single volume that is capable of affording any distinct account of the various events of their national career. This remarkable fact is thus accounted for in the learned work of Mr. Hardwick on "The Religions of the Ancient World": "One peculiarity in the mental condition of the Hindus prevented both the ancients and ourselves from gaining any accurate knowledge of their aboriginal condition. Rich as their literature is found to be in other products, it has never given birth to formal histories; and what is even more remarkable, the Hindu scholar is deficient in those very qualities which indicate the presence of historic consciousness. He gazes with a cold, if not contemptuous spirit on the varieties of sense and time; and therefore is disposed to treat all questions of chronology with arrogant indifference. He lives, or rather dreams away his lifetime, in the midst of intellectual problems; laboring hard to measure the immeasurable, to circumscribe the absolute. Compared with such recondite speculations every incident of life is but a mere ripple upon a boundless ocean, as fleeting as phenomenal. What now is, may, for aught he cares, have been a thousand times already, and may frequently come round afresh. The object of his interest is reunion with Divinity, a re-absorption of the finite soul into the primal source of being; and that destiny, according to the various creeds of Hindostan, implies obliviousness in reference to all earthly knowledge, and entire abstraction from all shadows and illusions of the past." In addition to this, we have the high authority of Forbes' Oriental Memoirs for the statement that "The origin of the Hindus, like that of most other nations buried in obscurity and lost in fable, has baffled the researches of the most persevering investigators." The learned Sir William Jones, after the fullest examination, pronounced it as his firm conviction that no established dynasty in the East, can be traced farther back than 2,000 years before the Christian era, the age of Abraham. The Pre-Adamite and Antediluvian dynasties of China and India have vanished, therefore, before the light of investigation, like frost-work in the sunbeam, and the objection is heard no more.

But again the note of triumph was heard in the infidel camp, in token of a fresh assault upon the citadel of Divine truth, the materials for which were found among the mysterious and colossal remains of Egypt. The celebrated scientific expedition which, under the auspices of the first

Napoleon, explored the wonders of that ancient land, met with some monuments, which to them spoke of times long anterior to the records of history, whether sacred or profane. These were the zodiacs of Esneh and Denderah, which were supposed to represent the state of the heavens at the time when the temples in which they were found were erected, and to indicate a very remote antiquity. The presumed discovery was at once made public, as decisive of the question, and as assigning a period to Egyptian civilization far beyond the time of Abraham, or even the deluge. French savans eagerly claimed it as a demonstration that the statements of Moses were erroneous. "M. Jomard proved to his own satisfaction that these zodiacs were three thousand, and M. Dupuis that they were, at the very least, four thousand years older than the Christian era, while M. Gori would not abate a week of seventeen thousand years." The discrepancies in their conclusions proved the unsoundness of their theories, and investigations of learned and scientific men exposed the fallacy of their assumptions. Still the adversaries of Revelation were unwilling to acknowledge defeat, and persisted in ascribing to the zodiacs an antiquity of more than six thousand years. The apprehensions of the Christian world from this source were, however, soon relieved. In August, 1799, a French artillery officer, named Bouchard, belonging to that army under whose protection Denon and his company of savans had made their explorations, when digging near Rosetta in Egypt for the foundation of a military work, came upon a huge block of basalt, marked with various strange characters and hieroglyphics. These characters were found to exhibit three inscriptions, in three different languages, one in Greek, another in hieroglyphic or sacred, and a third in the ancient Coptic, called also enchorial or demotic, like the trilingual inscription affixed by Pilate to the Cross. This was the celebrated Rosetta stone, now in the British Museum, which has been the subject of diligent investigation by learned antiquarians of every nation in Europe; and this stone, under the ingenious labors of Doctor Young in England, and Champollion in France, yielded, by a comparison of the characters found in the different inscriptions, a key to decipher the hieroglyphics that covered the obelisks, temples, and tombs of Egypt. A small obelisk discovered on the Isle of Philoe in the Nile in 1816 by M. Caillaud, containing the names of Ptolemy and Cleopatra in the Enchorial and Greek characters, still farther aided these researches, and at length the veil of mystery which had so long covered the monumental remains of the land of Mizraim, was lifted. That language which had been unknown for ages, and whose meaning it was supposed was forgotten forever, now disclosed the fact that the celebrated zodiacs extended no farther back than the times of the early Roman emperors. On the walls of the great temple at Denderah, in the ceiling of which the zodiac or planisphere had been placed, Champollion read the titles, names and surnames of the emperors Tiberius, Claudius, Nero and Domitian; and on the portico of Esneh, the zodiac of which was reputed to be older than that of Denderah, he read the imperial names of Claudius and Antoninus Pius. Consequently, these monuments for which Volney and other infidel literati had claimed an incalculably remote antiquity, belong to that period when Egypt was under the domination of the Romans, and they cannot be dated earlier than the first or second century of the Christian era. As soon as the Rosetta stone furnished the key to the hieroglyphics, the objections from the zodiacs, and the temples of Egypt, with their fabulous antiquity, lost their power and are heard no more.

But it has been sought on other grounds to establish an antiquity for Egypt irreconcilable with the Chronology of the Bible. The means for this have been supplied by the fragments of the Chronicles of Manetho, an Egyptian priest and historian, who lived 300 years B. C. Though his statements were once considered as almost wholly fabulous, he is now recognized by scholars as a reliable authority as far as it respects his honesty of intention and opportunities for information. His history has been lost, but his dynasties remain tolerably entire. These appear to claim a national existence for Egypt of nearly 30,000 years previous to this time! Twenty-five of these millenniums, however, are ascribed to the time when gods, demi-gods and spirits bore rule on earth; while the actual history of Egypt does not commence until Menes, the first human king, ascended the throne.[1] He is considered as identical with Mizraim, the son of Ham, and Manetho fixes the date of his accession, according to Lepsius, at 3,892 B. C.; while Baron Bunsen, correcting Manetho by the numerical data of a fragment of Eratosthenes, places it at B. C. 3,643. Other authorities, such as Brugsch and Böckh, following different methods of computing the dynasties, assign that era, respectively, to 4,455 B. C. and 5,702 B. C. The lowest of these dates, that of Bunsen, involves a discrepancy with the Scripture chronology, even if we follow the system of the Septuagint. This, however, is disposed of by the statement of Syncellus, a Byzantine monk of the ninth century, who informs us that in a corrected list of the Egyptian dynasties, fifteen hundred years were stricken off by Manetho himself. The remoter dates have been obtained by regarding

[1] Berosus, a Chaldean writer of whom Eusebius has preserved some fragments, has a yet more extravagant Chronology. He undertakes to give the annals of the Medes and the Chaldeans for upward of 400,000 years! But omitting from his scheme what is plainly mythic computation, the eras of gods and demi-gods, we have remaining a period which mounts up no higher than 2,458 years before Christ. If the accuracy of this be assumed, it can readily be reconciled with the Septuagint Chronology.

the dynasties of Manetho as consecutive; but later investigations have proved that several of them were in reality *contemporaneous* lists of petty sovereigns of parts of Egypt. While admitting this, Baron Bunsen, upon a theory of his own founded upon mere fancy, claimed that the historic records of Egypt reached far beyond the accession of Menes, up to the year B. C. 9,085. But, says Mr. Rawlinson, "if it be still thought that the mere opinion of men so well acquainted with the Egyptian monuments, as Bunsen and Lepsius, ought to have weight, despite the weakness of the argumentative grounds on which they rest their conclusions, let it be remembered that others, as deeply read in hieroglyphic lore, and as capable of forming a judgment, have come to conclusions wholly different. Sir Gardner Wilkinson inclines to place the accession of Menes about B. C. 2,690, and Mr. Stuart Poole gives as his first year B. C. 2,717. These writers believe that the number of contemporaneous dynasties has been much underrated by the German *savans*, who have especially erred in regarding the Theban dynasties as, all of them, subsequent to the Memphite. They consider that Manetho's first and third Theban dynasties were contemporary with his third, fourth, and fifth Memphite; that the first and second Shepherd dynasties ruled at the same time in different parts of Lower Egypt; and that the dynasty of Chörtes (Manetho's 14th) was contemporary with the two Shepherd dynasties above mentioned, and with the second Theban. They do not deny that their arrangement of the dynasties is to some extent conjectural; but they maintain that, while the idea of it was derived from a close inspection of Manetho's lists, it is also strikingly confirmed by the monuments. While names of such weight can be quoted on the side of a moderate Egyptian chronology, it can not be reasonably argued that Egyptian records have disproved the Biblical narrative." The remote antiquity of Egypt is, indeed, indisputable; but this is perfectly reconcilable with the statements of the Mosaic narrative, which imply that the Egyptians had attained a high point of arts, government and knowledge, when Abraham, the father of the Hebrew nation, was still leading a nomadic life.

It should also here be noted, that the high reputation of Baron Bunsen as a scholar gave an authority to the long lists of kings and dynasties and the consequent vast antiquity of Egypt, which they would not otherwise have had. But, says an eminent authority,[1] "when we come to examine the researches of Bunsen, we actually find that to this day he has never discovered the true Hieroglyphic alphabet. His whole system is built on a series of conjectures and assumptions, which, moreover, he varies and contorts, without rule or order, at every new sentence."

Another fragment of antiquity called "the Table of Abydos," from its discovery in 1818, by Mr. William Bankes, among the ruins of Abydos, an ancient city of note on the western bank of the Nile, corroborates the above conclusion. Having been deciphered by competent scholars, it was found to yield evidence of only twenty-five sovereigns predecessors of Rameses-Sesostris; and allowing to each of these an average of twenty years, we shall have five hundred years from the first king, probably Menes. Now, if the great monarch, to whose honor this tablet was engraven, died about fifteen hundred years before the Christian era, a short time before the Exodus, we bring the reign of Menes to about three hundred and fifty years after the deluge, a period when the descendants of Mizraim the son of Ham, would have become sufficiently powerful to form a great nation. And so far is this monument from confirm-

[1] Rev. J. L. Porter, the able author of "Five Years in Damascus and Murray's Hand Book for Syria and Palestine."

ing the theories built upon the statements of Manetho, that, so far as it goes, it is a witness against them, and confirmatory of the Chronology derived from sacred history.

But while infidelity has appealed to the zodiacs and hieroglyphics of Egyptian temples for evidence wherewith to overthrow the authority of the Bible, a remarkable verification of the date of its most ancient portion has been deciphered in the starry vault above us.

In the same striking chapter of Job, to which repeated reference has already been made, we find another interrogatory: "Canst thou bind the sweet influences of the Pleiades or loose the bands of Orion? Canst thou bring forth Mazzaroth in his season or canst thou guide Arcturus with his sons?" The rising and setting of certain constellations with the sun, were to the ancients marks for determining the seasons,[1] and it is known that the heliacal rising of the Pleiades was by the Egpytians associated with the spring. Accurate calculations, founded on the usual precession of the equinoxes, have ascertained that the star Taigette, the northernmost of the constellation, was precisely on the colure of the vernal equinox 2,136 years before Christ. This was before the birth of Abraham according to the common Chronology, and in his youth, according to the Chronology of Dr. Hales. And consequently, for several centuries thereafter, in the same latitude, the Pleiades would be esteemed as the cardinal constellation of spring. "Mazzaroth" designated the zodiac, or series of constellations through which the sun passes, bringing on the seasons in their annual order. Arcturus was the pole-star, and his sons the stars that move with him. Job is asked if he could hinder those "sweet influences" to which nature yields when the rising of the Pleiades announces the approach of spring; or whether he could loosen or retard that rigidity which contracts and binds up her fertile bosom, when the approach of winter is made known by the appearance of Orion. There is abundant internal evidence for assigning the book of Job to a very early period in the history of the world, and the patriarch is generally held by scholars to have lived not far from the time of Jacob.[1] As the calculations of Astronomy, carried back to that period, confirm this conclusion, they assist in dispelling the cloud of fabulous antiquity with which infidelity would obscure the credibility and authority of the Bible.

And not only in the heavens above, but in the earth beneath, may evidence be found to overthrow the infidel theories of the vast antiquity of man.

"To any one," wrote Bishop Berkeley, more than a century ago, "who considers that, on digging into the earth, such quantities of shells and, in some places, bones and horns of animals, are found sound and entire, after having lain there in all probability some thousands of years; it should seem probable that guns, medals, and implements in metal or stone might have lasted entire, buried under ground forty or fifty thousand years, if the world had been so old. How comes it then to pass that no remains are found, no antiquities of those numerous ages preceding the Scripture accounts of time; that no fragments of buildings, no public monuments, no intaglios, no cameos, statues, basso-relievos, medals, inscriptions, utensils, or artificial works of any kind are ever discovered, which may bear testimony to the existence of those mighty empires, those successions of monarchs, heroes, and demi-gods for so many thousand years? Let us look forward and suppose ten or twenty thousand years to come, during which time we will suppose that plagues, famine, wars and *earthquakes* shall have made great havoc in the world,—is it not highly probable that, at the end of such a period, pillars, vases, and statues now in being, of granite or porphyry or jasper (stones of such hardness as we know them to have lasted two thousand years above ground, without any considerable alteration), would bear record of these and past ages? Or that some of our current coins might then be dug up, or old walls and the foundations of buildings show themselves, as well as the shells and stones of the *primeval world*, which are preserved down to our own times."

Up to a recent period, this conclusion was supposed to be unimpeachable by Geological evidence. The "testimony of the rocks," as read by its most eminent expositors, was, that if there be any fact well established in Geology, it is that the advent of man upon earth can not be dated further back than about six thousand years. Sir Charles Lyell, after quoting the above passage from Bishop Berkeley with approval, adds to the same effect: "That many signs of the agency of man would have lasted at least as long as 'the shells of the primeval world,' had our race been so ancient, we may feel as fully persuaded as Berkeley; and we may anticipate with confidence that many edifices and implements of human workmanship, and the skeletons of men, and casts of the human form, will continue to exist when a great part of the present mountains, continents, and seas have disappeared. Assuming the future duration of the planet to be indefinitely protracted, we can foresee no limit to the perpetuation of some of the memorials of man."[1] This distinguished author has since withdrawn his support from the Scriptural view, and is now a strenuous advocate for an opposite theory. In a work which he has recently published on the "Geological Evidence for the Antiquity of Man," he maintains that "memorials" have been found, establishing a period of duration for the past existence of our race on the earth, so vast, that even the extravagant chronology of Baron Bunsen would be inadequate to fill it. A considerable amount of details respecting discoveries of "flint im-

[1] Lyell's Princ. of Geol. 8th edit. p. 740. See also pp. 144, 145, 773.

plements" near Amiens and Abbeville, in France, and of human remains in caves near Liege, Dusseldorf, at the foot of the Pyrenees, and in other places, is brought forward in the volume in justification of this hypothesis.[1] It is alleged that proofs have been thus obtained "that remains of mammoths occur in undisturbed alluvium, so imbedded with works of human art, and sometimes with human bones, as to admit of no doubt that man and mammoths co-existed." As the mammalian tribes are supposed to have been extinct ages before the era of Adam, the inference is that the "popular," i. e. the Biblical chronology is altogether deficient and unreliable. But the premises from which it is sought to draw this conclusion are still matters of doubt and dispute among men of science. An able writer in Blackwood's Magazine [No. 540, pp. 422–439], has clearly shown, that before extreme human antiquity can be predicated of the "remains" discovered in the "drift deposit," there are two questions yet to be solved. 1. Are they of the same age as the formation in which they are found? And 2. Is that formation itself of an antiquity very remote? The affirmative of these questions, he claims, is "not proven." And even granting that man was contemporaneous with ancient elephants and mammoths no longer found among the animal tribes of our globe, is it certain and beyond doubt that those gigantic races did not live down to a much later period in the earth's history, than has been hitherto supposed? "All these are problems awaiting solution. Meanwhile, it would be presumptuous and unwarrantable, on the part of any man, to assert the high antiquity of our race upon such

[1] As it respects the recent discoveries of peat deposits and *Kjoeckken modding* (kitchen leavings) in the Scandinavian peninsula, and of lake dwellings in Switzerland, although, unquestionably, memorials of pre-historic races, it is conceded that they furnish no data to militate with the Scripture chronology.

slight and insufficient evidence. All the negative testimony, even of geological science, omitting these alleged exceptions, is in favor of that comparatively modern epoch known as the *annus mundi.* We have no wish to contend for any very strict interpretation of the Scripture chronology; but the addition of a few thousand years would go only a little way to meet the hypothesis of those who contend that these are human relics of vast antiquity, while all profane as well as sacred history utters a silent but consistent protest against an extension so indefinitely great. We have every reason, then, to suspend our final judgment. If divines have their prejudices, so philosophers have their moments of enthusiasm; and it is only just that time should be allowed to arbitrate between them."[1]

On this subject, it is believed, that the great majority of scientific men still accord with the opinion expressed by the eminent Professor Sedgwick in his Discourse on the Studies of the University: "Geology tells us, out of its own records, that man has been but a few days a dweller on the earth; for the traces of himself and of his works are confined to the last monuments of its history. Independently of every written testimony, we therefore believe that man, with all his powers and appetencies, his marvellous structure and his fitness for the world around him, was called into being within a few thousand years of the days in which we live."

Even the heathen poet, Lucretius, though an advocate of the Epicurean hypothesis of the formation of the world by a fortuitous concourse of atoms, could see reasons for believing that the present system of things could not be of unlimited antiquity.

[1] Eclectic Mag. June, 1860.

CHAPTER VI.

PRIMITIVE HISTORICAL TRADITIONS.

THE shadowy uncertainty which the preceding results of Chronological research have shown to rest upon the early history of the most ancient nations, naturally suggests the obligations we owe to the Bible considered simply as a record of the past. Man is a being who looks both before and after, and as the mind awakens to the realities of the scene in which we find ourselves placed, the desire is irresistibly excited to know something of those who have occupied it before us, and by the monuments of whose existence and labors we find ourselves surrounded. "Not to know what happened before we were born," as Cicero has said, "is to remain always children." "Human and mortal though we are, we are, nevertheless, not mere insulated beings, without relation to the past or future. Neither the point of time nor the spot of earth, in which we physically live, bounds our rational and intellectual enjoyments. We live in the past by a knowledge of its history, and in the future by hope and anticipation. By ascending to an association with our ancestors; by contemplating their example, and studying their character; by partaking their sentiments, and imbibing their spirit; by accompanying them in their toils; by sympathizing in their sufferings and rejoicing in their successes and their triumphs,—we mingle our own existence with theirs, and seem to belong to their age. We become their contemporaries, live the lives which they lived, endure what they endured, and partake in the rewards which they enjoyed."[1] We cannot comprehend the part we are called to act ourselves, unless we know the character of those whose places we take. History, therefore, must ever possess an undying fascination for the minds of men, for its subject is the story of their race and the gradual unfolding of that mighty scheme of Providence and Grace, which, beginning with the creation and fall of man, "runs onward through successive generations, binding together the past, the present and the future, and terminating, at last, with the consummation of all things earthly, at the throne of God."

But while this interest is attached to Universal History, it is especially felt with respect to that period with which the poets have linked the legends of the golden age,—the world's childhood and early youth. Those opening scenes of our race have a charm with which none other can vie, and every line, every word, is eagerly welcomed that bears their faintest impress. But were it not for the Holy Scriptures, our knowledge of those scenes would be scant indeed. Take away the books of Moses, and the early history of mankind is almost utterly a blank. But for them, "the patriarchs of the infant world, with kings, the powerful of the earth, the wise and good, fair forms and hoary seers" of those long vanished ages, would have left no trace to tell us that they once had been.

"Vixere fortes ante Agamemnona
Multi; sed omnes illacrimabiles
Urgentur ignotique longâ
Nocte, carent quia vate sacro."
Hor. Car. L. iv. c. 12.

Before great Agamemnon reign'd
Reigned kings as great as he and brave,
Whose huge ambition's now contain'd
In the small compass of a grave:

[1] Daniel Webster.

In endless night they sleep, unwept, unknown:
No bard had they to make all time their own."

FRANCIS' *Translation.*

"The reptiles that crawled upon the half finished surface of our planet have left memorials of their passage enduring and indelible, but the line of march of mighty conquerors and their armies which once desolated the earth, has been utterly obliterated." And so of ancient empires and the primitive seats of power. Barbaric dwellings occupy the shattered sites of their vanquished grandeur, from the scattered symbols of their old renown the meaning has departed, and the tongue of gray tradition has long ceased to utter their once memorable names. Chaldea was the earliest seat of science; but the sun of Babylon has set; the golden city has ceased; and her lofty towers, her hanging gardens, her impregnable walls, are but as the memory of a dream. The populous Nineveh is extinct, and only tells the tale of her ancient glory in the ruins which have recently been uncovered from the dust of ages. The monumental records of Egypt, it is true, carry us back to the morning of the world, and sustain the traditions of her early wisdom and proficiency in the arts; but though the Hieroglyphic key has drawn from them highly valuable and important confirmation of the statements of Holy Writ; yet, as even Baron Bunsen acknowledges, "Egypt has, properly speaking, no history." "In those monuments," says Stanley, and the same is true of recent Assyrian discoveries, "the traveller sees great kings and mighty deeds —the father, the son, and the children,—the sacrifices, the conquests, the coronations. But there is no before and after, no unrolling of a great drama, no beginning, middle and end of a moral progress, or even of a mournful decline." Phœnicia, Tyre, Sidon, and Carthage, were early seats of commerce and of letters, but have left no historian to detail their discoveries or record their fame. The rock-built palaces and temples of Petra, and the splendid and extensive ruins of Persepolis and Palmyra testify the skill of their architects and the magnificence of which they were once the abodes; but the names and deeds of their princes and heroes, unconsecrated by the muse of History, have faded from the knowledge of men. The civilization and refinement of the ancient Etruscans have left no traces save in the painted tombs of their chiefs and nobles. The imperishable writings of Greece and Rome appear at first to present a torch to illumine the midnight of the past, but upon examination we find that there is only light to render "darkness visible." The early annals of Rome, which, though called "the Eternal City," compared with the Hebrew polity was but of yesterday, perished during its capture by Brennus and his Gauls; and Grecian History beyond the Olympiads, which commenced but 776 years before the Christian era, about 23 years before the foundation of Rome, is involved in an impenetrable tissue of cloud and fable.

Thus, says Sir Thomas Browne, "Time sadly overcometh all things, and is now dominant, and sitteth on a sphinx, and looketh upon Memphis and old Thebes, while her sister Oblivion reclineth demi-somnous on a pyramid, gloriously triumphing, making puzzles of Titanian erections, and turning old glories into dreams. *History sinketh beneath her cloud.* The traveller as he paceth amazedly through these deserts, asketh of her, who builded them, but what it is he heareth not."

> "The spider has woven his web in the imperial palace,
> And the owl has sung her watch song on the towers of Afrasiab."

From this silence of Profane History respecting the primitive ages of mankind, infidelity has drawn the objection that the writings of Moses are corroborated by no concurring testimony. To this assertion of Hume, Dr. Campbell, of Aberdeen, has replied, "neither are they invalidated by any contradictory testimony; and for the plain reason that there is no human composition that can be compared with them in point of antiquity." The "Father of history" lived more than a thousand years posterior to Moses, and Thucydides has declared that there were no authentic annals of his nation prior to the Trojan war. But although the Mosaic records are not corroborated by the concurrent testimony of any coeval histories, because if there were any such histories, they are not now extant; they are not, therefore, destitute of all collateral evidence. "In the theogonies of Greece and Rome, in the puranas and vedas of the East, the shasters of ancient Mexico, the mythology of Egypt, and the sagas of the Scalds, are to be found glow-worm glimmerings of truth, flickerings of light among clouds of error" or rather "shadows of realities contained in that Book, whose shadows themselves are true. Chaos the beginning of all things; darkness preceding light; the spirit of deity infused into the mass; the world so fashioned as the bird comes from its egg; man formed out of clay and touched with the Promethean spark of Heaven; the dominion he claims over the brutes; the golden age; the deluge of Ogyges; a race of giants engaged in warfare with the gods and attempting to scale Olympus; the descent of One to bring back his bride from Hades; the recognition of a triple deity, and of the power of sacrifice to free from sin, and of a brighter hope to fallen man, what are these but mythical versions of the facts and disclosures of the Bible?"[1] The learned Faber has shown that "the various systems of Pagan Idolatry in different parts of the world correspond so closely, both in their evident import and in numerous points of arbitrary resemblance, that they cannot have been struck out independently in the several countries where they have been established, but must all have originated

[1] Lecture on Religion and Science, by Rev. H. M. Mason, D. D.

from some common source. But if they all originated from a common source (he argues), "then either one nation must have communicated its peculiar theology to every other people in the way of peaceful and voluntary imitation, or that same nation must have communicated it to every other people through the medium of conquest or violence; or, lastly, all nations must in the infancy of the world have been assembled together in a single region, and in a single community, must, at that period and in that state of society, have agreed to adopt the theology in question, and must thence, as from a common centre, have carried it to all quarters of the globe. These are the only three modes. . . . . As the incredibility of the first, and as the equal incredibility and impossibility of the second, may be shown without much difficulty, the third alone remains to be adopted."[1]

Some of the more important of the "broken echoes and memorial fragments" which have floated down to us from the wreck of bye-gone ages and have been collected by the labors of the learned, will now be given. Examination of them will prove that they are strongly corroborative of the inspired narrative.

Thus, the wide spread tradition of a primeval chaos from which the world arose—the production of all living creatures out of water and earth by the efficiency of a supreme Mind—the formation of man last of all in the image of God, and his being vested with dominion over the inferior animals, so strikingly concurs with the first chapter of Genesis, that Ovid, in whose pages it is recounted, seems to be the paraphrast of Moses. (Metamorphoses, lib. i., v. 5–86.) This tradition can be traced in whole or in part to the ancient Chaldeans, Egyptians, Phœnicians, Hindoos, Chinese, Etruscans, Greeks, and the Indians of America.

[1] Faber's Origin of Pagan Idolatry.

Grotius says that "the nations which most rigidly retained ancient customs, reckoned by nights, darkness having originally preceded light, as Thales taught from the ancients. The remembrance of the completion of the work of creation on the seventh day was preserved by every nation of whom any records or traditions have come down to us. Hesiod, who lived about nine hundred years before the Advent of Christ, says: "The seventh day is holy." Homer, who sang about the same period, and Callimachus, likewise a Greek poet, who flourished about seven hundred years later, allude to the seventh day as holy. Theophilus of Antioch says, concerning the seventh day, "The day which all mankind celebrate." Porphyry says, "The Phœnicians consecrated one day in seven as holy." Lucian remarks, "The seventh day is given to schoolboys as a holiday." Eusebius observes, "Almost all the philosophers and poets acknowledge the seventh day as holy." Clemens Alexandrinus says, "The Greeks as well as the Hebrews, observe the seventh day as holy." Josephus, the Jewish historian, says, "No city of Greeks or barbarians can be found which does not acknowledge a seventh day's rest from labor." Philo testifies, "The seventh day is a festival to every nation." It was found (as ancient authors testify) in the calendars of the Hindus, Egyptians, Arabs and Assyrians. All these vestiges unquestionably point to the institution of the primeval Sabbath in Paradise, which has survived the fall of empires, and has existed among all successive generations, another proof, in addition to those already given, of the common origin of mankind.

From the Egyptians we have a tradition that man's life at the beginning was simple or innocent, and that his body was naked; hence the golden age, in which holiness and happiness prevailed, and the garden of the Hesperides with its golden apples, so beautifully sung by ancient poets. Maimonides has remarked that the history of Adam, of

Eve, of the tree, and of the serpent, existed in his time among the idolatrous Indians; and witnesses likewise of our own age (says Grotius) testify that the same tradition exists among the inhabitants of Peru and of the Philippine islands, who derived their origin from India. In the mythology of Egypt, the serpent bears an important character; represented in an upright form, it entered into all its rites and ceremonies. Among the coins of Augustus there is a remarkable one of a female with a mural crown, a palm branch in her hand, and a dove by her side, while her feet trample upon a serpent. Upon a Tyrian coin there is the figure of a serpent twisted round a tree; and upon a silver medal found in one of the sepulchral monuments of Mexico, a man and woman are represented in a garden with a serpent near them. This is obviously a picture record of the first pair in Eden, the serpent and the fall.

"In the ancient mysteries of Greece, it is well known that the people used to carry about a serpent, and were instructed to cry out *Eva*, whereby the devil seemed to exult over the fall of our first mother. Even now, says Stackhouse, in idolatrous nations, there are evidences of the triumph of the devil under the form of a serpent.

"Plutarch says the great serpent Python signifies destruction, and that serpent Greek mythology represents to have been slain by the son of Zeus or Jupiter. Porphyry and others among the Greeks, speak of "evil demons," whose wish is to be gods, and the power which presides over them aspires to be the greatest of gods; but the Most High, with a mighty arm, restrains their machinations.

"In the Gothic theology, the god Thor, whom they esteem as their middle divinity, or mediator between God and man, is said to have 'bruised the head of the great serpent with his mace, but so severe was to be the contest, that he himself would be suffocated with the flood of venom from the mouth of the serpent.' What can this mean but the seed of the woman bruising the serpent's head, and the serpent biting his heel?

"In India, also, two sculptured figures are yet extant, in one of their oldest pagodas, one of which represents Chrishna, an incarnation of Vishnu, trampling on the crushed head of the serpent, while the other exhibits the poisonous reptile encircling the deity in its folds and biting his heel."[1]

And in the ancient legend of Pandora's box, on the opening of which by the hand of a woman, all evils spread throughout the world, we recognize a significant emblem of the origin of evil; while hope at the bottom, was as significant a symbol of the prophetic promise, that by the seed of the woman, evil would finally be destroyed.

Grotius farther informs us, that "Berosus, in his history of the Chaldeans, Manetho, in that of the Egyptians, Hæstiæus, Hæcateus, Halbanicus, in their histories of Greece, and Hesiod among the poets, have related that the life of those who were descended from the first man extended to nearly a thousand years, which is the less incredible, as the histories of a great many nations, and especially Pausanius and Philostratus among the Greeks, and Pliny among the Romans, relate that the bodies of men in ancient times were much larger, as was found by opening the tombs. Catullus, following many of the Greek writers, relates that divine visions appeared to man before the frequency and enormity of his offences secluded him from converse with Deity and his angels."

In his valuable work on "the Bible and the Classics," already quoted, Bishop Meade says, "The ancient poets and philosophers speak of four successive ages through which the world passes,—the Golden, the Silver, the Brazen, and the Iron,—representing their characters by the

[1] The Bible and the Classics, by Bishop Meade.

comparative value of the pure metals. The last is the worst, and ends in the destruction of the world by the deluge. But in many of the ancient writings there are two series of such ages, set forth by the same four metals, —gold, silver, brass and iron. The facts mentioned show clearly that the second series commenced immediately after the flood, with Noah and his family—as the first did with Adam and his, immediately after the creation. That the first age in each was the purest; that each successive period was marked by gradual deterioration, sacred and profane history attest most clearly. As to the event terminating the first series, there is no doubt. The deluge was sent to purify the earth from the deep corruption which covered it. The human race began anew with the family of Noah, and was for a time comparatively pure in religion and morals.

Sometimes the ancients confound together the two series of ages, those before and those after the flood, as they do indeed (according to their doctrine of a succession of worlds) Creation and the Deluge, Adam and his children with Noah and his. We only state the general result of the researches of such men as Sir William Jones and others, in saying that they abound with references to the comparative character and condition of the different ages. The first, as we have said, was that of paradise itself, when all things abounded spontaneously, when men were called "the supreme and happy inhabitants of the earth." Then came a time when they were called the "moderately happy" inhabitants of the earth; and then a time when the least happy inhabitants of the earth lived. Then came the iron age,—the age of war, and lust and violence and rapine; of heroes and giants, of which Ovid says,

> "De duro est ultima ferro,
> Protinus erupit venæ pejoris in ævum
> Omne nefas: fugere pudor verumque fidesque.

Vivitur ex rapto. Non hospes a hospite tutus,
Non socer a genero. Fratrum quoque gratia rara est.
Victa jacet pietas."

" Stubborn iron, the last:
Then blushless crimes, which all degrees surpast.
All live by spoil: the host his guest betrays,—
Sons, fathers-in-law,—'twixt brethren love decays:
Foiled piety, trod under foot, expires."

The daring wickedness of these giants in sin as well as in stature, has given rise to poems in ancient days called the " Wars of the Titans," in which they are represented as actually assaulting heaven as we assault a stronghold upon earth; but there are circumstances in the war which have led to differences of opinion as to the time and place of the same. Some think it to be the rebellion of the wicked antediluvians, which led to their overthrow by the deluge; others, that it was the rebellion of the builders of Babel, which ended in the confusion of language and their dispersion through the earth. In either case we have the testimony of Pagan poets to two most important events in Mosaic history.

The tradition of a deluge has been found in every nation from one extremity of the globe to the other; it mingles with the legends of countries the most remote; and whose striking diversity of language would seem to have interdicted any interchange of communication. The Hindu and the Mexican, the Greek and the Roman, all attest and acknowledge a penal flood, which has swept their forefathers away and consigned them to destruction.

The Jewish historian Josephus says, that "all the writers of the barbarian histories make mention of the ark and of this flood." He instances Berosus, collector of the Chaldean monuments, Hieronymus, an Egyptian, who wrote the Phœnician antiquities, Mnaseas, and Nicolaus of Damascus. He adds, a great many more make mention of the same event. Berosus, who was contemporary with Alexander the Great, in his history of the Babylonians, relates the following circumstances in regard to a general deluge: "It happened in the reign of King Xisuthrus, who was *the tenth in descent from the first created man.* Saturn advised him of the *approaching* calamity in a dream. He instructed him to build an immense ship, to furnish it with provisions, and to enter it with his family and friends, and a number of quadrupeds and birds. These instructions he obeyed. Then the flood began. The whole world perished. When the waters began to abate, Xisuthrus sent out some of the birds. They could find neither food nor resting place and immediately returned. In a few days he sent them out again. They returned with their feet covered with mud. He sent them out a third time and they returned no more. He concluded, from this, that the earth was reappearing, made an opening in the side of his vessel, and saw that it was approaching a mountain on which it soon rested. He then came forth, adored the earth, erected an altar, and offered sacrifices to the gods. Xisuthrus himself having suddenly disappeared, a voice in the air informed his family that the country in which they were was Armenia, and commanded them to return to Babylon."

The account given by the witty Lucian, a professed scoffer at all religions, who lived in the second century, is, perhaps, still more remarkable. In a treatise entitled "The Syrian Goddess," while speaking of a very ancient temple to her honor at Hierapolis, he remarks, "It is generally believed that this temple was erected by Deucalion, the Deucalion in whose time there was an immense mass of waters." He proceeds to give the history of this Deucalion, as he had heard it in Greece from the Greeks themselves. The present race of men (they said) was not the original race. That race entirely perished, with the exception of Deucalion, from whom the present inhabitants of the earth, numerous as they now are, all descended. That former race were men of a contumelious bearing, who perpetrated the most heinous crimes. They neither listened to the voice of the suppliant, exercised the rites of hospitality, nor regarded the sanctions of an oath. They were, therefore, surprised by an overwhelming calamity. Suddenly, the waters burst forth from the earth, immense rains fell from the skies, the rivers overflowed their banks, the ocean discharged its stores upon the dry land,—there was one universal scene of waters. All men perished. Deucalion alone, preserved for his justice and for his piety, was left to repeople the earth. He placed his children and his wives in a great Ark, which he had, and also entered it himself. Then came to it by pairs, swine, and horses, and lions, and serpents, and other terrestrial animals, and he admitted them within the Ark. There they remained harmless. Through a divine influence a friendship arose between them, and they all sailed together in harmony while the waters remained upon the earth. This, Lucian remarks, is what the Greeks say of Deucalion. But the inhabitants of Hierapolis relate a wonderful event which subsequently happened. In their country, the earth opened and absorbed all the water. Deucalion observing it, erected altars, and built a temple to Juno over the chasm. The chasm, says Lucien, I saw, now small, and whether it ever was greater I know not. In commemoration of this event, not only the priests, but all Syria and Arabia, twice a year, bring water from the sea to this temple. Men go even from the Euphrates to the sea for this purpose. They pour it into the temple. It descends into the chasm, which, though small, receives it in great quantity. This rite, they say, was instituted by Deucalion in memory at once of the deluge and of his preservation. Plato believes that there was a universal deluge, which occurred before the partial inundations celebrated by the Greeks. Plutarch, in a treatise upon the sagacity of animals, has this remark: "The dove sent out of the Ark, it is said, by returning gave Deucalion a sure indication of the continued existence of the storm; by not returning, she assured him of restored serenity." A similar legend to that related by Lucian, no doubt borrowed from the Greeks, is found in the pages of the Roman poet Ovid, who has adorned it with the embellishments of fancy.

Nicolaus of Damascus, to whom Josephus refers, has this passage: "There is a great mountain in Armenia over Minyas, called *Baris*, upon which it is reported that many who fled at the time of the deluge were saved; and that one who was carried in an Ark, came on shore upon the top of it; and that the remains of the timber were a great while preserved. This might be the man about whom Moses the legislator of the Jews wrote."

With the foregoing accounts, it will be interesting to compare the ancient Aztec tradition as given by Humboldt. According to this, "Coxcox, or Tezpi, the American Noah, embarked in a spacious *acalli* or ark, with his wife and children, many animals and grain, the preservation of which was dear to the human race. When the Great Spirit commanded the waters to retire, Tezpi sent forth from his bark a vulture. This bird, nourished by dead flesh, did not return, on account of the great number of carcasses which were scattered upon the newly-dried earth. Tezpi sent out other birds, of which the humming-bird alone returned, bearing in its beak a branch covered with leaves. After which Tezpi seeing that the soil began to be covered with new verdure, left his bark near the mountain of Cothuacan." "Everywhere," adds Humboldt, "the traces of a common origin, the opinions concerning cosmogony, and the primitive traditions of nations, present a striking analogy even in minute circumstances. Does not the humming-bird of Tezpi call to mind the dove of Noah, that of Deucalion, and the

10*

birds, according to Berosus, which Xisuthrus sent forth from the Ark, to try if the waters had subsided, and if as yet he could erect altars to the gods of Chaldea? The raven no less than the dove and the order no less than the name; the first the ravenous beast not returning; the second, forever afterward the bird of peace, re-appearing and re-entering, identify each narrative as that of the selfsame fact with a speciality of circumstances which sober reason cannot misinterpret or mistrust."

From the same high authority, we have also this striking acknowledgment: "These ancient traditions of the human race, which we find dispersed over the surface of the globe, like the fragments of a vast shipwreck, are of the greatest interest in the philosophical study of our species. Like certain families of plants, which, notwithstanding the diversity of climates and the influence of heights, retain the impress of a common type, so the traditions respecting the primitive state of the globe, present among all nations a resemblance that fills us with astonishment: so many different languages, belonging to branches which have no connection with each other, transmit the same facts to us. The substance of the traditions respecting the destroyed races and the renovation of nature, is everywhere almost the same, although each nation gives it a local coloring. In the great continents, as in the smallest islands of the Pacific Ocean, it is always on the highest and nearest mountains, that the remains of the human race were saved; and this event appears so much the more recent, the more uncultivated the nations are."[1]

There is manifestly but one natural and satisfactory explanation of this wonderful harmony in the traditions of all nations in all parts of the earth—nations, the most diverse in language, religion, laws, and manners; and that is, that all of them must have had their origin in one event, whose

[1] Humboldt's Travels and Researches, pp. 190–92.

memory neither the power of time nor the dispersion of the human family over all the continents and islands of the earth, has been able to obliterate, though as the stream advanced from its source, it necessarily became mingled with many absurdities and fictions.

As we proceed, we find other traces and resemblances which point unmistakably to succeeding facts and events in the sacred history. Grotius farther says, that "Japhet, primogenitor of the Europeans, and from him Jon, or as it was formerly pronounced, Javon of the Greeks, also Hammon of the Africans, are names to be found in the writings of Moses, and others are traced by Josephus and other writers in the names of nations and places. Which of the poets does not mention the attempt to climb the heavens?" The following remarkable confirmation of the Scripture narrative of the Tower of Babel and the confusion of tongues is given by Mr. Rawlinson from an old writer, Abydenus, who either drew directly from the Chaldean historian Berosus, or had access to the sources which he used: "At this time the ancient race of men were so puffed up with their strength and tallness of stature that they began to despise and contemn the gods, and labored to erect that very lofty tower which is now called Babylon, intending thereby to scale heaven. But when the building approached the sky, behold the gods called in the aid of the winds, and by their help overturned the tower and cast it to the ground. The name of the ruins is still called Babel, because, until this time, all men had used the same speech, but now there was sent upon them a confusion of many and diverse tongues."

The burning of Sodom is mentioned by Diodorus Siculus, Strabo, Tacitus, Pliny, and Solerinus. Tacitus relates that "a tradition still prevailed in his days of certain powerful cities having been destroyed by thunder and lightning, and of the rich plains in which they were situated having been burnt up. He adds, that evident traces of such a catastrophe remained, while the parched and burnt soil had lost its fertility. This historian concludes with expressing his own belief in that awful judgment, derived from an attentive consideration of the country in which it was said to have happened. In a similar manner, Strabo, after describing the nature of the lake Asphaltis, adds, that the whole of its appearance gives an air of probability to the *prevailing tradition*, that thirteen cities, the chief of which was Sodom, were once destroyed and swallowed up by earthquakes, fire, and an inundation of boiling sulphurous water."

"Herodotus, Diodorus, Strabo, and Philo Biblius bear testimony to the very ancient custom of circumcision, which was practised among the descendants of Abraham; not the Hebrews only, but also the Idumæans, Ishmaelites, and others. The history of Abraham, Isaac, Jacob, and Joseph, in accordance with that of Moses, formerly existed in Philo Biblius, taken from Sanchoniathon, in Berosus, Hecatæus, Damascenus, Artaphanus, Eupolimus, Demetrius, and partly in the very ancient writers of the Orphic songs, and something is still extant in Justin taken from Trogus Pompeius."

References to Moses, the Hebrew lawgiver, are found in various Pagan historians: Diodorus Siculus calls him a man of most superior wisdom and courage. He mentions the departure of Israel from Egypt; of their advance into Palestine, and seizure of a number of cities, particularly Jerusalem. He speaks of their worship, their tribes, their code of laws, by which they were kept separate from every other people; of the priesthood established in one family; of judges, instead of kings, being appointed to decide all their controversies, and the supreme authority being vested in the chief priest; he adds, that Moses concluded the volume of his laws by claiming for them divine inspiration.

Strabo also mentions various particulars respecting Moses. Eupolimus likewise celebrates him as being the first wise man, and the inventor of letters, which the Phœnicians received from the Jews, and the Greeks from the Phœnicians. The Orphic songs also expressly mention that he was drawn out of the water, and the two tables were given him from God.

In the decree issued by the magistrates of Pergamos, forty-four years B. C., the following statement is found: "Our ancestors were friendly to the Jews, even in the days of Abraham, who was the father of all the Hebrews, as we have also found it set down in our public records."

We have also the testimony of Josephus already noticed that in the public records of different nations, and in a great number of books extant in his time, evidences were to be found that the most remarkable events in the history of Israel were admitted generally by the Heathen world, as veritable and indisputable facts.

Not a few of the memorable incidents in the career of the great Hebrew lawgiver are mentioned in the pages of Artapanus, a Greek historian of uncertain, but very ancient date. The oppression of the Israelites; the flight of Moses into Arabia, and his subsequent marriage; a circumstance similar to that of the burning bush; his Divine commission to deliver his countrymen; the transformation of his rod into a serpent; the various plagues of Egypt; the spoiling of the Egyptians; the passage through the Red sea; the destruction of Pharaoh and his host; and the support of the Israelites by manna in the wilderness, are all related in his narrative. Moses is further said to be the person whom the Greeks call Musæus, the preceptor of the celebrated Orpheus. The same author asserts, that the passage of the Israelites through the Red sea was not unknown to the Heliopolitans, who gave the following account of that supernatural transaction: "The king of Egypt, as soon as the Jews had departed from his country, pursued them with an immense army, bearing along with him the consecrated animals. But Moses having by the Divine command struck the waters with his rod, they parted asunder, and afforded a free passage to the Israelites. The Egyptians attempted to follow them, when fire suddenly flashed in their faces, and the sea, returning to its usual channel, brought a universal destruction upon their whole army." The circumstance of the Egyptians being struck with lightning, as well as being overwhelmed by the waves, is mentioned in the 77th Psalm, although not noticed in the Pentateuch.

From Diodorus Siculus we learn that the Ichthyophagi, who lived near the Red sea, had a tradition handed down to them through a long line of ancestors, that the whole bay was once laid bare to the very bottom, the waters retiring to the opposite shores; and that they afterward returned to their accustomed channel with a most tremendous revulsion. Even to this day, the inhabitants of the coast of Corondel preserve the remembrance of a mighty army having been once drowned in the bay which Ptolemy calls Clysma.

In the fragments of Manetho, we meet with a distinct though distorted notice of the departure of the Israelites out of the house of bondage. The Hebrews are represented as leprous and impious Egyptians, who, under the conduct of a priest of Heliopolis, named Moses, rebelled on account of oppression, occupied a town called Avaris, or Abaris, and having called in the aid of the people of Jerusalem, made themselves masters of Egypt, which they held for thirteen years; but who were at last defeated by the Egyptian king, and driven from Egypt into Syria. Upon this passage Mr. Rawlinson remarks: "We have here the oppression, the name Moses, the national name Hebrew, under the disguise of Abaris, and the true direction of the retreat; but we have all the special circumstances of the occasion concealed under a general confession of disaster; and we have a claim of triumph which consoled the wounded vanity of the nation, but which we know to have been unfounded. On the whole, we have perhaps as much as we could reasonably expect the annals of the Egyptians to tell us of transactions so little to their credit; and we have a narrative fairly confirming the principal facts, as well as very curious in many of its particulars."

In the characteristics ascribed to Hermes or Mercury in the Grecian Mythology, we find some remarkable coincidences with the Scripture narrative of the life and character of Moses, which it is difficult to account for except upon the supposition that the heathen legend is an adaptation of the inspired account of the illustrious leader of the Hebrews. The Caduceus of Hermes, with the serpents twining around his rod, is at once suggestive of the appearance of Moses armed with the credentials of his mission. If Moses descended from the Mount with the commands of God, and was emphatically God's messenger, so was Hermes the messenger from Olympus; his chief office was that of messenger. If Moses is known as the slayer of the Egyptian, so is Hermes (and so is he more frequently called in Homer) Argiphontes the slayer of Argus, the overseer of a hundred eyes. Moses conducted through the wilderness to the Jordan, those who died and reached not the promised land; nor did he pass the Jordan. So was Hermes the conductor of the dead, delivering them over to Charon (and here note the resemblance of the name with Aaron, the brother and associate of Moses); nor was he to pass to the Elysian fields. In the hymn of Hermes ascribed to Homer, other coincidences may be found.

The remarkable miracle by which Joshua was enabled to complete the overthrow of the confederate enemies of Israel, is also another event corroborated by tradition, and in such a manner as to shame the cavils of the scorner. It is recorded that Joshua commanded the sun to stand still on Gibeon. The slaughter of the armies of the five kings commenced after he had "gone up all night from Gilgal." He came upon the enemy "suddenly." It was during the pursuit which immediately commenced, that Joshua, in the strength of the God of Israel, uttered the command which must have confounded the worshippers of the sun and moon. The sacred writer declares that "there was no day like that, before it or after it." The fabled fall of Phæton and the history of Hercules both establish the fact, that it was known to the recorders of ancient tradition, that there had been a *night*, like which was no night before it or after it. In the history of Hercules, it is fabled that Jupiter caused a long night—a night equal to three ordinary nights. Now, in consequence of the miracle wrought in Palestine, it is obvious that throughout the greater part of the known world, instead of the return of the *day*, they had continued *night*. At the time the revolution of the globe was suspended, while "the sun stood still in the midst of Heaven," over the land of Canaan, the western world must have remained in darkness. To this then may be traced the fabled destruction of Phæton, when he attempted to direct the chariot of the sun. Conflicting accounts would, however, be received from the more eastern countries, some of which would have had twilight, and part even might have just seen the sun arrested in his rising, or heard that it might be seen during the period of their long night.

"But still more extraordinary testimony to the occurrence of the miracle has been lately brought to light from the records of Hindoo mythology. As in the fables of Western Paganism, we read of an extraordinary *night*, so in the traditions of the eastern hemisphere, we hear of a day of extraordinary length. This fact is incontestably proved by the Skanda Purana, where it is related, that at the end of the Suttya Jug, or golden age, a mountain arose, and for a time impeded the progress of the sun, till by miraculous agency, at the prayer of Agastya, the obstacle was removed, the mountain sunk into its place, and the sun was permitted to pursue his wonted course."

In addition to the above, it has been suggested that the sacrifice of Iphigenia is a mythical version of the story of Jephthah's daughter, and that the Prometheus Bound of Æschylus is a Pagan conception of the promised deliverer whose sufferings would accomplish the reconciliation of divine justice and divine love.

Such are the most important traditionary fragments that have come down to us from profane sources, respecting the early ages of the world. They are at least sufficient to refute the infidel charge that the principal facts related in the books of Moses depend merely upon his solitary testimony. On the contrary they show that the concurrent voice of all nations witnesses in their behalf. From the Nile to the Ganges, and from China to Peru, whatever of ancient record or tradition can be found, supports the truth of the facts recorded in the Bible. And though the enemies of Christianity, with the most perverse ingenuity, have ransacked all the archives of antiquity, their efforts have been in vain. Not the slightest contradictory evidence can be produced. And can this be the work of chance? Can we believe that the combination of the traditions of all heathen nations in support of the truth of Scripture is nothing more than a curious coincidence? Surely, the Epicurean hypothesis, according to which a fortuitous concourse of atoms produced the glorious universe, is hardly more absurd. Testimony from such sources cannot be impeached, and it is impossible to reconcile it with any other conclusion than that the Bible is the Book of God.

But though valuable as auxiliary evidence, these classic and heathen legends are in themselves shadowy and unsubstantial. They do not dispel the darkness of primeval history, and, had we no other source of information, we should know nothing respecting the dawn of the human race. In the Bible we find the realities of these shadows and are brought out of darkness into light. It has no mythical ages of gods and demi-gods, claims no fabulous antiquity for its people, asserts no divine origin for its heroes. As it is free from the absurdities of false physical science, so neither does it contain even an allusion to the fabulous animals and races in which the Greeks and Romans believed. It tells of no nation of Pigmies, or Cimmerians, who live in perpetual darkness; no men "whose heads grew beneath their shoulders!" no griffins or phœnixes or other monsters. It has no tales of water carried in a sieve or of olive trees transplanting themselves, like those which Pliny relates with such trustful credulity. It relates, indeed, many marvels and wonders, but they are all wrought by the hand of the Omnipotent Creator, and are worthy in themselves of the putting forth of his might. It takes us back to what was ere Time began his career, and enables us to behold the Heavens and the Earth arise out of nothing at the word of God. It tells us when and where the original man emerged from the dust under the forming hand of the Creator. It tells us of his glorious original endowments, how he was made upright and in the image of God. It then tells the sad story of his fall, and thus solves that enigma so perplexing to the lofty piercing intellects of Pagan sages, who saw that some terrible disaster, some dire calamity, must have happened to the physical and moral system of the world, but who could not interpret "the groans of nature." The numerous and wide spread traditions of the flood, which left to ourselves we should have guessed in vain, here in the graphic description of the inspired Hebrew historian find their true significance. By the same volume we are assisted in accounting for the multiplicity of languages which now exist in the world, and for that remarkable method of attempting to appease the divine wrath by sacrifice, once so universal, until the light of Christianity made known the only prevailing sacrifice of the Redeemer. Here also is recorded the original dispersion of those primitive races, whose descendants now people the globe, and here we read of the rise and fall of ancient empires which had run their race of glory ere Greece and Rome had won a place in history. And here, above all, are recorded the gradual unfoldings of that wondrous plan of grace, whose consummation "kings and prophets waited for," which reveals hope to those who were ready to perish, and a way to everlasting joys to those who "sat in darkness and the shadow of death."

Thus while the legends of the primitive ages which are found in the Heathen writers are "but a tissue of dream and fable, and may be compared to the scanty shrubs of the desert in a mirage, which will often enlarge themselves into distant groves of palms and cedars, watered by clear lakes, and cheat the eye with their grandeur and beauty; the early history of the Old Testament stands out alone, like a solitary column amidst broken ruins, or one opening of clear sky amid the dense mists of the morning, which everywhere else conceal the origin of nations and primeval antiquity in mysterious darkness."[1]

Truly then does ancient Fuller say: "Without this history the world would be in total darkness, not knowing whence it came or whither it goeth. In the first page of this sacred book a child may learn more in one hour, than all the philosophers of the world in a thousand years."

[1] Christian Observer.

CHAPTER VII.

ANCIENT HISTORY.

As the era of the New Testament falls considerably within the historic period, it becomes a matter of high and grave importance to ascertain whether the facts which it relates bear the undeniable impress of authenticity and truth. As far more abundant materials are at hand, wherewith to sift and verify its statements, than in the case of the Old Testament, the more imperative the necessity to show that it is prepared to sustain the scrutiny. This is a point which modern scepticism has assaulted with all its resources of subtilty and art. It has labored to show that we know nothing of the rise of Christianity "as a matter of certain history—that it was not till a comparatively late period that some floating legends, half romance and half parable, spun in the brain of Asiatic visionaries, assumed at last a definite form, and came to be mistaken for history, when it was too late to look back and test historically whether or no the things reported had really occurred." Evidently, this objection, if it could be maintained, would be a fatal one to the cause of revelation; for it is a peculiar feature of our religion that it is indissolubly bound up with facts, so that it must stand or fall with them. "We may concede," says Mr. Rawlinson in his Bampton Lectures, "the truth of the whole story of Mahomet as it was related by his early followers, and this concession in no sort carries with it even the probable truth of the religion. But it is otherwise with the religion of the Bible. There, whether we look to the Old or the New Testament, the Jewish dispensation or the Christian, we find a scheme of doctrine which is bound up with facts; which depends absolutely upon them; which is null and void without them; and which may be regarded for all practical purposes, established, if they are shown to deserve acceptance." Let the advent and life of Jesus Christ, his miracles, his resurrection from the dead, and the miracles wrought by his apostles after his ascension to Heaven, be disproved as matters of fact, and the whole fabric of Christianity, with all its peculiar doctrines, is a manifest imposture.

A point of no little importance is gained, toward establishing the historic verity of those facts, when it is shown that in the times of the New Testament, with the exception of our Lord's resurrection, they were *uncontradicted.* For let it be noted that in those times detection in case of error or fraud was inevitable. The events of Scripture are detailed with the greatest minuteness as to time, place, and circumstances, connected with numerous public facts, and names of public men. The occasions also on which the miracles were wrought are stated, and the names of the persons who were the subjects of them,—some of them well known characters,—with their places of abode, are often given,—while the general facts respecting Jesus Christ, as claiming to be the Messiah, were of the most public nature, connected with the government, and involving the interests and characters of the whole Jewish nation, especially of the chief men and rulers.

Can it be supposed then that with all the intense malignity and opposition that were enkindled by the Christian religion, those facts would have remained unchallenged, if their truth could have been successfully impugned? That the numerous enemies of the Gospel in the early ages of our faith, refrained from attacking the truth of the facts upon which Christianity rested, is a tacit admission that their notoriety rendered a contradiction hopeless.

But there is also abundance of positive testimony. "As an historical question," says Isaac Taylor, "Christianity is distinguished from others of a like nature by nothing, unless it be the multiplicity and the force of the evidence it presents. The Gospels demand a verdict according to the evidence, in a firmer tone than any other ancient histories that can be put to the bar of common sense. From those who are convinced of its truth, Christianity does, indeed, ask the surrender of assent to whatever it reveals of the mysteries of the unseen world; but to its impugners it speaks only of things obvious and palpable as the objects and occupations of common life; and in relation to matters so simple, it demands what cannot be withheld—the same assent which we yield to the same proof in all other cases."

Dr. Lardner and others have filled numerous volumes with evidence drawn from the writings of the early centuries, Jewish, Profane, and Christian, corroborating the matters of fact recorded in the Gospels. A brief abstract of the more important portions of this evidence is all that can here be given.

The remarkable fact will be first adverted to, of the wide spread anticipation of the coming of some illustrious Personage, which prevailed in the world contemporaneously with the Advent of Christ. Not only were the Jews looking for the fulfilment of the Messianic prophecies, but throughout the Roman empire there was an anxious expectation of some wonderful event, and even the oracles and sybils of heathenism became instinct with prophetic mutterings of a new dawn in human affairs. Whether this expectation is to be attributed to lingering traditions of the original promise made to our fallen progenitor, or to knowledge of the prophecies derived from the dispersed Jews or the Greek version of the Old Testament Scriptures, there is the most unexceptionable historical evidence of its existence. The beautiful lines in the fourth Eclogue of Virgil are well known. He begins the poem with saying, that "the last age of the Cumean prophecy is come; the great order of ages again commences; the virgin is already returning, and the Saturnian reign."

"The last great age, foretold by sacred rhymes,
Renews its finished course; Saturnian times
Roll round again; and mighty years, begun
From their first orb, in radiant circles run.
The base degenerate iron offspring ends;
A golden progeny from heaven descends;
O, chaste Lucina, speed the mother's pains,
And haste the glorious birth!"

According to this eclogue, the son to be born was to be the offspring of the gods, the great seed of Jupiter. He was to command the world, and to introduce peace. He was to abolish violence and injustice, and to restore the life of man to its original innocence and happiness. He was to Kill the Serpent. The blessings of his reign were to extend to the animal and vegetable kingdoms. The latter was to be purged of its noxious poisons, and the nature of the most savage beasts was to be changed, so that the lowing herds should feed secure from lions. Still there were to remain some traces of ancient fraud. Great cities should still be encompassed with walls, and war should be excited; but at length, under this Sovereign, all was to be composed and happy,—when

"No plough shall hurt the glebe, no pruning hook the vine.
The Fates, when they this happy web have spun,
Shall bless the sacred clew, and bid it smoothly run.
Mature in years, to ready honors move,
O, of celestial seed! O foster son of Jove!
See, lab'ring Nature calls thee to sustain
The nodding frame of heaven, and earth, and main:
See to their base restor'd, earth, seas, and air,
And joyful ages from behind, in crowding ranks appear."

This poem proves, not only the expectation which at that time prevailed of the great king who was to arise, but describes the precise features of Messiah's reign, as delineated by the Hebrew prophets, and especially the peculiar characteristics of its effects on the world, which were to be most remarkable, not at the commencement, but after the conclusion of a certain period.

The flatterers of Vespasian professed to find the fulfilment of this general expectation in the accession of that emperor to the throne of the Cæsars. Josephus expressly assigns it as the principal cause of the revolt of the Jews against the Roman government, and of the provocation of that war which terminated in the destruction of Jerusalem.

Tacitus, speaking of the time when Vespasian waged war with the Jews, asserts that "a firm persuasion prevailed among a great many that it was contained in the ancient sacerdotal writings, that about this time it should come to pass that the East should prevail, and that those who should come out of Judea should obtain the empire of the world."

Suetonius, in his life of the Emperor Vespasian, relates that "there had prevailed, all over the East, an ancient and constant opinion, that it was in the fates, that at that time there should come out of Judea those who should obtain the empire of the world."

"It is thus established as an undoubted fact, that at the period of the Advent of the Redeemer, there existed a *general* expectation of the coming of some great and distinguished Personage; that it was *uniform*, that it was *ancient*, that it was founded on what was believed to be the *decree of heaven*, and contained in the sacerdotal writings, that he who should appear was to come *out of Judea*, and that he was to obtain *the empire of the world*. And this gives a striking significancy to the declaration of the prophet, which in 'the fulness of time' was fulfilled at Bethlehem, that 'the Desire of all nations should come.'"

Josephus, the celebrated Jewish historian, was contemporary with the Apostles, having been born in the year 37. His abilities were considerable, and he had the best opportunities for information respecting the early rise of the Christian Religion.

In his Antiquities there is a remarkable passage respecting the character and claims of Jesus, which, however, as it is objected to by the enemies of Christianity as spurious, though upon insufficient grounds, we will not urge it as evidence.[1] His silence elsewhere respecting the Founder of our faith and the Christian religion is accounted for by his being a Jew, and is confirmatory of Christianity. Had he told what he knew he would have condemned himself. The minute description he has given of the other religious sects in Judea, fully proves that this important omission was one of design, to which he was compelled by circumstances.

The account, however, which Josephus has given us in his Antiquities and in his history of the Jewish War, of the state of Judea, civil, political, and moral during his times, is in perfect accordance with the representations which we have in the Gospels. He supplies, moreover, a fact which had been passed over in the Gospel account, probably as belonging to secular history, but which is strikingly corroborative of the sacred narrative. We read in St. Matthew, that on the death of Herod, Joseph "arose and took the young child and his mother, and came into the land of

[1] The passage is as follows: "Now there was about this time Jesus, a wise man, if it be lawful to call him a man; for he was a doer of wonderful works, a teacher of such men as receive the truth with pleasure. He drew over to him both many of the Jews and many of the Gentiles. He was (the) Christ. And when Pilate, at the suggestion of the principal men among us, had condemned him to the cross, those that loved him at the first did not forsake him; for he appeared to be alive again the third day; as the divine prophets had foretold these, and ten thousand other wonderful things concerning him. And the tribe of Christians, so named from him, are not extinct at this day."

Israel. But when he heard that Archelaus did reign in Judea, in the room of his father Herod, he was afraid to go thither." The particular cause of this sudden fear, the evangelist does not mention. But Josephus relates, that the first act of Archelaus was the cruel murder of three thousand Jews at the festival of the Passover—a deed of savage atrocity, the knowledge of which, on the return of the Jews to their respective cities, could not fail of being instantly carried to every part of Judea, and which accounts most naturally for the suspension of the sacred journey.

The testimony of Josephus to the appearance of John the Baptist and his execution by Herod is still more important, while his omission of all reference to his doctrine and his mission as forerunner of the Messiah, is strikingly significant. His words are: "Some of the Jews thought Herod's army was destroyed by God, he being justly punished for the slaughter of John, who was surnamed the Baptist. For Herod had put that good man to death, although he exhorted the Jews, after having exercised virtue and righteousness towards one another, and having performed the duties of piety towards God, to come to baptism. For thus baptism would be acceptable to him, not if they abstained from some sins only, but if, to purity of body, they joined a soul first cleansed by righteousness. But when many gathered round him, for they were much pleased with the hearing of such discourses, Herod, fearing lest the people, who were greatly under the influence of his persuasion, might be carried to some insurrection (for they seemed to do nothing but by his counsel), judged that it might be better to seize him, before any insurrection was made, and to take him off, than, after affairs were disturbed, to repent of his negligence. Thus he, by the jealousy of Herod, being sent bound to Machærus, was there put to death; and the Jews thought that, on account of the punishment of this person, destruction had befallen the army,

God being displeased with Herod." In this passage, while Josephus assigns such a reason for John's death as might be expected from a courtier, there is an entire coincidence as to the historical facts, between his narrative and that of the sacred historian.

Under the Roman government, it was usual for rulers of provinces to send to Rome accounts of remarkable transactions occurring during their administration, which were preserved as official documents among the archives of the empire. Referring to this custom, Eusebius says: "Our Saviour's resurrection being much talked of throughout Palestine, Pilate informed the emperor of it, as likewise of his miracles, which he had heard of, and that, being raised up after he had been put to death, he was already believed by many to be a God." The same fact is further attested by Justin Martyr in his first Apology, which in the year 140 was presented to the Emperor Antoninus Pius and the senate of Rome. Having mentioned the crucifixion of Jesus, and some of the circumstances of it, he adds: "And that these things were so done, you may know from the acts made in the time by Pontius Pilate." Tertullian, in his Apology, about the year 198, having spoken of our Saviour's crucifixion and resurrection, his appearances to his disciples, and his ascension to heaven in the sight of the same disciples, who were ordained by him to preach the Gospel over the world, says: "Of all these things relating to Christ, Pilate, in his conscience a Christian, sent an account to Tiberius, then emperor." In another part of the same Apology he adds: "There was an ancient decree, that no one should be received for a deity unless he was first approved by the senate. Tiberius, in whose time the Christian religion had its rise, having received from Palestine in Syria an account of such things as manifested our Saviour's divinity, proposed to the senate, giving his own vote first in his favor, that he should be placed among the gods. The senate refused, because he had himself declined that honor. Nevertheless, the emperor persisted in his own opinion, and ordered, that if any accused the Christians they should be punished."

The probability that such an official record as is thus referred to, would be made, is certainly very great, and as great is the improbability that in their Apologies, these Christian fathers would have appealed to its testimony, had there been the least doubt as to its existence. It was not made public for the reason that such accounts were intended only for the government. The publication of the acts of the senate was forbidden by Augustus.

Important confirmatory evidence is also derived from the writings of opponents to Christianity.

Celsus, a heathen philosopher, wrote a book against Christianity in the second century, during the reign of Hadrian (A. D. 118 to 138, soon after the death of St John), the title being "The True Word," which was answered by Origen. In this work he introduces a Jew declaiming against Jesus Christ and against such Jews as were converted to Christianity. His attack is conducted *not by denying the facts* contained in the Scriptures, of which he all along *admits* the truth, but by reasoning from such as the following topics: That it was absurd to esteem and worship one as God, who was acknowledged to have been a man, and to have suffered death; that Jesus Christ invited sinners to enter the kingdom of God; that it was inconsistent with his supposed dignity to come and save such low and despicable creatures as Jews and Christians; that he spake dishonorably and impiously of God; and that the doctrines and precepts of religion are better taught by the Greek philosophers than in the Gospels, and without the threatenings of God. He has no less than eighty quotations from the New Testament, and so numerous are his references to the life of Christ, that it has been said an abridgment of the evangelic history could be formed from them; beginning with the star in the East and the massacre of the innocents, and continuing down to the crucifixion and resurrection. It is true, he speaks of these events with resentment and scorn, but he does not venture to dispute the authenticity of the Scripture account of them. His objections only prove that these histories and doctrines existed antecedently to his cavils. The theory by which he would account for that which he cannot deny or disprove, is that Jesus, being "brought up obscurely, and obliged to serve for hire in Egypt, learned there certain powerful arts, for which the Egyptians are renowned; then returned greatly elated with his power, on account of which he declared himself a God."

Tacitus, the celebrated Roman historian, was born in the year 61 or 62. He was prætor of Rome under Domitian in 88, and consul in the short reign of Nerva in 97. In his account of the great fire at Rome in the 10th of Nero, about thirty years after our Lord's ascension, he says—"To suppress, therefore, this common rumor" (viz., that the emperor himself had set fire to the city), "Nero procured others to be accused, and inflicted exquisite punishments upon those people who were abhorred for their crimes and were commonly known by the name of Christians. They had their denomination from Christus, who, in the reign of Tiberius, was put to death as a criminal by the procurator Pontius Pilate. This pernicious superstition, though checked for a while, broke out again, and spread not only over Judea, the source of this evil, but reached the city also, whither flow from all quarters all things vile and shameful, and where they find shelter and encouragement. At first, they only were apprehended who confessed themselves of that sect; afterwards a vast multitude, discovered by them; all of whom were condemned, not so much for the crime of burning the city, as for their enmity to mankind. Their executions were so contrived as to expose them to derision and contempt. Some were covered over with the skins of wild beasts, and torn to pieces by dogs; some were crucified; others, having been daubed over with combustible materials, were set up as lights in the night time, and thus burnt to death. Nero made use of his own gardens as a theatre upon this occasion, and also exhibited the diversions of the circus, sometimes standing in the crowd as a spectator in the habit of a charioteer; at other times driving a chariot himself, till at length these men, though really criminal, and deserving exemplary punishment, began to be commiserated as people who were destroyed, not out of a regard to the public welfare, but only to gratify the cruelty of one man."

Such is the testimony of Tacitus, who lived in the same age with the Apostles, to the principal facts which relate to the origin of the Gospel, as well as to its rapid progress. He here attests that Jesus Christ was put to death as a malefactor, by Pontius Pilate, procurator under Tiberius; that, from Christ, the people called Christians took their name; that this religion had its rise in Judea; that thence it was propagated into other parts of the world, as far as Rome, where Christians were very numerous; and that they were reproached and hated, and underwent many and grievous sufferings.

Suetonius, a Roman historian who flourished in the reign of the Emperor Trajan, A. D. 116, in his history of the life of Claudius, who reigned from the year 41 to 54, says that "the emperor banished the Jews from Rome, who were continually making disturbances, Christus being their leader." The first Christians, being of the Jewish nation, were for a while confounded with the rest of that people, and shared in the hardships that were imposed on them. This account, however, attests what is related in the Acts of the Apostles (xviii, 2), that Claudius had commanded all

Jews to depart from Rome, when Aquila and Priscilla, two Jewish Christians, were compelled to leave that city. In the life of Nero, whose reign began in 54, and ended in 68, Suetonius says: "The Christians were punished; a sort of men of a new and malignant superstition."

On the foregoing passage of Tacitus, and in reference to the persecution of the Christians under Nero, Gibbon remarks: "The most sceptical criticism is obliged to respect the truth of this extraordinary fact, and the integrity of this celebrated passage of Tacitus. The former is confirmed by the diligent and accurate Suetonius, who mentions the punishment which Nero inflicted upon the Christians." Nothing but the force of undeniable truth could have wrung so ample an admission from such an inveterate enemy of Christianity.

The second great persecution of the Christians is recorded to have taken place in the reign of the Emperor Domitian, having begun in the year 81, and terminated in the year 96. During that time an interesting and well authenticated incident is said to have occurred. Domitian made inquiry after the posterity of David, and two men were brought before him of that family. "At that time," says Hegesippus, "there were yet remaining of the kindred of Christ the grandsons of Jude, who was called his brother according to the flesh. These some accused as being of the race of David, and Evocatus brought them before Domitianus Cæsar; for he too was afraid of the coming of the Christ, as well as Herod." Of these men, the historian Gibbon says: "They frankly confessed their royal origin, and their near relation to the Messiah; but they disclaimed any temporal views, and professed that his kingdom which they devoutly expected, was purely of a spiritual and angelic nature. When they were examined concerning their origin and occupation, they showed their hands, hardened with daily labor, and declared that they derived their whole subsistence from the cultivation of a farm near Cocaba, of the extent of about twenty-four English acres, and of the value of three hundred pounds sterling. The grandsons of St. Jude were dismissed with compassion and contempt."

A remarkable historic testimony to the truth of Christianity has been preserved in the correspondence of Trajan and Pliny. Trajan became emperor A. D. 98, and in the year 100 the third great persecution of the Christians commenced. The younger Pliny was appointed proconsul of Bithynia, a province of the Roman empire on the Euxine Sea. In that distant region there were now vast numbers of Christians, against whom the proconsul, according to the emperor's edict, used great severity. Being desirous of more full information how to proceed against them, and "being moved," as Eusebius says, "at the multitude of those who were slain for the faith," he wrote the following letter to Trajan, in the year 107, and in the same year received the emperor's rescript:

"Pliny to the Emperor Trajan, health and happiness. It is my constant custom, Sir, to refer myself to you, in all matters concerning which I have any doubt. For who can better direct me where I hesitate, or instruct me where I I am ignorant? I have never been present at any trials of Christians; so that I know not well what will be the subject-matter of punishment or inquiry, or what strictness ought to be used in either. Nor have I been a little perplexed to determine whether any difference ought to be made upon account of age, or whether the young and tender, and the full-grown and robust, ought to be treated all alike; whether repentance should entitle to pardon, or whether all who have once been Christians ought to be punished, though they are no longer so; whether the name itself, although no crimes be detected, or crimes only belonging to the name, ought to be punished. Concerning all these things I am in doubt. In the mean time, I have taken this course with all who have been brought before me, and have been accused as Christians. I have put the question to them, whether they were Christians? Upon their confessing to me that they were, I repeated the question a second and a third time, threatening also to punish them with death. Such as still persisted I ordered away to be punished; for it was no doubt with me, whatever might be the nature of their opinion, that contumacy and inflexible obstinacy ought to be punished. There were others of the same infatuation, whom, because they are Roman citizens, I have noted down to be sent to the city. In a short time, the crime spreading itself, even whilst under persecution, as is usual in such cases, divers sorts of people came in my way. An information was presented to me, without mentioning the author, containing the names of many persons, who, upon examination, denied that they were Christians, or had ever been so; who repeated after me an invocation of the gods, and with wine and frankincense made supplication to your image, which, for that purpose, I had caused to be brought and set before them, together with the statues of the deities. Moreover, they reviled the name of Christ, none of which things, as is said, they who are really Christians can by any means be compelled to do. These, therefore, I thought proper to discharge. Others were named by an informer, who at first confessed themselves Christians, and afterwards denied it; the rest said they had been Christians, but had left them some three years ago, some longer, and one or more above twenty years. They all worshipped your image, and the statues of the gods; these also reviled Christ. They affirmed that the whole of their fault or error lay in this, that they were wont to meet together on a stated day, before it was light, and sing among themselves alternately a hymn to Christ as God; and bind themselves by an oath not to the commission of any wickedness, but not to

11*

be guilty of theft, or robbery, or adultery, never to falsify their word, nor to deny a pledge committed to them, when called upon to return it. When these things were performed, it was their custom to separate, and then to come together again to a meal, which they ate in common, without any disorder; but this they had forborne since the publication of my edict, by which, according to your commands, I prohibited assemblies. After receiving this account, I judged it the more necessary to examine, and that by torture, two maid-servants, which were called ministers. But I have discovered nothing beside a bad and excessive superstition. Suspending, therefore, all judicial proceedings, I have recourse to you for advice; for it has appeared unto me a matter highly deserving consideration, especially upon account of the great number of persons who are in danger of suffering; for many of all ages, and every rank, of both sexes likewise, are accused, and will be accused. Nor has the contagion of the superstition seized cities only, but the lesser towns also, and the open country. Nevertheless it seems to me that it may be restrained and corrected. It is certain that the temples, which were almost forsaken, begin to be more frequented. And the sacred solemnities, after a long intermission, are revived. Victims likewise are everywhere bought up, whereas for some time there were few purchasers. Whence it is easy to imagine what numbers of men might be reclaimed, if pardon were granted to those who repent."

To this letter of Pliny the following reply was returned by Trajan:

"Trajan to Pliny, health and happiness. You have taken the right method, my Pliny, in your proceedings with those who have been brought before you as Christians; for it is impossible to establish any one rule that shall hold universally. They are not to be sought for. If any are brought before you, and are convicted, they ought to be punished. However, he that denies his being a Christian, and makes it evident in fact; that is, by supplicating our gods; though he be suspected to have been so formerly, let him be pardoned upon repentance. But in no case of crime whatever, may a bill of information be received, without being signed by him who presents it; for that would be a dangerous precedent, and unworthy of my government."

The date of this memorable correspondence was about seventy years after the death of Christ. "We have herein," says Mr. Haldane, "a public and authentic attestation to the amazing growth of the Christian religion, which had made such progress in the remote country of Bithynia, that the pagan temples were, according to Pliny, 'almost forsaken;' he also mentions that there had been Christians in that country twenty years before. Their blameless lives, the purity of their religious worship, their meeting together on a certain day, their adoration of Jesus Christ as God, their obedience to their civil rulers, in giving up what they did not consider to be enjoined by Divine authority, and their fortitude in suffering, and steady perseverance in the faith of Christ, are all unequivocally attested by their persecutors."

The Emperor Hadrian succeeded his kinsman Trajan, A. D. 117. As the edict of Trajan had not been repealed, the Christians still suffered persecution under his reign, although he issued no new edict against them. Upon occasion, however, of the Apologies which Quadratus and Aristides presented to him at Athens, in the year 128, that persecution was moderated. Of Aristides, Jerome says: "He was a most eloquent Athenian philosopher, and in his former habit he presented to the Emperor Hadrian, at the same time with Quadratus, a book containing an account of our sect, that is, an Apology for the Christians which is still extant, a monument with the learned of his ingenuity." This Apology is now lost. To Quadratus was ascribed the gift of prophecy, and he is said to have been "a disciple of the apostles." The following is all that remains of the Apology which he presented to Hadrian: "The works of the Saviour were always conspicuous, for they were real, both they that were healed and they that were raised from the dead; who were seen not only when they were healed or raised, but for a long time afterwards; nor only whilst he dwelt upon this earth, but also after his departure, and for a good while after it, insomuch that some of them have reached to our times."

We will now again call up testimony which history has preserved, contributed by decided enemies of the Christian faith, Porphyry and the Emperor Julian.

Porphyry was a pupil of Longinus, who flourished in the third century. He wrote a book against the Scriptures, which was burnt in the following century, by order of Constantine, and afterwards by that of Theodosius the Younger. He admits the working of miracles by the apostles, but ascribes them, like Celsus, to magical arts. This was the common excuse for rejecting the Gospel, supported as it was by these wonders, which could not be controverted. A work containing such objections deserved only contempt, and hardly needed the edict of the civil power for its suppression. It was already fully met by our Lord's reply to a similar taunt: If Satan sustain the cause which can only prevail by his overthrow, how shall his kingdom stand?

Julian, A. D. 361, mentions Paul by name, and treats of the first chapter of St. John. While he speaks contemptuously of Christ, as having made a few proselytes from among the dregs of the people, and as not having been known for more than three hundred years, he admits the cure of the halt and the blind, and the exorcism of demoniacs at Bethesda and Bethany. His whole book is a bitter invective against the Christians. He admits the holy life of the Christians, and holds up their charity to imitation. Their zeal, their fortitude, their pure notions of religion receive his honorable mention; and while his arguments against the Gospel are perfectly harmless, he has undesignedly borne important testimony to the truth of many of its facts.

How complete the chain of evidence that has been adduced! Not only have we the contemporaneous narratives of friends; but enemies, Jews and Pagans, the Roman emperor and senate and Pilate, the very judge who condemned our Lord, all bear witness that there was such a person as Jesus Christ, that he lived at the time the Gospel relates, that he wrought miracles, that he was crucified, and that he had numerous disciples and followers, of whose affairs many of them make mention. They cannot deny the facts—are forced to admit that miracles were wrought by our Lord, and can only allege against them the absurd cavil that has been noticed—that they were the result of magic arts.

This chain of evidence might be greatly lengthened; but enough has been given to warrant the assertion that Ancient History, as far as it extends, is a witness to the truth of Holy Scripture, and that no discovery in the annals of the past can disturb the solid masonry of fact on which it rests. I will only add a brief notice of two most interesting historical monuments, which have come down to us from the very times of the New Testament.

On what was the Via Sacra in ancient Rome, still stands in proud decay a Triumphal Arch beneath which, it is said, no Jew will pass, though it spans one of the thoroughfares of the city, but turns from it in silent aversion.

Of this majestic ruin, a modern traveller says: "The voice of the sceptic has nothing to say of Him with whom is no variableness nor shadow of turning." But the very *stones* do speak. Who could have thought that Domitian, that cruel persecutor of the Christians, should erect an arch which should confirm for ages the veracity of that God whom they worshipped? But God brings to nought the wisdom of men.

We are told that this arch of triumph was erected by Domitian and the Roman people in honor of Titus for his conquest of Jerusalem. On the interior are two bass-reliefs. On one Titus is represented borne on a triumphal car, which Rome, under the figure of a woman, conducts; whilst victory crowns the conqueror. On the opposite side is represented the triumphal pomp with the Jewish spoils: first the prisoners; then the table of the shewbread with the sacred vessels; the silver trumpets; the candlestick with seven branches; the ark of the covenant, which the Roman soldiers, crowned with the wreath of victory, bear on their shoulders.

"Who that gazes on that relic of Roman grandeur can avoid recalling the sound of that voice which once said: 'Seest thou these great buildings? there shall not be left one stone upon another, that shall not be thrown down?'"

The other historical monument referred to as having come down to us from the very times of the New Testament is that of the Jew of the present day, bearing as he does incontrovertible evidence, in every line of his oriental features, of the authenticity of his descent through uncounted generations. In him we have a living argument of the truth of divine revelation; in him we behold a literal fulfilment of the prophecies; with him may we ascend the stream of time until, by an emanation from that same light which was to his nation "a pillar of cloud by day and a pillar of fire by night," we witness the division of the sea; the angels' food; the rock that followed them; the opening of the earth and the fire from heaven; the parting of the waters of Jordan; the walls of Jericho; the sun standing still in the valley of Ajalon. Their whole career as a people, from Egypt down to the destruction of Jerusalem by Titus and their final dispersion, is full of wonders. Yet, perhaps, there is nothing more marvellous in their history than their present condition, scattered as we find them through almost every habitable portion of the globe. Eighteen centuries have now passed away since they ceased to exist as a state, and when, according to the ordinary laws which determine such events, they ought to have disappeared among the mass of nations. Their oppressors, the Egyptians, Assyrians, Babylonians, Syro-Macedonians and Romans, have all in their turn long ago been razed from the list of principalities and powers. Since the extinction of their polity, the Byzantine empire has succeeded to the Roman and the Mussulman to the Byzantine; Goths and Vandals have expelled the ancient settlers of more than half of the kingdoms of Europe, and have themselves been succeeded by fresh invaders; all have changed again and again their names, laws, dynasties, character, languages, and religion. Yet, during the whole of that immense period, the fallen Jews, without a home or a government, unacknowledged in most parts of Europe, and scarcely tolerated in some, hated and persecuted by all, have still preserved their faith, their institutions, their exclusive habits, and their numbers entire. How shall this extraordinary vitality be explained, except as the fulfilment of the promise of God that He would "not make a full end of His people"—that He "would not destroy them utterly," and that even in their lowest estate, He would not "break His covenant with them?" Truly might the great Condé have said, in reply to certain infidel arguments, that "it was perfectly vain to assail the credibility of the Christian revelation, so long as so singular a miracle as that of the existing Jewish people could be alleged in its support."

CHAPTER VIII.

OBJECTIONS AND REPLIES.

The opponents of Revelation have endeavored to invalidate the authority and impugn the credibility of the sacred writers, by the charge of discrepancy and contradiction in their statements. As truth is one and must always be consistent with itself, if this charge could be substantiated, it would at once annul the claim of inspiration for the Bible. When we apply this test to the Koran of Mahomet, we find that its pages contain more than one hundred and fifty palpable contradictions, admitted even by learned Mussulmen, who account for them by saying that in all these instances the Almighty changed his mind! But of the numerous alleged contradictions that have been brought against the Bible, it may safely be affirmed that there is not one of them that is not capable of a rational solution. Through the mistakes of transcribers, errors no doubt at times crept into manuscripts of the sacred writings, before the invention of printing, and such may also be found in printed copies; but the contradictions objected, are only apparent, not real. The slightest examination will show that the greater portion of these are frivolous, while the difficulties of the remainder will vanish upon a more profound acquaintance with the facts. "It is by no means uncommon" (says Professor Lee), "to find in the accounts of two perfectly honest historians referring to the same events from different points of view, certain peculiarities in the structure of their compositions, which, when noticed, at once reconcile the seeming variance which such peculiarities may have occasioned; or some fact may have been omitted which lends an air of opposition to their statements—an opposition which the mention of the omitted fact by a third writer instantly clears up." The following solution of a difficulty in ordinary history, together with the application of the principle on which it rests, to a parallel case in the Evangelical record, will amply confirm what has just been stated.

Aristobulus, the friend of Alexander the Great, and who watched by his death bed, relates that he died on the 30th of the Macedonian month Dæsius. On the other hand, Eumenes and Diodotus, who kept the journal of Alexander, and who recount the progress of his malady, place his death on the evening of the 28th of the same month. Here is an obvious variance in statement, and yet no critic has for a moment considered that there is any real contradiction, although the solutions which have been given are very different. Thus, it is shown by some, how the variance will disappear if we call to mind the manner of counting the days of the month by the Greeks; while the explanation of another writer is founded upon the difference in the point of time from which the beginning of the day was reckoned—whether from sunrise as at Babylon, or from sunset according to Grecian usage. Other explanations are also supplied, and any one among them is considered to remove every appearance of contradiction. The history of the Gospel harmony supplies an example exactly parallel. The case is one of peculiar interest, and from a very early period it has presented a difficulty to Christian apologists. I allude to the statements of St. Mark and St. John as to the hour of Christ's passion—"a question," says St. Augustine, "which, above all others, is wont to stir up the shamelessness of the contentious, and to disturb the unskilfulness of the weak." St. Augustine himself proposed two methods whereby the accounts might be reconciled; and, while admitting the difficulties with which his suggestions were encumbered, he lays down the principle for which I now contend. Referring to a supposed objection to one of his solutions, he asks: "If we both alike believe the Evangelists, do you point out how their accounts can be otherwise reconciled, and I will acquiesce most cheerfully; for I love not my own opinion, but the truth of the Gospel. Until some other explanation is discovered, this of mine shall suffice; and when that other is demonstrated, I too will adopt it." It has been reserved for modern times to suggest a solution which has been almost universally accepted, and which removes every shade of difficulty from the case: St. Mark asserts that our Lord was crucified at "the third hour," or at nine o'clock in the forenoon; while, according to St. John, Pilate "about the sixth hour" was still sitting in judgment. The explanation of this apparent discordance in time—an explanation which even Strauss, while exaggerating "the difficulty" to the utmost, allows to be "possible"—is, that St. John has given the hour according to the Roman calculation of time, which counted, as we do, from midnight; while St. Mark adheres to the Jewish custom of counting from sunrise.

And thus it will be found that, in all the apparent discrepancies of Scripture, the difficulty arises from our not having the *clue* which unites the different statements. As soon as that is obtained, their harmony is established.

Another sceptical objection is founded upon the alleged collision between the statements of Scripture and those of Profane History. It is not to be denied that such instances are to be found, but what can be more unfair than to take it for granted that the sacred narrative must be necessarily false? Did a tribunal of appeal exist, in the shape of authentic, reliable records of those times, it might then be satisfactorily shown, in such cases of contradiction, on which side lay the error. Without such a tribunal, when probabilities are weighed, and the characters of the writers are considered, the truth of the Biblical statements cannot be successfully impugned.

The following are instances of what at first appeared to be historical discrepancies, but in which subsequent discovery has vindicated the minute accuracy of the sacred writers.

It is related in the Second Book of Kings (xx. 12), and in the historical chapters of Isaiah (xxxix. 1), that Merodach Baladan, king of Babylon, sent letters and a present to Hezekiah, because he heard that he had been sick. As previous to the publication of the Chronicle of Eusebius in the early part of this century, there was no other known record of such a monarch, it was objected that he was a mythical personage, and moreover that Babylon at that time was merely a dependent province of the Assyrian empire. A fragment of Berosus, however, preserved in that chronicle, supplies the desired information and removes all the difficulty. We learn from it that Merodach Baladan was an usurper, who reigned independently at Babylon for six months, and was then overthrown by Sennacherib. From another passage of the same Berosus, it has been sought to disprove the historical narrative of Belshazzar in Daniel. Berosus makes the last Babylonian monarch absent from the city at the time of its captivity by the Persians, and also speaks of him as taken prisoner afterwards at Bersippa, and as then not slain, but treated with much kindness by Cyrus. The two narratives of the fall of Babylon were thus in appearance wholly irreconcilable; and some were driven to suppose two falls of Babylon, to escape the seeming contrariety. But out of all this confusion and uncertainty, a small and simple but most important discovery, which was made by Sir Henry Rawlinson, from documents obtained at *Mughur*, the ancient Ur of the Chaldees, has delivered us. From these he learned that Nabonadius, the last of the kings of Babylon, associated with himself on the throne during the later years of his reign his son Bel-shar-uzar, and allowed him the royal title. That this was the prince who conducted the defence of Babylon, and who was slain in the massacre that followed upon its capture, cannot be doubted; while his father, who was at the time in Borsippa, surrendered and experienced the clemency which was generally shown to fallen kings by the Persians. Nor is this all. The discovery of Belshazzar's position as joint-ruler of the empire, throws light upon another passage in the narrative which had been the cause of some perplexity, and thus imparts additional confirmation to its historical credibility. We are therein told that Belshazzar promised to the successful interpreter of the handwriting on the wall, that he should be promoted to be the third ruler in the kingdom. Why his position should not be the same as it seems to have been under Nebuchadnezzar, or as that of Joseph was in Egypt, or of Mordecai in Persia, it would have been impossible to tell until the above discovery. But as there were two joint sovereigns reigning at the time, it is now seen that the reward proffered by Belshazzar was the highest position tenable by a subject.

In the work I have already quoted, Professor Lee gives a remarkable instance of the minute accuracy of St. Luke, which he prefaces "by a parallel example illustrative of the apparent contradictions so constantly to be met with in ordinary history. The medals struck for the coronation of Louis XIV give a different day from that which all contemporary historians agree in fixing for the date of that event. Of all these writers, one only has noticed a circumstance which accounts for this discrepancy, for he alone mentions that the coronation had been appointed to take place on the day given by the medals, which were accordingly prepared,—but that circumstances caused a delay till the date assigned by the historians. Nothing can be more simple than this; and yet, in a thousand years, had no such explanation been given, antiquarians would have been sadly perplexed in their efforts to reconcile the contradiction. Let us now turn to the parallel case in the Acts of the Apostles. St. Luke in the thirteenth chapter, gives the title of Proconsul to the Governor of Cyprus. In the division, however, of the Roman Empire by Augustus, this island had been reserved for his own jurisdiction, and, consequently, its governor must have borne the rank of procurator; —that of proconsul being appropriated to those who ruled the provinces which the emperor had ceded to the senate. The title here assigned by St. Luke to Sergius Paulus had for a long time perplexed commentators, who knew not how to reconcile the statement of the sacred historian with the assumed facts of the case. Some coins, however, were found bearing the effigy of the Emperor Claudius; and in the centre of the reverse there appears the word ΚΥΠΡΙΩΝ, while the surrounding legend gives the title in question of proconsul to an individual who must have been the immediate successor or predecessor of Sergius Paulus. In addition to this evidence, a passage has been pointed out in the writings of Dion Cassius, who mentions that Augustus, subsequently to his original settlement, had changed Cyprus and Gallia Narbonensis into senatorial provinces; the historian adding, as if with the design of establishing St. Luke's accuracy, "And so it came to pass that proconsuls began to be sent to these nations also." Had the writings of Dio Cassius perished amid the wreck of ancient literature, and the coins alluded to never been found, we should unquestionably have seen this hypothetical blunder of the inspired historian foremost among the array of cases adduced by such writers as Strauss. Is not the Christian apologist, therefore, fully justified in deprecating the precipitancy of criticism? Has he not ample grounds for maintaining that difficulties, such as those we have considered, arise from our ignorance of the whole of the case; and that we have good reason to expect that they will eventually disappear as similar evidence accumulates.

Equally untenable is the sceptical objection which has been drawn from the *silence* of Profane History as to some of the facts of the New Testament. Of the leading and more important of those facts, it is not true; for as we have seen, they are abundantly corroborated in the pages of Tacitus, Suetonius, and others. For the omission of some others, such as the massacre of the innocents and the supernatural darkness at the crucifixion, a sufficient reply is furnished in the following extract from the recently published diary of Varnhagen von Ense:

"Humboldt confirms the opinion I have more than once expressed, that too much must not be inferred from the silence of authors. He adduces three important and perfectly undeniable facts, as to which one finds no evidence in places where one would naturally, above all others, expect to find it. In the records of Barcelona there is not a trace of the triumphal entry made by Columbus; in Marco Polo, no mention of the great wall of China; and in the archives of Portugal, nothing about the voyage of Amerigo Vespucci in the service of that crown."—History of the Geography of the New World, part iv, p. 160, *et seq.*

To this it may be added that Pliny makes no mention whatever of the destruction of Herculaneum and Pompeii—large and populous cities. Even Tacitus merely glances at the event in these words: "Haustæ aut obrutæ urbes"—*cities were consumed or burned.* Suetonius is silent as to the cities, though the eruption is incidentally mentioned. Martial has a slight allusion to them; and Dion Cassius, about one hundred and fifty years after Pliny, adverts to the *traditional* account of them. "A multitude of things," says Montfaucon, "are daily found out, which have been hitherto unobserved and not mentioned; such as the temple of Mithras, in the Viminal vale, of which not one word is met with in authors."

The weakness and fallacy of the above objections having been demonstrated, let us proceed to examine two arguments in behalf of the historic verity and divine authority of the Holy Scriptures, drawn from their internal evidence, which cannot fail to carry irresistible conviction to the mind of the earnest and sincere inquirer after truth.

The first of these is the wonderful *unity and harmony of design* which is found in the Bible, from the beginning of Genesis to the close of the Apocalypse.

The absurdity of supposing that this could be the effect of fraud is thus strongly urged by Mr. Haldane. He says: "Let any set of men combine to write such a book as the Bible. Let their plan be laid so as to extend through a period of fifteen hundred years. Let those who shall first enter upon the work obtain others to succeed them during that space of time. Let them write history, poetry, theology, and prophecies concerning the state of the world. Let them at length procure some one to come forward in whom all that they have written shall find its accomplishment. Let him be born in the place they had foretold, of the family they had singled out, at the exact period they had predicted. Let him be exhibited in the most critical situations, in the midst of enlightened, powerful, and determined adversaries, while they still uphold him as perfect, and defy his enemies to prove the contrary. Let his own death be a part of their plan, which he himself shall foretell. Let a number of persons arise immediately afterwards to carry forward the design, charge the government under which he suffered as his murderers, affirm that he is alive, and has given them convincing evidence that he will reward them in a future world. Let these men support their doctrines by an appeal to miracles openly performed before enemies armed with civil power; and let them adhere to their testimony at the expense of life, and all things dear in this world. Let them promulgate a new religion and code of laws, completely subversive of every existing religion on earth, and directly opposed to the indulgence of the strongest propensities of the human heart. Let this religion, by the force of its own evidence, win its way through the world, overthrow every opposing system, extend its triumphs, and finally establish itself in the most civilized nations, in spite of the most learned, the most determined, and the most powerful adversaries; and let the character of the leader, as set forward by his associates, be thus vindicated as 'the light of the nations.' Who does not see the total impracticability, the absolute absurdity of such an attempt? As soon might men of understanding be induced to climb up to the stars, as to propose to themselves such a scheme."[1]

Yet all this is the true and wondrous story of that Book which Christians claim to be from God.

The Bible contains sixty-six books, to the composition of which thirty different persons have contributed. These books were written amidst the strangest diversity of time, place, and condition,—among the sandy deserts of Arabia, the fields and hills of Palestine, in the courts of the Jewish Temple, in the palace of Shushan, in the dungeons of Rome, and one of them in a lonely island of the Ægean Sea. They were written in a variety of forms,—in history, biography, and parable; proverbs, poems, and letters. They were written by persons occupying various conditions in life—princes and peasants, warriors and fishermen, learned men and unlearned. And from the time that Moses took his pen to write the story of the creation, to the record by

[1] Haldane's Evidences of Christianity, vol. ii, p. 486.

St. John of the visions which he saw in Patmos, a period of fifteen hundred years had intervened.

Under such circumstances, collusion and preconcert were utterly impossible. Yet so far from one contradicting what another inculcates, there is on the contrary the most perfect harmony. Every book both in the Old and New Testaments is a link in the same golden chain. They are one uniform whole, though beginning at the creation and extending to the consummation of all things. "As in Beethoven's matchless music there runs one idea, worked out through all the changes of measure and of key; now almost hidden, now breaking out in rich natural melody, whispered in the treble, murmured in the bass, dimly suggested in the prelude, but growing clearer and clearer as the work proceeds, winding gradually back till it ends in the key in which it began, and closes in triumphant harmony; so throughout the whole Bible there runs one great idea: man's ruin by sin and his redemption by grace; in a word, Jesus Christ the Saviour. This runs through the Old Testament, that prelude to the New; dimly promised at the fall, and more clearly to Abraham; typified in the ceremonies of the law; all the events of sacred history paving the way for his coming; his descent proved in the genealogies of Ruth and Chronicles; spoken of as Shiloh by Jacob, as the Star by Balaam, as the Prophet by Moses; the David of the Psalms; the Redeemer looked for by Job; the Beloved of the Song of Songs. We find him in the sublime strains of the lofty Isaiah, in the writings of the tender Jeremiah, in the mysteries of the contemplative Ezekiel, in the visions of the beloved Daniel, the great idea growing clearer and clearer as the time drew on. Then the full harmony broke out in the song of the angels: 'Glory to God in the highest, and on earth peace, good will towards men.' And evangelists and apostles taking up the theme, the strain closes in the same key in which it began—the devil, who troubled the first paradise, forever excluded from the second; man restored to the favor of God, and Jesus Christ the key-note of the whole."

"The silver sounding instruments did meet
With the base murmur of the water's fall;
The water's fall with difference discreet,
Now soft, now loud, unto the wind did call;
The gentle warbling wind low answered to all."—SPENSER.

Does not this wondrous unison make it evident that the Bible must have had its origin in the infinite Mind of that God who sees the end from the beginning, and who is without variableness or shadow of turning—from eternity to eternity the same? Truly might the poet ask:

"Whence but from Heaven could men unskill'd in arts,
In several ages born, in several parts,
Weave such agreeing truths? or how, or why,
Should all conspire to cheat us with a lie?
Unask'd their pains, ungrateful their advice,
Starving their gain, and martyrdom their price."—DRYDEN.

Another argument of hardly less weight has been drawn from what have been called the "undesigned coincidences" of the Bible. These, it has been said, "involve a test of truth which is acknowledged almost instinctively, by the human mind, and which every day's experience serves to strengthen and to impress; a test which advocates are always glad to seize upon and to urge whenever they have it in their power, and judges and juries are not less ready to acknowledge; and no one who observes the state of his own mind, or that of others, in the reception of evidence, can shut his eyes to the fact, how much more strongly coincidences, which come out accidentally, and are free from all suspicion of collusion, prevail in the establishment of a fact, than the most exact agreement in points, which would naturally have presented themselves beforehand, as prominent features of the story, and necessary to be shaped and fitted by those who were fabricating a falsehood."

A few of these coincidences gleaned from the numerous collections made by Paley and Blunt, will be sufficient to show that the Bible is its own witness.

Thus, in his account of the crucifixion, St. Matthew tells us that "the soldiers smote Jesus with the palms of their hands, saying, Prophesy unto us, thou Christ, Who is he that smote thee?" And in this challenge there seems nothing very difficult. There is apparently neither force nor meaning in the insult, if Christ had the offender before his eyes. But when we learn from St. Luke (xxii. 64), that "the men that held Jesus *blindfolded* him" before they asked him to prophesy who it was that smote him, we discover what St. Matthew intended to communicate, namely, that they proposed this test of his divine mission, whether, without the use of sight, he could tell who it was that struck him.

All the evangelists agree in telling that when the high priest's officers came out to arrest Jesus, Peter drew a sword, and smote off a servant's ear. And yet both St. Matthew and St. Mark agree in relating, that when Christ's persecutors sought all sorts of evidences against Him, so as to make out a case before the Roman Governor, they could procure none. But is it not very strange, that when the high priest had in his own palace such a striking proof of the violent character and dangerous designs of these Galileans, he should not have called as a witness his own wounded servant? Had we possessed no information beyond the narratives of St. Matthew and St. Mark, this would have been a flagrant difficulty. You say that "the whole effort of the priests was to prejudice Pilate against Jesus, as a seditious and turbulent character; but they could substantiate nothing." Why was not this recent and conclusive witness forthcoming? Especially, when Jesus said to Pilate, "My kingdom is not of this world; if my kingdom were of this world, *then would my servants fight*, that I should not be delivered to the Jews,"—why did none of his accusers reply, "Yes, but your servants did fight, and one of them has inflicted a wound on the sacred person of the high priest's servant"? Now had we possessed no Gospels except these two, we could not have accounted for so strange an oversight on the part of the priestly faction. But St. Luke mentions a circumstance which sufficiently explains it. From his account we find that as soon as Peter smote off the ear *Jesus healed it again;* and by doing this he effectually disqualified the wounded servant from appearing as a witness against him. The priests were in this dilemma. If next morning they produced the servant as a proof of the violence of Christ and his followers, how could Pilate credit them? That wound was never inflicted overnight, or it could not be healed so soon. Or if, to explain this latter circumstance, they acknowledged that Christ had instantaneously healed it, they would at once have trod on dangerous ground, and would have given Pilate another reason for suspecting—what he was already very apt to surmise—the supernatural character of his prisoner.

In St. Matthew (viii. 16) we read, that "when the even was come, they brought unto him many that were possessed with devils, and he cast out the spirits with his word, and healed all that were sick." But why was it *evening* when they brought to Jesus these demoniacs and sick persons? From St. Mark (i. 21–32), we find that it was the Sabbath-day; and from St. Luke (xiii. 14), we find that the Jews thought it sinful for "men to come and be healed on the Sabbath-day." But we also know that the Jewish Sabbath ceased at sunset; so that when the evening was come the people would feel no scruple in bringing their afflicted friends to Jesus to be healed. But observe how far we have to travel before we can complete Matthew's simple statement. He merely mentions that it was in the evening Jesus wrought these cures; and had we possessed Matthew's narrative alone, we might have laid no particular stress upon the time of day. But we go on to Mark, and we find that it was the Sabbath evening, "when the sun was set." And we go on to Luke, and find, though in a totally different connection, that these Jews would have thought it very wicked to carry the sick or to accept a cure on the Sabbath.

Again, the Evangelist St. John tells us (vi. 5), that on one occasion, when surrounded by a weary multitude, Jesus said: "Whence shall we buy bread that these may eat?" And in putting this question he addressed himself to Philip. But John hints no reason why he should have put this inquiry to Philip rather than to any other apostle. Luke, however, mentions (ix. 10) that the place was a desert near to Bethsaida; and John himself happens to have mentioned, in the opening of his Gospel (i. 44), that Bethsaida was the city of Philip. And laying these three insulated passages together, we see how natural it was to put the question, "Where is bread to be bought?" to one acquainted with the neighborhood. Had we not possessed St. John's Gospel, we should never have known that such a question was asked; and had we not possessed St. Luke's Gospel, we should never have seen the special propriety of asking it of Philip.

Of these latent harmonies of Holy Scripture, Dr. James Hamilton has unanswerably said: "It is just because the particulars are so minute that the coincidence is so valuable. They are just such trifles as a true historian is apt to omit, and just such trifles that a fabricator would never think of applying. These delicate agreements of one evangelist with another show that their story is an extract from the Book of Truth,—a leaf from the volume of actual occurrences,—a derivation from a counterpart original. And though all coeval literature had perished,—though all the external confirmations were destroyed,—though all the monuments of antiquity were annihilated, strong in its intrinsic truthfulness, the New Testament would still hold its lofty place—a tower of self-sustaining integrity. And though the efforts of enmity were to succeed as they have signally failed,—though learned hostility were to undermine its documentary foundations, and blow up that evidence of manuscripts and early versions on which it securely reposes, so finely do its facts fit into one another, so strongly are its several portions clamped together, and in the penetration and interfusion through all its parts of its ultimate inspiring Authorship, into such a homogeneous structure has it consolidated, that it would come down again on its own basis, shifted, but nowise shattered. Such a book God has made the Bible, that, whatever theories wax popular, or whatever systems explode, "the Scripture cannot be broken."

CHAPTER IX.

SACRED GEOGRAPHY—TOPOGRAPHICAL ACCURACY OF THE INSPIRED WRITERS.

"Those holy fields
Over whose acres walk'd those blessed feet,
Which *eighteen* hundred years ago were nail'd
For our advantage, on the bitter cross."—*First Part K. Henry IV.*

"The pathways of Thy land are little changed
Since thou wert there;
The busy world through other ways has ranged
And left these bare.

"The rocky path still climbs the glowing steep
Of Olivet;
Though rains of two millenniums wear it deep,
Men tread it yet.

"And as when gazing, Thou didst weep o'er them,
From height to height,
The white roofs of discrown'd Jerusalem
Burst on our sight.

"The waves have washed fresh sands upon the shore
Of Galilee;
But chisell'd in the hillsides evermore
Thy paths we see.

"Man has not changed them in that slumb'ring land,
Nor time effaced;
Where Thy feet trod to bless, we still may stand;
All can be traced."—*The Three Wakings.*

Much has been written by philosophic historians respecting the correspondency which is alleged to exist between the scenery, the features, and boundaries of countries and the national characteristics of the peoples who inhabit them. And in the case of nations such as the Greeks and Romans, who have played a great part on the world's stage, it is maintained that a prophetic forecast of their destiny can be read in the hills, the plains, the rivers and the seas, which cradled and fostered their birth and infancy. This is especially true of the local features of that land, which was the divinely appointed home of the chosen people and the cradle of a faith designed to be universal. "No one can study the geography of Palestine without perceiving that this narrow strip of territory was designed by Providence for some important purpose in the history of man. At the head of the Mediterranean, the gateway of Asia for the nations of the west, and the natural outlet of the great caravan commerce of Western Asia with the sea, lying in the highway of all ancient trade and conquest, the very pivot about which the intercourse of nations and continents revolves, it is yet isolated by natural causes from all adjacent countries which might swallow up its individuality. The great mountain barrier upon the north, the sea upon the west, the deep crevasse of the Ghor and the Dead Sea upon the east, and the desert also to the east, and on the south, these physical characteristics of the country, stamp it in perpetuity as a land apart from all lands—fitted at once to be the theatre of great events, and to keep their unchanging record upon its unchanging features. Those features are photographed upon every page of the Bible, and the original remains to certify the fidelity of the copy. Indeed, there seems even to be the same relation of the Land and the Book which exists between the two revealed economies. In order to the complete revelation of God in the incarnation and atonement of Christ, it was necessary that a particular people, separated for this end, should be made familiar with theophanies, with prophetic inspiration, with miraculous endowments, sacrificial offerings, and a representative, priestly intercession, and should thus form a sacred language as the groundwork of the revelation of God in Christ.—The comparative isolation of the Jews in their territory, and their complete isolation by that economy and polity which were given to them by Jehovah before their entrance into the promised land, prepared the typical moulds in which the great thoughts of Divine love and mercy should be fully conveyed to an unbelieving world. And since, as compared with that disclosure of God which is made to those who see him face to face, the Bible is but the Pictorial Primer of our faith, there was need also that its symbols and illustrations should be run into some physical mould prepared to contain so much of spiritual truth as we, in this period of childhood, might be able to receive. What were the Bible to man without its Eden and Jerusalem; its tree of life forfeited in the one, restored with perennial fruitfulness in the other? What were the incarnation, had not the human life of Christ been circumscribed within familiar and unchanging scenes;—Nazareth and Bethany, Gennesaret, and its romantic shores, Jerusalem and its Temple? What were the impression of the atonement itself, had it been enacted in some spirit world, without the visible agony of the garden, and the Cross lifted up on Calvary? And so in the land of Palestine, as would hardly be possible in any other land, there existed in its physical features and its every-day life, materials for a pictorial alphabet of spiritual truths;—the rock, the tower, the fountain, the stream, the mountain, the forest, the desert, the cave, the gulf, the sea, the shepherd, the watchman, the husbandman, the vinedresser, the robber, and the beast of prey, whatever could furnish a similitude for a religious truth or duty, compressed into a little territory, and there made permanent by the finger and the providence of God. The land where the incarnate Word dwelt with men, is, and must even be, an integral part of the Divine

Revelation. Her testimony is essential to the chain of evidences, her aid invaluable to exposition. The very hills and mountains, rocks, rivers, and fountains are symbols and pledges of things far better than themselves. In a word, Palestine is one vast tablet whereupon God's messages to men have been drawn and graven deep in living characters, by the great Publisher of glad tidings, to be seen and read of all to the end of time."[1]

The value of this testimony to the truth of the Bible will be perceived, when it is considered that romancers always place the scene of their fictions in a distant region or a departed time; the sacred writers recount events happening in their own country and during the period of their own lives. Impostors avoid details, and keep to general statements, taking care to introduce no names, places or distances, which might serve to betray the fraud and publish the imposition. But the Bible, in almost every chapter, stands committed on all these points, and its narratives are accompanied with all the minute circumstances of time, place, situation, habit, etc., conveying an impression of reality beyond the reach of fiction. Thus in the Old Testament we read that it was "between Bethel and Hai," whence the valley of the Jordan can be seen, that Abraham parted with Lot, and it was from the heights near Hebron that the patriarch beheld the smoke denoting the overthrow of the cities of the plain. In the New Testament, it was as our Lord was "coming down" from Cana to Capernaum, that news arrives of the healing of the nobleman's son; it was on the road from Jericho to Jerusalem, and on the eve of a memorable Passover, that Bartimeus, the blind beggar, the son of Timeus, is restored to sight; and it was at Bethany, a village two miles from the capital, that a few days afterwards Lazarus is recalled from the tomb.

[1] The substance of the above introductory paragraph is from Dr. Thomson's "Land and the Book."

These are a few of innumerable examples that might be cited, showing the fearlessness with which the sacred writers commit themselves to statements, always avoided in Apocryphal works, and which could be so readily disproved if untrue. Yet in no one known instance has geographical incorrectness or even indistinctness been detected. Each new traveller is adding fresh confirmation of its precision and accuracy. "It is impossible not to be struck," says Canon Stanley, "by the constant agreement between the recorded history and the natural geography both of the Old and New Testament. To find a marked correspondence between the scenes of the Sinaitic mountains and the events of the Israelite wanderings is not much, perhaps, but it is certainly something towards the truth of the whole narrative. To meet in the Gospels allusions, transient but yet precise, to the localities of Palestine, inevitably suggests the conclusion of their early origin, while Palestine was still familiar and accessible, while the events themselves were still recent in the minds of the writers. The detailed harmony between the life of Joshua and the various scenes of his battles, is a slight but a true indication that we are dealing not with shadows, but with realities of flesh and blood. Such coincidences are not usually found in fables, least of all in fables of Eastern origin."

During the last half century this interesting department of testimony to the Bible has been sedulously cultivated, and the observations of intelligent Eastern travellers have furnished numerous and striking confirmations of its truths and narratives. "The truth is," says a learned writer,[1] "the Providence of God, which is never more worthily employed than about his Word, seems now to be directing the eyes of his servants, as with a pointed finger, to the immense stores of elucidation constantly accumulating from this quarter. Animated either by the noble spirit of missionary

[1] Professor Bush.

enterprise, of commercial speculation, of military adventure, or laudable curiosity, men of intelligence and observation have made their way into every region on which the light of revelation originally shone; exploring its antiquities, mingling with its inhabitants, detailing its manners and customs, and displaying its physical, moral and political features. From these expeditions they have returned laden with the rich results of their industry; and the labors of the pen and pencil have made thousands partakers of the benefit."

A selection of some of the more important of these "results" gleaned from various authentic and reliable sources, will occupy the remainder of the present chapter.

MANNERS AND CUSTOMS.

The testimony of the Land to the Book may be read in the existing frame-work of manners and usages. It has been beautifully ordered, in Divine Providence, that while the nations of the West are notorious for perpetual fashion and change, those of the East are, to a great extent, immutable in their customs, and social habits, and arrangements. The Bedouin tents are still the faithful reproduction of the outward life of the patriarchs. During the heat of the day, the Sheik of the tribe, with his flowing robes and reverend beard, will still be found, as Abraham in the plains of Mamre, sitting by the tent door, ready to receive the stranger, to bring him a little water that his feet may be washed, to break bread for him, and to bid him tarry for the night. The wandering Arab of the desert may often be seen laying himself down after sunset on his bed of sand, like Jacob in the wilderness of Padan-aram, with a stone only for his pillow. At the well are still also to be seen the troughs for the camels, the stone on the well's mouth, and the camels kneeling with their burdens and waiting patiently till their troughs are full. The close veil, the forehead ornaments, the earrings, the anklets, the burden carried on the head, the children carried on the shoulder, still mark the Eastern woman as in the days of Isaiah. Companies of Ishmaelites still come from Gilead, with their camels and dromedaries, bearing spicery and balm and myrrh, as in the days of Reuben and Judah. The description of Elijah and of the Baptist, finds a parallel in the startling appearances, familiar to all travellers in those lands, of the strange wild figures, who, as Santons or Dervishes, still haunt the solitary places of the East, their only clothing being a cloak of camel's hair thrown over the shoulders and a girdle of skin tied round the waist. All this may still be seen among the pastoral tribes of the unchanging Orient:

> "Where the lone desert rears its craggy stone,
> Where suns unblest their angry lustre fling;
> And way-worn pilgrims seek the scanty spring."
>
> BISHOP HEBER'S *Palestine.*

The vineyards, the corn fields, the houses, the wells of Syria, moreover, still retain the outward imagery of the teaching of Christ and his apostles; while the dress of the people, the customs of society, the idioms of thought, the salutations of courtesy, are living records of even yet remoter times. The unmuzzled ox still treads out the corn as in the most distant ages of the past; shepherds watch their flocks by night, while the sheep know their voice and follow them: women are seen grinding at the mill, and still come with their pitchers and talk with them who sit by the well. The beds of the people are a simple mat or carpet, and even a child may take them up and walk; their bottles are of leather; the grass is cast into the oven; the tombs are inhabited; there are lodges in the garden of cucumbers; grass grows on the houses; and the inhabitants walk, sleep, and meditate on the roofs of their dwellings. At night the gay marriage procession, with torches and music, may often be seen on their way to the wedding festival. The mourners also go about the streets and make lamentations for the dead. "At every step," says Morier, "some object, some idiom, some dress, or some custom of common life, reminds the traveller of ancient times; and confirms above all, the beauty, the accuracy, the propriety of the history of the Bible."

THE FACE OF NATURE.

The natural phenomena and features of the country also remain the same. The hills still stand round about Jerusalem, as in the days of David and Solomon. The dew falls on Hermon; the cedars grow on Libanus; and Kishon, "that ancient river," draws its streams from Tabor as in the times of old. The sea of Tiberias still lies imbedded bright and blue, amid the hills of Galilee; the fig tree springs up by the wayside; the sycamore spreads its branches; and the vines and olives still climb the sides of the mountains. The wells of Elim with their overshadowing palm trees still refresh the weary traveller of the desert, and the waters of Marah are as bitter now as they were before the miracle of healing. Flocks of quails from some unknown region still alight in the desert, and from the top of Carmel, the cloud "no bigger than a man's hand," is still at times descried emerging from the horizon, as seen by the prophet, and always heralds the coming rain. Abana and Pharpar still water and fertilize the plain of Damascus as in the days of Naaman, and the swellings of Jordan are not less regular than when the Hebrews first approached its banks. The brook still wanders through the valley of Elah, where the Philistines were once encamped, and which supplied the smooth pebbles for the sling of David. Bashan is still renowned for its oaks, and Sharon for its roses. The willow still weeps by the Euphrates as when the captives of Judah hung upon it their harps; the pelican and the bittern are still found in desert places. Mount Tabor still overlooks the fertile plain of Esdraelon, where the tribe of Issachar rejoiced in their tents, and where Barak fought and discomfited Sisera and his hosts. Ebal and Gerizim still guard the vale of Shechem. Pisgah still overlooks the land of promise, and Sinai frowns in awful majesty amid its desert solitude. "Among all the stupendous works of nature," says Mr. Stephens, "not a place can be selected more fitted for the exhibition of Almighty power."

"Extraordinary appearances," says Chateaubriand, in describing Palestine, "every where proclaim a land teeming with miracles; the burning sun, the towering eagle, the barren fig tree; all the poetry, all the pictures of Scripture are here. Every name commemorates a mystery, every grotto proclaims the future, every hill re-echoes the accents of a prophet. God himself has spoken in these regions; dried up rivers, riven rocks, half open sepulchres attest the prodigy. The desert still appears mute with terror, and you would imagine that it had never presumed to interrupt the silence, since it heard the awful voice of the Eternal."

The present rocky and barren appearance of the greater part of Palestine, at first sight strikes the observer as contradictory to the inspired description of it as "a land flowing with milk and honey,—the glory of all lands." Upon examination, however, this apparent difficulty vanishes, or rather yields additional testimony to the truth of the Bible.

"It would be wrong," remarks a modern traveller, "to argue the former capabilities of the Holy Land from its present appearance, as it is now under the curse of God, and its general barrenness is in full accordance with prophetic denunciation. The Israelite in our street, whose appearance was delineated with graphic precision by Moses in the fifteenth century before Christ, is not a surer evidence of the inspiration of the holy volume, than the land as it now exists, cursed as it is in all its products, its heaven shut up, and comparatively without rain. The prophecies concerning Canaan are numerous, and have been so literally fulfilled that they may now be used as actual history."—HARDY'S *Notices of the Holy Land*, p. 283.

Great, however, as is the change which has been wrought in the appearance of Palestine, there are not wanting indications of what it was before divine judgments made it desolate, and of what it may again become when those judgments shall be removed. "Even in those parts where all is now desolate," remarks Dr. Robinson, "there are everywhere traces of the hand of men of other days. . . . Most of the hills, indeed, exhibit the remains of terraces built up around them, the undoubted signs of former cultivation." Again, when travelling towards Hebron, he observes: "Many of the former terraces along the hill sides are still in use; and the land looks somewhat, as it may have done in ancient times." "There are elements in the land of Palestine," writes Lieut. Van de Velde, "for the production of the richest abundance of useful plants. The ground is untilled by mortal hands, and yet what a profusion of charms does nature offer!" (He is speaking of the plain of Sharon.) "The same elements are to be found existing in the soil elsewhere; but there the land is inhabited—inhabited by a race of men whose track is followed by barbarism and desolation. It is thus, in a certain sense, a blessing for the country to be uninhabited. It will have been remarked, perhaps, that the want of water, more than any other cause, makes the land lie dry and dead. No doubt, scarcity of water is the immediate cause; but in the days of Israel's prosperity water was to be had every where by means of wells and water courses, and the greater cultivation of trees at once increased the rain and diminished the evaporation from the ground. Such, however, is the natural disposition of the present inhabitants of Palestine, that with all this-want of water, they allow the wells and fountains that existed from of old to be ruined and stopt up, and leave the water courses of former days broken down and neglected. And all this that God's word may be fulfilled, and God's curse upon the land accomplished: "Then shall the land enjoy her sabbaths, as long as it lieth desolate . . . because it did not rest in your sabbaths, when ye dwelt upon it."—*Syria and Palestine*, vol. i. p. 344.

"In ages past all glorious was the land,
And lovely were thy borders, Palestine!
The heavens were wont to shed their influence bland
On all those mountains and those vales of thine;
For o'er thy coasts resplendent then did shine
The light of God's approving countenance,
With rapturous glow of blessedness divine,
And 'neath the radiance of that mighty glance,
Basked the wide-scattered isles o'er ocean's blue expanse.

"But there survives a tinge of glory yet,
O'er all thy pastures and thy heights of green,
Which, though the lustre of thy day hath set,
Tells of the joy and splendor which hath been:
So some proud ruin, 'mid the desert seen,
By traveller, halting on his path awhile,
Declares how once beneath the light serene
Of brief posterity's unclouded smile,
Uprose in grandeur there some vast imperial pile."

Lays of Palestine.

Desolate as for the most part it now appears, the sacred soil awaits but the appointed hour (so we may gather from every narrative) to sustain its millions as of old; to flow again with milk and honey; to become once more "a land of brooks of waters, of fountains and depths that spring out of valleys and hills; a land of wheat and barley, and vines, and fig-trees, and pomegranates, and of oil olive;" and to resume its ancient and rightful titles, "the garden of the Lord," and "the glory of all lands."

When from the general features of the country, we descend to the minutest topographical details, we find the same marvellous accuracy. In order that the strength of this argument may be more fully estimated, I propose to select the more prominent and interesting localities of sacred history, and show from the testimony of the most learned and accomplished travellers, that so exact is the agreement, that the Bible may be said to be written on the scenes which it describes.

THE LAND OF GOSHEN.

"In the best of the land . . . in the land of Goshen let (the Israelites) dwell . . . And Joseph placed his father and his brethren . . . in the land of Rameses, as Pharoah had commanded."—GEN. xlvii. 6, 11.

"The land of Goshen lay on the east of the Delta, and was the part of Egypt nearest Palestine; this tract is now comprehended in the modern province Esh-Shurkîyeh. That the land of Goshen lay upon the waters of the Nile, is apparent from the circumstance that the Israelites practised irrigation; that it was a land of seed, figs, vines, and pomegranates; that the people ate of fish freely; while the enumeration of the articles for which they longed in the desert, corresponds remarkably with the list given by Mr. Lane as the food of the modern fellahs. 'We remember the fish we did eat in Egypt freely, the cucumbers, and the melons, and the leeks, and the onions, and the garlic.' All this goes to show that the Iraelites, when in Egypt, lived much as the Egyptians do now, and that the land of Goshen probably extended further west, and more into the Delta than has usually been supposed. They would seem to have lived interspersed among the Egyptians of that district, perhaps in separate villages. . . . This appears from the circumstance of their borrowing 'jewels of gold and silver' from their Egyptian neighbors; and also from the fact, that their houses were to be marked with blood, in order that they might be distinguished and spared in the last dread plague of the Egyptians. The immediate descendants of Jacob were doubtless shepherds, like their forefathers, dwelling in tents; and probably drove their flocks for pasture far up in the valley of the desert, like the present inhabitants of the same region. Even now there is a colony of Arabs, about fifty families, living (in those parts), who cultivate the soil, and yet dwell in tents. They came thither from Mount Sinai, and acquired such a taste for the good things of Egypt, that, like the Israelites, they could not live in the desert. The land of Goshen was 'the best of the land;' and such too the province Esh-Shurkîyeh has ever been, down to the present time (being now famous for its fertility). There are here more flocks and herds than anywhere else in Egypt; and also more fishermen."—ROBINSON'S *Researches*, vol. i, pp. 76–79.

ON—HELIOPOLIS.

"(Pharoah gave Joseph to wife) Asenath, the daughter of Poti-pherah, priest of On."—GEN. xli. 45.

"The ride from Cairo to Heliopolis, the On of Scripture, is delightful; the first part is across the skirt of the desert. . . . Farther on, the road lies through green fields and shady avenues of acacia trees, and the whole air is redolent of the delicious perfumes of bean blossoms, and alive with the hum of wild bees. The 'land of Goshen' is opening upon you, and its actual aspect bears out the ancient renown for pastoral fertility, which caused it to be conceded by Pharoah as an abode to Jacob and his sons, when Joseph persuaded them to leave their own country, and to bring their flocks and herds with them, that they might dwell near him in the land of Egypt. I cannot describe the deep and reverential interest with which one treads the ground rendered sacred by its associations with Bible history; and while the imagination of the traveller is carried back to the days of the patriarchs, and fancy peoples the land with the venerable forms of Joseph's kindred; no pert innovation of modern times, in the shape of recent civilization, is visible, to dispel the momentary illusion. The swarthy Arab, with turbaned head and naked limbs, laboriously irrigates his fields by means of the primitive *shadoof;* the patient ox, unmuzzled, treads out the corn; and long strings of camels and asses bear home loads of green provender, exactly in the same manner as in the days of the pastor patriarchs.

"No vestige of the ancient On remains, except an obelisk sixty-five feet high, of a far less beautiful description than those of Luxor and Karnae, the sole remaining one (with the exception of Cleopatra's Needle), now to be seen in Lower Egypt. The cartouches upon its four sides show it to have been erected by Osirtasen, the Pharaoh of Joseph; and as some indications formerly existed of an avenue of sphinxes leading from it, and part of a sphinx was lately found there, most probably this solitary obelisk formed one of the pair which stood before the entrance of the celebrated Temple of the Sun, at Heliopolis. . . . I in vain looked around me for some other trace of the famous city where Joseph dwelt, and where Moses became 'learned in the wisdom of the Egyptians.' All is now on a level blank, and the words of prophecy have been illustrated to the letter in On, as in Noph and No,—the pomp of Egypt is destroyed, and she is destitute of that of which she was full."—MRS. ROMER'S *Temples and Tombs of Egypt.*

ZOAN OR TANIS.

"Marvellous things did he in the sight of their fathers in the land of Egypt, in the field of Zoan."—PSALM lxxviii. 12.

"We landed at the village of San, anciently called Tanis, and in Scripture Zoan, one of the most ancient cities in the world. The fine alluvial plain around was no doubt 'the field of Zoan,' where God did marvellous things in the days of Moses. We pitched our tents upon the bank, to shelter ourselves from the rays of an almost vertical sun, while the wild Arabs came round, some to gaze upon the strangers, and some to offer old coins and small images for sale. In the cool of the day we wandered forth, and Mr. Bonar, passing over some heaps of rubbish a few minutes' walk from the village, started a fox from its lair. Following after it, he found himself among low hills of alluvial matter, full of fragments of pottery, while beyond these lay several heaps of large stones, which on a nearer inspection he found to be broken obelisks, and ruins of what may have been ancient temples, the relics of a glory that is departed; but darkness came on, and obliged him to return to the tent. It was a very lovely moonlight night, and very pleasant it was to unite in prayer and in singing psalms amid the wild Arabs, in the very region where God had wrought so many wonders, long ago. We read over Isaiah xix., 'The burden of Egypt,' in our tent, and when we looked out on the paltry mud village of San, with its wretched inhabitants, we saw God's word fulfilled before our eyes. 'Surely the princes of Zoan are fools. . . . Where are they? Where are thy wise men?' Isa. xix. 11, 13. . . . . At sunrise next morning we took a full survey of all that now remains of ancient Zoan. We found that the large mounds of alluvial matter which cover the ruins of brick and pottery, extend about two miles from east to west, and one mile and a half from north to south. The whole country round appeared to be covered, not with sand, but with soil that might be cultivated to the utmost if there was water. The most remarkable relics of this ancient city lie at the western extremity. We came upon immense blocks of red granite lying in a heap. All had been hewn, some were carved, and some were still lying regularly placed one above another. Here probably stood the greatest temple of Zoan, and there seems to have been an open square round it. Possibly, also, a stream flowed through the very midst of the city, for at present there is the dry channel of a torrent. Farther to the north we found ten or twelve obelisks, fallen and prostrate, and two sphinxes, broken and half sunk in the ground. Among the mounds we could clearly trace buildings of brick, the bricks still retaining their original place. The remains of pottery, however, were most remarkable, consisting of jars of the ancient form without number, all broken into fragments, many of them bearing the clearest marks of the action of fire, showing that God has literally fulfilled the word of the prophet, 'I will set fire in Zoan.'" Ezek. xxx. 14.—*Mission to the Jews.*

THE PASSAGE OF THE RED SEA.

"And Moses stretched out his hand over the sea; and the Lord caused the sea to go back by a strong east wind all that night, and made the sea dry land, and the waters were divided. And the children of Israel went into the midst of the sea upon the dry ground: and the waters were a wall unto them on their right hand and on their left."—EXODUS xiv. 21, 22.

No part of Holy Scripture, probably, has been more a source of cavil to the sceptic than the account of the passage of the Red Sea by the Israelites, and not a few Christian writers even, have endeavored to explain away its miraculous character. To those, however, who are willing to receive the literal statements of the inspired narrative, it is gratifying to know that the geographical features of that wonderful event can still be identified.

"It has always been our opinion," says Dr. Kitto, "confirmed more and more by the results of progressive inquiry, that the passage was effected a few miles below the town of Suez, across the sea itself, where it is about ten miles in width. How could the Israelites have been 'entangled in the land,' so as to become an easy prey to their pursuers, if they had only a narrow and fordable frith before them? Whence the consternation and distress of the Israelites? How could the waters be '*a wall*' unto them on the right hand and on the left, so as to justify the expression, 'the waters stood upright as an heap, and the depths were congealed in the heart of the sea.' Why the triumphant song of Moses at the miraculous overthrow of the Egyptians, if this was occasioned mainly by the regular return of tidal waters? 'The dukes of Edom shall be amazed; the mighty men of Moab, trembling shall take hold of them; all the inhabitants of Canaan shall melt away with fear.' And why? Because the Israelites went at low water, over a narrow pass, in safety, as is customary to this day, and the Egyptians in pursuit were drowned by the returning tide!

"To obviate these objections, the children of Israel are supposed to have turned their course from Etham, and passed either in a circuitous route around the Attakah, which rises 'lofty and dark,' in a bold bluff, from the western shore below Suez, or else directly down the coast, passing between this head land and the sea. This mountain is supposed to have been the Baal-Zephon of the Exodus, and the valley on the south of it Pi-hahiroth. A German writer, Von Raumer, in an able and laborious work on Scripture Geography, supposes them to have made their final exit from the south-western border of Goshen, near Cairo, and to have pursued their course to the sea through a valley, still called the Valley of Wandering, south of a chain of mountains which runs from Cairo eastward, and terminates in the Attakah. According to this theory, Rameses was near the present Cairo; Succoth and Etham were in the valley; and Migdol, the Deraj, a lofty mountain south of Attakah.

"Here they would be beset with dangers on every side. On the right a wide waste of mountains and desert; on the left the impassable Attakah; before them the sea; and behind them the Egyptians in eager pursuit, with a regular military force, and six hundred chariots of war. On the supposition that the waters were divided by the direct and immediate power of Jehovah, the Israelites could have eight or ten hours to make their way through the channel opened to them by the hand of Omnipotence, a space amply sufficient for a march of about ten miles. An escape so miraculous, through the depths of the sea, and the fearful overthrow of Pharaoh and his hosts, might indeed strike 'the dukes of Edom' and the surrounding nations, far and near, with the fear of Jehovah, and a dread of his people."

THE WELLS OF MOSES.

The first spot where the Israelites probably encamped after their passage, was that which is still called the "Wells of Moses."

"We rode in the clear moonlight to the Wells of Moses, where our tents were ready for our reception. (Here) we read the song of Moses and of the children of Israel, with feelings and emotions such as we had never before experienced.

"(Next morning), before assembling for breakfast, we particularly examined the wells, in the midst of which we were encamped. They rise in mounts elevated a little above the level of the neighborhood, and less than a couple of miles inland. . . . Only one of them appeared to be regularly dug and built. . . . The others, six in number at present, are nothing more than fountains rising in small basins formed in the sands. . . . The supply of water is considerable."—WILSON'S *Lands of the Bible.*

"I am much inclined to think that Ayún Mousa is really the spot on which the foot of rescued Israel rested, and from which they beheld their enemies dead on the sea shore. . . . I am persuaded . . . that the people of Israel entered their pathway just to the north of Rás Attakah, and that they passed straight onward to Ayún Mousa."—FISK'S *Pastor's Memorial.*

MARAH.

"And when they came to Marah, they could not drink of the waters of Marah, for they were bitter: therefore the name of it was called Marah" (or bitterness).—EXODUS xv. 23.

From the Red Sea, Moses led the people into the wilderness of Shur. Many parts of the great Arabian desert were called by the name of distinct wildernesses; such as the Wilderness of Shur, into which they now went out. They continued their march for three days in a south-easterly direction, along the coast, through sterile and hilly parts. They appear to have suffered much from want of water during those three days; and when at length it was discovered, it proved bitter or brackish.

"We came to the 'Ain Howárah, the 'well of destruction,' a fountain on a small knoll close to the track which we were pursuing. It occupies a small basin, about five feet in diameter, and eighteen inches deep, and to some extent it oozes through the sands, leaving, like the wells of Moses, a deposit of lime. The Arabs, on observing me about to drink of the water, exclaimed, 'It is bitter, bitter, bitter!'

"This fountain has been almost universally admitted by travellers since the days of Burkhardt, to be the true Marah of Scripture, as it is found in a situation about thirty miles from the place where the Israelites must have landed on the eastern shore of the Red Sea, a space sufficient for their march, when they were three days in the wilderness and found no water. No other constant spring is found in the intermediate space. It retains its ancient character, and has a bad name among the Arabs, who seldom allow their camels to partake of it."—WILSON'S *Lands of the Bible.*

ELIM.

"And they came to Elim, where were twelve wells of water, and three score and ten palm trees; and they encamped there by the waters."—EXODUS xv. 27.

About eight or nine miles south by east from the 'Ain Howárah is the Wady Ghurandel, generally believed to be identical with the Elim of Scripture, where the Israelites encamped. It is described by recent travellers as "a gracefully undulated, sandy territory, scattered over with thick clumps of the tamarisk tree and small palms, which give it the appearance of an ornamental plantation." Dr. Shaw discovered here nine wells, and supposed the other three to have been filled up by drifts of sand so common in Arabia. Burckhardt says, "The non-existence of *twelve* wells at Ghurandèl must not be considered as evidence against the foregoing conjecture, for Niebuhr says that his companions obtained water here by digging to a very great depth, and there was a great plenty of it when I passed; water, in fact, is readily found by digging in every valley in Arabia, and wells are thus easily formed, which are as quickly filled up again by the sands."

MOUNT SINAI.

" . . . And Mount Sinai was altogether on a smoke, because the Lord descended upon it in fire; and the smoke thereof ascended as the smoke of a furnace, and the whole mount quaked greatly."—Exodus xix. 18.

"On a sudden a broad quadrangular plain, but of much greater length than breadth, lay before us. It is bounded at its farthest extremity by a mountain of surpassing height, grandeur, and terror; and this was the very 'Mount of God,' where He stood when He descended in fire, and where rested the cloud of His glory, from which He spake 'all the words of the law.' The plain itself was the Wádi, or Ráhah, the Valley of Rest, where stood the whole congregation of the sons and daughters of Israel, when gathered together before the Lord. As of old, the everlasting mountains, by which it was bounded on every side, were the walls, and the expanse of Heaven itself, the canopy, of this great temple. Entered within its courts, so sacred in its associations, we felt for a time the curiosity of the traveller lost in the reverance and awe of the worshipper. We walked through the valley of Ráhah, occasionally stopping to survey the interesting scene around us.

"The mountain is of deep red granite. It rises from the plain almost perpendicularly about 1,500 feet. From the monks it receives the name of Horeb, which in Hebrew means 'dry, desert, and desolation.' The Mount of Moses (Jebel Músá) was not visible. It is not, however, it is to be observed, a distinct mountain, but only the highest peak of this one, at the parts most remote from the valley. Rounding the eastern corner of Horeb . . . we had a narrow defile before us called 'The valley of Jethro.'"—Wilson's *Lands of the Bible.*

"I made the ascent of Mount Sinai. . . . As to the precise pinnacle of the Sinaite group from which the law was given to Moses, I must frankly confess that it would only be a choice of conjectures, or a balance of probabilities. That it was indeed the Sinaite group which invited my footsteps, there could be no doubt. Not a particle was there of this wilderness of granite that had not quaked at the mysterious and awful presence of Jehovah: not one of its numberless clefts and caverns, in which was not heard and echoed the voice of the trumpet which sounded long and waxed louder and louder. And was there not enough . . . in this certainty? . . . Scripture withholds all but the *general* certainty to which I have referred. . . . I retired—still gazing on the venerable and solemn scene, and read, with a humbled heart, the law as written by the finger of God upon the two tables of stone."—FISK'S *Pastor's Memorial.*

"How sternly desolate! the Deity,
Methinks, has fix'd upon that awful height
His grandest signature of majesty,
And chronicled his Godhead's changeless might.
And as the tempest, in its lurid path,
Sweeps over thee unheeded, we behold
Fit emblem of that throne, which earthly wrath
And change affect not, resting, as of old,
Upon the strong foundations; truth sublime,
And wisdom infinite, and power unchang'd by time.

"Still thou art holy. God's appointed throne,
Where mortal man held audience with Him.
Here, lightning-girt, his high pavilion shone,
Here his own thunder roll'd its awful hymn.
Here, while unutterable awe did thrill
The souls of Israel's breathless multitude,
As if the heart of that great host grew still
In one concentred pulse; the prophet stood
Commission'd to receive the laws of heaven,
For man's instruction, strength, and guidance given."

REV. J. W. BROWN.

THE WILDERNESS

"And thou shalt remember all the way which the Lord thy God led thee these forty years in the wilderness."—DEUT. viii. 2.

"The general name by which the Hebrews called 'the wilderness,' including always that of Sinai, was 'the pasture.' Bare as the surface of the Desert is, yet the thin clothing of vegetation, which is seldom entirely withdrawn, especially the aromatic shrubs on the high hill sides, furnish sufficient sustenance for the herds of the six thousand Bedouins who constitute the present population of the Peninsula.

'Along the mountain ledges green,
The scatter'd sheep at will may glean
The Desert's spicy stores.'—KEBLE.

"So were they seen following the daughters or the shepherd-slaves of Jethro. So may they be seen climbing the rocks, or gathered round the pools and springs of the valleys, under the charge of the black-veiled Bedouin women of the present day. And in the Tiyâḥa, Towâra, or Alouin tribes, with their chiefs and followers, their dress and manners, and habitations, we probably see the likeness of the Midianites, the Amalekites, and the Israelites themselves in this their earliest stage of existence. The long straight lines of black tents which cluster round the Desert springs, present to us on a small scale the image of the vast encampment gathered round the one Sacred Tent, which with its covering of dyed skins, stood conspicuous in the midst, and which recalled the period of their nomadic life long after their settlement in Palestine. The deserted villages—marked by rude enclosures of stone, are doubtless such as those to which the Hebrew wanderers gave the name of 'Hazeroth,' and which afterwards furnished the type of the primitive sanctuary at Shiloh. The rude burial-grounds, with the many nameless head stones, far away from human habitation, are such as the host of Israel must have left behind them at the different stages of their progress—at Massah, at Sinai, at Kibroth-hattaavah, 'the graves of desire.' The salutations of the chiefs, in their bright scarlet robes, the one 'going out to meet the other,' the 'obeisance,' the 'kiss' on each side the head, the silent entrance into the tent for consultation, are all graphically described in the encounter between Moses and Jethro. The constitution of the tribes, with the subordinate degrees of sheikhs, recommended by Jethro to Moses, is the very same which still exists amongst those who are possibly his lineal descendants—the gentle race of the Towâra."—STANLEY'S *Sinai and Palestine.*

THE APPROACH TO PALESTINE.

"Everything told us that we were approaching the sacred frontier. That wide plain with its ruins and walls was the wilderness of Beersheba; with wells such as those for which Abraham and Isaac struggled; at which, it may be, they had watered their flocks; the neutral ground between the Desert and the cultivated region which those shepherd patriarchs would most naturally choose for their wanderings, before the idea of a more permanent home had yet dawned upon them. That long line of hills was the beginning of 'the hill country of Judea,' and when we began to ascend it, the first answer to our inquiries after the route told that it was 'Carmel,' not the more famous mountain of that name, but that on which Nabal fed his flocks: and, close below its long ranges, was the hill and ruin of 'Ziph;' close above, the hill of 'Maon.' That is to say, we were now in the heart of the wild country where David wandered from Saul like those very 'partridges in the mountains,' which we saw abounding in all directions. . . . And to the east, towering high into the hazy sky, what looked like the Alps of Moab; and between us and them a jagged line of lower hills, the rocks of Engedi; and, in the misty depths which parted these nearer and those further mountains, there needed no guide to tell that there lay, invisible as yet, the Dead Sea."—*Sinai and Palestine.*

BEERSHEBA.

"So Abraham returned unto his young men; and they rose up, and went together to Beersheba; and Abraham dwelt at Beersheba."—GEN. xxii. 19.

This ancient settlement was on the southern limits of Judah and Palestine. Hence the phrase, "from Dan (in the extreme north) to Beersheba" (in the extreme south), to describe the whole extent of the land. It was a favorite station of Abraham, and occurs so often in the history of the patriarchs, that much interest had long been felt in it, although its site had been forgotten, and no traces of its existence were known until it was discovered by Dr. Robinson.

Upon coming up from the desert so graphically described by Mr. Stanley, he soon reached a wide watercourse, or bed of a torrent. Upon its northern side, close upon the bank, he found two deep wells, still called Bir-es-sheba. The water was sweet and abundant, and flocks were gathering round them to drink. On some low hills a little to the north, he found ruins indicative of a considerable village in the remote days of its prosperity.

"Here then," says Dr. Robinson, "is the place where the patriarchs Abraham, Isaac, and Jacob dwelt! Here Abraham dug perhaps this very well; and journeyed from hence with Isaac to Mount Moriah to offer him up there in sacrifice. From this place Jacob fled to Padan-Aram after acquiring the birthright and blessing belonging to his brother; and here too he sacrificed to the Lord, on setting off to see his son Joseph in Egypt. Here Samuel made his sons judges; and from here Elijah wandered out into the southern desert, and sat down under a shrub of Retem, just as our Arabs sat down under it every day and every night. Over these smiling hills the flocks of the patriarchs once roved by thousands, where now we found only a few camels, asses, and goats."—*Biblical Researches.*

HEBRON.

"Abraham buried Sarah his wife in the cave of the field of Machpelah before Mamre: the same is Hebron in the land of Canaan."—GEN. xxiii. 19.

This venerable city stands second to Jerusalem alone, in high and sacred associations. "It was the earliest seat of civilized life," says Mr. Stanley, "not only of Judah but of Palestine. It was the ancient city of Ephron the Hittite, in whose 'gate' he and the elders received the offer of Abraham, when as yet no other fixed habitation of man was known in Central Palestine. It was the first home of Abraham and the patriarchs; their one permanent resting place when they were gradually exchanging the pastoral for the agricultural life. It was the city of Arba—the old Canaanite chief, with his three giant sons, under whose walls the trembling spies stole through the land by the adjacent valley of Eshcol. Here Caleb chose his portion, and gave it the new name of Hebron, when at the head of his valiant tribe he drove out the old inhabitants, and called the whole surrounding territory after his own name; and there, under David, and at a later period under Absalom, the tribe of Judah always rallied when it asserted its independent existence against the rest of the Israelite nation. It needs but few words to give the secret of this early selection, of this long continuance of the metropolitan city of Judah. Every traveller from the desert will have been struck by the sight of that green vale, with its orchards and vineyards, and numberless wells, and in earlier times we must add the grove of terebinths or oaks, which then attracted from far the eye of the wandering tribes. This fertility was in part owing to its elevation into the cooler and the more watered region, above the dry and withered valleys of the rest of Judæa. Commanding this fertile valley, rose Hebron on its crested hill. Beneath was the burial place of the founders of their race. Caleb must have marked out the spot for his own, when with the spies he had passed through this very valley. When David returned from the chase of the Amalekite plunderers on the desert frontier, and doubted 'to which of the cities of Judah he should go up' from the wilderness, the natural features of the place, as well as the oracle of God, answered clearly and distinctly, 'unto Hebron.'"—*Sinai and Palestine.*

The present town of Hebron is described by travellers as lying low down on the sloping sides of a narrow valley (Mamre), chiefly on the eastern side, but in the southern part stretches across also to the western side. The houses are all of stone, high and well built, with windows and flat roofs, and on these roofs are small domes, sometimes two or three to each house. "No city in Palestine," says Dr. Thomson, "so carries one back to the earliest patriarchal times. Manners, customs, modes of action, and even idioms of speech have changed but little from what they were when Abraham dwelt here." An aged oak or terebinth in the adjacent plain of Mamre, where the patriarch's tent was often pitched, is still called Abraham's tree. The valley through which leads the road to Jerusalem is generally considered to be the Eshcol of the Old Testament, and the character of its fruits still corresponds to its ancient celebrity. The largest and best grapes of Palestine are still produced there. In Hebron itself two ancient pools are still to be seen, one of which is supposed to be referred to (2 Sam. iv. 12) as the place where David hung up the murderers of his rival Ishbosheth.

That, however, which imparts to Hebron its highest interest is a massive structure entitled the Haram or Sacred Place, and which is honored by Moslems, Jews, and Christians alike as the Tomb of the Patriarchs. It is described by Dr. Robinson as "a large and lofty building . . . . The walls are built of very large stones, all bevelled and hewn smooth, and similar in all respects to the most ancient parts of the walls around the Haram at Jerusalem . . . . There are no windows in any part of these walls. The places of entrance are at the two northern corners, where a long and broad flight of steps, of very gentle ascent, built up and covered along each side of the building externally, leads to a door in each wall opening into the court within." . . . . "I know of nothing," says that eminent traveller, "that should lead us to question the correctness of the tradition which regards this as the place of sepulture of Abraham and the other patriarchs as recorded in the book of Genesis. On the contrary, there is much to strengthen it. Josephus relates that Abraham and his descendants erected monuments over the sepulchres in question, which implies, at least, that in his day the place was marked by some ancient memorial. In another passage he says expressly that the sepulchres of the patriarchs were still to be seen in Hebron, built of marble and of elegant workmanship. In the days of Eusebius and Jerome, the monument of Abraham was yet pointed out; and the Bordeaux Pilgrim, in A. D. 333, describes it as a quadrangle, built of stones of admirable beauty . . . . It appears to me, we may rest with confidence in the view that this remarkable external structure of the Haram is indeed the work of Jewish hands, erected, long before the destruction of the nation, around the sepulchre of their revered progenitors, 'the friend of God,' and his descendants. The cave of Machpelah is described in Scripture as at the 'end of the field,' over against Mamre, the same is Hebron; and all the later writers above quoted speak of the sepulchre of the patriarchs, as *at* or *in* Hebron, not near it. Here, then, the 'Father of the faithful,' as also Isaac and Jacob, rested from their wanderings."—*Biblical Researches.*

The following observations of another traveller upon this vicinity bring out other Biblical associations: "From Hebron we climbed a steep terraced hill. At the top was a grove of fine old fig-trees, reminding one of the groves which crowned the 'high places' in ancient days. The view from this was rich and beautiful, and might be taken as some faint likeness of what it must have been in David's time, when the industrious Jews had entered on the olive gardens and vineyards of that earlier race, which, with all its crimes and savage idolatries, must have possessed elements of material civilization lost to the lawless Arab peasants who people the land now. The royal city lay below us, not far off, in the luxuriant plain, from a centre in the valley radiating up three separate hills. Its white roofs, domes, and airy minarets, and especially the great mosque over Machpelah, blended beautifully with the olives, vines, and figs which surrounded them. Around was the lovely, rich Plain of Mamre, and beyond, cornfields were still golden on the lower uplands.

"Again, a night under the shelter of Abraham's oak, and in the morning once more across the hill country of Judea on the way back by Bethlehem and Jerusalem.

"The especial interest of this day's journey was that it lay through the heart of the scenery of David's Psalms. The rocks and hill-fortresses, the 'thousand hills,' and the quiet valleys, the green pastures by the still waters, the wild caves and ravines of the shadow of death, amidst which we journeyed this day, were precisely those which have from our earliest childhood been made allegorical to us by the inspired poetry of the shepherd king."—*Wanderings in Bible Lands.*

THE LAND OF THE PHILISTINES.

"And Abraham sojourned in the Philistines' land many days."—GENESIS xxi. 34. "Woe unto the inhabitants of the sea-coast, the nation of the Cherethites! the word of the Lord is against you; O Canaan, the land of the Philistines, I will even destroy thee, that there shall be no inhabitant. And the sea-coast shall be dwellings and cottages for shepherds and folds for flocks."—ZEPHANIAH ii. 5.

The land of the Philistines was a narrow strip of territory lying on the coast of the Mediterranean sea, west and southwest of Judæa. The Philistines appear to have been a colony of foreign settlers, who, at some remote period, had crossed the sea from Asia Minor or Crete. The name "Cherethites" is given them by the prophets, and imported their strange worship of Dagon, the Fish-god, a divinity unknown to the other tribes of Canaan. As early as the time of Abraham they had become a powerful people. When the Israelites were on their way to the Promised Land, it is recorded that "God led them not through the way of the Philistines, although that was near; for God said, Lest peradventure the people repent when they see war, and they return to Egypt." The Philistines, however, were not of the Canaanite races, doomed to extirpation. They were left, we are told, to teach Israel war, and for a trial of the faithfulness and obedience of the chosen people, whom, for their sins and idolatry, they were often permitted to chastise.

The localities of the interesting events associated with this mutual warfare, may now be traced. The rough mountain-road by which Samson "went down" from the hill forts of his native Dan into the "low country" beneath, —the tangled thickets close to the vineyards where the young lion in the path roared against him,—the waving wheat-fields on the level interspersed with olives and vines, which he set on fire, are all there, and the wild animals he made use of as living fire-brands, still infest the neighborhood. The caves which exist in the lime-stone cliffs around give an idea of his place of retreat in "the top of the rock Etam," as well as of David's sojourn, in the same locality, in the cave of Adullam. There amid the palm trees and gardens of pomegranates and mulberry, which surround the ruins of what once was Gaza, was the scene of Samson's later deeds and of his fall. There, too, he drew down upon himself and the pride of Philistia, in its hour of insolent triumph, the temple of Dagon; so that "the dead which he slew at his death were more than they which he slew in his life."

The present state of Philistia could not be expressed more truly and forcibly than in the very words spoken as prophecy five hundred years before the coming of our Lord. . . . "Thou, whole Palestina, *art dissolved!*" It is emphatically a land of ruins, and both the villages and their inhabitants are poor and wretched.

Of the once famous Gath, the birthplace of Goliath and his giant brethren, not a vestige remains. A probable site has been assigned for it by Dr. Robinson, but it has been literally swept from the face of the earth. Amos vi. 2.

"Nor has prophecy been less strikingly verified in the case of the other cities of the Philistine plain. All vestiges of the ancient walls and former strength of Gaza have disappeared. Columns of marble and granite are scattered in the streets and gardens of the modern village, and used as thresholds at the gates and doors of houses. 'Baldness is come upon Gaza.' Jer. xlvii. 5.

"Ashdod, where the ark of God was brought into the

temple of Dagon, and humbled, 'that twice battered god of Palestine' in the eyes of his worshippers,—a city famous in history, as having sustained a siege of twenty-nine years by one of the kings of Egypt, is now an insignificant village. A succession of calamities has abased its pride, and thinned its population. 'They shall drive out Ashdod at noon-day.' Zeph. ii. 4.

"The modern village of 'Akir represents the Ekron of former days, the town from which the ark was conveyed on a new cart, drawn by two milch-kine, who took the straight way to Beth-shemesh, the nearest point in the hills of Judah. It was the shrine of Baalzebub, the 'lord of flies;' but the flies have outlived their lord. The town is built of un-burnt bricks or mud, with no mark of antiquity to tell of its ancient greatness. 'Ekron shall be rooted up.' Zeph. ii. 4.

"The decay that has come upon the Philistian cities is not written in blight or barrenness upon the land. The country is everywhere fertile and luxuriant, abounding in rich tracts of pasturage, and numerous flocks are seen near the villages, giving an aspect of life and cheerfulness to the landscape. The bow of its old fighting men has been broken, and the spear cut in sunder, but the pastoral life the people led in the days of Abimelech still holds its quiet round through the seasons: the shepherd's crook is more enduring than the warrior's sword. And this was the picture of its future fortunes drawn by a Hebrew prophet long ago—'The sea-coast shall be dwellings and cottages for shepherds, and folds for flocks.'"

BETHLEHEM.

"But thou, Bethlehem Ephratah, though thou be little among the thousands of Judah, yet out of thee shall he come forth unto me that is to be ruler in Israel; whose goings forth have been from of old, from everlasting."—MICAH v. 2.

The associations which cluster around the little town of Bethlehem, and which are familiar as household words wherever the Bible has come, equal, perhaps exceed in interest, those of any other spot on the whole earth. Apart from these, it possesses little claim to consideration. "It was," says Stanley, "but the ordinary type of a Judæan village, not distinguished by size or situation from any amongst 'the thousands of Judah.' All the characteristics of Bethlehem are essentially of this nature. Its high position on the narrow ridge of the long gray hill would leave 'no room' for the crowded travellers to find shelter; its southern situation made it always a resting-place, probably the first halting-place from Jerusalem on the way to Egypt. 'By Bethlehem' in ancient times was the Caravanserai or Khan of Chimham (Jer. xli. 17), son of Barzillai, for those who would 'go to enter into Egypt;' and from Bethlehem, it may be, from that same caravanserai, Joseph 'arose and took the young child and his mother and departed into Egypt.' The familiar well appears close by the gate, for whose water David longed. Eastward extend the wild hills, where the flocks and herds of David, and of Amos, and of 'the shepherds abiding with their flocks by night,' may have wandered. Below lie the corn-fields, the scene of Ruth's adventures, from which it derives its name, the 'house of Bread.'"—STANLEY'S *Sinai and Palestine.*

"We entered the plains of Bethlehem; it was early in the morning, yet there were shepherds abiding in the fields, who had been keeping watch over their flocks by night, and the black tents of the Bedouins were clustered on the side of a hill, while their sheep and goats pastured round them. Every shepherd lad here seemed to possess an interest, and to represent to us the youthful David as he kept his father's sheep on these plains, and fearless slew the lion and bear who came to rob his flock."—WOODCOCK'S *Scripture Lands.*

"What a mighty influence for good," says another traveller, "has gone forth from this little spot upon the human race, both for time and for eternity. The legends and puerilities of monastic tradition may be safely disregarded. It is enough to know that this is Bethlehem, where Jesus the Redeemer was born. Generation after generation has, indeed, since that time passed away, and their places know them no more. For eighteen hundred seasons and more the earth has renewed her carpet of verdure, and seen it again decay. Yet the skies and the fields, the rocks and the hills and the valleys around remain unchanged, and are still the same as when the glory of the Lord shone round about the shepherds, and the song of a multitude of the heavenly host resounded among the hills, proclaiming, 'Glory to God in the highest, on earth peace, good will towards men.'"—ROBINSON'S *Biblical Researches.*

JERUSALEM.

"The city which I have chosen me to put my name there."—1 KINGS xi. 36.

"Of earth's dark circlet once the precious gem
Of living light—O fallen Jerusalem!"—SOUTHEY.

"On reaching the rocky heights of Beer," writes Mr. Jowett, "travelling towards Jerusalem, the country began to assume a more wild appearance. Uncultivated hilly tracts in every direction, seemed to announce that not only Jerusalem, but its vicinity for some miles round, was destined to sadden the heart of every visitor. Even the stranger that should come from a far land, it was predicted, should be amazed at the plagues laid upon the country; and this became more than ever literally fulfilled in my feelings as I drew near to the metropolis of this chosen nation. Expectation was indeed wrought up to a high pitch as we ascended hill after hill, and beheld others yet more distant rising after each other. Being apprehensive lest I should not reach the city gate before sunset . . . I repeatedly desired the guides to ask the Arabs whom we met, how far, or, according to the language of this country, how many hours, it was to Jerusalem? The answer we received from all was, 'We have been at the prayers at the mosque of Omar, and we left at noon;' to-day being the Mohammedan sabbath. We were thus left to calculate the distance. The reply sounded very foreign to the ears of one who knew that formerly there were scenes of purer worship on this spot. 'Thither the tribes go up, the tribes of the Lord, to the testimony of Israel, to give thanks unto the name of the Lord.' At length, while the sun was yet two hours high, my long and intensely interesting suspense was relieved. The view of the city burst upon me as in a moment; and the truly graphic language of the Psalmist was verified in a degree of which I could have formed no previous conception. Continually the expressions were bursting from my lips—'Beautiful for situation; the joy of the whole earth is Mount Zion! They that trust in the Lord shall be as Mount Zion, which cannot be removed, but abideth forever! As the mountains are round about Jerusalem, so the Lord is round about his people, from henceforth, even forever!' "—JOWETT's *Chr. Researches.*

"Apart from all associations," says Warburton, "the first view of Jerusalem is a most striking one. A brilliant and unchequered sunshine has something mournful in it, when all that it shines upon is utterly desolate and drear. Not a tree or green spot is visible; no sign of life breaks the solemn silence; no smile of nature's gladness ever varies the stern scenery around. The flaming, monotonous sunshine above, and the pale, distorted, rocky wastes beneath, realize but too faithfully the prophetic picture—"Thy sky shall be brass and thy land shall be iron." To the right and left, as far as the eye can reach, vague undulations of colorless rocks extend to the horizon. A broken and desolate plain in front is bounded by a wavy, battlemented wall, over which towers frown, and minarets peer, and mosque-domes swell; intermingled with church turret and an indistinguishable mass of terraced roofs. High over the city, to the left, rises the Mount of Olives; and the distant hills of Moab, almost mingling with the sky, afford a background to the striking picture. . . .

"I am not sure that this stern scenery did not present the only appearance that would not disappoint expectation. It is unlike anything else on earth—so blank to the eye, yet so full of meaning to the heart; every mountain round is familiar to the memory; even yon blasted fig tree has its voice, and the desolation that surrounds us bears silent testimony to fearful experiences. The plain upon which we stand looks like the arena of deadly struggle in times gone by—struggles in which all the mighty nations of the earth took part, and in which Nature herself seems to have shared.

"As we advanced, some olive trees appeared, and deep valleys on the left, slightly marked with pale, green gardens. An enclosure concealed the prospect for a while, and then again the City of Zion appeared, shadowing with its battlemented walls the barren rocks around. As we approached, nothing but these walls were visible, presenting probably, with their massive gates and lofty towers, the same appearance as they wore when they first opened to the desiring eyes of the Crusaders"—a scene which Tasso has so vividly described.

"Swiftly they march'd, yet were not tired thereby,
For willing minds make heaviest burdens light.
But when the gliding sun was mounted high,
Jerusalem (behold) appear'd in sight;
Jerusalem they view, they see, they spy,
Jerusalem with merry noise they greet,
With joyful shouts, and acclamations sweet.

"To that delight which their first sight did breed,
That pleased so the summit of their thought,
A deep repentance did forthwith succeed,
That reverend fear, and trembling with it brought.
Scantly they durst their feeble eyes dispreed,
Upon that town, where Christ was sold and bought,
Where for our sins he faultless suffer'd pain,
There where he died, and where he lived again.

"Their naked feet trod on the dusty way,
Following th' ensample of their zealous guide.
Their scarfs, their crests, their plumes and feathers gay
They quickly cleft, and willing laid aside,
Their moulten hearts their wonted pride allay;
Along their watery cheeks warm tears down slide."

Fairfax's Tasso, Cant. iii. v. 6, 7.

Although the denunciations of divine prophecy have been so remarkably fulfilled in the desolations which have overtaken the holy city, yet there are certain ineffaceable features which still remain to attest the fidelity of the sketches so frequently drawn in the Book of Truth. The hills which surround it for nearly twenty miles on every side, forcibly image forth the security that encompasses the people of God. The two parallel ridges upon which the ancient city was built, with a valley between them, are the grand land marks of the present city. The eastern is Mount Moriah on which the Mosque of Omar occupies the place of the Temple of Solomon. Within under the dome, is a mass of limestone rock, the natural surface of the mount, on which may be seen marks of chiselling. The place where the Jewish altar of burnt-offering stood, has been identified by a bore in the solid rock, which "corresponds exactly with the description given in the Mishna of the drain and cesspool communicating with the sewer that ran off into the Kidron."—Conybeare and Hewson, ii. 257.

In the huge foundation stones of the wall enclosing the Haram area, now the Jewish waiting place, we have undoubted portions of the original temple. To the west of Moriah is Mount Zion, on which an oblong castle represents the ancient tower of David, and probably may have sprung out of its ruins. The valley between is that of the Tyropœon, once spanned by the magnificent viaduct erected by Solomon, "the ascent by which he went up to the house of the Lord," which so impressed the Queen of Sheba with the wise king's greatness "that there was no more spirit in her." Unequivocal remains of this noble work, it is said, have been recently discovered. Rising to the east, is seen the gray ridge of Olivet over which David once fled from Absalom, and on whose brow a greater than David once paused and dropt his tears, on the wayside stones. "As now the dome of the mosque rises like a ghost from the earth, so then must have risen the temple tower; as now the vast enclosure of the Mussulman sanctuary, so then must have spread the temple courts; as now the gray town on its broken hills, so then the magnificent city, with its background of gardens and suburbs on the western plateau behind. It is hardly possible to doubt that this rise and turn of the road, this rocky ledge, was the exact spot where the multitude paused again, and 'He beheld the city, and wept over it.'" Beneath the rocky side of Moriah is still found the pool of Siloam, and the well of En Rogel where Jonathan and Ahimaaz tarried yet marks the ancient border between Judah and Benjamin. The valleys of Gihon, Hinnom, and Jehosaphat still intrench the city round about, and the brook Kidron pursues its course as of old, where a grove of ancient and magnificent olive trees still marks the garden of Gethsemane. However apocryphal may be the sites which have been for many ages associated with scenes of the most sacred interest, there are features so strongly marked and unmistakable as to make it absolutely certain that most of the prominent localities of the holy city may still be identified. Scepticism may smile at the superstitions connected with alleged holy places, but here, it cannot be doubted, is the City of David and Solomon—where the visible presence of Jehovah was vouchsafed—where prophets were wrapped in heavenly visions—where the chosen tribes came up to worship—and above all where that death was perpetrated which has opened our way to life. How terribly the atrocities which marked that event have been avenged, the desolations which have continued even to the present time, bear impressive testimony.

"Mourn, Salem! mourn! Low lies thine humbled state;
Thy glittering fanes are levelled with the ground;
Fallen is thy pride—thine halls are desolate!
Where erst was heard the timbrel's sprightly sound,
And frolic pleasure tripped the nightly round.
There breeds the wild fox lonely, and aghast
Stands the mute pilgrim at the void profound;
Unbroke by noise—save when the hurrying blast
Sighs like a spirit, deep along the cheerless waste!

"It is for this, proud Solyma, thy towers
Lie crumbling in the dust; for this, forlorn
Thy genius wails along thy desert bowers;
While stern destruction laughs, as if in scorn,
That thou didst dare insult God's eldest born;
And with most bitter persecuting ire
Pursued his footsteps, till the last day dawn
Rose on his fortunes—and thou saw'st the fire
That came to light the world, in one great flash expire."

THE ROAD FROM JERUSALEM TO JERICHO.

The parable of the good Samaritan has rendered the long and rugged pass which leads from Jerusalem to Jericho forever famous, and its incidents still find striking illustration in the wild and gloomy scenery. "The road winds through the bottom of savage gorges, or rises steeply along the edge of the precipices, only to sink deeper into narrow passes and glens still more desolate, cloven through naked cliffs of limestone. Here, without an escort, sometimes with one, the traveller may still 'fall among thieves;' and none can pass that way, through the heart of these stern and rugged solitudes, without a sensation of awe and peril. A particular part of the road, the scene of many a murder, was called *the red or bloody way;* and here in Jerome's time a fort was placed with a Roman garrison, for the protection of travellers." "The region," says an American writer, "is so scarred, gashed, and torn, that no work of mankind can save it from perpetual desolation. It is a wilderness more hopeless than the desert. If I were left alone in the midst of it, I should lie down and await death without thought or hope of rescue." "The heat reflected from those ghastly walls of rock, the sultry ash-colored vapor brooding over the white hollows like the smoke of a furnace, with no breath of air to lift it, the scorching sirocco blowing in fiery gusts, rendering the 'going down' into the Jordan valley a most fatiguing journey; and the frightful sterility and silence of the place gives one an impression, till then unfelt, of the horrors of the situation in which a traveller would find himself stretched bleeding by the wayside and left to die."—REV. J. D. BURNS.

THE DEAD SEA.

This sea is called in sacred writ the Salt Sea, the Sea of the Plain, and the East Sea. It occupies what was formerly the valley of Siddim, in which stood the five cities of the plain—Sodom, Gomorrah, Admah, Zeboiim, and Bela. These guilty cities were utterly destroyed by the righteous vengeance of the Almighty, and their very sites have been hid from the face of heaven by waters that are unique among all the waters of the earth.—Vid. Gen. xiii. xiv. xix.

"The inference from the Bible," says Lieut. Lynch, "that the entire chasm was a plain sunk and 'overwhelmed' by the wrath of God, seems to be sustained by the extraordinary character of the soundings. The bottom of this sea consists of two submerged plains, an elevated and a depressed one; the former averaging *thirteen*, the latter about *thirteen hundred* feet below the surface. Through the northern, and largest and deepest one, in a line corresponding with the bed of the Jordan, is a ravine, which again seems to correspond with the Wady el-Jeib, at the south end of the sea.

"Between the Jabbok and this sea, we unexpectedly found a sudden break down in the bed of the Jordan. If there be a similar break in the water-courses to the south of the sea, accompanied with like volcanic characters, there can scarce be a doubt that the whole Ghôr has sunk from some extraordinary convulsion; preceded, most probably, by an eruption of fire, and a general conflagration of the bitumen which abounded in the plain. I shall ever regret that we were not authorized to explore the southern Ghôr to the Red Sea. . . .

"It is for the learned to comment on the facts we have laboriously collected. Upon ourselves the result is a decided one. We entered upon this sea with conflicting opinions. One of the party was sceptical, and another, I think, a professed unbeliever of the Mosaic account. After twenty-two days' close investigation, if I am not mistaken, we are unanimous in the conviction of the truth of the Scriptural accounts of the destruction of the cities of the plain. I record with diffidence the conclusions we have reached, simply as a protest against the shallow deductions of *would-be* unbelievers."—LYNCH'S *Expedition.*

"Yes, on that plain, by wild waves covered now,
Rose palace once, and sparkling pinnacle;
On pomp and spectacle beamed morning's glow,
On pomp and festival the twilight fell.

"Lovely and splendid all—but Sodom's soul
Was stained with blood, and pride, and perjury;
Long warned, long spared, till her whole heart was foul,
And fiery vengeance on its clouds came nigh.

"And still she mocked, and danced, and taunting, spoke
Her sportive blasphemies against the Throne:
It came!—the thunder on her slumber broke—
God spake the word of wrath!—Her dream was done."

CROLY.

ENGEDI.

"And David went up from thence, and dwelt in strongholds at Engedi."—1 SAMUEL xxiii. 29.

This locality has always, until recently, been sought at the north end of the Dead Sea; but Seetzen, a Russian traveller, having recognized the ancient name in the Ain-jidy of the Arabs, ascertained its true situation at a point of the western shore, nearly equidistánt from both extremities of the lake. It was here that David and his men lived among the "rocks of the wild goats," and where the former cut off the skirts of Saul's robe in a cave. 1 Sam. xxiv. 1–4.

"We had no question," writes Dr. Robinson, "that this spot is the ancient En-gedi. With this name the present 'Ain Jidy of the Arabs is identical, and like it also, signifies the 'Fountain of the Kid.' The more ancient Hebrew name was Hazazon-Tamar. As such it was first mentioned before the destruction of Sodom, as being inhabited by Amorites and near to the cities of the plain. Under the name En-gedi, it occurs as a city of Judah in the desert, giving its name to a part of the desert to which David withdrew for fear of Saul. At a later period, bands of the Moabites and Amorites came up against King Jehosaphat, apparently around the south end of the Dead Sea, as far as to En-gedi; by the very same route, it would seem, which is taken by the Arabs in their marauding expeditions at the present day, along the shore as far as to 'Ain Jidy, and then up the pass and so northwards below Tekoa. According to Josephus, En-gedi lay upon the lake Asphaltis, and was celebrated for beautiful palm-trees and opobalsam; while its vineyards are likewise mentioned in the Old Testament. From it towards Jerusalem there was an ascent 'by the cliff Ziz,' which seems to have been none other than the present pass. In the days of Eusebius and Jerome, En-gedi was still a large village on the shore of the Dead Sea."—*Bib. Res.*, vol. ii.

THE JORDAN.

"And Joshua . . . came to Jordan, he and all the children of Israel, and lodged there before they passed over."—JOSH. iii. 1.

"This celebrated stream, which, though it cannot boast, like other famous rivers, of splendid cities and marts of commerce on its banks, yet far surpasses them all in illustrious and hallowed associations, is probably little altered, since Joshua with the Israelites approached the fords or passages about two miles from its mouth. At that time, the sacred writer informs us, the river Jordan 'overflowed all its banks,' in the first month, or at the time of harvest. The original Hebrew expresses in these passages nothing more than that 'the Jordan was full (or filled) up to all its banks,' meaning the banks of its channel; it ran with full banks, or was brimfull.' . . .

"Thus understood, the Biblical account corresponds entirely to what we find to be the case at the present day. The Israelites crossed the Jordan four days before the Passover (Easter). . . . Then, as now, the harvest occurred during April and early in May, the barley preceding the wheat harvest by two or three weeks. Then, as now, there was a slight annual rise of the river, which caused it to flow at this season with full banks, and sometimes to spread its waters even over the immediate banks of its channel, where they are lowest, so as in some places to fill the low tract covered with trees and vegetables along its sides.

"The low bed of the river, and the absence of inundation and of tributary streams, combine to leave the greater portion of the Ghôr a solitary desert. Such it is described in antiquity, and such we find it at the present day. Josephus speaks of the Jordan as flowing 'through a desert;' and of this plain as in summer scorched by heat, insalubrious, and watered by no stream except the Jordan." Lieut. Lynch describes its banks as exhibiting "a bright line of verdure amid a cheerless waste."

"Such is the Jordan and its valley; that venerated stream celebrated on almost every page of the Old Testament as the border of the Promised Land, whose floods were miraculously 'driven back' to afford a passage for the Israelites. In the New Testament it is still more remarkable for the baptism of our Saviour; when the heavens were opened, and the Spirit of God descended upon him, and, lo, a voice from Heaven, saying, 'This is my beloved Son!' We now stood upon its shores, and had bathed in its waters, and felt ourselves surrounded by hallowed associations. The exact places of these and other events connected with this part of Jordan, it is vain to seek after; nor is this necessary, in order to awaken and fully to enjoy all the emotions which the region around is adapted to inspire."—ROBINSON'S *Bib. Res.*

CHAPTER X.

TOPOGRAPHICAL ACCURACY OF THE INSPIRED WRITERS—CONTINUED.

Not the least interesting among the results of topographical discovery in the Holy Land is the identification of ancient

GIBEON.

"The high place at Gibeon."—1 Chron. xxi. 29.

This town, so celebrated in Old Testament History, seems to have derived its name from the natural locality of its site, its meaning being the hill place or city. It is first mentioned in connection with the deception practised by the inhabitants upon Joshua, by which, although belonging to the accursed race of the Canaanites, they induced the Jewish leader not only to make a league with them, and to spare their lives and cities, but also in their defence to make war upon the five kings by whom they were besieged. It was in the great battle that followed, that the sun stood still upon Gibeon. (Joshua x. 12–14.) See also Joshua xi. 19, xviii. 25, xxi. 17; 2 Sam. ii. 12–23, iii. 30, xx. 8–12; 1 Kings iii; Jer. xli. 12, etc.

"The situation of Gibeon has fortunately been recovered with as great certainty as any ancient site in Palestine. The traveller who pursues the northern camel-road from Jerusalem, turning to the left at Tuleil el-fûl (Gibeah), finds himself . . . in a district . . . where the hills are more isolated than those through which he has been passing. . . . Retaining its ancient name almost intact, El-Jîb stands on the northernmost of a couple of these hills, just at the place where the road to the sea parts into two branches. . . Its distance from Jerusalem by the main road is six and a half miles; but there is a more direct road reducing it to five miles."—SMITH'S *Biblical Dictionary*.

After the conquest by Joshua, says Dr. Robinson, "the place fell to the lot of Benjamin, and became a Levitical city, where the tabernacle was set up for many years under David and Solomon. The ark at this time was at Jerusalem. Here the latter youthful monarch offered a thousand burnt-offerings; and in a dream by night communed with God, and asked for himself a wise and understanding heart, instead of riches and honor. Here, too, it was that Abner's challenge to Joab terminated in the defeat and flight of the former, and the death of Asahel; and here, also, at a later period, Amasa was treacherously slain by Joab.

"The village of El-Jîb is situated upon an isolated oblong hill or ridge, which rises in a beautiful plain, bounded on the west and south by mountains.

"This hill is in some parts steep and difficult of access, and capable of being everywhere very strongly fortified. . . It may be said to stand in the midst of a basin, composed of broad valleys or plains, cultivated, and full of grain, vineyards, and orchards of olive and fig trees. It was decidedly the finest part of Palestine that I had yet seen. . .

"We reached the village of El-Jîb, situated on the summit of this hill. . . . It is of moderate size; . . . the houses stand very irregularly and unevenly, sometimes almost one above another. They seem to be chiefly rooms in old massive ruins, which have fallen down in every direction. One large massive building still remains, perhaps a former castle or tower of strength; . . . the whole appearance is that of antiquity. Towards the east the ridge sinks a little; and here, a few rods from the village, just below the top of the ridge, is a fine fountain of water. It is in a cave excavated in and under the high rock, so as to form a large subterranean reservoir. Not far below it, among the olive trees, are the remains of another open reservoir. . . . It was doubtless anciently intended to receive the superfluous waters of the cavern. At this time no stream was flowing from the latter. It is not difficult to recognize in El-Jîb and its rocky eminence the ancient Gibeon of the Scriptures; . . . (and) the 'Pool of Gibeon,' mentioned in the story of Abner, may well be the waters of the fountain described (above); and these are also probably 'the great' (or many) 'waters in Gibeon,' spoken of in Jeremiah xli. 12."—ROBINSON'S *Bib. Res.*, v. ii. pp. 135–8.

The ancient Gibeon "is situated on the top of a remarkably round hill, the sides of which are so completely terraced, not by art, but by nature, that they present the appearance of a flight of steps all round, from the top to the bottom. The buildings are mostly on the western brow of the hill, the rest of the summit being covered with fine olive trees. Many of the terraces are also set with vines and fruit trees. . . . The scene of Joshua's miracle was vividly set before us. The glorious sun was sloping westward, about to sink in the Mediterranean Sea, and his horizontal rays were falling full upon the hill of Gibeon; at the same time the moon was rising, and soon after poured her silver beams into the quiet vale (beneath). It was strangely interesting to look upon the scene where 'the Lord hearkened unto the voice of man.'"—*Narrative of Mission to the Jews*, pp. 201, 202.

Of the valley beneath Gibeon, the traveller Carne writes that it "is of sufficient breadth and compass to allow of a numerous host engaging in its bosom, and presents as fine a field of battle as two armies could desire. The Amorites were probably surprised by Joshua, as they were encamped in this valley, and hemmed in by hills on each side; as it is said, 'he came suddenly upon them;' and after a bloody combat, they fled along the valley, whose enclosed space afforded great advantage to the pursuers, as it appeared to be from twelve to fifteen miles in length. On the summit of a lofty hill, in the bosom of the valley, Gibeon is supposed to have stood, as there is a hamlet of the name of El-Jib still standing on the site; and this site agrees with the description given. The peculiar and bold aspect of this memorable valley must have greatly aided the effect of the miracle. The high hill of Gibeon, towards the west, overlooked the whole region; and the royal city on its summit, just before besieged by the confederate kings, was the meed for which both armies fought—the one to save, the other to destroy. It may be inferred that the day was waning on the slaughter of the vanquished, who fled along the valley to the opposite extremity to which their conqueror had entered; and while the declining rays were thrown redly on the lofty hill and the city that crowned it, Joshua uttered the command: Sun, stand thou still on Gibeon, and thou, moon, in the valley of Ajalon. It would seem, too, that the destroying storm from on high fell not on the flying Amorites, until, issuing from the valley, they descended on the wide plain beyond. Here, scattering themselves on every side, they could more easily avoid the pursuer's sword, from whose edge the greater part would have escaped, but that they fell by a Divine arrest.

In what manner the sword of Israel was seconded by the artillery of Heaven, whether by a hail storm of uncommon fierceness or by the falling of the bodies called aërolites, it is impossible to determine. The effects were the same in the destruction of the Canaanites, and on either supposition we must recognize the finger of God, since the timing of the tempest to that end, and its not touching the Israelites, sufficiently indicated a supernatural interposition. That hailstones have descended of force enough to destroy life, is proved by the account of one of the plagues of Egypt having been a storm of that description, and is confirmed by other historians. Thus Albertus Aquensis relates that Baldwin I. and his army, when in the vicinity of the Dead Sea, "suffered incredibly from horrid hail, and other atmospheric influences, so that many lives were lost."

The other miracle wrought upon this memorable occasion has been a fruitful source of cavil to the sceptic and unbeliever. The objection drawn from its want of scientific accuracy of statement—that it seems to represent the sun as moving round the earth instead of the earth moving round the sun—is readily met by the answer that the language used is adapted to the appearance, not the reality of things. But a more serious objection to the narrative is the derangement which the alleged occurrence must have occasioned. The course of nature would have been generally interrupted. Such a sudden check to the earth's motion would have been, by means of the atmosphere, to crush at once all animal and vegetable existence—to level with the ground the loftiest and most massive structures, and, in fact, to sweep the whole surface of the globe as with the besom of destruction. To this perhaps it were sufficient to reply that He who was able to work so great a miracle was also able to counteract any evil consequences that might result from it. But another explanation has been suggested which, without resorting to such an interference, entirely obviates the difficulty. The expression rendered in our English version "the midst of heaven," may be rendered the *division of heaven*, or the visible horizon. Also the word rendered *sun* may be rendered *solar* light. The account admits, therefore, of being read thus: The solar light lingered on the horizon, and hastened not to go down about a whole day. Now it is well known that through the operation of the laws of refraction and reflection, the sun's disc is ordinarily seen above the horizon some time after he has really sunk below it. Without, therefore, the progress of nature having been either delayed or accelerated, it is evident that Almighty power could on this memorable occasion have so altered the medium through which the sun's rays passed, as to render it visible above the horizon longer after it would, under ordinary circumstances, have disappeared. This, to the apprehension of the Israelites, would have had all the visible effects of staying the career of the sun; and to ours that of arresting the earth's revolution on its axis; and this is all that the sacred text requires, while it satisfies all the conditions of the miracle.

MIZPEH.

"And Samuel said, Gather all Israel to Mizpeh."—1 Sam. vii. 5.

Mizpeh of Benjamin is probably to be found at the spot now called Neby Samwîl, or the Tomb of Samuel, at which tradition (but without sufficient reason) asserts that the prophet was buried.

The name Mizpeh, which signifies "a place of look-out—a watch tower," implies that it was situated on an elevated spot. Neby Samwîl is on a conspicuous height, and is visible from Jerusalem and many other parts. Traces of an ancient town are visible upon it.

"We now had before us the elevated ridge of Neby Samwîl. Our way led us directly to the summit, up the steep but not difficult ascent of the northwestern side. The top is crowned by a small miserable village and a neglected mosque. The mosque is here the principal object; it is now in a state of great decay. There are few houses now inhabited, but many traces of former dwellings. In some parts the rock, which is soft, has been hewn away for several feet in height, so as to form the walls of houses:

two or three reservoirs are, in like manner, hewn in the rock. These cuttings and levellings extend over a considerable space. The view from the roof of the mosque is very commanding in every direction; the deep Wady Beît Henîna, Jerusalem, the Mount of Olives, the Frank Mountain, and a large portion of the eastern slope, with the mountains beyond the Jordan and the Dead Sea. In the northwest the fertile plain of Gibeon lies immediately below; and farther on the eye embraces a large extent of the great lower plain along the coast, as well as of the Mediterranean itself. In a clear day Jaffa may be distinctly seen. A large number of villages were visible on every side."—ROBINSON'S *Res.*, vol. i. pp. 139, 140.

"The hill on which the village and mosque of Neby Samwîl now stand is not only the most conspicuous object round El-Jîb, but also in the surrounding country. It rises abruptly to a height of 500 or 600 feet above the little plain of Gibeon; and its sides, though here and there broken by cliffs, are almost everywhere cultivated in terraces, along which the fig and the vine grow luxuriantly . . . From the summit we gain a wider view than from any other peak in southern Palestine."—PORTER'S *Hand Book*, p. 225.

The best and latest investigators now unite in attesting that here was the ancient Mizpeh, a famous city of Benjamin, where the tribes often assembled; where Samuel offered sacrifice and judged the people; where Saul was chosen king by lot; and where, under the Chaldeans, Gedaliah the governor resided and was assassinated. "Of all the points of interest about Jerusalem," says Stanley, "none perhaps gains so much from an actual visit to Palestine as the lofty peaked eminence which fills up the northwest corner of the table land; seen in every direction, the highest elevation in the whole country south of Hermon, commanding a view far wider than that of Olivet, inasmuch as it includes the western plain and Mediterranean Sea on one side, as well as Olivet and Jerusalem in the distance backed by the range of Moab. It is in fact the point from which travellers mounting by the ancient route through the pass of Beth-horen obtained their earliest view of the interior of the hills of Palestine. 'It is a very fair and delicious place,' says Mandeville, 'and it is called Mount Joy, because it gives joy to pilgrims' hearts; for from that place men first see Jerusalem.'" Canon Stanley also identifies this locality with Mizpeh.

SHILOH.

"Go ye now to my place which was in Shiloh, where I set my name at the first, and see what I did to it for the wickedness of my people Israel." —JER. vii. 12.

The site of this most interesting locality was entirely unknown until its discovery by Dr. Robinson, A. D. 1848. An old tradition had placed it at Neby Samwil, in quite a different district of the country, though the slightest reference to the statement of Scripture regarding its actual position would have shown it to be untenable.

"A prominent object of our inquiries in this region (Dr. Robinson was travelling from Jerusalem to Sichem, and was now about half way between Bethel and the latter place) was the ancient Shiloh, celebrated in the history of the Israelites as the place where the ark remained from the time of Joshua to Solomon. Our guide yesterday spoke of a ruin called Seilûn; of which there was a saying among the people that, were the Franks to visit it, they would deem it of such importance that they would not go away in less than a day. On inquiring farther, we found that the place in question lay not very far from the road, and might be visited by a small circuit. As the position seemed to answer well to that of Shiloh, we determined to go thither. . . . The ruins of Seilûn are surrounded by hills, but looking out through a small valley towards a beautiful plain . . .

The position is in itself a fine one for strength, if it were ever fortified, though it is commanded by the neighboring hills. Among the ruins of modern houses are many large stones and some fragments of columns, showing the place to have been an ancient site. Our guide told us of a fountain up through the narrow valley towards the east. We went thither, and found that the valley here breaks through a ridge, and is at first shut in by perpendicular walls of rock; then follows a more open tract; and here, at the left, fifteen minutes from Seilûn, is the fountain. The water is excellent, and issues from the rocks first into a sort of artificial well, eight or ten feet deep, and thence into a reservoir lower down. Many flocks and herds were waiting round about. In the sides of the narrow valley are many excavated tombs, now much broken away; near the fountain are also several.

"The position of Shiloh is very definitely described in the Book of Judges as 'on the north side of Bethel, on the east side of the highway that goeth up from Bethel to Shechem, and on the south of Lebonah.' (Judges xxi. 19–23.) These circumstances correspond exactly to Seilûn; for we were on the east of the great road between Bethel and Shechem; and in passing on towards the latter place we came, after an hour, to the village of Lebonah, now El-Lubban. Here, then, was Shiloh, where the tabernacle was set up after the country had been subdued before the Israelites; and where the last and general division of the land was made among the tribes. The ark and tabernacle long continued here from the days of Joshua, during the ministry of all the judges, until the close of Eli's life; and here Samuel was dedicated to God, and his childhood spent in the sanctuary. In honor of the presence of the ark there was 'a feast of the Lord in Shiloh yearly, during which the daughters of Shiloh came out to dance in dances; and it was on such an occasion that they were seized and carried.

off by the remaining Benjamites as wives. The scene of these dances may not improbably have been somewhere around the fountain above described. From Shiloh the ark was at length removed to the army of Israel; and being captured by the Philistines, returned no more to its former place. Shiloh henceforth, though sometimes the residence of prophets, as of Ahijah, celebrated in the history of Jeroboam, is nevertheless spoken of as forsaken and accursed of God. It is mentioned in Scripture during the exile, but not afterwards; and Jerome speaks of it in his day as so utterly in ruins, that the foundations of an altar could scarcely be pointed out."—*Biblical Researches.*

"Shiloh is so utterly featureless, that, had it not been for the preservation of its name (Seilûn), and for the extreme precision with which its situation is described in the Book of Judges, the spot could never have been identified; and, indeed, from the time of Jerome till the year 1838, its real site was completely forgotten, and its name was transferred to that commanding height of Gibeon, which a later age naturally conceived to be a more congenial spot for the sacred place, where for so many centuries was the tent which He had pitched among men,—

'Our living Dread, who dwells
In Silo, his bright Sanctuary.'

Its ruins were scattered over a slight eminence which rises in one of those softer and wider plains before noticed as characteristic of this part of Palestine, a little removed from the great central route of the country."—STANLEY'S *Sinai and Palestine.*

SHECHEM.

"And Abram passed through the land unto the place of Sichem."—GEN. xii. 6.

This celebrated locality is distant from Jerusalem between thirty and forty miles, about ten from Shiloh and seven from the city of Samaria. Its present name is Nâblus, a corruption of the word Neapolis, or new town, the Greek name given it by the Romans, and this is one of the rare instances in which the ancient Oriental appellation has been superseded in popular language by a more modern one. It is believed that the present town occupies the site of the ancient one, but is probably of more contracted dimensions. The sacred associations of Shechem are co-extensive with the history of the entire Church, as recorded both in the Old and in the New Testaments. Here Abraham first halted when he had crossed the Jordan on his way from Chaldæa to the land which God should give him, and here God distinctly told him that this was the country destined to be the sure possession of his descendants. It was afterwards the scene of many memorable events in the history of Israel. And here at last came One, whose "day Abraham saw afar off and was glad," and who was himself "the way" to the everlasting rest prepared for the people of God, of which the earthly Canaan was but the type.

At the entrance of the narrow pass which leads to Shechem, stand the two mounts known as the mounts respectively of the curses and of the blessings, Mount Ebai and Mount Gerizim. "It was here the affecting ceremony took place which was commanded by Moses, carried into effect by Joshua, and never afterwards repeated. Six of the tribes stood over against Gerizim to bless the people, and the other six upon Ebal to curse. It would appear that the whole of the law was read over by Joshua, and that the Levites spoke unto all the men of Israel with a loud voice the words of the curse, to which the people answered and said Amen. A better situation could not be conceived for this purpose, as the hills are at such a distance from each other, that the hosts of Israel might stand between, and the voice from either side be heard distinctly on a calm day throughout the whole assembly. It must have been an imposing spectacle: the ark of the covenant in the centre, surrounded by the elders, officers, and judges, with the venerable Joshua at their head; the banners of the tribes marking their different positions, as appointed by God, which they were now to occupy for the last time, and the millions of Israel extending in firm phalanx as far as the eye could reach; it must also be remembered that every individual of that vast company had but a little time before beheld the most striking wonders performed in their own behalf, the falling down of the walls of Jericho, and the dividing of the stream of the Jordan,—and when the men, women, children, and strangers, thinking on these things, with one voice shouted Amen, the acclaim must have reverberated among the rocks around with true sublimity, and have swelled in majestic volumes towards heaven. . . . .

"The hills are of equal height, about 800 feet above the plain, and are neither of them cultivated, but Gerizim has the more pleasing appearance."—HARDY'S *Notices of the Holy Land.*

Between these mountains, in its hallowed seclusion lies the spot which links together the sacred history of more than three thousand years, but which is specially memorable from the fact that here took place the first recognition of the Son of God, as not only the Jewish Messiah, the Christ, but the Desire of all nations, the Saviour of the world. The whole valley is still remarkable for its beauty, and excites the admiration of travellers. It abounds in rich gardens, delightful groves, stately trees, and fragrant bowers. "One could fancy," says an elegant writer, "that the powers of life in nature had been unfettered here ever since, in virtue of that acknowledgment; and that the valley of Sychar (Shechem) was ever after to be a fragment and foretaste of paradise,—a place of streams and rest, full of all manner of trees pleasant to the eyes, and good for food, a little spot of earth visibly subject to the life-giving sceptre of the 'second Man,' the Lord from Heaven. No place to be compared with this in fertility and beauty exists, it is said, in Palestine."

"We inquired of the Samaritans respecting Jacob's Well. They said they acknowledged the tradition, and regarded it as having belonged to the patriarch. It lies at the mouth of the valley, near the south side, and is the same which the Christians sometimes call 'Well of the Samaritan woman." They acknowledge, also, the tomb near by as the place of Joseph's burial; though the present building is only a Mohammedan tomb. Late as it was, we took a Christian guide and set off for Jacob's Well. . . . . The well bears evident marks of antiquity, but was now dry and deserted; it was said usually to contain living water, and not merely to be filled by the rains. A large stone was laid loosely over, or rather in its mouth; and as the hour was now late, and the twilight nearly gone, we made no attempt to remove the stone and examine the vaulted entrance below. We had also no line with us, at the moment, to measure the well; but by dropping in stones we could perceive that it was *deep*. . . .

. . . . "I think we may rest with confidence in the opinion that this is Jacob's Well, and here the parcel of ground which Jacob gave to his son Joseph. Here the Saviour, wearied with his journey, sat upon the well, and taught the poor Samaritan woman those great truths which have broken down the separating wall between Jews and Gentiles: 'God is a spirit, and they that worship him must worship him in spirit and in truth.' Here, too, as the people flocked from the city to hear him, He pointed his disciples to the waving fields which decked the noble plain around, exclaiming, 'Say not ye, there are yet four months, and then cometh harvest? behold I say unto you, Lift up your eyes, and look on the fields; for they are white already to the harvest."—ROBINSON'S *Bib. Res.*

"About a hundred yards off (from the well) is Joseph's Tomb. Whether by accident or design, a luxuriant vine had made its way over the wall that encloses the tomb, and was now waving its branches from the top, as if to recall to mind the prophetical description of this favored tribe, 'Joseph is a fruitful bough, even a fruitful bough by a well, whose branches run over the wall.' The beautiful field around it is, no doubt, the parcel of ground that Jacob gave to his son Joseph, taking it out of the hand of the Amorite with his sword and with his bow."—WILSON'S *Lands of the Bible.*

SAMARIA.

"And (Omri) bought the hill Samaria ot Shemer for two talents of silver, and built on the hill, and called the name of the city which he built, after the name of Shemer, owner of the hill, Samaria. . . .

"And Ahab the son of Omri reigned over Israel, in Samaria, twenty and two years."—1 KINGS xvi. 24, 29.

The above Scripture statement respecting the origin of Samaria has received a remarkable confirmation by a discovery of Mr. Layard. In exploring the ruins of Nineveh, he met with a tablet on which the city was named Beth Khumri or Omri. As he was the builder of the city, it was in accordance with Eastern custom that it should be called after its founder. The presence of such a tablet at Nineveh is accounted for by the fact that the Assyrians destroyed Samaria after a siege of three years, and carried its inhabitants into captivity. (2 Kings xvii. 5).

Samaria became the capital of the ten revolted tribes. "It had the winter house, and the summer house, and the houses of ivory. The wicked Ahab erected on this hill an altar to Baal; in this plain Benhadad, king of Assyria, was routed; in the gate of this city sat the king of Israel and the king of Judah, each in his robes, and upon a throne, when the false prophets delivered their ambiguous prediction, and Micaiah declared the word of the Lord; in that pool the dogs licked the blood of Ahab, as they had formerly licked the blood of Naboth his victim; up that ascent have often toiled the prophets Elijah and Elisha, bearing messages of wrath from the Most High; within these walls there has been a great famine, so that 'an ass's head sold for four score pieces of silver, and a woman boiled her own son and did eat him'; it was from hence that the host of the Syrians fled, because the Lord made them to hear a noise of chariots and a noise of horses, leaving their camp, as it was, a prey to the famished Samaritans; it was here that Jehu slew the worshippers of Baal, and brake down their images; it was after enduring a siege of three years in this capital that Hoshea, the last of its kings, was carried away captive by the king of Assyria; it contained the royal sepulchre of Israel; the Gospel was here preached by Philip, and confirmed by Peter and John, to whom Simon, the sorcerer, offered money, that he might receive the Holy Ghost; and it suffered in common with its more guilty rival, when Palestine was subdued by the Roman power."—HARDY'S *Notices of the Holy Land.*

Dr. Keith, after visiting Samaria, writes: "Few seats of royalty can rival its princely site. Its local position is most peculiar, of a finely varied and oblong form. The isolated hill of Samaria, with a flattened summit, seems as if it had been raised by nature at 'the head of the fat valley,' to be at once a stronghold and royal seat. But now Samaria is become 'as an heap of the field, and as plantings of a vineyard.' Stones abound in the mountainous regions of Israel; and it is evident that in their terraced vineyards the stones have been gathered out of the level spaces which are occupied only by the soil, and when freed from them were fitted for planting. In some fields in the valleys, the stones have been gathered up, and have been cast into heaps which thus form literally 'heaps of the field.' Samaria, it is recorded, was utterly demolished after its first siege, and must then have formed a great mass of ruins. Herod rebuilt it, and it has again been laid low and reduced to be as an heap of the field. The stones, which yet lie on its surface, bereaved of the glory that might seem to hover around a *ruin*, however defaced, have been gathered singly, and cast into heaps, as if they were heaps of a field, and not the remains of a capital. The ground has been cleared of them to form the gardens or patches of cultivated ground possessed by the inhabitants of the wretched village, which stands on the extremity of the site of the ancient city. The stones, as if in a field or vineyard, have manifestly been gathered up in heaps, to prepare the ground for being sown or planted. Lines of columns now stand in a *field* which was covered when we saw it with a crop of ripe barley, that was overtopped in various places with sixteen heaps of stones within the space enclosed by the ancient colonnade. The foundations of buildings remain in some places, in long lines, low as when they first were laid; and the beasts of the field browse among the trees in the bottom of the valley and hills, and pasture upon the terraces, where once were vineyards, but where now, after much searching, the leaf of a *wild* vine only was found."—*Incidents of Travel*, vol. ii. p. 301.

"The vast temple of Baal was there erected, which Jehu destroyed; and in later times, Herod chose it alone out of the ancient capitals of the north, to adorn with the name and with the temple of Augustus, from which time it assumed the appellation which with a slight change it has borne ever since, 'Sebaste.' And now, although its existence has but been brought fully to light within the last few years, it is the only site in western Palestine, besides Jerusalem, which exhibits relics of ancient architectural beauty. A long avenue of broken pillars, apparently the main street of Herod's city, here, as at Palmyra and Damascus, adorned by a colonnade on each side, still lines the topmost terrace of the hill. The Gothic ruin of the church of St. John the Baptist, parent of the numerous churches which bear his name throughout the West, remains over what Christians and the Mussulman inhabitants still revere as the grave 'of the Prophet John, son of Zacharias,' round which in the days of Jerome the same wild orgies were performed which are now to be seen round 'the Holy Sepulchre.' "—STANLEY'S *Sinai and Palestine.*

"The prophecy concerning Samaria is most distinct, and its fulfilment has been exact. I wish an infidel could have stood with me and compared the present state of Samaria, even in minute particulars, with the prophecy of Micah, which I read on the spot. Though Israel's monarchs there swayed the sceptre—though there Herod reigned and revelled—though pomp and splendor and the glory of this world there shone and dazzled the thousands of Israel—yet, Samaria is a desolation. The sceptres are broken—the revel is hushed—the splendor has faded. Samaria is as an heap in the field, and as the plantings of a vineyard; her stones have been literally poured down into the valley—her foundations have been indeed discovered—and there they now lie; while from every heap and from every fragment there goes forth as it were a testimony which cannot be silenced, to the righteous severity of an angry God."—FISK'S *Pastor's Memorial.*

DOTHAN.

"And Joseph went after his brethren, and found them in Dothan."—GEN. xxxvii. 17.

About twelve miles north of Samaria, one of the most interesting scenes in Old Testament history has recently been discovered. "A few years ago, M. Van de Velde, when passing through the plain of Jenin, had his attention arrested by a singular looking *tell* (height), rising up like an island near the margin of the level ground, and evidently covered with ruins. 'What place is that?' said he to the sheikh who was at that time his guide. *Haida-Dothan*—'That is Dothan,' was his immediate and unhesitating reply. 'Dothan'? said Van de Velde, in an inquiring tone, to make sure that he had not mistaken the sheikh's answer. *Nahm, Dothan—Dothan—Dothan*—'Yes, Dothan,' was his reply, repeating the word three times over, and evidently piqued at what he supposed to be a doubting of his word. This important fact of the still surviving name, when put alongside also of the testimony of Eusebius and Jerome, may be considered as having conclusively settled the point of its identification. It is certain that the Dothan of Scripture stood on an isolated height. The following facts plainly prove this: When Benhadad sent a military force to seize Elisha in Dothan, they 'came by night, and compassed the city *round about*.' In the morning, when the prophet's servant looked down from his master's place of refuge, and saw that they were hemmed in on every side, he was filled with terror. To relieve his fear, the Lord, at the request of the prophet, opened the servant's eyes, and showed him the multitudes of the heavenly host by whom they were defended; in describing whom the sacred historian says that 'the *mountain* (or *mount*) was full of horses of fire and chariots of fire round about Elisha.' The whole Scripture statement conveys just such an idea of the position of Dothan, as answers most exactly to the isolated eminence to which Abû Monsûr, the guide of Van de Velde, gave that name. Further still, the Scripture Dothan must have stood near the leading thoroughfare by which the Ishmaelite merchants of the East were wont to cross the land of Canaan on their way to Egypt.

It was to a caravan of these merchants that Joseph was sold by his envious brethren. They had cast him into a pit or dry well at Dothan, intending apparently to leave him to die there, when 'they lifted up their eyes and looked, and behold a company of Ishmaelites came from Gilead with their camels bearing spicery, and balm, and myrrh, going to carry it down to Egypt.' (Gen. xxxvii. 25). Now, this *tell* of Van de Velde is in just such a position. The camel road in the direct line from the country of Gilead, that leads across the country to the plain of Sharon, and so southward along the seacoast to Egypt, passes to this day within a few hundred yards of the place."—BUCHANAN'S *Clerical Furlough.*

MOUNT CARMEL.

"The excellency of Carmel."—ISAIAH xxxv. 2.
"The top of Carmel shall wither."—AMOS i. 2.

The word Carmel is derived from a verb signifying to be noble, and answers to the English word "park." It was used to indicate a fruitful field, or a well wooded country, in contradistinction to a wilderness or forest land. There are two places of this name mentioned in Scripture, which should be carefully borne in mind to prevent a confusion of ideas in reading the Old Testament. "That long line of hills," says a modern traveller, describing his entrance into Canaan from the south, "was the beginning of the hill country of Judea; and when we began to ascend, the first answer to our inquiries about the route told that it was Carmel; not the more famous mountain of that name, but that on which Nabal fed his flocks." Carmel is, indeed, mentioned in the Bible in connection with the conquest and division of Canaan by Joshua. But it is in the reigns of David and Ahab, kings of Israel, that the name

"Carmel" becomes associated with instructive events of sacred history.

The northern Carmel, or that of Ahab and Elijah, was the boundary of the possessions of the tribe of Asher westward, and forms one of the most remarkable headlands on the whole coast of the Mediterranean. "It is no place," writes Mr. Carne, "for crags and precipices, or rocks of the wild goats; it is the finest and most beautiful mountain in Palestine—in many parts covered with trees and flowers." To its woods were compared, by Solomon, the glossy tresses of his bride's head. Its rich garniture is regarded by Isaiah as the type of natural beauty; and the withering of its fruits is considered by him and other prophets as the type of national desolation. It is not so much a mountain as an upland park. It extends from the sea many miles into the interior of the country. On the top of the part close to the sea is now a convent of barefooted monks, deriving their distinctive name from the locality, and celebrated throughout Europe as the Carmelite monks. Below, towards the sea, i. e., in the cliffs that front the water, are caverns, many in number and curiously constructed. These, it is supposed, were the hiding places of the prophets of the true God when persecuted by the idolatrous Jezebel. The remarkable adaptation of these caverns, close to the sea, for the purpose of concealment, is confirmed by Amos, when he says that even *their* intricate and dark recesses could not conceal the wicked from the eye of the Omniscient One: "Though they hide themselves in the top of Carmel, I will search and take them out thence; and though they be hid from my sight in the bottom of the sea, thence will I command the serpent, and he shall bite them."

The excellency of Carmel has passed away, and the prophet's curse has fallen upon it; the top of Carmel has withered. Its steep sides are often barren and desolate, while wild vines and olives (showing that it had formerly been cultivated), met with among the brambles, together with oaks and cedars, attest its former luxuriance.

Lamartine thus describes a storm on Mount Carmel: "I have witnessed few so terrible. The clouds rose perpendicularly, like towers above Mount Carmel, and soon covered all the length of the summit of this chain of hills. The mountain just now so brilliant and serene, was plunged by degrees in rolling waves of darkness, split here and there by trains of fire. The horizon seemed to close around us,—the thunder did not burst in claps—it threw out one single majestic rolling, continual and deafening. The lightning might be truly said to rush like torrents of fire from the heavens, on the black flanks of Carmel. The oaks on the mount and on the hill on which we were journeying, bent like young plants. The winds which rushed from the caverns, and from between the hills, must have swept us from our horses, if we had not speedily alighted, and found a little shelter behind a fragment of rock in the then dry bed of a torrent. The withered leaves, upraised in masses by the storm, were carried above our heads like clouds, and the slender, broken branches of the trees showered around us. I remembered the Bible and the prodigies of Elijah. . . . The storm abated in about half an hour. We continued our route along the foot of Mount Carmel, which we traced in this way, during a march of about four hours. It presented everywhere the same severe and solemn aspect. It is a gigantic rock, rising almost perpendicularly, and everywhere covered by a bed of shrubs and odoriferous herbs. The rock is seldom entirely naked."
"In Leviticus xxvi. 22, we read that wild beasts were to be sent amongst the people of that land for their iniquities; even that has a present accomplishment. The monks of Mount Carmel reported that in consequence of the disarming of the people, and the great decrease of their numbers,

wild beasts were increasing on Mount Carmel to an alarming degree."—*Travels*, pp. 255, 358.

"From this we descended into a valley, passed over a plain, and after that again ascended another valley, all belonging to the finest parts of Carmel. At every step the ancient glory of Carmel now became more and more evident to me. What a memorable morning in this wild flower garden! It was at the most inviting season, too, for it was spring. The verdure is now fresh and vivid; the vertical sun of summer has not yet scorched it. The hawthorn, the jasmin, and many another tree and shrub, whose sweetly odorous and elegant bunches of blossom are unknown to me by name, are now in flower. Now it is that the fir tree exhales its resinous particles most powerfully; the oak, the myrtle, and the laurel have tempered their dark winter green with glittering leaflets of a lighter hue. And what a variety of sorts of flowers are trodden upon by the traveller on his way! There is not one that I have seen in Galilee, or on the plains along the coast, that I do not find here again on Carmel, from the crocuses on the rocky grounds to the fennel plants and narcissuses of the Leontes; from the intense red, white, and purple anemones of the plains to the ferns that hide themselves in the dark sepulchral caves. Yes; Carmel, indeed, is still Carmel; the fruitful, the graceful, the fragrant, the lovely mountain that he was in the days of old. But his glory, his attire, is hidden, is 'withered,' according to God's word, so that the traveller along the common highways beholds it not."—VAN DE VELDE'S *Syria and Palestine*, vol. i. p. 347.

It is at the eastern extremity of Carmel that we are to look for the scene of its grand and lasting associations. Its summit there commands the last view of the sea behind, and the first view of the great plain of Esdraelon in front. This spot is, to this day, called in Arabic language, the *burning*, or the *sacrifice*. The tradition which thus points it out as the place of the sacrifice of Elijah, is corroborated by the fact that the localities adapt themselves to the event in every particular. "There, on the highest ridge of the mountain, may well have stood," says Mr. Stanley, "on its sacred 'high place,' the altar of the Lord which Jezebel had cast down. Close beneath, on a wide upland sweep, under the shade of ancient olives, and round a well of water, said to be perennial, and which may therefore have escaped the general drought, and have been able to furnish water for the trenches round the altar, must have been ranged, on one side the king and people, with the eight hundred and fifty prophets of Baal and Astarte, and on the other side the solitary and commanding figure of the Prophet of the Lord. Full before them opened the whole plain of Esdraelon, with Tabor and its kindred ranges in the distance; on the rising ground, at the opening of its valley, the city of Jezreel, with Ahab's palace and Jezebel's temple distinctly visible; in the nearer foreground, immediately under the base of the mountain, was clearly seen the winding stream of the Kishon, working its way through the narrow pass of the hills into the bay of Acre. Such a scene, with such recollections of the past, with such sights of the present, was indeed a fitting theatre for a conflict more momentous than any which their ancestors had fought in the plain below. This is not the place to enlarge upon the intense solemnity and significance of that conflict which lasted on the mountain height from morning till noon, from noon till the time of the evening sacrifice. It ended at last in the level plain below, where Elijah brought the defeated prophets 'down' the steep sides of the mountain 'to the "torrent" of the Kishon, and slew them there.'

"The closing scene still remains. From the slaughter by the side of the Kishon, the king 'went up' at Elijah's bidding once again to the peaceful glades of Carmel, to join in the sacrificial feast. And Elijah, too, ascended to 'the top of the mountain,' and there, with his face upon the earth, remained wrapt in prayer, whilst his servant mounted to the highest point of all, whence there is a wide view of the blue reach of the Mediterranean Sea, over the Western shoulder of the ridge. The sun was now gone down, but the cloudless sky was lit up with the long bright glow which succeeds an Eastern sunset. Seven times the servant climbed and looked, and seven times there was nothing; the sky was still clear, the sea was still calm. At last, out of the far horizon there rose a little cloud—the first that had for days and months passed across the heavens—and it grew in the deepening shades of evening, and at last the whole sky was overcast, and the forests of Carmel shook in the welcome sound of those mighty winds which in Eastern regions precede a coming tempest. Each from his separate height, the king and the prophet descended. And the king mounted his chariot at the foot of the mountain, lest the long-hoped-for rain should swell the torrent of the Kishon, as in the days when it swept away the host of Sisera; and 'the hand of the Lord was upon Elijah,' and he girt his mantle round his loins, and, amidst the rushing storm with which the night closed in, 'ran before the chariot,' as the Bedouins of his native Gilead still run, with inexhaustible strength, to the entrance of Jezreel, distant, though still visible, from the scene of his triumph—the top of Carmel."—STANLEY'S *Sinai and Palestine*, pp. 354–356.

JEZREEL.

"And Ahab rode, and went to Jezreel."—1 KINGS xviii. 45.

The city to which Ahab rode from Carmel, attended by Elijah, was his favorite residence and the chief seat of his dynasty for three successive reigns. It has been identified with the modern Zer'in, which is a mere collection of hovels; but though its splendor has vanished, enough remains in its natural features to illustrate the most striking incidents in the scenes in which it appears in the Sacred History, of the overthrow of the house of Ahab.

"Our grand object to-day was the position of the ancient Jezreel. . . . Setting out from Jenin (at a quarter to five in the morning) we struck out upon the noble plain . . . towards the western extremity of the mountains of Gilboa. . . . At seven o'clock we reached Zer'în. . . . As we approached (it) there was only a very gentle rise of the surface, like a low swell; and it was therefore unexpected to us, on reaching Zer'în, to find it standing upon the brow of a very steep rocky descent, of one hundred feet or more towards the northeast, where the land sinks off at once into a great fertile valley, running down along the northern wall of the mountains of Gilboa. This valley is itself a broad deep plain . . . enclosed between the ranges of Gilboa and little Hermon, (and) about an hour in breadth; and below Zer'în continues down quite to the plain of the Jordan at Bethshan. We could see the acropolis of Bethshan lying much lower than Zer'în.

"In the valley directly under Zer'în is a considerable fountain; and twenty minutes further east another larger one, under the northern side of Gilboa, called 'Ain Jâlûd. Zer'in itself thus lies comparatively high, and commands a wide and noble view; extending down the broad low valley on the east to Beisân, and to the mountains beyond the Jordan; while towards the west it includes the whole great plain quite to the long ridge of Carmel. It is a most magnificent site for a city; which, being itself such a conspicuous object in every part, would naturally give its name to the whole region. There could, therefore, be little question that we had before and around us the city, the plain, the valley, and the fountain of the ancient Jezreel.[1]

[1] *Valley* of Jezreel, Josh. xvii. 16; Judges vi. 33; Hos. i. 5. *Fountain* at Jezreel, 1 Sam. xxix. 1.

"Jezreel is first mentioned as belonging to the tribe of Issachar; and it constituted afterwards a part of the kingdom of Ishbosheth. It became more notorious under Ahab and Jezebel, who, though residing at Samaria, had a palace here; and it was to enlarge the grounds of this palace that the king desired the vineyard of Naboth, and gave occasion for the sad story of the latter.

"In the retributions of Divine Providence, the same place became the scene of the massacre of Jezebel herself, her son Joram, and all the house of Ahab, by the hand of Jehu."—ROBINSON'S *Bib. Res.* vol. iii, p. 168.

It has already been noticed that the surrounding localities illustrate the sacred narrative of these awful scenes. "We see how up the valley from the Jordan, Jehu's troop might be seen advancing,—how in Naboth's 'field' the two sovereigns met the relentless soldier,—how, whilst Joram died on the spot, Ahaziah drove down the westward plain, towards the mountain-pass by the village of En-gannim (Jenin), but was overtaken in the ascent, and died of his wounds at Megiddo; how in the open place, which, as usual in Eastern towns, lay before the gates of Jezreel, the body of the queen was trampled under the hoofs of Jehu's horses; how the dogs gathered round it, as even to this day, in the wretched village now seated on the ruins of the once splendid city of Jezreel, they prowl on the mounds without the walls for the offal and carrion thrown out to them to consume."—STANLEY'S *Sinai and Palestine*, p. 342.

"The valley of Jezreel is celebrated in Scripture history for the remarkable victory of Gideon, and the last fatal overthrow of Saul. The Midianites, the Amalekites, and the children of the East had come over Jordan and pitched in the valley of Jezreel: and Gideon had gathered the Israelites of the northern tribes together, and encamped at the well of Harod, probably on Mount Gilboa; since the host of Midian was beneath him in the valley. Here Gideon went down to the host, and heard the dream; and then, with his three hundred men, attacked and miraculously routed the whole host of Midian. Against Saul, the Philistines came up and pitched in Shunem, and Saul and all Israel pitched in Gilboa; afterward the Philistines are said to be at Aphek, and the Israelites at a fountain in Jezreel, doubtless the present 'Ain Jâlûd. Forsaken of God, and in the depth of his despair, Saul now crossed over the ridge of the little Hermon to Endor, to consult the sorceress. The battle took place next day; 'the men of Israel fled from before the Philistines, and fell down slain in Mount Gilboa;' and Saul and his three sons were found among the dead. The Philistines cut off his head, stripped the dead body, and then fastened it to the wall of Beth-shan. Thus, in the language of David's pathetic elegy, 'The beauty of Israel was slain upon thy high places!' and hence the curse upon the scene of slaughter: 'Ye mountains of Gilboa, let there be no dew, neither rain upon you, nor fields of offering.'

"Leaving Jezreel at half-past seven, we descended to the fountain below the village, by a steep and rocky path. The water is copious and good. From here we proceeded down the valley twenty minutes to 'Ain Jâlûd, a very large fountain, flowing out from under a sort of cavern in the wall of conglomerate rock, which here forms the base of Gilboa. The water is excellent; and, issuing from crevices in the rocks, it spreads out at once into a fine limpid pool, in which great numbers of fish were sporting. From the reservoir, a stream sufficient to turn a mill flows off down the valley. There is every reason to regard this (or the other fountain below the town, as Dr. Wilson thinks) as the ancient fountain of Jezreel, where Saul and Jonathan pitched before their last fatal battle; and where, too, in the days of the crusades, Saladin and the Christians successively encamped."—ROBINSON'S *Bib. Res.* vol. iii, p. 173.

NAZARETH.

"And he came to *Nazareth*, where he had been brought up."—LUKE iv. 16.

This hallowed spot, in which the first thirty years of our Lord's earthly life were spent in tranquil seclusion, lies embosomed in a quiet valley among the hills of Galilee, about six miles north-west from Mount Tabor. "Fifteen gently rounded hills seem as if they had met to form an enclosure for this peaceful basin; they rise round it like the edge of a shell to guard it from intrusion. It is a rich and beautiful field in the midst of these green hills—abounding in gay flowers. . . . The expression of the old topographer, Quaresmius, was as happy as it was poetical: 'Nazareth is a rose, and like a rose has the same rounded form, enclosed by mountains as the flower by its leaves.'

"From the crest of the hills which thus screen it, especially from that called Nebi-Said, or Ismail, on the western side, is one of the most striking views in Palestine: Tabor, with its rounded dome on the south-east; Hermon's white top in the distant north; Carmel and the Mediterranean Sea to the west; a conjunction of those three famous mountains probably unique in the views of Palestine: and in the nearer prospect, the uplands in which Nazareth itself stands, its own circular basin around it. . . . On the south and south-east, lies the broad plain of Esdraelon, overhung by the broad pyramidal hill, which as the highest point of the Nazareth range, and thus the most conspicuous to travellers approaching from the plain, has received, though without any historical ground, the name of the 'Mount of Precipitation.' These are the natural features which for nearly thirty years met the almost daily view of Him who 'increased in wisdom and stature' within this beautiful seclusion. It is the seclusion which constitutes its peculiarity and its fitness for these scenes of the Gospel history. Unknown and unnamed in the Old Testament, Nazareth first appears as the retired abode of the humble carpenter. Its separation from the busy world may be the ground, as it certainly is an illustration, of the Evangelist's play on the word 'He shall be called a Nazarene.' Its wild character, high up in the Galilean hills, may account both for the roughness of its population, unable to appreciate their own Prophet, and for the evil reputation which it had acquired even in the neighboring villages, one of whose inhabitants, Nathanael of Cana, said: 'Can any good thing come out of Nazareth?' There, secured within the natural barrier of the hills, was passed that youth, of which the most remarkable characteristic is its absolute obscurity; and thence came the name of Nazarene, used of old by the Jews, and used still by Mussulmans, as the appellation of that despised sect which has now embraced the civilized world."—STANLEY'S *Sinai and Palestine*, p. 366.

"The sun was now fast declining; and . . . we hastened on; and at length, when it was nearly dark, having entered the streets of Nazareth, proceeded to the Latin Convent. . . .

"Nazareth is situated on the side, and extends nearly to the foot of a hill, which, though not very high, is rather steep and overhanging. . . . At the foot of the hill is a modest, simple plain, surrounded by low hills, reaching in length nearly a mile; in breadth, near the city, a hundred and fifty yards; but, further on, about four hundred yards. . . . Then follows a ravine, which gradually grows deeper and narrower, till, after walking about another mile, you find yourself in an immense chasm with steep rocks on either side, from whence you behold, as it were, beneath your feet and before you, the noble plain of Esdraelon. The situation of Nazareth is very romantic. The scenery around is of the kind in which one would imagine the Saviour of the world delighted to wander, and to withdraw himself when meditating on His great mission—deep and secluded dells, covered with a wild verdure—silent and solemn paths, where overhanging rocks shut out all intrusion. No one can walk round Nazareth without feeling thoughts like these enter his mind, while gazing often on many a sweet spot, traced perhaps by the Redeemer's footsteps, and embalmed by His prayers."—JOWETT'S *Researches*, pp. 154–156, 165.

. . . "I walked out alone to the top of the hill over Nazareth. . . . Here, quite unexpectedly, a glorious prospect opened on the view. The air was perfectly clear and serene, and I shall never forget the impression I received, as the scene burst suddenly upon me. There lay the magnificent plain of Esdraelon, . . . on the left was seen the round top of Tabor over the intervening hills, with portions of the little Hermon and Gilboa, and the opposite mountains of Samaria. . . . Then came the long line of Carmel. . . . In the west lay the Mediterranean, gleaming in the morning sun; . . . below, on the north, was spread out another of the beautiful plains of northern Palestine; . . . beyond it, long ridges rise one higher than another, until the mountains of Safed overtop them all, on which at that place is seen, 'a city set upon an hill.' Further towards the right is a sea of hills and mountains, backed by the higher ones beyond the Lake of Tiberias, and in the north-east by the majestic Hermon with its icy crown. Carmel here presented itself to great advantage, extending far out into the sea, and dipping his feet into the waters.

. . . "I remained for some hours upon this spot, lost in the contemplation of the wide prospect, and of the events connected with the scenes around. In the village below, the Saviour of the world had passed His childhood; and although we have few particulars of His life during those early years, yet there are certain features of nature which meet our eye now, just as they once met His. He must often have visited the fountain near which we had pitched our tent; his feet must frequently have wandered over the adjacent hills; and His eyes doubtless have gazed upon the splendid prospect from this very spot. Here the Prince of Peace looked down upon the great plain, where the din of battles so often had rolled, and the garments of the warrior been dyed in blood; and he looked out, too, upon that sea, over which the swift ships were to bear the tidings of His salvation to nations and to continents then unknown. How has the moral aspect of things been changed! Battles and bloodshed have indeed not ceased to desolate this unhappy country, and gross darkness now covers the people; but from this region a light went forth which has enlightened the world and unveiled new climes; and now the rays of that light begin to be reflected back from distant isles and continents, to illuminate anew the darkened land where it first sprung up."—ROBINSON'S *Bib. Res.* vol. iii, pp. 181–191.

SEA OF GALILEE.

"And it came to pass, that, as the people pressed upon him to hear the word of God, he stood by the lake of Gennesaret."—LUKE v. 1.

This hallowed sheet of water, associated with so much of the Saviour's life on earth, has several names in the Bible. In the Old Testament it is called the *Sea of Chinnereth*, from a town of that name upon its shores. It is thus called in the Old Testament only. In the Apocryphal books it is called the *Water of Genessar;* in Josephus the Sea of Gennessar; and in the New Testament, where it is very often mentioned, the Sea of Gennesareth, or, according to another reading, Gennesar, or the Sea of Galilee.

"We reached the brow of the height above Tiberias, where a view of the whole sea opened at once upon us. It was a moment of no little interest; for who can look without interest upon a lake on whose shores the Saviour lived so long, and where He performed so many of his mighty works? Yet to me, I must confess, so long as we continued around the lake, the attraction lay more in those associations than in the scenery itself. The lake presented indeed a beautiful sheet of limpid water, in a deep depressed basin, from which the shores rise, in general, steeply and continuously all around, except where a ravine, or sometimes a deep wady, occasionally interrupts them. The hills are rounded and tame, with little of the picturesque in their form; they are decked by no shrubs nor forests. . . . One interesting object greeted our eyes—a little boat, with a white sail, gliding over the waters; the only one, as we afterwards found, upon all the lake. . . .

"As we sat at evening in the door of our tent, looking out over the placid surface of the lake, its aspect was too inviting not to allure us to take a bath in its limpid waters. The clear and gravelly bottom shelves down in this part very gradually, and is strewed with many pebbles. In or after the rainy season, when the torrents from the neighbouring hills and the more northern mountains stream into the lake, the water rises to a higher level, and overflows the courtyards of the houses along its shores in Tiberias. The lake furnished the only supply of water for the inhabitants; it is sparkling, and pleasant to the taste; or at least it was so to us, after drinking so long of water carried in our leathern bottles. . . .

"The lake is full of fish of various kinds; we had no difficulty in procuring an abundant supply for our evening and morning meal; and found them delicate and well flavored."—ROBINSON'S *Bib. Res.* vol. iii, pp. 252–253.

"My experience in this region enables me to sympathize with the disciples in their long night's contest with the wind. I spent a night in the Wady Shukaiyif, some three miles up it. The sun had scarcely set when the wind began to rush down toward the lake, and it continued all night long with constantly increasing violence, so that when we reached the shore next morning, the face of the lake was like a huge boiling caldron. The wind howled down every wady from the north-east and east, with such fury that no efforts of rowers could have brought a boat to shore at any point along that coast. In a wind like that, the disciples must have been driven quite across to Gennesaret, as we know they were. To understand the causes of these sudden and violent tempests, we must remember that the lake lies low—six hundred feet lower than the ocean; that the vast and naked plateaus of the Jordan rise to a great height, spreading backward to the wilds of the Hauran, and upward to snowy Hermon; that the water-courses have cut out profound ravines and wild gorges, converging to the head of this lake, and that these act like gigantic funnels to draw down the cold winds from the mountains. On the occasion referred to we subsequently pitched our tents at the shore, and remained for three days and nights exposed to this tremendous wind. We had to double-pin all the tent-ropes, and frequently were obliged to hang with our whole weights upon them, to keep the quivering tabernacle from being carried up bodily into the air. No wonder the disciples toiled and rowed all that night; and how natural their amazement and terror at the sight of Jesus walking on the waves! The faith of Peter in desiring and daring to set foot on such a sea is most striking and impressive; more so, indeed, than its failure after he made the attempt. The whole lake, as we had it, was lashed into fury: the waves repeatedly rolled up to our tent door, tumbling over the ropes with such violence as to carry away the tent-pins. And, moreover, those winds are not only violent, but they come down suddenly, and often when the sky is perfectly clear. I once went in to swim near the hot baths, and, before I was aware, a wind came rushing over the cliffs with such force that it was with great difficulty I could regain the shore. Some such sudden wind it was, I suppose, that filled the ship with waves, 'so that it was now full,' while Jesus was asleep on a pillow in the hinder part of the ship; nor is it strange that the disciples aroused Him with the cry of 'Master! Master! carest thou not that we perish?' 'But he arose and rebuked the wind, and said unto the sea, Peace, be still; and the wind ceased, and there was a great calm. And the disciples feared exceedingly, and said one to another, What manner of man is this, that even the wind and the sea obey him?'"—Dr. Thomson's *Land and the Book*, vol. ii, p. 32.

"Yet one scene was perhaps more present with us than any other through that Sunday,—and especially at each of the three sunrises we saw over the lake,—the scene which almost more vividly and familiarly than any other brings before us our risen Saviour, the first fruits in whose likeness all that sleep in Him shall be raised.

"It was the time when Jesus showed himself again to the disciples by the Sea of Tiberias, that last supplementary chapter of St. John's Gospel, which seems to lead us beyond the grave to the shores of life on 'the other side,' and yet whose chief delight it is that its scene was here on this actual, familiar, untransformed earth, on one of these very sandy or shingly beaches. We could not but recall continually the solitary figure seen dimly from the boat after the night of toil and disappointment in the grey of the morning; the voice recognized at last by its power in the repetition of the old miracle; old, yet new in the significant variety of the safe landing of the unbroken net with all its contents at the feet of Jesus; the simple meal which the Master provided from his stores, not from theirs; and afterwards, more than all, the familiar converse as the little band, 'when they had dined,' walked along this shore.

"Yes, along this shore; with the quiet music of these waters rippling against the beach, and the golden outlines of the opposite hills reflected on the lake in the early morning, that little band walked on, conversing as they went; and before them the risen Lord, the One who had died was alive again, and would die no more, speaking, as he walked, to Peter in few and quiet words which went to the depths of the heart. The past three-fold denial, recalled by the three-fold question, but only recalled to stamp a deeper consecration on the service of the future. This was the scene which, more than any other, seemed before us.

"The fire of charcoal smouldering on this beach to welcome the weary fishermen; the fishes laid thereon, and the flat unleavened cakes (such as were often prepared for us) baked on the ashes; the Lord himself taking the bread and fish and giving them to the disciples; and after the simple meal the quiet conversation as they walked along the shore—and then the gleams of allegoric meaning which flash through all these homely details, lifting the heart to the heavenly shore; and the net which, 'when it is full,' the angels shall come forth and lay at the feet of Jesus, no more treading the stormy sea, or tossed in the frail boat, but standing in majesty on the eternal shore. And afterwards the 'feast,'—not a morning meal then, but a 'supper,' an evening feast when the long day of toil is over; and when the 'Lovest thou me?' shall be exchanged for the 'In that thou didst it unto me;' and the 'Feed my sheep' for 'Well done, good and faithful servant, thou hast been faithful in a few things, I will make thee ruler over many things; enter thou into the joy of thy Lord.'

"Thus if through the night the Sea of Galilee seems to echo with the heart-calming assurance, 'It is I, be not afraid,' its shores at morning seem no less to resound with the heart-stirring question, 'Lovest thou me?'"

SCENERY OF THE PARABLES.

"And he sat down and taught the people out of the ship."—LUKE v. 3.

"The greater part of the parables delivered in Galilee, are grouped in the discourse from the fishing vessel off the beach of the plain of Gennesareth. Is there anything on the spot to suggest the images thus conveyed? So (if I may speak for a moment of myself) I asked, as I rode along the track under the hill side, by which the plain of Gennesareth is approached, so I asked at the moment, seeing nothing but the steep sides of the hill alternately of rock and grass. And when I thought of the parable of the sower, I answered, that here at least was nothing on which the Divine Teaching could fasten. It must have been the distant corn-fields of Samaria or Esdraelon on which His mind was dwelling. The thought had hardly occurred to me, when a slight recess in the hill side, close upon the plain, disclosed at once, in detail, and with a conjunction which I remember nowhere else in Palestine, every feature of the great Parable. There was the undulating corn-field descending to the water's edge. There was the trodden pathway running through the midst of it, with no fence or hedge to prevent the seed from falling here and there on either side of it, or upon it; itself hard with the constant tramp of horse and mule, and human feet. There, near at hand, were all kinds of aquatic fowl by the lake side, immediately recalling the 'birds of the air' which 'came and devoured the seed by the way side,' or which took refuge in the spreading branches of the mustard tree. There was the 'good' rich soil, which distinguishes the whole of that plain and its neighborhood from the bare hills elsewhere descending into the lake, and which, where there is no interruption, produces one vast mass of corn. There was the rocky ground of the hill side protruding here and there through the corn-fields, as elsewhere through the grassy slopes. There were the large bushes of thorn—the 'Nabk,' that kind of which tradition says that the Crown of Thorns was woven,—springing up, like the fruit trees of the more inland parts, in the very midst of the waving wheat.

"This is the most detailed illustration of the Galilean parables. But the image of the corn-fields generally must have been always present to the eye of the multitude on shore, of the Master and disciples in the boat—as constantly as the vineyards at Jerusalem. 'The earth bringeth forth fruit of herself,'—'the blade, the ear, the full corn in the ear,'—'the reapers coming with their sickles for the harvest,'—the tall green stalks still called Zuwan by the Arabs (in the Greek N. T. 'zizania' and in our version rendered 'tares') at first sight hardly distinguishable from the wheat, could never be out of place in the plain of Gennesareth. It is mpossible, moreover, to see even the relics of the great fisheries, which once made the fame of Gennesareth, the two or three solitary fishermen casting their nets into the lake from its rocky banks, without recalling the image which here alone, in inland Palestine, could have a meaning; of the net which was 'cast into the sea and gathered of every kind,' from all the various tribes which still people these lonely waters."—STANLEY.

LEBANON.

"The glory of Lebanon shall come unto thee."—ISA. lx. 13.

"The first mention of Lebanon is in the prayer of Moses, when he besought the Lord that he might see 'that goodly mountain and Lebanon.' It was then inhabited by the Hivites. There is frequent reference to the fountains, wells, and streams of Lebanon, as well as to its vines, flowers, roots, fir trees, box trees, and cedars; and in one description of the latter day glory, it is said, that 'the fruit thereof shall shake like Lebanon.' The allusions of the prophets appear very striking to those acquainted with the circumstances of the place. We learn from Hosea, that Israel shall one day be 'as the vine of Lebanon;' and its wine is still the most esteemed of any in the Levant. What could better display the folly of the man who had forsaken his God, than the reference of Jeremiah to the cold flowing waters from the ices of Lebanon—the bare mention of which must have brought the most delightful associations to the inhabitants of the parched plain? The Psalmist declares, that 'the voice of the Lord breaketh the cedars; yea, the Lord breaketh the cedars of Lebanon;' and a more sublime spectacle can scarcely be conceived than the thunder rolling among these enormous masses, and the lightning playing among the lofty cedars, withering their foliage, crashing the branches that had stood the storms of centuries, and with the utmost ease hurling the roots and trunks into the distant vale. But by Isaiah the mountain is compared to one vast altar, and its countless trees are the pile of wood, and the cattle upon its thousand hills the sacrifice; yet, if a volcanic eruption were to burst forth from one of its summits, and in torrents of liquid fire to enkindle the whole at once, even this mighty offering would be insufficient to expiate one single crime: and the sinner is told that 'Lebanon is not sufficient to burn, nor the beasts thereof for a burnt-offering.' The trees of Lebanon are now comparatively few, and with them are gone the eagles and wild beasts to which they afforded shelter; and it is of its former state, and not of its present degradation, that we are to think, in reading the glowing descriptions of the prophets."—HARDY'S *Notices of the Holy Land*, pp. 271–273.

"His countenance is as Lebanon."

"Such is the figure used by Solomon to indicate the

dignity, beauty, and majesty of the great Head of the Church. They who have gazed upon Lebanon from the heights about Beyrout must have felt how noble an image it is. Lebanon is a little world in itself. It is still abundantly populated, notwithstanding the ravages of war; and its fertility is very great, by means of the terraced manner of cultivation, which has so generally prevailed in the East. From Beyrout the eye traces numberless villages, scattered about even on the higher ridges, amidst forests of pine and majestic oaks. The loftiest peak of Lebanon is called Sannin, and is computed at 10,000 feet above the sea level. There is an indescribable air of grandeur pervading this grand mass of mountain. But what must Lebanon have been, when the prophet Isaiah referred to it as an image to illustrate his announcement of gospel blessing and gospel glory—'The glory of Lebanon shall be given unto it'?"—*Mission to the Jews*, p. 240.

. . . "I have travelled in no part of the world where I have seen such a variety of glorious mountain scenes within so narrow a compass. Not the luxurious Java, not the richly wooded Borneo, not the majestic Sumatra or Celebes, not the paradise-like Ceylon, far less the grand but naked mountains of South Africa, or the low impenetrable woods of the West Indies, are to be compared to the southern projecting mountains of Lebanon. In yonder lands all is green or all is bare. An Indian landscape has something monotonous in its superabundance of wood and jungle, that one wishes in vain to see intermingled with rocky cliffs or with towns or villages. In the bare table lands of the Cape Colony, the eye discovers nothing but rocky cliffs. . . . It is not so, however, with the southern ranges of Lebanon. Here there are woods and mountains, streams and villages, bold rocks and green cultivated fields, land and sea views. Here, in one word, you find all that the eye could desire to behold on this earth. . . . The whole of northern Canaan lies at our feet. Is not this Sidon? Are not those Sarepta and Tyre, and Ras-el-Abial? I see also the Castle of Shukif and the gorge of the Leontes, and the hills of Safed, and, in the distance, the basin of the Sea of Tiberias, with the hills of Bara, far, far away; and all these hundreds of villages between the spot we are at and the sea coast. . . . Half a day would not suffice for taking the angles of such an ocean of villages, towns, castles, rivers, hills and capes."—Van de Velde, vol. ii, p. 488.

. . . "Wherever one may wander over the sunny hills and valleys into which the romantic region of 'the Lebanon' is cloven, will he find himself in presence of a living picture of ancient times and ever fresh associations. He will find the venerable mountain incrusted with a rich and sacred symbolism. The waving of its golden harvests will speak to him of 'an handful of corn on the top of the mountains, the fruit thereof shall shake like Lebanon.' Its vineyards purpling in the clear heat of the summer, the mellow fruitage of its load of orchards, the brilliant colors of its wayside flowers, the sweetness of its odorous thickets and beds of thyme, the balsamic fragrance of its cedars, will give more vivid force to holy words which have rung from childhood through the memory: 'I will be as the dew unto Israel: he shall grow as the lily, and cast forth his roots as Lebanon. His branches shall spread, and his beauty shall be as the olive tree, and his smell as Lebanon. They that dwell under his shadow shall return: they shall revive as the corn and grow as the vine; the scent thereof shall be as the wine of Lebanon.' Stability, fragrance, fruitfulness, types of the highest graces that beautify and exalt the life of man, dwell in pure and endless companionship beneath the cedars of Lebanon."

MOUNT HERMON.

"As the dew of Hermon."—PSALM cxxxiii. 3.

This celebrated mountain, though the subject of frequent allusion, is not associated with any historical event in the Old Testament. It was however the most probable scene of one of the most interesting events in the life of our Lord related in the New. "In the turning point of his history, when 'from that time many of his disciples went back and walked no more with him,' when even the twelve seemed likely 'to go away;' and He could no more walk in Judæa 'because the Jews sought to kill Him;' then He left His familiar haunts on the Sea of Galilee, to return to them, as far as we know, only once more. He crossed to the north-eastern corner of the lake, and passed, as it would seem, up the rich plain along its eastern side, and came into 'the parts,' into 'the villages' of Cæsarea Philippi. It is possible that He never reached the city itself; but it must at least have been in its neighborhood that the confession of Peter was made; the rock on which the Temple of Augustus stood, and from which the streams of the Jordan issue, may possibly have suggested the words which now run round the dome of St. Peter's. And here one cannot but ask what was the 'high mountain' on which six days from that time, whilst still in this region, 'He was transfigured' before His three disciples? It is impossible to look up from the plain to the towering peaks of Hermon, almost the only mountain which deserves the name in Palestine, and one of whose ancient titles was derived from this circumstance, and not be struck with its appropriateness to the scene. That magnificent height—mingling with all the views of Northern Palestine from Shechem upwards—though often alluded to as the northern barrier of the Holy Land, is connected with no historical event in the Old or New Testament. Yet this fact of its rising high above all the other hills of Palestine, and of its setting the last limit to the wanderings of Him who was sent only to the lost sheep of the house of Israel, falls in with the supposition which the words inevitably force upon us. High up on the southern slopes there must be many a point where the disciples could be taken 'apart by themselves.' At any rate, the remote heights above the sources of the Jordan witnessed the moment, when His work in His own peculiar sphere being ended, He set his face for the last time 'to go up to Jerusalem.'"—STANLEY'S *Sinai and Palestine*, pp. 391–392.

The same view is also adopted and ably supported by Dr. Buchanan in his "Clerical Furlough." . . . . "Upon the whole, in so far as its known history is concerned, the one event which sheds a glory around it, is the visit and the transfiguration of our Lord. As regards the natural beauties of the scene, they can hardly be exaggerated. From the edge of the grove where our tents were pitched the view all around was of the noblest kind. Immediately behind us, on the east, and looking right down upon us from a height of 1,000 feet, were the massive ruins of the singularly picturesque and majestic fortress of Subeibeh. Thousands and thousands of feet above it, and running along the whole north side of our position, towered up the mighty Hermon, his vast sides cleft by tremendous chasms and shaggy with dark woods, his swelling breast rising black and bare over these primeval forests; and higher still his broad and gigantic shoulders and hoary head white with eternal snow! Who could look at him and fail to acknowledge his right to be called the Jebel-es-Sheikh—the mountain monarch of the land?"

The view from the summit of Hermon is thus finely given by Mr. Porter: "I shall not soon forget the feelings that filled my breast as I gazed on the magnificent panorama spread out before me. I could scarce realize the thought that my feet stood on that sacred mountain of which inspired penmen had written; and that the Land of Israel, God's gift to Abraham's seed, was before me. And yet it was so! Looking westward, that expanse of water, now gleaming like burnished gold beneath the rays of the sinking sun, is the 'Great Sea,' the border of the 'Promised Land.' On that low promontory jutting out behind those mountains stands Tyre, the ancient queen of the sea; and those mountains are called Lebanon. That blue ridge far away to the south is Carmel, and the broad plain of Esdraelon stretches along its base, with Jezreel and Shunem, Endor and Tabor, Nain and Nazareth on its borders. Here on the south, deeply depressed, are the still waters of the Sea of Galilee, and the narrow valley running away beyond, marks the course of the Jordan. The picturesque hills on the left bank of the Jordan are the hills of Gilead; and the elevated plateau on this side of them, extending far eastward, is the 'Land of Bashan.' On the north are the lofty parallel ridges of Libanus and Antilibanus, rising peak over peak far as the eye can see, and enclosing between them the rich valley of Cœle-Syria. At the eastern base of Antilibanus is a broad plain covered with verdure; and the eye can just detect a bright speck in the centre of it—that is Damascus, the oldest city in the world.

"What a multitude of wondrous events does memory crowd together in this narrow space! Through these mountains and plains roamed the patriarchs with their flocks and herds. This country was witness to the prowess of Samson, the valour of David, and the wisdom of Solomon. Here God's ancient people were cheered by revelations of eternal truth from on high; and they were awed and solemnized by wondrous manifestations of Divine power and love. The feet of the Son of God and Saviour of the

World trod these cities and villages, while their inhabitants beheld His miracles, His sufferings, and the heavenly purity of His life. Here too was consummated the glorious work of man's redemption, when Jesus died and rose again, having vanquished death and Satan, and brought life and immortality to light. Of incidents venerable for their high antiquity, of events celebrated for their display of valour and patriotism, and of acts hallowed by the loftiest manifestations of Divine power and love, this land was the scene."—*Five Years in Damascus*, vol. I. pp.291, 292.

The details above given are but a selected portion of the testimony of the Land to the Book gathered from the observations of different travellers. Many volumes would be required, fully to present the evidence arising from this source. The argument which it sustains has been thus forcibly stated by the learned Professor Stuart: "How obviously every thing of this kind serves to give confirmation to the authority and credibility of the sacred record. Do sceptics undertake to scoff at the Bible, and aver that it is the work of impostors who lived in later ages? Besides asking them what *object* impostors could have in forging a book of such high and lofty principles, we may ask—and ask with an assurance that need not fear the danger of being put to the blush—whether impostors of later ages could possibly have so managed as to preserve all the *localities* in complete order which the Scriptures present? Rare impostors they must indeed have been—men possessed of more knowledge of antiquity than we can well imagine could ever be possessed by such as would condescend to an imposition of such a character. In fact, the thing appears to be morally impossible, if one considers it in the light of *antiquity*, when so little knowledge of a geographical kind was in existence, and when mistakes respecting countries and places with which one was not personally familiar were almost, if not altogether, unavoidable.

"How happens it now that the authors of the Old Testament Scriptures should have possessed such a wonderful tact in geography, as it would seem they did, unless they lived at the time and in the countries of which they have spoken? This happens not elsewhere. It is but yesterday since one of the first geological writers in Great Britain published to the world that our Mississippi and Missouri rivers belong to *the tropics*. Respectable writers, even in Germany, the land of classical attainments, have sometimes placed Cœle-Syria on the east of the Antilibanus ridge, or even seemed to transfer Damascus over the mountains, and place it between the two Lebanon ridges in the valley. No such mistakes occur in the sacred writers. They write as men who were familiar with the geography of places named; they mention places with the utmost familiarity; and after a lapse of almost three thousand years, every successive traveller who visits Bible lands, does something to confirm the accuracy of the Hebrew prophets. Towns bearing the same name, or the ruins of towns, are located in the same relative position in which they said they were; and the ruins of once splendid cities, broken columns, dilapidated walls, trodden-down vineyards, half-demolished temples and fragments broken and consumed by time, proclaim to the world that those cities are what they said they would be, and that they were under the inspiration of God."

CHAPTER XI.

ARCHÆOLOGICAL DISCOVERIES—OLD TESTAMENT.

THE constant agreement which has been shown to exist between the recorded history and the natural geography of both the Old and New Testament, proves undeniably, the *accuracy* of the sacred writers. But does it also establish the *historic reality* of the events which they narrate? That it does so when candidly viewed, seems also undeniable. To find the Scripture notices, not only of distant regions, but of valleys, fountains, mountains, rivers, so exactly confirmed in the minutest details, is irreconcileable with any other supposition than that the men and the occurrences of those distant times which the Bible brings before us, were not less true and living than the human realities which are now around us.

Against this point, as has been already noticed, the special and most strenuous efforts of modern infidelity have been directed. It has laboured to show that the events of the Bible history are so enveloped in the mists and clouds of the remote ages in which they transpired, that it is impossible to separate them from the unsubstantial fancies of myth and legend. The additional and overwhelming evidence stored up in memorials of dead empires, that lay forgotten and unknown until needed for the vindication of God's word, will furnish the materials for the present chapter.

It will be instructive, however, first to consider the rise

of the peculiar school of scepticism which rendered the production of that evidence timely and opportune.

"The close of the last and the beginning of the present century," says Mr. Rawlinson,[1] "saw the rise of a new science,—the science of historical criticism, identified in Germany with the name of Niebuhr, and adopted and applied by such English scholars as Thirlwall, Grote, Arnold, and others. Under the application of its new and shifting principles of historical investigation, many of the hitherto recognized verities of ancient history, Greek, Roman, and Egyptian, fell back into the region of the legendary and the fabulous. The domain of real history was circumscribed; facts once received melted down into fables, heroes receded into gods and demi-gods, and their feats and triumphs were proved to be but the fancies of poets or the dreams of national vanity. An unreasoning and uncritical faith had received with equal satisfaction the narratives of the campaigns of Cæsar and of the doings of Romulus, the account of the marches of Alexander and of the conquests of Semiramis, the story of the conspiracy of Cataline and the tale of the Trojan settlements at Latium. The light had not been sufficiently bounded off from the darkness, the dreamy cloud-land of legend and fable from the clear, perfect historic day. In dividing between these and clearing the historic field of its long legendary occupants, although in some instances the pruning knife of the critic may have overdone its work, it cannot be denied that an important service has been rendered to historical science, and reliable principles for the conduct of historical inquiry have been fixed and ascertained.

"The successful demolition of errors in this part of the historic field, suggested the inquiry—'Might not this new science be made available for a fresh assault upon historical Christianity?' If it could be wielded in that direction,

[1] Bampton Lectures.

the attack would fall in with the humour of the times, with the movement in the world of philosophy. It would cover itself with the plausible shield of historical inquiry. Criticism had reduced the dimensions of Grecian and Roman history; it had disintegrated the true from the false, the really historical from the fabulous. Might it not be applied with equal success to the Jewish and Christian histories? Might they not be shown to have their fabulous excrescences to be cut off by the modern critical pruning-knife, their large account of facts to be thrown back into the dim twilight region of myths and legends? There was no want of will to make the attempt. The great master-mind to whom the new science owed, if not its existence, its advancement to the place it held, had indeed distinctly accepted the mass of the Scripture history as authentic, and was a sincere and earnest believer. But there were minds of a different order among his countrymen, neither guided by his caution nor restrained by his reverence, and whose faith had already given way in all that was essential in Christianity. Having cast away the kernel, their next struggle was to dispose of the shell, and the new science was pressed into their service to accomplish the work of demolition." The result has been the rise of the German mythical school of infidelity, which with an erudition and acumen never surpassed, have brought all the resources of learning against the historical statements of Holy Writ. By these writers, the miracles in the sacred narrative have been compared with the prodigies and divine appearances related by Herodotus and Livy. Because the names of kings were frequently apposite to their character or the events of their career, they have argued that the monarchs supposed to have borne them, must be regarded as fictitious personages like Theseus and Numa. Portions of the sacred history were early declared to present every appearance of being simply myths; and by degrees it was sought to give the whole history from first to last a legendary and unreal character. Did any of the particular narratives in the sacred books seem to the rationalistic mind objectionable or improbable, it was deemed a sufficient account of any such narrative to say that its main source was oral tradition—that it first took a written shape many hundreds of years after the supposed date of the circumstances narrated, the authors being poets rather than historians, and bent rather on glorifying their native country than on giving a true relation of facts—and that in places they had not even confined themselves to the exaggeration, but had allowed imagination to step in and fill up the blanks in their annals. This school of writers have not hesitated to claim the possession of "a verifying faculty," —an infallible tact, which enables them to decide at once as to what is, and what is not, historical and literal truth. Armed with this spear of Ithuriel, De Wette was empowered to relegate a great part of the Old Testament Histories into the region of the mythical; and Schleiermacher did not hesitate to characterize those narratives out of the life of our Lord, which the Evangelists have preserved respecting his childhood and early youth, as "no more than the poetical expression of the truth, that the beginning and end of his marvellous life were not to be measured by the laws of common experience." At length the system may be said to have culminated in the remarkable work entitled "The Life of Christ," by Strauss, in which the entire New Testament is turned into a myth and Christ himself becomes a mere name.

From Germany this school of infidelity has spread to England and America, exerting in both countries a widely pernicious influence among the cultivated classes of society. In circles which would turn with disgust from the vulgar productions of the Paine school, works of a far more dangerous character are now freely circulated,—works whose avowed object it is to "extirpate all faith in the supernatural; to account for the origin of every form of religion, not excepting Christianity itself, on purely natural principles; to undermine all creeds, and overthrow every existing form of worship; and to substitute for them either the simplest and most practical code of utilitarian morals, or the vague and mystic generalities of Pantheism." Among the more prominent of these may be mentioned Mackay's "Progress of the Intellect," a work bearing the marks of erudition, more ingenuity and labour, and very slender judgment. The author attempts to dispose of the supernatural claims of Christianity by applying the theory of myths alike to the systems of Polytheism and the Scriptures of Truth; all mythology being in his estimation, "but the exaggerated reflection of our own intellectual habits." The Polytheism of the Greeks and the Christianity of the New Testament, were equally the products or creations of the human mind; and each of the two may be satisfactorily accounted for by the same natural law or tendency which leads mankind every where and in all circumstances to give form and body to their ideal conceptions, to personify abstractions, and to endow these imaginary beings with attributes akin to their own. In attempting to develop this fundamental idea, he not only compares the mythology of the Greeks with the mythology of the Hebrews, as contained in the Jewish and Christian Scriptures, but he places both on precisely the same level, and ascribes to them a common origin. As a specimen of what the beautiful narratives of Scripture become by the application of this theory, his interpretation of the history of Joseph may be subjoined. This, he suggests, "is simply the myth of the Arabian phœnix in another form, because the moon and the stars bowed down to him in the dream, and he was carried away amidst bales of myrrh, as that bird was said to make its funeral pyre of spices, and after marrying a daughter of the priest of the sun, representative of the sun himself, a command was given respecting his bones, like those of the Nature God, symbolized by Osiris, Orestes and Pelops!" 'Ex uno disce omnes.' Subjected to this crucible, the whole of those simple and touching histories which delight the opening mind of childhood and charm to the last the dull ear of old age, are transmuted into a mere mass of legends, on a par with the Arabian Nights or the adventures of the Odyssey. They are but phantasmata—as unreal as the vision that mocked the efforts of the Trojan hero:—

> "Ter frustra comprensa manus effugit imago,
> Par levibus ventis volucrique simillima somno."

A dim haze settles down upon the Scripture landscape, and all its scenes and events—the actors and the stage—become "such stuff as dreams are made of," and, like Fairy-land with King Arthur and his knights, are floated off to some

> ——"island valley of Avilion
> Where falls not hail, or rain, or any snow,
> Nor ever wind blows loudly."

Were it possible for this attempt to "rationalize" the Bible and transform its histories into "myths" to be successful, then, indeed, would the Gospel refuge for sinners be dismantled and levelled to the dust. For, as we have already seen, Christianity must stand or fall with the facts with which it is intertwined. But the waves of profane speculation and the winds of sentimental fancies burst in vain against this building of God. It is founded on the rock of eternal truth, and cannot be overthrown. This phase of infidelity has been made in the wisdom of Providence, to serve what seems its natural end, to lead to a more accurate study of Scripture than was ever before engaged in; and to broaden and deepen the foundations of all the defences of the faith. The subtile and insidious methods of undermining the vital truths and facts of revelation, devised by Strauss, Bruno Bauer and other rationalistic leaders, roused such men as Tholuck, Hengstenberg, Neander, Olshausen and Stier to rally to the standard of the truth. These great scholars, and not they alone, have met the mythical school of infidels upon their own ground, and with their own weapons have fully discomfited them. By the application of the principles of a legitimate and just criticism, the weakness and fallacy of their objections have been fully demonstrated, the historic verity of the Scriptures vindicated, and not a jot or tittle has fallen to the ground.

The internal evidence on this point is alone sufficient to carry conviction to every unprejudiced mind. "The Scriptures shine bright with the amiable simplicity of truth. They set forth things just as they happened, with the minute circumstances of time, place, situation, gesture, habits, &c., in such a natural manner that we seem to be actually present."[1] "When we compare the early Scriptures with the Grecian and Eastern fables, we feel just the same contrast as between a crowd of meteors, appearing and disappearing suddenly in all directions, and the calm, steady, onward progress of the stars, that move silently and irresistibly in their course through the dark blue heavens. There is no hurry and yet there is no pause, in the view of the Divine Providence, and of the moral government of the world, which these simple histories set before us. If wonders are recorded, there is no pausing to dwell upon them, as if strange works of power were strange and surprising even to the Divine Historian. There is no lingering in the far distant past, where a human fancy would have loved to disport itself amidst the rivers of Paradise, and gorgeous visions of Hesperian gardens, homes of beauty, and islands of the blest. The giants, 'the mighty men of

* Jonathan Edwards' Works, vol. viii, p. 197.

old, men of renown,' haye their transitory fame just indicated in one sentence, and pass at once out of view. The peopling of the old world by the sons of Noah, and the dispersion from the tower of Babel, are briefly recorded; but no details of the journeyings which followed, whether to the lands of the East, or the islands of the West; no geographical romance, like that of the Odyssey, so attractive to half-civilized ears, intrudes on the narrative, and interferes with the rigid unity of its moral purpose. And when the fathers of the chosen race are set before us, there is no element in the description to feed the pride of their children, though much to animate their faith and kindle their love towards the God of their fathers. They are men of like passions with ourselves—not, like the demi-gods of Greece, heroes in power, and profligates in character. The faith of Abraham fails him twice under the pressure of temptation. Isaac, in his old age, betrays a weakness most unworthy of the son of Abraham, and heir of the promises. Jacob steals first the birth-right from his brother, and afterward the blessing; and his whole life is like one severe discipline, to root out duplicity as well as to strengthen his faith. Amidst all these sins or follies of the Patriarchs, the purpose of God who chose them and their seed to be witnesses for His truth in the deepening idolatry of the nations, advances slowly and calmly to its fulfilment. When the appointed centuries have expired, 'that selfsame night' the hosts of the Lord come forth from the iron furnace of their Egyptian bondage. Every fresh book from Genesis to Nehemiah, adds a new link to the golden chain. It reveals the constant progress of a plan of moral government and spiritual recovery, which sweeps aside at every step the dreams and falsehoods of men, till the twilight yields at length to a joyful daybreak, in the fuller message of the Gospel, and the Sun of Righteousness rises upon the heathen darkness with healing in his wings."

But had the voice of human vindication been silent, it is gratifying to know that an answer most convincing and indisputable, had been laid up for the confusion of the assailant of Old Testament History in the depositories of Egypt, in remote desert places where for ages traveller's foot had not trodden, and in those vast and mysterious mounds by the banks of the Tigris and Euphrates, on which wandering Kurd and Bedouin for centuries had gazed with superstitious awe, and which tradition had associated with Nimrod, Nebuchadnezzar, and other mighty conquerors of old. When that answer was needed it appeared. Egypt from her tombs and temples, Edom and Moab from the wilderness, Assyria from her ruined mounds, bore testimony to the truth of that Word which, in their days of power and prosperity, pronounced their overthrow and desolation.

The nature of this testimony may be illustrated by the discoveries made among the ruins of Herculaneum and Pompeii, and the use to which they have been applied. From the excavations carried forward in these two Roman towns, overwhelmed eighteen hundred years ago by the scoriæ and ashes of Vesuvius, a lifelike picture is obtained of Roman arts and manners. The structure of the dwellings and gardens—the household furniture—the mosaics and paintings—the theatres and baths—the shops and their utensils—all unite to give us a perfect insight into the social condition of the Romans of the Empire in all its circumstantial reality.

"Returns the Past, awakening from the tomb?
Rome—Greece!—O, come!—Behold—behold! For this
Our living world—the old Pompeii sees;
And built anew the town of Dorian Hercules!
House upon house—its silent halls once more
Opes the broad Portico——how lone
The clear streets glitter in the quiet day—
The footpath by the doors winding its lifeless way!

The roofs arise in shelter, and around
The desolate Atrium—see
The marble-tesselated floor—and there
The very walls are glittering livingly
With their clear colors.
The earth, with faithful watch, has hoarded all!
Still stand the mute Penates in the hall;
Back to his haunts returns each ancient god.
Why absent only from their ancient stand
The Priests?—waves Hermes his Caducean rod,
And the wing'd victory struggles from the hand."—SCHILLER.

No one would think of disputing the obvious inferences which these discoveries enable us to draw. The strong, clear light shed from Pompeii's opened vaults, has dispelled the obscurity which had hitherto rested on many points connected with the private life and economy of the ancients, and helped to explain many dark passages in the Roman poets and historians. It has also served to confirm much which they have written.

What reason can be assigned why a like use should not be made of the far more ancient remains of Egypt and Assyria? Why should not, for instance, those of Egypt, contemporaneous as they were with the era of Moses, be accepted as evidence, whether for or against the credibility and trustworthiness of his statements? Could it be made to appear that they did not tally or correspond—that the one contradicted the other—at once would the infidel claim that the writings of the Hebrew lawgiver were thereby proved unworthy of credit. But, as in the famous controversy occasioned by the Zodiacs of Esneh and Denderah already noticed, all attempts to falsify Moses from this source have proved signal failures. It is one of the most remarkable phenomena in the annals of mankind that on the walls of the ruined temples and sepulchral chambers of Egypt, there is still preserved a more extensive and varied reproduction than even that of Pompeii, of a civilization dating back to within a few centuries of the flood. Not only the regal state and warlike achievements of their kings, with their civil and religious ceremonies, command an interest,—but the people, with all their private and domestic occupations, and in all their various castes, civil, military, and religious; in their feasts and their funerals; in their fields and their vineyards; in their amusements and their labors; in their shops, in their kitchens; by land and by water; in their boats and their palanquins; in the splendid public procession, and the privacy of the household chamber—seem to live again before us,—the almost unchanging climate having preserved the paintings in all their original freshness and vividness of color. Yet in all the unnumbered details there presented, no discrepancy with the sacred history can be found. There is nothing but agreement. "The whole monumental wonders and antiquities of the land seem to have been preserved," says Dr. Wilson, "as if for the express purpose of evincing the authenticity and illustrating the narratives of the Bible; every single allusion of which, either to the circumstances of the country or of the people, is seen to have the minutest consistency with truth,—so strikingly so, indeed, as to have attracted the attention of every Egyptian antiquary." "The memorials of their manners, customs, and institutions," says another writer, "which the people of the Pharaohs depicted on the walls of their sepulchres, afford a decisive because an unsuspicious test of the historical veracity of the Old Testament, and they have furnished confirmations of its minute accuracy, which must silence where they do not convince the most sceptical."

Through the visit of Abraham, the history of the ancient Church became at a very early period connected with the land of Egypt. Driven thither by a famine which prevailed in Canaan, as he approached near its borders, he became alarmed respecting Sarah his wife, fearing that they would not scruple to put him to death in order to get her into their undisturbed possession. The cause of his fear appears to have been the circumstance of her complexion being so much fairer than that of the women of Egypt. "Behold now, I know that thou art a *fair* woman to look upon; therefore it shall come to pass when the Egyptians shall see thee, that they shall say, this is his wife; and they will kill me, but they will save thee alive." The pictorial representations on the monuments now show that a fair complexion was deemed a high recommendation in the age of the Pharaohs. Almost always the lighter tints with which females of high rank are drawn, are in striking contrast to their swarthy attendants. Thus does pagan art of that remote antiquity confirm the history of the Bible.

The apprehensions of Abraham were partly realized. The beauty of Sarah attracted the notice of the Egyptians and of Pharaoh's court, and led to her being temporarily taken from him. This account apparently conflicts with the immemorial custom of the East requiring that the women should go closely veiled and be kept in careful seclusion from the society of men other than their husbands and nearest relatives. The answer is, that the social system of the Egyptians differed in this respect from that of other oriental nations. The monuments show that the Egyptian women in the days of the Pharaohs went unveiled, and were permitted to enjoy as much freedom as the females of modern Christendom. We may suppose, therefore, that prudence dictated Sarah's conforming to the customs of the land upon which she had now entered.

From the account of the gift which Pharaoh bestowed upon Abraham at his departure, it has been sought to draw an inference hostile to the Mosaic narrative, because no mention is made in it of horses, though they were common in Egypt. This very omission is, however, a confirmation of the truthfulness of the history. It is accounted for by the fact that horses, though common in Egypt, were not yet in use among the Hebrews, and did not come into employment until the time of the kings. In Solomon's reign a cavalry force was for the first time employed, and then it was comparatively small and an unwarranted innovation. Even in Egypt the horse is introduced into the monuments chiefly if not exclusively in cases of war; and it was not under such auspices that Abraham appeared before Pharaoh. Hence the propriety of horses being omitted in the gift which Pharaoh made to him. In harmony with this and Abraham's character as a shepherd, there is a striking pastoral scene depicted in the sides of a tomb hewn in a rock, on which, according to Mr. Wilkinson, "First came the oxen, over which is the number 834, cows 220, goats 3,234, and sheep 974. There are no horses. The Hebrews were shepherds in Egypt, and sheep appear on the monuments in great numbers."

Ignorance of the condition of Egypt has been alleged against the relation of the dream of the chief butler of Pharaoh, because it supposes the cultivation of the vine, whereas Herodotus expressly asserts that in Egypt there were no vineyards, and Plutarch assures us that the natives of that country abhorred wine, considering it as the blood of Typhon. Could it be shown that those ancient writers were infallible, a serious difficulty would here be presented. But not only are they contradicted on this point by other authorities, such as Diodorus and Athenæus, but discoveries among the monuments have decided the question beyond a doubt in favor of the sacred historian. According to Champollion, there are to be seen in the grottoes of Beni Hassan, minute representations of the vintage in all its parts, from the dressing of the vintage to the drawing off of the wine. There have also been found among the ruins of the old cities of the Pharaohs, remains of wine-vessels with unmistakable marks of having contained wine, and since the key to the hieroglyphics has been discovered, the very word, *wine*, has been deciphered, and thus proved to have been familiarly known to the people.

It has also been objected that the sacredness of animals prevented the use of animal food, of which we read in the book of Genesis; but on referring to the monuments, we find delineations of feasts and kitchen scenes, unanswerably confirming the sacred record. From the employment of bronze instruments among the Egyptians, even from the earliest ages, a case has been attempted to be made out against the statement that Tubal Cain was the father of all workers in iron, and to show that its use did not arise till a much later age. A sufficient answer to such an objection is, that there is no proof that the Egyptians did not use iron. Long after iron was known, implements continued to be made of bronze, from the great facility in working it. The obelisks and hieroglyphics would scarcely have been cut or the pyramids built, as Herodotus himself suggests, without the use of iron. And lastly, there are representations on the walls of Thebes which have the appearance of being those of steel. Thus the very objections of scepticism, upon investigation, have confirmed the truth of revelation.

Many incidents in the interesting history of Joseph receive valuable illustration from the scenes depicted on the monuments. Slaves were procured for Egypt, not merely in war, but also in trade with other nations, and in accordance with usage Joseph was brought there as an article of merchandise by an Arabian caravan. The buyer of the youthful slave was Potiphar, chief of Pharaoh's body guard and one of the high officers of his court. In existing paintings of marches and battle scenes, this kind of officer may be seen in attendance upon his sovereign, and he is always represented as a very important and influential person, one who possessed in a very high degree the royal confidence. This will account for the arbitrary power he possessed over Joseph, even supposing his state of servitude not sufficient for the purpose. Potiphar's licentious wife plotted the seduction, and then the imprisonment and death of Joseph, and many representations of the Egyptian women convey an equally bad idea of their character, and prove that in Egypt the restraints on the females in the household were not those which prevailed generally in oriental countries. The situation which Joseph held in the house of Potiphar was that of steward, and in the tombs of Beni Hassan this kind of officer is represented discharging his duties and overseeing the domestic slaves. In other pictures the Egyptians carry flat baskets on their heads, placed one above another, in accordance with the custom alluded to by the chief baker of Pharaoh, in his account of his dream.

When, in consequence of the chief butler's favorable account of Joseph, the king sent for him, we read that he shaved himself and changed his garments, and came to Pharaoh. Here, as we learn from the monuments, is an essentially Egyptian characteristic. It was not the custom of the Hebrews to shave the beard, except in cases of mourning, while that of the Egyptians was just the reverse. Joseph, probably, had hitherto adhered to his own national custom, yet, when he was called to the royal presence, it was necessary that he should conform to the usages of the court and kingdom. In this account, we have, therefore, a clear proof that the sacred historian had a minute acquaintance with the usages of the land.

On being introduced to Pharaoh, Joseph is told of dreams which the king had dreamed, and which none of his magicians and wise men could interpret. This order of men is to be distinguished on the monuments, and from the inscriptions we learn that they were applied to for explanation and aid in all things which lay beyond the circle of common knowledge and action. Nothing, therefore, can seem more natural than that when the king was perplexed by a very remarkable and repeated dream, his first impulse should be to summon the magicians and wise men. But in the very substance and description of the dreams themselves, we find convincing proof of the authenticity of the narrative which relates them. There appeared seven fat and seven poor kine (cows), to indicate years of plenty and years of famine. The cow was the peculiar Egyptian symbol of the earth, with its cultivation and produce. Kine, lean and fat, would consequently, in the region of the Nile, form the most expressive signs of coming abundance and of coming scarcity. Nor is this all. Not only does the coming of the fat and the lean kine out of the river correspond with the well known fact that the Nile is the source of plenty or starvation to the whole land, but there is another circumstance, lost to English readers by the inaccuracy of our translation, which proves the sacred writer's familiarity with the minute peculiarities of Egypt. The fat kine, it is added, fed in a "meadow,"—but this word does not convey the exact meaning. The original means the aquatic plants of the Nile, particularly those of the litus kind, which were considered so valuable that they were reaped and gathered in as regular a harvest as the flax and corn. Evidently the history of Joseph could only have been penned by one who was well acquainted with the natural productions of the valley of the Nile.

Upon the elevation of Joseph, he was clothed with garments of byssus or fine linen, which were highly esteemed in Egypt, and appropriated exclusively to those of high rank. The signet ring, as an emblem of authority, and a necklace of gold, such as the monuments show betokened rank and eminence, were given to him. He was married to the daughter of Potipherah, a name not wanting on the monuments. This Potipherah, a person quite distinct from Potiphar to whom he was sold, was high priest of Heliopolis, and as such occupied a very exalted position in the state. The marriage was effected under the direct sanction of the king, who, as high priest as well as king, exercised authority over the priesthood. If it be thought improbable that a foreigner like Joseph should ally himself with the daughter of so high a family, it is to be remembered that Joseph had become naturalized in Egypt, and there is evidence on the monuments that distinguished foreigners were sometimes admitted into the priesthood.

Of the labors rendered by Joseph in collecting the produce of the country, we have clear and remarkable illustration in the Egyptian paintings. There are to be seen representations of vast granaries, before the door of which lie large heaps of corn already winnowed, while "a registrar of bushels" takes an account of the number of bushels brought to him by another man, who is engaged in measuring. The scene of entertainment in which Joseph is represented as eating separately from the other Egyptians, is in accordance with the principle of caste, to the highest class of which Joseph belonged; and the position of the guests, that of sitting at table, though not oriental or patriarchal, is verified by the Egyptian monuments. A remarkable parallel to the migration of the family of Jacob into Egypt is depicted in a tomb at Beni Hassan, which some have even supposed to have a direct reference to that event. The scene is an arrival of strangers over whom the number 37 is written in hieroglyphics, bringing their goods with them upon asses. The first figure is an Egyptian scribe, who presents an account of their arrival to one of the chief officers of the king. They are then ushered into his presence, and two of the strangers advance, bringing presents of the wild goat and the gazelle. Four armed men follow leading an ass, on which there are two children in panniers, accompanied by a boy and four women. Another laden ass follows accompanied by two men, one of whom carries a bow and club, and the other musical instruments. Whatever the scene may actually represent, it is in striking harmony with the narrative of Genesis.

Similar illustrations from the monuments of the wonderful accuracy of incidental allusions and references in the Mosaic history to Egyptian antiquities might be greatly multiplied, did our limits permit. There are, however, two *direct* illustrations of Scripture history so remarkable as justly to claim special attention.

The first has reference to the state of humiliation and oppression to which the Israelites were reduced in Egypt, when another king arose who knew not Joseph or his services. The Scripture statement is that "the Egyptians made the children of Israel to serve with rigor; and they made their lives bitter with hard bondage in mortar and in brick, and in all manner of service in the field; all the service wherein they made them serve was with rigor." All this is represented to the letter in a painting which was found upon the walls of a tomb at Thebes. A copy and explanation of it was first furnished by the distinguished Italian scholar Rosellini in his great work on the monuments of Egypt. His account of it is headed—"Explanation of a picture representing the Hebrews as they were engaged in making brick." In this picture some of the laborers are employed in transporting the clay in vessels; some in working it up with the straw: others in taking the bricks out of the moulds and setting them in rows to dry; while others, by means of a yoke upon their shoulders, from which ropes are suspended at each end, are seen carrying the bricks already dried. The physiognomy of the Jews it is impossible to mistake; and the splashes of clay with which their bodies are covered, the air of close and intense labor that is conveyed by the grouping on the left side of the picture, and, above all, the Egyptian taskmaster seated with his heavy baton, whose remorseless blows would doubtless visit the least relaxation of the slaves he was driving from their wearisome and toilsome task of making bricks, and spreading them to dry in the burning sun of

Egypt, give a vivid impression of the exactitude of the Scripture phrase—"all their service, wherein they made them serve, was with rigor."

The group of Egyptians to the right of the picture affords also a confirmation of the literal correctness of the inspired narrative and of the uniformity of all things in Egypt. We read in the 5th chapter of Exodus that when Moses and Aaron had been before Pharaoh, "he said, Behold the people of the land now are many, and ye make them rest from their burdens. And Pharaoh commanded the same day the taskmasters of the people and their officers, saying, Ye shall no more give the people straw to make brick, as heretofore; let them go and gather straw for themselves. And the tale of bricks which they did make heretofore ye shall lay upon them; ye shall not diminish aught thereof." In consequence of this arbitrary and cruel order, the taskmasters hastened them, saying, "Fulfil your works, your daily tasks, as when there was straw. And the officers of the children of Israel which Pharaoh's taskmasters had set over them were beaten, and demanded, Wherefore have ye not fulfilled your task, in making brick both yesterday and to-day, as heretofore?" The picture referred to shows the actual carrying out of this cruel mode of procedure. Two of the Egyptian officers over the Israelites, sufficiently distinguished from them by their head-dresses and complexions, are compelled by the blows of the taskmasters over them, to bear themselves the vessels of clay and the brick yoke, and to complete the work which they had failed to exact from the captives committed to their charge. That these men had not come forth to labor is sufficiently indicated by the right hand figure with the yoke, who, having not yet taken up his burden, has not yet girt his loins, like his companions and all the other laborers in the picture, and also according to the invariable custom in the East, but still wears his dress loose, after the fashion of the officer who is sitting in the centre with the baton, and of the supreme taskmaster (probably the personage by whom the tomb was excavated), who is represented as beating the officer his companion.

So close is the representation by Egyptian artists of the very scene which the sacred Book describes!

But the existing evidence of the bondage in which the Israelites were held during the latter part of their sojourn in Egypt, is probably of far wider extent than this single picture. A learned writer[1] on the antiquities of Egypt has forcibly presented the considerations which support this view.

"The great works of Egypt in that age were chiefly of a monumental character, and on these would the Israelites be employed. The quarries whence the stones were obtained were in the Sinaitic wilderness. Thither would the Israelites be marched in gangs, and the blocks of granite which were hewn in these quarries they would afterwards have to transport across the desert. Others of the oppressed race were employed, doubtless in making bricks of Nile mud, so extensively used in the walls of huge quadrangular precincts of the temples, and the cloisters and cells attached to them. And as at that epoch the mechanical arts were extremely simple, the amount of work done depended mainly upon the amount of human force which the sovereign of Egypt could bring to bear in the construction of his works. If, then, there be truth in the Bible narrative, and if Rameses be the 'king who knew not Joseph,' we should expect to find that the monuments erected during his reign surpassed those of any other of the Pharaohs, seeing none of them had such an amount of forced labor at their command.

"Now we do not shrink from the test. There is a Pharaoh who is distinguished from all his predecessors and

[1] Osburn's Israel in Egypt, pp. 196–205.

from all who came after him by the enormous number of the monumental memorials of his reign. There is a Pharaoh whose name is stamped on every crumbling mound in Egypt and Nubia, and on almost every Coptic monument in the museums of Europe. There is a Pharaoh whose existing monuments actually surpass those of all the other sovereigns of Egypt put together. That Pharaoh is Rameses. Every crumbling heap that dots the valley of the Nile—every ruined temple, almost every statue and sphinx in that land of wonders, proclaims that there was an epoch of fearful bondage in Egypt—an epoch when millions of slaves were urged by the lash to their daily tasks—and that there was a king in that land who reduced the full half of his subjects into slavery, and set them to work in the construction of cities, and strongholds and gigantic monuments, which, after four thousand years, excite the spectator's astonishment. Over and over the soil is written, in ineradicable characters, the great fact of the oppression. The whole land cries aloud that once it was a 'house of bondage.' What a convincing and overwhelming proof of the truth of the Bible!"

The other direct illustration from the monuments of Egypt of the inspired history is the invasion of Judea by Pharaoh Shishak in the reign of Rehoboam, the son of Solomon,—the history of which is given in the twelfth chapter of the second book of Chronicles. We there find him marching against Jerusalem with chariots and horsemen and people without number—the Lubims, the Sukkims, and the Ethiopians. The humiliation and penitence of Rehoboam, under the warnings of Shemaiah the prophet, averted from him the calamity of the entire loss of his kingdom; but while the Lord declared that he should not utterly be destroyed, he nevertheless added, that the people should be servants of Shishak,—that is, should taste the bitterness of a foreign yoke. Shishak came and took away the treasures of the house of the Lord, and the king's treasures—"he took all"—and though his stern purpose was mollified by Him in whose hand are the hearts of kings, that he did not retain Judea in subjection, yet for the time it was reduced to the condition of a conquered province.

On the walls of the great Temple at Karnak this successful invasion of Judah is commemorated. Copies of some of the inscriptions there remaining having found their way to Europe, the celebrated Champollion without ever having seen Egypt was enabled to detect the hieroglyphic name of this monarch and read it—"Beloved of Amon, Sheshouk." It was four years afterwards before Champollion saw Egypt, during which interval, says Mr. Gliddon, "the name of Sheshonk and his captive nations had been examined times without number by other hieroglyphists, and the names of all the prisoners had been copied by them and published, without any of them having noticed the extraordinary biblical corroboration thence to be deduced." On his passage toward Nubia, Champollion landed for an hour or two, about sunset, to snatch a hasty view of the ruins of Karnak; and on entering one of the halls, he found a picture representing a triumph, in which he instantly pointed out in the third line of a row of sixty-three prisoners (each indicating a city, nation or tribe) presented by Sheshonk to his god Amon, a figure with this inscription attached in hieroglyphic characters, "Judah melek kah," or "king of the country of Judah."

This picture had been executed by the order of Shishak or Sheshonk, so that here was found the sculptured record of the invasion and the conquest recorded in the Chronicles. On the same picture were shields, containing in hieroglyphics the names Bethhoron, Megiddo, Mahanaim, and some others, all towns through which Shishak passed on his invasion of Judea.

What more complete and unambiguous corroboration of the Scripture history could be required?

Leaving Egypt, we will now proceed to another region in which remarkable discoveries confirmatory of the truth of the Bible have been unveiled.

Half a century ago, the once famed capital of the Edom of Scripture was only known by the references to it in the ancient writers, and by some wild Arabian legends, which recognized the existence of a petrified city in the desert, whose inhabitants had been swept away by the vengeance of the Almighty. In the year 1812, the traveller Burkhardt first found a clue to the labyrinth in which the long lost city lay concealed.

The value of that discovery as confirmatory of Holy Scripture, a brief sketch of the Bible record concerning Edom will enable us the better to understand.

Desolate as Mount Seir now appears, it was one of the earliest seats of civilization, power and grandeur. Its history goes back to the time of Esau, "the father of Edom;" and we read that princes and dukes, eight successive kings, and again a long line of dukes, dwelt there before any king "reigned over Israel." At a period coeval with the Exodus, the land of Edom was in a highly cultivated state, with fields, vineyards, highways, and a numerous population, and Petra was probably even then the central point of an extensive caravan trade, which was conducted for many ages afterward between the countries of the Persian Gulf, Egypt, and the shores of the Mediterranean. According to allusions in the book of Job, himself an Edomite, the year and the months were regularly defined, kings and great men had been accustomed to build for themselves splendid tombs, and the people were in possession of great wealth in gold and silver. They were acquainted with the weaver's shuttle, and the use of scales, and made cheese from milk; gardens were protected by ground traps and snares; inscriptions were cut on tablets, attached to the faces of the rocks; archers had steel bows, with quivers for their arrows; the spear, shield, and sword were ordinary weapons in battle; while the sound of the trumpet called to the combat, in which the war horse figured, finely described as having his "neck clothed with thunder." For many ages after the time of Job this people held and retained no mean eminence in arts and in arms, in science and in commerce, and in the wealth, refinement, and luxury which extensive and prosperous commerce brings along with it. But it lacked that righteousness which alone permanently exalteth a people. For numerous acts of treachery and hostility, committed at different periods against the descendants of Jacob, though a kindred race, a malediction of the most awful description was pronounced upon the land of Esau's posterity. From the height of worldly prosperity it was doomed to fall into the most abject state of wretchedness and desolation. While it was yet a land of palaces and fortresses, of wise men and mighty men, the word of prophecy had thus spoken its fate:

> "From generation to generation it shall lie waste,
> None shall pass through it forever and ever.
> But the cormorant and the bittern shall possess it;
> The owl also and the raven shall dwell in it:
> And He shall stretch out upon it the line of confusion,
> And the stones of emptiness.
> They shall call the nobles thereof to the kingdom,
> But none shall be there.
> And all her princes shall be nothing.
> And thorns shall come up in her palaces,
> Nettles and brambles in the fortresses thereof:
> And it shall be a habitation for dragons,
> And a court for owls."—ISAIAH xxxiv. 10–13.

> "The pride of thine heart hath deceived thee,
> Thou that dwellest in the clefts of the rock, whose habitation is high;
> That saith in his heart, Who shall bring me down to the ground?

Though thou exalt thyself as the eagle,
And though thou set thy nest among the stars,
Thence will I bring thee down, saith the Lord.
How are the things of Esau searched out! . . .
How are his hidden things sought up!
Shall I not in that day, saith the Lord,
Even destroy the wise men out of Edom,
And understanding out of the mount of Esau?
And thy mighty men, O Teman, shall be dismayed,
To the end that every one of the mount of Esau
May be cut off by slaughter."—OBADIAH.

So exactly did the ruined city which was brought to view among the desert ranges of Mount Seir answer to the description given by the prophets, that if a painter had sought to depict a city from the words of the prophecy, he could hardly have failed to give some resemblance to her present appearance. The travellers found her *holding the heights of the hill*, her dwellings *in the clefts of the rocks*, like the nests of the eagle, *set among the stars*, and, viewing the strength of her position, could imagine her former boast: *Who shall bring me down to the ground?* Yet the extent of her desolation manifested how fully Jehovah had redeemed his word—*thence will I bring thee down.* Laborde describes the first view of the city, bursting upon the eye of the traveller approaching from the south, from the heights above, as presenting "the most singular spectacle, the most enchanting picture, which nature has wrought in her grandest mood of creation; which men, influenced by the vainest dreams of ambition, have yet bequeathed to succeeding generations. At Palmyra, nature renders the works of man insignificant by her own immensity, and her boundless horizon—here she appears delighted to set in her own noble frame-work his productions, which aspire, and not unsuccessfully, to harmonize with her own majestic yet fantastic appearance. The spectator hesitates for a moment whether is most worthy of admiration: nature who invites his attention to her matchless girdle of rocks, wondrous as well for their colors as for their forms, or the men, who feared not to intermingle the works of their genius with such splendid efforts of creative power." The city is situated in a hollow, surrounded by a superb enclosure of rocks, pierced with myriads of tombs. The ravine into which the traveller enters from the east is represented as becoming more and more imposing at every step, and the excavations and sculptures more frequent on both sides, till it presents at last a continued street of tombs; beyond which the rocks, gradually approaching each other, appear all at once to close without any outlet. There is, however, one frightful chasm for the passage of the stream, which furnishes, as it did anciently, the only avenue to Petra on this side. This passed, the traveller reaches an area once filled with its close ranged dwellings, and loud with its busy life—now silent and strewn with heaps of ruin, fragments of foundations, pavements, and arches; while all around the precipitous cliffs hewn into pillared façades, and honey-combed with sumptuous chambers, show where the princes of Edom once dwelt "in the clefts of the rock, and held in pride the heights of the hill." (Jer. xlix. 16.) The cry of the bittern alone now disturbs the awful desolation—"the line of confusion and the stones of emptiness." The whole territory of the descendants of Esau has been swept as by "the besom of destruction," and presents a miracle of evidence which defies cavil or contradiction.

"I would," says Mr. Stephens, "that the sceptic could stand as I did among the ruins of this city among the rocks, and there open the sacred book, and read the words of the inspired penman, written when this desolate city was one of the greatest cities in the world. I see the scoff arrested, his cheek pale, his lips quivering, and his heart quaking for fear, as the ruined place cries out to him in a voice loud and powerful as that of one risen from the dead;

though he would not believe Moses and the prophets, he believes the handwriting of God himself in the desolation and eternal ruin around him."

"Many prophets," says Laborde, "have announced the misery of Idumæa, but the strong language of Ezekiel can alone come up to the height, or reach the acme of this great desolation." "Every one that passeth by Edom is astonished at it," as the prediction intimated. And the first sentiment of "astonishment" in the contemplation of it is, how such a region could ever have been adorned with cities, or tenanted for ages by a powerful and opulent people. "Its present aspect would belie its ancient history," says Dr. Keith, "were not that history corroborated by the many vestiges of former cultivation, by the remains of walls and paved roads, and by the ruins of cities still existing in this ruined country. The total cessation of its commerce; the artificial irrigation of its valleys wholly neglected; the destruction of all the cities, and the continued spoliation of the country by the Arabs; the permanent exposure for ages of the soil, unsheltered by its ancient groves, and unprotected by any covering from the rays of the sun; the unobstructed encroachments of the desert, and of the drifted sands from the borders of the Red Sea; the consequent absorption of the water of the springs and the springlets during summer—are causes which may have all combined their baneful operation in rendering Edom most desolate, the desolation of desolations."

"Perfect as has been the fulfilment of the prophecy in regard to Idumæa, in no one particular has its truth been more awfully verified than in the complete destruction of its inhabitants, in the extermination of the race of the Edomites. In the same day, and by the voice of the same prophets, came the separate denunciations against the descendants of Israel and of Edom, declaring against both a complete change of their temporal condition; and while the Jews have been dispersed in every country under heaven, and are still in every land, a separate and unmixed people, 'the Edomites have been cut off forever, and there is not any remaining of the house of Esau.'

"'Wisdom has departed from Teman, and understanding from the mount of Esau;' and the miserable Arab who now roams over the land cannot appreciate or understand the works of its ancient inhabitants."

To the north of Edom, in a region now called the Hauran, but formerly comprising the countries of Bashan and Moab, surprising discoveries of a most interesting character have recently yielded fresh evidence of the reality of the Scripture history.

In an inaugural address at Belfast, Dr. Porter[1] says: "I remember well, how in former days I studied the geography of Palestine; and with what intense interest I read of the great cities and warlike exploits of Og, the giant king of Bashan. I observed, with no little surprise, that a single province of his little kingdom contained 'three score cities fenced with walls, besides unwalled towns a great many.' I remember how on turning to my atlas, I found that the whole of Bashan was not larger than an ordinary English county. I was astonished, and though my faith in the divine record was not shaken, yet I thought that some strange statistical mystery hung over the passage. That one city, nourished by the commerce of a mighty empire, might grow till her people could be numbered by millions, I could well believe; that two or three might spring up in favored spots, clustered together, I could also believe; but that sixty walled cities, besides unwalled towns a great many, should exist at such a remote age, far from the sea, with no rivers, and little commerce, appeared altogether inexplicable. Inexplicable though it seems, it was strictly true. On the very spot, with my own eyes, I have verified it.

[1] Author of "Five Years in Damascus."

More than thirty of these great cities I have myself visited. When standing, on one occasion, on the summit of the mountain range of Bashan, I could see at a single glance every city the sacred penman referred to. Many of them, though deserted for centuries, have their massive walls and massive old houses still perfect. The Cyclopean architecture of the aboriginal inhabitants of Palestine—of the Emim, and Anakim and Rephaim—still stands to bear testimony to the facts of revelation."

Elsewhere, the same learned writer says: "In the minutest particulars my researches bear testimony to the faithfulness of Bible narrative and description. The numerous and extensive ruined cities and villages scattered over its surface tell of its former populousness, and are the present memorials of its ancient strength and greatness. The oak forests still cover its mountain sides; its pastures are still celebrated for their richness, and its soil is proverbial for its fertility. The ancient names, too, cling to it yet; and we have Bashan, and Golan, and Kenath, and Salchah, and Bozrah, and Kerioth, and Hauran and Edrei, but little changed by the lapse of long centuries. Thus does it appear that the more extensive our research, and the more minute our investigations, the more full and accurate will be our illustrations of the Word of God."—*Five Years in Damascus*, vol. ii. pp. 271, 272.

Beyond Salchah, the frontier town of Bashan, which was the farthest point reached by Dr. Porter, discoveries of equal if not greater interest have since been made in the neighboring country—the old land of Moab. Scarcely anything was known of its interior, and especially of the eastern portion, until the year 1857, when for the first time it was explored by a modern traveller, Mr. Graham, of Cambridge. The following extract from his contribution to the Cambridge Essays for 1858, will give some idea of the result of his researches: "Perhaps of all those which we saw in our journey, none struck us more than the large towns in the plain south and east of Salchah. Among them there was one in particular which made an impression on us we shall never lose—it was Um-el-Jemul, the ancient Beth-Gamul, a very large city, and to be compared almost with the modern Jerusalem. It is very perfect; and as we walked about among the streets, and entered every house, and opened the stone doors, and saw the rooms as if they had just been left, and then thought that we were actually in the private dwellings of a people who for two thousand years had 'ceased to be a people,' we felt a kind of awe, and realized in a manner that we never, perhaps, could feel elsewhere, how perfectly every tittle of God's word is carried out; and whether it be a blessing that is spoken or a curse, it continues to be so—nothing is remitted until all be fulfilled. These cities of Moab, which are still so perfect that they might again be inhabited to-morrow, have been during many centuries unpeopled. The land about them, rich and fruitful as any in Syria, has long ceased to produce aught but shrubs and herbs, the food of the camel and the antelope. The sound of the rejoicing at harvest-time, and the song of the grape-gatherers, has long since died away; and for centuries, these old cities, which were once the scene of so much life and so much rejoicing, have been still; and no sound, save the cry of wild animals, has been heard in them. How wonderfully true are these words—'Moab is destroyed. Give wings unto Moab, that it may flee and get away; for the cities thereof shall be desolate, without any to dwell therein. Moab is spoiled and gone out of her cities. Moab is confounded, and judgment is come upon the plain country. Upon Beth-Gamul . . . and upon Kerioth, and upon Bozrah, and upon all the cities of the land of Moab far and near, the horn of Moab is cut off, and his arm is broken, saith the Lord.' Again, in all this country there is now no fruit except at

Salchah, where there are some wild vines and pomegranates and figs, but before they are quite ripe the Arabs of the desert plunder them. Is not this predicted? 'The spoiler has fallen upon thy summer fruits and upon thy vintage. And joy and gladness is taken from the plentiful field, and from the land of Moab. And I have caused wine to fail from the wine-press; none shall cry with shouting; their shouting shall be no shouting. And Moab shall be destroyed from being a people, because he hath magnified himself against the Lord. Woe unto thee, O Moab! . . . for thy sons are taken captives and thy daughters captives.' Can we have stronger evidence of the accurate fulfilment of prophecy than by comparing what we see in this country with the words of Jeremiah spoken 2,500 years ago? When he spoke these words Moab was powerful and proud, and laughed at the thought of what he said. They cried—'We are strong and mighty, and no enemy can overcome us! How say ye, we are mighty, and strong men for the way! We have heard of the pride of Moab (he is exceeding proud), his loftiness and his arrogancy, and his pride, and the haughtiness of his heart.'"

No less than fourteen of these ancient towns were visited by Mr. Graham, and in connection with them he further remarks: "When we find (such) great stone cities (Deut. iii), walled and unwalled, with stone gates, and so crowded together that it becomes a matter of wonder how all the people could have lived in so small a tract of country; when we see houses built of such huge and massive stones that no force which could ever have been brought against them in that country, would have been sufficient to batter them down; when we find rooms in those houses so large and lofty that many of them would be considered fine rooms in a large house in Europe; and lastly, when we find some of these towns bear the very name which cities in that country bore before the Israelites came out of

Egypt, I think we cannot help feeling the strongest conviction that we have before us the cities of the giants (Rephaim), the cities of the land of Moab. They have been gradually deserted as the Arabs of the desert have increased in number, and now, south and east of Salkhad, not one of these many towns is inhabited." . . .

. . . "Very different is the present condition of the towns of Moab from those of the neighboring Edom—from those heaps of rubbish which are strewn over the basin of Petra—the nest of the eagle that built in the crags torn to pieces, in token that it will be built no more. In this contrast there would seem to be some special design of Providence; and it is in accordance with prophetic hints and foreshadowings of changes that yet lie in the obscurity of future time. For while Idumea is to be a 'perpetual desolation,' it is written, 'I will bring again the captivity of Moab in the latter days, saith the Lord.' The tide of life has ebbed forever from the one, and left it empty and forlorn as a naked beach; but here it may return to its former channels, and flow with a fuller current than of old. The household lamp may once more be lighted in the dwellings; the cheerful stir and murmur of men he heard in the streets; the song of the reaper, the joy of the vintage, the innocent mirth of children; and, sweeter than all, the melodies of Sabbath praise."

The neighboring land of the kindred people of Ammon has also yielded up its quota of evidence for the Bible. "We descended," writes Lord Lindsay, "a precipitous strong slope into the valley of Ammon, and crossed a beautiful stream, bordered by a strip of stunted grass. The hills on both sides were rocky and bare, and pierced with excavations and natural caves. Here, at a turning in the narrow valley, commence the antiquities of Ammon. It was situated on both sides of the stream,—the dreariness of its present aspect is quite indescribable, it looks like the abode of Death. The valley stinks with dead camels; one of them was rotting in the stream; and though we saw none among the ruins, they were absolutely covered in every direction with their dung. That morning's ride would have convinced a sceptic. How runs the prophecy? 'I will make Rabbah a stable for camels, and the Ammonites a couching place for flocks; and ye shall know that I am the Lord.'

"Nothing but the croaking of frogs, and screams of wild birds, broke the silence as we advanced up this valley of desolation. We examined the ruins more at detail the following morning. It was a bright and cheerful day; but still the valley is a very dreary spot, even when the sun shines brightest. Vultures were garbaging on a camel, as we slowly rode back through the glen. Ammon is now quite deserted, except by the Bedouins, who water their flocks at its little river. Re-ascending the slope, we met sheep and goats by thousands, and camels by hundreds, coming down to drink. 'Ammon shall be a desolation, and Rabbah of the Ammonites shall be a desolate heap.'"

But the crowning discovery of the century has been in a yet more distant region, yielding an amount of additional illustration and confirmation of the sacred word as great and important as it was unexpected.

A thousand miles remote from the highways of modern commerce and the routes of ordinary travel, a far mightier city than the rock-built metropolis of Edom lay buried in the sandy earth of a half-desert Turkish province, with no certain trace of its place of sepulture. Vague tradition said that it was hidden somewhere near the river Tigris; but when Xenophon with his Greeks in their celebrated retreat passed by the mound of Nimroud which he describes, the name of Nineveh was already forgotten on its very site. It afterwards reappears on the pages of Greek and Roman writers, but for ages the former queen of nations was nothing more than a name, suggesting the idea of an ancient capital of fabulous splendor and magnificence; a mighty collection of palaces and other buildings, vast but scarcely real.

More than two thousand years had it thus lain in its unknown grave, when an English traveller and a French consul, Layard and Botta, sought the seat of the once powerful empire, and searching 'mid

"Hillocks heap'd
On what were chambers, arch crush'd column strown
In fragments, choked-up vaults and frescoes steep'd
In subterranean damps"—

discovered the buried city, disentombed her temple palaces from the sepulchre of ages, and unveiled to an astonished and curious world, the pomp and pageantry of Assyrian monarchs. The Nineveh of Scripture, the great city "of three days' journey," that was "laid waste and there was none to bemoan her," whose greatness sank ere the coming orb of Roman dominion had ascended the horizon, the Nineveh in which the captive tribes of Israel had labored and wept, was, after a sleep of twenty centuries, again brought to light. The long lost was found. The regal halls were once more trodden; the proofs of ancient splendor were again beheld by human eyes, and the gorgeous description of the poet drawn in colors borrowed from the sacred page, shown to have been a reality:

"The days of old return;—I breathe the air
Of the young world;—I see her giant sons
Like to a gorgeous pageant in the sky
Of summer's evening, cloud on fiery cloud
Thronging up heaped,—before me rise the walls
Of the Titanic city—brazen gates—
Towers—temples—palaces enormous piled—
Imperial Nineveh, the earthly queen!
In all her golden pomp I see her now."—ATHERSTON.

That he may the better understand the range and extent of these discoveries, let the reader suppose himself standing on the highest part of the city of Mosul on the west bank of the Tigris. Looking across the river, the eye rests on a long range of ancient mounds. At the southern end is the irregular platform on which stands the village of Nebby Yeonas, with its spacious mosque and capacious cemetery. Towards the northern extremity rises the huge plateau of Kouyunjik, whose ample surface, though the palace of ancient Nineveh lies entombed beneath, has long rewarded the toil of the cultivator as richly as the plain below. This mound is but one of many. Others are found at Nimroud, about eighteen miles lower down the river, near the junction of the Greater Zab; at Karasules, about twelve miles north of Nimroud, and at Khorsabad, nearly the same distance north of Kouyunjik. These points form the four corners of a rhomboid, the circumference of which is sixty miles, which answers to the three days' journey of the prophet Jonah, twenty miles being as in ancient days the computation of a day's journey. Within this space a vast number of smaller mounds, remains of pottery, bricks and other fragments, indicate where once stood the private habitations of the great city.

Other mounds of great extent are found at Kalah Sherghat, supposed to be the ruins of Calah (Gen. x. 11) on the opposite bank of the Tigris, forty miles below Nimroud, at Babylon and Borsippa, Seukerah and Niffer. They are also found along the Khabor and Euphrates, and on the plains of Babylonia and Chaldea as well as Mesopotamia and Assyria.

Many of these have been recently explored, and the most precious treasures that ever rewarded the labors of the antiquary have been brought to light; for deep down in their interior have been buried for thousands of years, palaces of monarchs who reigned from the time when

Abraham went forth from Ur of the Chaldees until near the close of Israel's captivity in Babylon, or for a period dating back a thousand years before the Trojan war and extending to the early dawn of Roman greatness.

Most of the huge mounds already explored contain, buried up at various depths, extensive remains of ancient palaces. The walls of these are of great thickness, with a panelling to the height of about ten feet of slabs of alabaster. Every portal is guarded by strange mythic figures (winged bulls or lions with human heads), while the slabs are adorned with sculptures of the most elaborate workmanship, painted in gorgeous colors, and in many cases as fresh in their sharp and delicate lines as if newly from the chisel and pencil of the artist. These sculptures are the records of the empire, and under each picture are engraved, in characters filled up with bright copper, inscriptions describing the scenes represented. The visitor to these chambers, so long lost not merely to the sight but to the knowledge of mankind, sees spread before him a highly illustrated historical volume, in which are minutely and effectively, though often most grotesquely, displayed all the leading pursuits and characteristics of an extinct nation; while the incidental details, no less than the prominent features, strikingly and impressively illustrate Scripture statements, and that to such an extent that there is scarcely an obscure fact or expression in the Old Testament that is not made clear by the knowledge we have already derived, or may hope hereafter to obtain from the prosecution of these discoveries. "Three thousand years their cloudy wings expand," and the men who then trod these halls again live before him. There he sees them "portrayed upon the wall, the images of the Chaldeans, portrayed with vermilion, girded with girdles upon their loins, exceeding in dyed attire upon their heads, all of them princes to look to, after the manner of Babylonians of Chaldea" (Ezek. xxxiii. 14,

15)—such as idolatrous Jerusalem saw when she "doted upon the Assyrians her neighbors, captains and rulers, clothed most gorgeously, horsemen riding upon horses, all of them desirable young men" (ver. 12). There are to be seen, as is believed, the "mighty hunter," Nimrod himself, strangling a young lion by pressing it against his chest—the eunuch in the palace of the king of Babylon—the king's cupbearer, to whom was appointed "a daily provision of the king's meat and of the wine which he drank,"—"the governors, treasurers, and rulers of provinces," such as surrounded Nebuchadnezzar's image of gold—"the most mighty men" in the army, such as obeyed the behests of the same monarch in casting Shadrach and his heroic companions into "the burning fiery furnace"—while figures of the great kings of Assyria, in all their pomp and magnificence, everywhere presented, seem again to exact the awe and veneration which they once inspired.

As might be expected in the case of so warlike a people, warlike exploits occupy the largest portion of this illustrated gallery. All the incidents of the successful campaign are registered with a circumstantiality and minuteness indicative of the national vanity. Horsemen "lifting up both the bright sword and the glittering spear," and horses "swifter than the leopards, and more fierce than the evening wolves"—bowmen, shield bearers, and slingers, for whom were prepared "shields and spears, and helmets, and habergeons, and bows, and slings to cast stones"—chariots and battering rams, the assault, the charge, the retreat and the pursuit, the burning fort, and the sacked city—bearded warriors "furiously driving their chariot in pursuit of the remnant of the inhabitants, who are flying over a rocky plain, strewn with headless bodies"—the soldier "deliberately plunging his sword into the breast of an adversary whom he has driven down upon his knees"—the king stopping his chariot "to command a register to be made of the number of the heads of the slain piled up in a heap before him" (2 Kings x. 8), and, hovering over dead and dying, "the ravenous beasts of every sort" (Ezek. xxxix. 4)—these horrid accompaniments of a horrid system are represented with surprising vigor and effect. It is as if, instead of reading the wonderfully graphic description of Ezekiel (chap. xxvi. 7–12), the visitor actually looked on "the king of kings coming from the north with horses, with chariots, and with horsemen, and companies, and much people; he slays with the sword the villages in the fields; he makes a fort against the city; he casts a mount against it, he lifts up a buckler against it; he sets engines of war against the walls, and with his axe breaks down the towers.

"The walls shake at the noise of the horsemen and of the wheels, and of the chariots, when he enters into the gates or through the breach with the hoofs of his horses, he treads down every street, he slays the inhabitants by the sword, and strong garrisons go down to the ground. His soldiers make a spoil of wealth and merchandise. They break down the walls and the pleasant houses." "A fire devoureth before them, and behind them a flame burneth. The land is as the garden of Eden before them, and behind them a desolate wilderness; yea, and nothing escapes them." (Joel ii. 3.)

To these stirring scenes succeed the treaty of peace, the triumphal march, the manacled prisoners supplicating for mercy, "the captive child and the mother that bare it cast out into another country" (Jer. xxii. 26), and tribute bearers enriching the imperial treasury with the spoils of enslaved provinces and conquered kingdoms.

The charge of cruelty which the sacred writings bring against ancient Nineveh are fearfully sustained by these sculptured scenes. In the disclosures made in the "Hall of Judgment" and the "Chamber of Judgment," the "woe" which the prophet Nahum denounced against "the bloody city," is shown to have been well deserved. In the bassi-rilievi here are to be seen prisoners, some of them supposed to be Jews or Samaritans, having rings in their lips, to which is attached a cord held by the king, embodying literally the metaphor in Isaiah's prophetic message sent in reply to the prayer of Hezekiah—" Because thy rage against me and thy tumult is come up into mine ears, therefore will I put my hook in thy nose, and my bridle in thy lips, and I will turn thee back by the way by which thou camest." (Isa. xxxvii. 29.) One prisoner, in addition to having his hands manacled, has on his ankles strong rings fastened by a heavy bar, the condition in which the Assyrian king took Manasseh to Babylon (2 Chron. xxiii. 11); and perhaps, resembling that of Zedekiah when bound, at a later period, with fetters of brass. (2 Kings xxv. 7; Jer. xxxix. 7.) In another group is a man naked, with limbs outstretched, and wrists and ankles fastened to pegs in the table or floor, while the "chief of the slayers" is, with a curved knife, beginning to remove the skin from the back of the arm of the prisoner, whose head is turned towards the king imploring pardon, the very words of which petition may possibly be contained in the cuneatic inscription above. In another scene may be recognized the fate of Zedekiah, the king thrusting the point of the spear into the eyes of the supplicating prisoner, while he holds in his left hand a cord attached to rings in the lips of two other captives. Well, therefore, did "the bloody city" merit the prophet's similitude of "an old lion, tearing in pieces his victims for his whelps, and strangling them for his lionesses, and filling his holes with prey, and his dens with ravin."

The early Assyrian kings, like the illustrious founder of their monarchy, were "mighty hunters," and their exploits in the chase of wild animals are vividly represented by the sculptures. Among this class of pictures, "the wild bull in a net," or enclosure of felled trees, as alluded to by Isaiah (ii. 20), is seen exhibiting his impotent rage.

The Assyrian gods also are there—Baal, Nisroch and Asherah—still the same as when their portraits were drawn five and twenty centuries ago—cut from the trees of the forest, decked with silver and gold, fastened with nails, and clothed with purple and blue. The very star to which Amos alludes (v. 26) is yet on those palace walls above the horned cup of the idol—her

> "Whom the Phœnicians called
> Astarte, Queen of Heaven, with crescent horns,
> To whose bright image, nightly by the moon,
> Sidonian virgins paid their vows and songs."

There too, the "grove" of Scripture has been identified with the "sacred tree" supposed to be an emblem or symbol of the same goddess who was the Oriental Venus. The winged bulls and other combinations of animal forms with gigantic human faces, so frequent in the sculptures, still faithfully guard these deserted halls, and are, probably, traditional representations of the cherubim that were placed by God as the guardians of Paradise, and which hence came to be symbolic guardians of things or places to which access was forbidden.—"Before those wonderful forms," says Dr. Layard, "Ezekiel, Jonah, and others of the prophets stood, and Sennacherib bowed; and even the patriarch Abraham himself may have possibly looked upon them." In the floor of the inner court, Botta found secret cavities containing small images of baked clay of repulsive hybrid forms; these being, it is suggested, the Teraphim or images such as Rachel took from her father and put in the camel's furniture, and sat upon them (Gen. xxxi. 19, 30, 34), the signification of the original word according with the terrifying aspect of these figures. In the "divine chamber" were found the figures of two magi with a gazelle in one hand and the other uplifted in prayer; and it is inferred that in this chamber they were wont to be consulted by the king, the blood of the victims being poured into a cavity in a slab in the floor. These magi, it is supposed from their form and features, are one of the four orders of Chaldeans mentioned by Daniel, to whom the Assyrian kings resorted, on occasions the most trivial or important, for the interpretation of dreams, or the solution of political problems.

The sumptuous convivialities of the Assyrian court are delineated in the "banqueting hall" in which the king was wont to entertain "the nobles and princes of the provinces (Esther i. 3–7), in celebration of his conquests when the harp and the viol were in their feasts;" and here too is probably the very recess in which stood the wine vase of a size to contain royal wine in abundance according to the state of the king, while his guests are in the act of drinking his health or of pledging each other in uplifted cups. "The scene exhibited on such occasions," says a recent visitor to these ruins, "especially at night, when these long galleries and richly sculptured chambers were illuminated by the light of lamps—'cressets fed with naphtha or asphaltum'—must have been gorgeous and imposing beyond measure."

The question as to the early origin of writing, which scepticism has brought to bear against the authenticity of the book of Genesis, is also settled by these discoveries. Some of the sculptures show manuscripts unrolled as they were read, telling us that the Assyrians were acquainted with writing on parchment or papyrus. Clay seals also, which seem to have been attached to such documents, burned up or long since decayed, and scribes writing down the long lists of the slain or the number of the captives, corroborate this testimony.

The art of printing even was in some degree known to those early ages, as is testified by the innumerable bricks stamped with the name of the king before they were burned, which have been brought up from the recesses of the mounds. Some of these are stamped with inscriptions more than three centuries older than Abraham.

The letters on the marble walls, as also the intaglios on seals and cylinders, were engraved with a sharp instrument; and when the inscription was on the floor of a palace, the letters were often filled up with some soft metal illustrating that passage of Job (xix. 23, 24), "O that my words were graven with an iron pen and lead in the rock forever!"

By a marvellous coincidence, just as the annals of the old Assyrian empire, engraved in alabaster and marble, were brought to light; the character and language in which they were written, were at length deciphered, after having baffled the ingenuity and learning of ages. By the profound study of some fragments of cuneiform or arrow-headed inscriptions brought from Persepolis, Professor Grotefend had succeeded in determining the names of Cyrus, Xerxes, Darius and Hystaspes, comprising nearly one third of the alphabet, and thus laid the foundation of the discovery. This was in 1802. Little farther progress was made until the year 1836, when a more perfect clue was found by Col. Rawlinson on a rock near the ruins of Behistan—the Bagistan of ancient history. Here, on the perpendicular face of a precipice more than 300 feet above the base, is sculptured King Darius holding his bow, with two state officers behind; under his feet lies one rebel, while a line of nine others stand before him, chained one behind another, with their hands tied. Accompanying these figures are several explanatory inscriptions, one of considerable length, written in the Persian, Median or Scythian and Assyrian languages. The reading of the Persian portion of these inscriptions, accomplished for the more difficult and complicated Assyrian versions, what the Greek of the Rosetta stone did for the hieroglyphics of Egypt; it furnished the key by the aid of which Col. Rawlinson, Dr. Hincks, and other scholars have unlocked the depositories of Assyrian and Babylonian lore, and deciphered their ancient records. The coincidence of their independent investigations, joined to the internal evidence of truth which the translations bear, places beyond question the general accuracy of the results at which they have arrived.

A striking verification of the truth of the Bible has been furnished by these discoveries in the identification of Scripture names.

In the tenth chapter of Genesis we read of the cities of "Erech, and Accad, and Calneh, in the land of Shinar;" "Calah and Resen;" and in the eleventh chapter, "Ur of the Chaldees" is mentioned. After that period these cities almost entirely disappeared from the page of history—nothing was known of their story, their fate, or even their sites. Now, however, the bricks and stones that lay buried for near three thousand years beneath the mounds of Mesopotamia have found a tongue, and have not only told us where each of these cities stood, but have added interesting details of their history.

The vast number of the inscriptions found will require a considerable length of time for their perfect elucidation; yet very important corroboration of the historical facts of Scripture has already been obtained from them.

In the Second Book of Kings, iii. 27, we read that the king of Moab, when he saw that the battle was too sore for him, and that he could not cut his way through the besieging army, took his eldest son that should have reigned in his stead, and offered him for a burnt-offering upon the wall. And Grotefend has deciphered an inscription of Nebuchadnezzar which contains the record of his offer to let his son be burned to death in order to ward off the afflictions of Babylon. Were not these, like the unconscious prophecy of Caiaphas, the blind groping and groaning of a fallen race after the alone perfect sacrifice that could avail with God?

Upon the walls of the palace of Khorsabad, excavated by the French, are to be read the annals of the reign of Sargon, or Shalmaneser, both of which titles are given in the inscriptions. In the first year of his reign, it is said, he came up against the city of Samaria (called Samarini), and the tribes of the country of Beth Homri (or Omri), being the name of the founder of Samaria. (1 Kings xvii. 16, *seq.*) He carried off into captivity in Assyria 27,280 families, and settled in their places colonists brought from Babylonia; appointing prefects to administer the country, and imposing the same tribute which had been paid to former kings.

In the second year of Shalmaneser's reign, he is stated to have subdued Libnah and Kahzitah (the Cadytis of Herodotus), dependencies of Egypt; and in the seventh year of his reign he received tribute direct from the king of that country, who is named Pirhu, probably for "Pharaoh," the title by which the kings of Egypt were known to the Jews and other Semitic nations. This punishment of the Egyptians by Sargon or Shalmaneser, is alluded to in the twentieth chapter of Isaiah.

Among the other exploits of Shalmaneser found in his annals are, the conquest of Ashdod, also alluded to in Isaiah xxi. 1; and his reduction of the neighboring city of Jumnai, called Jabneh, or Jamneh, in the Bible.

The entire annals of Shalmaneser have not yet been discovered; but a tablet erected by him towards the close of his reign in the palace at Nimroud, in which he claims to be the conqueror of Judæa, Colonel Rawlinson thinks refers to the expedition in which, after a three years' siege of Samaria, he carried off the great body of the tribes of Israel, and which is commemorated in the Bible as having occurred in the sixth year of Hezekiah.

But yet more striking coincidences are found in the annals of the son of Shalmaneser, Sennacherib. He commenced his career by subjugating the Babylonians under their king Merodach Baladan, who had also been the antagonist of his father. This is a confirmation of Scripture, but the most important points of agreement are found in the annals of his third year. Let us compare their disclosures with the Bible. In 2 Kings, chap. xviii., we read that Hezekiah sent an embassy to Sennacherib, the king of Assyria, at Lachish, and from the subsequent statements we infer that Lachish was taken and destroyed. What say the inscriptions? In the palace at Kouyunjik a beautiful and highly finished bas-relief has been found, representing the siege and capture by the Assyrians of a city of great extent and importance. The sculptures tell the whole story of the attack, the conquest, and the entire destruction of the enemy. The captives, as they appear in the bas-reliefs, have been stripped of their ornaments and fine raiment, are barefooted and half clothed. But it is impossible to mistake the race to which they belong. They are Jews; for the stamp is on the countenance as it is impressed on the features of their descendants at this very hour. The Assyrian sculptor has noted the characteristic lines, and drawn them with surprising truth. To what city they belong we likewise know, for above the figure of the king, who commands in person, it is declared, that Sennacherib the mighty king, the king of Assyria, sitting on the throne of judgment before the city of Lachish, gives permission for its slaughter.

The inspired record says, that Sennacherib came up against the fenced cities of Judah and took them (2 Kings xviii. 13), and that when Hezekiah offered to purchase a peace, the invader exacted from him 300 talents of silver and 30 of gold. This, it will be borne in mind, was the sum originally demanded, not from all the towns, but from Hezekiah and Jerusalem alone. The writer does not go on to specify the sum which Hezekiah actually gave, but only that he gave all the silver which was found in the house of the Lord and in the royal treasury. He also "cut off all the gold from the doors of the temple of the Lord, and from the pillars which Hezekiah king of Judah overlaid," but nowhere does he tell us of the amount that was thus procured and given to the Assyrian. Scripture also informs us how Sennacherib took advantage of this submissive spirit of Hezekiah, and after repeated insulting messages and threats, advanced to the destruction of Jerusalem. But Hezekiah, we are told, trusted in God, and in answer to his prayer the Lord slew 185,000 of the invaders in a single night, so that the king of Assyria returned to Nineveh without inflicting further injury upon the holy city.

Of the terrible blow which thus arrested his designs, we could scarcely expect to find any mention in the grandiloquent annals of an Oriental monarch. But he says, according to the inscriptions, "Because Hezekiah king of Judah did not submit to my yoke, forty-six of his strong fenced cities and innumerable smaller towns which depended on them I took and plundered, but I left to him Jerusalem his capital city, and the inferior towns around it,"—a very significant admission in view of the Scripture reason for his retreat,—"and because Hezekiah refused still to do me homage, I attacked and carried off the whole population, fixed and nomade, which dwelt around Jerusalem, with thirty talents of gold and eight hundred talents of silver, the treasures of Hezekiah's palace, besides his sons and his daughters, and his male or female servants or slaves; I returned to Nineveh, and I accounted their spoil for the tribute which he refused to pay me." The apparent discrepancy in the amount of silver here mentioned being a larger sum than that stated in the Bible, finds its ready explanation in the circumstance that, while the Bible merely states what was demanded of Hezekiah, the inscription states the whole amount carried off, which of course would include a great deal more. The amount of gold being the same in both accounts is an "historic coincidence," which Dr. Layard justly claims to be "one of the most remarkable coincidences of historic testimony on record."

Another discovery connected with the history of Sennacherib is perhaps even more remarkable. In a passage in the southwest corner of the Kouyunjik palace, Dr. Láyard stumbled upon a large piece of fine clay, bearing the impression of seals, which there can be no doubt had been affixed, like modern official seals of wax, to documents written on leather or parchment. The writings themselves have of course decayed, but, curiously enough, the holes for the string by which the seal was fastened are still visible; and in some instances the ashes of string itself may be seen, together with the unmistakable marks of finger and thumb. Four of these seals are purely Egyptian. Two of them are impressions of a royal signet. "It is," says Dr. Layard, "one well known to Egyptian scholars as that of the second Sabaco, the Ethiopian, of the 25th dynasty. On the same piece of clay is impressed an Assyrian seal, with a device representing a priest ministering before the king, probably a royal signet."

Of the mystery here involved, Scripture supplies the following solution.

Hoshea, king of Israel, made a treaty withSo, king of Egypt, to help him throw off the yoke of Shalmaneser, king of Assyria; but the result was an Assyrian invasion and the first great captivity of the kingdom of Israel. This So, or Sabaco II., was succeeded by Tirhakah in Egypt, and Shalmaneser in Assyria by Sennacherib, and hostilities existed during both reigns. (2 Kings xix. 9.) It would seem that, a peace having been concluded between the Egyptians and the Assyrians, the signets of the two kings thus found together were attached to the treaty, which was deposited among the archives of the kingdom.

The document itself and the cord by which it was attached to the seal, have long since turned to dust; but the seal, with its double impress, though buried for ages, has come to light and is now in the British Museum. The two kings affixed their seals to a document which has perished like themselves; but in their act the hand of the Most High affixed an additional seal to his Holy Word, which is true and abideth forever.

The annals of Ezar-haddon, the son of Sennacherib, have also been found in a tolerably perfect state. They are written upon a cylinder now in the British Museum, and contain an account of a further deportation of Israelites from Palestine, and a further settlement of Babylonian colonists in their place. This statement affords an explanation of a passage in Ezra (iv. 2), in which the Samaritans speak of Ezar-haddon as the king by whom they had been transplanted.

Another corroboration of Scripture furnished by these discoveries, has reference to the account in Daniel (iv.) of Nebuchadnezzar driven from among men and dwelling for a season with the beasts of the field. An inscription now in the East India House at London, according to Col. Rawlinson, describes the various works of that monarch at Babylon and Borsippa. The enumeration is doubtless the counterpart of that expression, "Is not this great Babylon which I have built for the house of my kingdom, by the might of my power and for the honor of my majesty?" In the midst of the list occurs a remarkable passage which the decipherer could not but regard as the official version of that terrible calamity.

Abruptly breaking off from the account of the architectural decoration of Babylon, it denounces the Chaldean astrologers. It says "the king's heart was hardened against them. He would grant no benefactions for religious purposes. He intermitted the worship of Merodach, and put an end to the sacrifice of victims. He *labored under the effects of enchantment.*" There is much more that is obscure in this episode, and at its close the architectural narrative is abruptly resumed. But how much clearer a narrative of that awful visitation could we expect from Nebuchadnezzar?

The more light that is thrown from researches in these monumental records upon the historic statements of Scripture, the more authentic and matter-of-fact are they made to appear. It is impossible to exaggerate the value of the mine thus opened to the biblical student. "Perhaps the time may come," says Mr. Rawlinson, "when through the recovery of the complete annals of Egypt, Assyria and Babylon, we may obtain for the whole of the Sacred History that sort of illustration, which is now confined to certain portions of it. God, who disposes all things 'after the counsel of his own will,' and who has given to the present age such treasures of long buried knowledge, may have yet greater things in store for us, to be brought to light at His own good time."

In the utter ruin and desolation which have overtaken Nineveh and Babylon, we have additional evidence that the word of the Lord is truth. The calcined alabaster and charred cedar of the Assyrian palaces (Khorsabad and Nimroud) bear witness that the prophetic denunciation against them was fulfilled to the very letter—that not only the flooding river and the destroying sword, but "the devouring fire" was made an instrument whereby "the rejoicing city that dwelt carelessly was made a desolation, a place for beasts to lie down." "She is empty and void and waste." (Nahum ii. 9, 10.) "Neither Botta nor Layard found any of that store of silver and gold and 'pleasant furniture' which the palaces contained; scarcely anything, even of bronze, escaped the spoiler, but he unconsciously left what is still more valuable; for to the falling in of the roofs of the buildings, by his setting fire to the columns and beams that supported them, and his subsequent destruction of the walls, we are indebted for the extraordinary preservation of the sculptures." A like testimony to the "sure word of prophecy" comes from the shapeless heaps of rubbish which mark the site where once stood "the lady of kingdoms," "the glory of the Chaldees' excellency." In her fate the seemingly opposite declarations of the prophet Jeremiah (li. 42, 43) have both been exactly accomplished. "The sea is come upon Babylon," while she is also "a desolation, a dry land, and a wilderness." "From the summit of the Birs Nimrod," says Dr. Layard, "I gazed over a vast marsh, for Babylon is made 'a possession for the bittern and pools of water.' In the midst of the swamps could be faintly distinguished the mat huts of the Kazail, forming villages on the small islands. The green morass was spotted with herds of the black buffalo. Light boats were skimming to and fro over the shallow water."

It is remarkable that in the region around these fallen seats of ruined empire, as in the case of Syria, the same unchanging frame-work of oriental life, its manners and customs, still exists, as when the Bible was written. There are still the lodges in the cucumber gardens which Isaiah describes; the oxen still tread out the corn; the vessels of bulrushes may still be seen; and the wild asses of the desert so poetically alluded to by Job, still watch the traveller from the distance, pause for him to draw near, and then gallop away to the shadowy horizon. The hot, stifling breath of the easterly wind or *sherki*, from which Jonah so grievously suffered, is still found singularly relaxing and dispiriting. Though three thousand years have passed away, the very scenes of the Old Testament are here faithfully reproduced, while, as if to confound the folly of modern scepticism, the famous capitals which were the seats of mighty kings, "when Egypt with Assyria strove in wealth and luxury," have been summoned from their graves. "The stone *hath* cried out of the wall, and the beam out of the timber *hath* answered it."

CHAPTER XII.

ARCHÆOLOGICAL DISCOVERIES—NEW TESTAMENT.

But the aim of the rationalistic school is not merely to destroy the historical character of the Old Testament. In the hands of Strauss, as has been already noticed, and of writers who have followed him, the New Testament also has been idealized. The incarnation of our Lord, His descent from David, the circumstances of His nativity, His temptation, transfiguration, His most remarkable miracles, including those attested by all the Evangelists,—all become mere myths, and never possessed an historical existence. The fact of His death is accepted, but His resurrection is a mere vision due to the excited imagination of His followers. And that death—how different the view in which the ideologists regard it, from that which brings heavenly peace and immortal hope to the soul of the believer! "The blood of sprinkling, the Cross of Calvary, the pierced hands, the wounded side—these have vanished from their eyes; they may suit inferior minds, incapable of supporting the clear atmosphere and unimpeded vision into which they think themselves to have entered."[1] They would have a Christianity without Christ.

Yet the internal evidence of the New Testament History alone could extort from the infidel Rousseau such a confession as the following: "If this be a fiction, the inventor is yet more wondrous than the hero of the narrative." If there were no other proof of the reality of the

[1] Bishop Wilberforce.

Gospel history than the character which the four Evangelists have ascribed to Christ, that alone would furnish evidence beyond all cavil and doubt.

"The brightness of the brightest names," says a great writer, "pales and wanes before the radiance which shines from the person of Christ. The scenes at the tomb of Lazarus, at the gate of Nain, in the happy family at Bethany, in the upper room, where He instituted the beautiful feast which should forever consecrate His memory, and bequeathed to His disciples the legacy of His love; the scenes in the garden of Gethsemane, on the summit of Calvary and at the sepulchre; the sweet remembrance of the patience with which He bore wrong, the gentleness with which He rebuked it, and the love with which He forgave it; the thousand acts of benign condescension by which He well earned for Himself, from self-righteous pride and censorious hypocrisy, the name of 'the friend of publicans and sinners;' these and a hundred things more which crowd those concise memorials of love and sorrow with such prodigality of beauty and pathos, will still continue to charm and attract the soul of humanity, and on these the highest genius as well as the humblest mediocrity will love to dwell. These things lisping infancy loves to hear on its mother's knee, and over them age, with its gray locks, bends in devoutest reverence. No; before the infidel can prevent the influence of these compositions, he must get rid of the Gospels themselves, or he must supplant them by fictions far more wonderful! Ah! what bitter irony has involuntarily escaped me! But if the last be impossible, at least the Gospels must cease to exist before Infidelity can succeed. Yes, before Infidels can prevent men from thinking as they ever have done of Christ, they must blot out the gentle words with which, in the presence of austere hypocrisy, the Saviour welcomed that timid guilt that could only express its silent love in an agony of tears; they must blot out the words addressed to the dying penitent, who, softened by the majestic patience of the mighty sufferer, detected at last the monarch under the veil of sorrow, and cast an imploring glance to be 'remembered by Him when He came into His kingdom;' they must blot out the scenes in which the demoniacs, or the maniacs, if the infidel will, for it does not help him—sat listening at His feet and 'in their right mind;' they must blot out the remembrance of the tears which He shed at the grave of Lazarus, not surely for him whom He was about to raise, but in pure sympathy with the sorrows of humanity, for the myriad myriads of desolate mourners, who could not with Mary fly to Him and say, 'Lord, if thou hadst been here, my mother —brother—sister—had not died!' They must blot out the record of those miracles which charm us not only as the proofs of His mission and guarantees of the truth of His doctrine, but as they illustrate the benevolence of His character, and are types of the spiritual cures His Gospel can yet perform; they must blot out the scenes of the sepulchre, where love and veneration lingered, and saw what has never been before, but shall henceforth be seen till the end of time,—the tomb itself irradiated with angelic forms and bright with the presence of Him 'who brought life and immortality to light;' they must blot out the scenes where deep and grateful love wept so passionately, and found them unbidden at her side,—type of ten thousand times ten thousand, who have 'sought the grave to weep there,' and found joy and consolation in Him 'whom though unseen they loved;'—they must blot out the discourses in which He took leave of His disciples, the majestic accents of which have filled so many departing souls with patience and with triumph; they must blot out the yet sublimer words in which He declares Himself 'the Resurrection and the Life'—words which have led so many millions more to breathe out their spirits with child-like trust, and to believe, as the gate of death closed behind them, they would see Him who is invested with 'the keys of the invisible world,' 'who opens and no man shuts, who shuts and no man opens,' letting in through the portal which leads to immortality 'the radiance of the skies;' they must blot out, they must destroy these and a thousand other such things, before they can prevent Him from having the pre-eminence who loved, because He loved us, to call Himself the 'Son of Man,' though angels called Him the 'Son of God.'"[1]

If all this be mythical, whence, let us ask, did the disciples of Christ draw the conception of the character of their Master? "It is a character so transcendently original in its mere conception, so thoroughly and profoundly consistent in its working out, so remarkable for its combination of seemingly opposite traits—so full of a mingled majesty and loveliness, firmness and gentleness, candor and reserve, and so radically free from every morbid tendency or sentiment, from fanaticism, pride, impetuosity, weakness, or one-sidedness of any kind, that, if not drawn from the life, it is the most stupendous and wonderful piece of art that was ever exhibited by the human mind. We may search the records of ancient and modern literature in vain to find anything like it." "It is related of a celebrated Grecian sculptor, that he searched all Greece with the view of modelling a perfect figure, and he borrowed here from the most beautiful a feature, and there from the most graceful a limb; but after all the patchwork was apparent; he could not so harmonize the different lineaments and members as to give congruity and symmetry to the whole; and just so the attempt to construct a perfect character out of virtues borrowed from all the best of human kind has ever failed, because men cannot combine, and adjust, and harmonize the materials. Under these circumstances, in the face of difficulties so insuperable, how could it have entered into

[1] Defence of the Eclipse of Faith by Rev. Henry Rogers.

the minds of a few Jewish fishermen, without education, without advantages of refinement or taste—men brought up in prejudice and bigotry—how could it have entered into their minds to conceive the idea of drawing, or, conceiving it, what possibility was there of their being able to draw a faultless character? And yet these fishermen of Galilee not only conceived, but realized the idea; they painted one of whom we may say, 'Behold the Lamb of God;' 'a lamb without blemish and without spot.' 'Behold the man!' 'holy, harmless, undefiled, and separate from sinners.'"[1] Surely there must have been a living model from which they drew. Truly says Neander, "As man's limited intellect could never, without the aid of God's revelation of Himself to the spirit of man, have originated the idea of God, so the image of Christ could never have sprung from the consciousness of sinful humanity, but must be regarded as the reflection of the actual life of such a Christ. It is Christ's self-revelation, made, through all generations, in the fragments of His history that remain, and in the workings of His Spirit which inspires these fragments, and enables us to recognize in them one complete whole."[2]

What honest and candid mind can avoid the conviction that if the Gospel narrative be a fiction, then is all history a fiction?

But in its behalf also, "truth has sprung out of the earth." While the historic verity of the Old Testament has been vindicated by exhumed remains of long lost cities in the depths of Asia, fresh confirmations of the historic character of the New have been brought to light from beneath the foundations of the old seven hilled city of the Cæsars.

So crowded is Rome with the treasured relics of the Past—so manifold the attractions of her temples, palaces and galleries of art—that few comparatively of those that

[1] Rev. H. Stowell. [2] Life of Christ, p. 6.

visit the Eternal City, bestow a thought upon the far more marvellous antiquities which lie beneath the streets they daily tread or under the majestic buildings whose objects of interest they eagerly explore.

It has long been known that Rome is undermined by subterranean excavations, but very indefinite views prevailed as to their extent and the ancient memorials which they concealed. Recent explorations have ascertained that they form a network beneath Rome and the Campagna of nearly nine hundred miles in extent, their narrow chambers in some parts rising in stories one above another, and that they formed a refuge and burial place for Christians during the persecutions of the first three centuries.

Evidence of the highest value in establishing the historical character of the religion of the New Testament, has been thence obtained. The following summary has been derived from the valuable Bampton lectures of Mr. Rawlinson, and it will be seen that the discoveries admit of no other inference than that in the first, second and third centuries, the facts of the New Testament were accepted as historical verities, and hence that there was no possible period when myths could have arisen.

Following out in detail the evidence of the Catacombs, Mr. Rawlinson holds it to be in the first place conclusive as to the vast numbers of Christians in the early ages—ages when there was nothing to tempt men, and everything to disincline them, towards embracing the persecuted faith. The calculation that the Catacombs contain seven millions of graves would imply, for the four hundred years they were in use, an average population of from 500,000 to 700,000,—an amount immeasurably beyond any estimate that has hitherto been made of Roman Christians at any portion of the period. Allowing the calculation of the number of graves to be somewhat exaggerated, and the proportion of deaths to the population under the circumstances to be unusually large, still the evidence cf vast numbers which the Catacombs furnish cannot wholly mislead. They establish, beyond all reasonable doubt, that in spite of the general contempt and hatred, in spite of the constant ill usage to which they were exposed, and the occasional fiery trials which proved them, the Christians, as early as the second century, formed one of the chief elements in the population of Rome.

Secondly, he holds that the Catacombs afford conclusive proof of the dangers and sufferings to which the early Christians were exposed. Without assuming that the phials which have contained a red liquid, found in so many of the tombs, must have held blood, and that therefore they are certain signs of martyrdom, and without regarding the palm branch as an unmistakable evidence of the same, the Catacombs yet furnish evidence confirmatory of those writers who estimate at the highest the number of Christians who suffered death in the great persecutions. The number of graves taken at the lowest, compared with the highest estimate of the Christian population that is at all probable, would give a proportion of deaths to population enormously above the average,—a result which at any rate lends support to those who assert that in the persecutions of Aurelius, Decius, Diocletian, and others, vast multitudes of Christians were massacred. Further, the word martyr is frequent upon the tombs; and often, when it is absent, the inscription otherwise shows that the deceased lost his life on account of his religion, and opens to us, besides the individual buried, a long vista of similar sufferers—as when one of Aurelius' victims exclaims—"O unhappy times, in which amid our sacred rites and prayers,—in the very caverns,—we are not safe! What is more wretched than our life? What more wretched than a death, when it is impossible to obtain burial at the hands of friends or relatives? Still at the end they shine like stars in Heaven. A poor life is his who has lived in Christian times!"

Thirdly, he holds that the Catacombs furnish a certain amount of evidence with respect to the belief of the early Christians. The doctrine of the resurrection is implied or expressed on almost every tombstone which has been discovered. The Christian is not dead—he "rests" or "sleeps;" he is not buried, but "*deposited*" in his grave; and he is always at peace (in pace). The survivors do not mourn his loss despairingly, but express trust, resignation, moderate grief. The anchor, indicative of the Christian's sure and certain hope, is a common emblem; and the phœnix and peacock are used as more speaking signs of the resurrection. The cross appears, though not the crucifix; and other emblems are employed, as the dove and the cock, which indicate belief in the sacred narrative as we possess it. There are also a certain number of pictures in the Catacombs, and these represent ordinarily, historical scenes from the Old or New Testament, treated in a uniform and conventional way, but clearly expressive of belief in the facts thus represented. The temptation of Eve, Moses striking the rock, Noah welcoming the return of the dove, Elijah ascending to heaven, Daniel among the lions, &c., are the favorite subjects from the Old Testament; while from the New Testament we find the adoration of the wise men, the interview with Herod, the baptism of Christ by John the Baptist, the healing of the paralytic, the turning of the water into wine, the feeding of the five thousand, the raising of Lazarus, the Last Supper, and many other miracles and facts of Gospel History. These early artists never tire of repeating the type of "the Good Shepherd," and ofttimes the sower appears going forth to sow, and the wise and foolish virgins with their lamps. Thus from these ancient and long hidden sepulchral remains, we derive indisputable evidence that the historic belief of the early Church was identical with that of orthodox Christendom at the present day.

Still more recently, a remarkable discovery has been made in Rome, affording another striking confirmation of the truth of Revelation. The following account of it is from an article in a late number of the Edinburgh Review on what are technically called the *graffiti* of Pompeii. These graffiti are the writings upon the street corners and places of public resort, which are now disclosed to the world, and throw great light upon the habits, tastes and manners of the ancients. The reviewer says:

"Mention has been made more than once of *graffiti* lately discovered in other localities, and especially at Rome. Of these, the most important have been found in the substruction of the palace of the Cæsars, recently excavated. It would carry us entirely beyond our allotted limits to describe these in detail. Some of them, indeed, were discovered several years since, and are embodied in P. Garucci's general collection. But there is one so exceedingly remarkable, and indeed of so deep and peculiar an interest, that it would be unpardonable to pass it over.

"The apartment in which it was found is one of several (now subterranean) chambers on the Palatine, which, in the course of the many alterations and extensions of plan during the progress of the building of the palace, were dismantled and filled up in order to form substructions for a new edifice to be erected on a higher level. The light and air being effectually excluded by this process, the walls have remained to this day in a state of preservation little inferior to that of the buildings of Pompeii. The particular apartment in question having been opened in December, 1856, some traces of Greek characters were observed upon the wall; and, on a fuller examination by P. Garucci, who was attracted to the spot by the news of the discovery, these characters proved to be an explanatory legend written beneath a rude sketch upon the wall, in which P. Garucci at once recognized a pagan caricature of the crucifixion of our Lord, and of the Christians' worship of their crucified God. This blasphemous sketch represents a figure with arm uplifted and outstretched (as if in the act of kissing the hand, a recognized attitude of worship or adoration), turned towards a cross, upon which is suspended a human figure with the head of a horse, or perhaps of an *onager*, or wild ass.

"If any doubt can be entertained as to the purport of this sketch, it would be dispelled by the legend underneath:

'ALEXAMINUS WORSHIPS GOD.'

Who this Alexaminus may have been, and what may have been the special occasion (if, indeed, there were any) of this rude caricature, it is of course impossible now to conjecture. From the name it may be inferred that, like a large proportion of the Christians of Rome in the early centuries, he was a Greek, and perhaps a slave. But whatever may be said as to the individual on whom it was meant to be a satire, the singular *graffito*, thus unexpectedly brought to light after so many centuries, is at once a most interesting illustration of the struggle between the Christianity of that early age and its yet powerful and contemptuous rival, and a literal verification of one of the most striking passages in the 'Apology' of Tertullian. It is impossible to doubt that this blasphemous caricature is, in one of its forms, the actual reality to which Tertullian alludes. It is not alone that this father defends himself and his fellow Christians from the general charge of having an ass's head as their God, and that he retorts upon the pagans themselves their charge against the Christians of 'being superstitious respecting the cross,' by showing that the pagans also worshipped the cross when they erected trophies, or took the military oaths upon their standards; he describes something closely resembling *the very picture which we have here before us in this rude graffito*, as a caricature of the Christian worship which was then popular among the pagan calumniators.

"We forbear to touch the higher associations which this strange discovery presses upon the mind. But even as a purely historical monument, the most unimaginative reader will regard it with the deepest interest. It opens to us with a distinctness which no written record could supply, a glimpse into those dark days of the infant Church, while her divine founder was still 'a folly to the Gentile,' and while it was still possible to present him to the popular mind of paganism under the hideous type of *folly* which is here depicted in all its revolting coarseness."

Our proposed comparison of the discoveries of science and the results of historic research and inquiry with the statements of the Bible, has here reached its termination; and we trust it has been shown that the Bible has stood every test which the refined scepticism of the present age has brought against it—the closer its claims have been scrutinized, the more triumphant has been its vindication. Did infidelity aspire to make its home among the stars? The glorious orbs of heaven have uttered solemn harmonies to redemption's anthem. Driven from thence, did it seek to erect a fortress down in the recesses of the earth? The rocks have uttered their testimony that the Author of creation and of revelation must be the same. Did it then strive to build up an array of proof that mankind was not a race of one blood and one brotherhood? Physiology has uttered her assent to the declaration of Scripture that "God has made of one blood all nations of men for to dwell upon the face of the earth," while other sciences have yielded a confirmatory testimony. The long successions of Oriental dynasties—the calculations of eclipses and planetary conjunctions—the Egyptian Zodiacs—with which it was sought to overthrow the Mosaic account of the world's duration, when examined by the light of true science, vanished into air, or rather went to confirm the Scripture narrative. And other objections with which it has been sought to impugn its credibility, have been found to supply internal evidence of its truth. And when a new school of philosophic scoffers has risen, who would treat the histories of the Bible as fables and its narratives of miraculous occurrences as myths, a species of evidence has been brought to light, precisely adapted to meet the emergency. Accomplished travellers have traversed to and fro through the lands of the East, and have returned to tell us that the Bible is, as it were, written upon the scenes which they have visited. The key to the Coptic tablets has been discovered, and across the gulf of forty centuries, the inscriptions have been read. The gates of Mount Seir have opened to disclose the rock-built palaces of Edom. The old cities of Bashan and Moab have been found still standing in massive greatness almost as they were in the days of Moses and Joshua. The mysterious mounds by the Tigris and Euphrates have been explored, and the old palaces of Assyrian and Chaldean monarchs have revealed their magnificence and grandeur. All there are like witnesses summoned from the grave. Their evidence is contemporaneous with the Scriptures, and it cannot be gainsayed or disputed. And what is their testimony? Wherever the same points are touched, it confirms the statements of the sacred records. It is thus found to the confusion of the infidel that if miracles are not now wrought to attest the truth of revelation, yet illustrations and evidences marvellous and manifold are laid up in the earth around him, and are brought forth at the moment of exigency, to vindicate the divinity of the Bible and to shed new beauty upon its hallowed pages.

APPENDIX.

THE AUTHENTICITY AND GENUINENESS OF THE SACRED WRITINGS.

Were the books of Holy Scripture the productions of the writers whose names they bear, and have they come down to us in a genuine and unadulterated form?

In the preceding pages, whose particular object it has been to vindicate the truth and authority of the Bible as a revelation from God, the affirmative of this question is necessarily assumed and implied. Its demonstration has occupied the labors of numerous scholars of the highest eminence, who have unanswerably shown that the authenticity and genuineness of the inspired oracles are sustained by a force and accumulation of evidence to which neither the Commentaries of Cæsar, the Æneid of Virgil, nor any of the classical writings of antiquity can even approach.

As this is, however, a fundamental point, and many readers are probably unacquainted with the facts and arguments by which the conclusion is reached, it is deemed proper to subjoin a brief sketch of the grounds upon which the learned consider the question as set at rest.

We will first inquire how we are to satisfy ourselves that we now possess the canonical writings of the Old Testament?

Canon is a Greek word signifying rule, and is used figuratively of that which governs or determines. As the Sacred Scriptures were at a very early period carefully distinguished from all human writings, and as they formed the only rule of faith and practice which Christians regarded as authoritative or safe, they were soon designated as the "canon," *i. e.*, the rule of God.

As to the present canon of the Old Testament, it is generally admitted that its formation is to be traced to Ezra and the prophets who returned with him to Babylon. This is the uniform tradition of the Jews, and it is strengthened by the fact that there were no prophets after Malachi, who was a contemporary of Ezra, and consequently no authority sufficient for the purpose. Josephus, moreover, distinctly states that after the time of Artaxerxes (the age of Ezra and Nehemiah), there had been no addition to the Jewish sacred books. "Fact has shown what confidence we place in our writings, for although so many ages have passed away, no one has dared to add to them, nor to take away any thing from them, or to make alterations."

To this collection of the inspired oracles, which were arranged in three classes, the Law, the Prophets, and the Sacred Writings, our Lord Jesus Christ and his apostles gave their explicit sanction. Our Saviour frequently reproved the Jews for disobeying and misinterpreting the sacred Scriptures, and adding their traditions thereto, but he never charged them with unfaithfulness or negligence in preserving the sacred books. On the contrary, he often speaks of the Scriptures (that is, of the Scriptures as then known) as an infallible rule which could not be broken, and from which not one jot or tittle should pass till all should be fulfilled. To these Scriptures he ever refers as the unerring truth of God. And so also the apostle Paul, alluding chiefly, if not wholly, to the Old Testament writings, says "all Scripture is given by inspiration of God," and again he speaks of them as "the oracles of God" and as "the teachings of the Holy Ghost." The testimony of the other apostles is equally plain and explicit. One important point, then, is established with the utmost certainty: that the volume of Scripture which existed in the time of Christ and his apostles was uncorrupted by the presence of any spurious works, and that the whole of it was expressly declared by them to be in-inspired and infallible. The question, then, becomes a mere question of fact; for if we can ascertain what were the particular books which were at that time received and known by the Jews as the Scriptures, we shall know with absolute certainty what books constitute the inspired canon of the Old Testament. If Christ and his apostles had given us the names of every one of the books then known as parts of the Old Testament, the question would at once be settled. But this they have not done. They have, indeed, distinctly quoted from several of these books, and so far the evidence is complete. And, more than this, they have recognized as inspired all the works known to the Jews of their day as "the Scriptures;" and still more particularly as "the Law," "the Prophets," and "the Psalms." But all this, even, is not of itself sufficient to inform us whether the Old Testament then contained precisely the same books that it now does, and no others; so that the question still remains, What were the books which all the Jews of that day received as included in the Scriptures in the threefold division which has just been mentioned? To ascertain this point, we should naturally resort, if possible, to the testimony of some Jew then living, just as, if we held any doubts of the orations of Cicero being rightly ascribed to him, we should examine the pages of contemporaneous history. In Josephus, the celebrated Jewish historian, who was contemporary with the apostles, we have the witness, and find the very information which we desire. He does not, indeed, name all the books of the Old Testament, but then he numbers and otherwise so accurately describes them, that there is no room for mistake. "We have," says he, in his first book against Apion, "only twenty-two books which we hold to be of divine origin, and which we are bound to believe. Of these, *five* are the books of Moses, which treat of the creation of the world, &c. From the death of Moses to the reign of Artaxerxes, king of Persia, the Prophets who succeeded Moses have written in *thirteen* books, and the remaining *four* books contain divine poems or hymns to God, and moral precepts or rules of life for men." According to the method of arrangement formerly in use among the Jews, the twenty-two books mentioned by Josephus, though numbered differently, are, in fact, precisely the same with those of the Old Testament as now received by us. Shakspeare or Blackstone's Commentaries is still the same work whether in one or in four volumes; and so is the Old Testament whether arranged in twenty-two or in thirty-nine divisions. The whole argument, in a word, then, is this: Jesus Christ and His Apostles expressly and repeatedly declared that the Scriptures, as received by the Jews at the time when they lived, were inspired. Jewish history written at that very time informs us what books *were* then contained in the Jewish Scriptures. These books, though differently arranged and numbered, are found, on examination, to be the very same which are contained in our English version of the Old Testament. Therefore, the Old Testament, as received by us, is expressly sanctioned by Jesus Christ and His Apostles, its canonical authority is established, and to every book of it we may safely trust as the inspired words of the Holy Spirit.

To the Christian believer, this testimony of the Saviour and His Apostles is abundantly sufficient. It is necessary, however, to use another method to parry the assault of the infidel, who asserts that these sacred books are forgeries, and that their author or authors surreptitiously palmed them off upon the ignorance and credulity of the Jewish people.

This charge is conclusively met and its absurdity demonstrated, in the following admirable argument condensed from the Evidences of Dr. Gregory.

"No forgery was ever yet so complete as wholly to escape detection for any great length of time. In fictitious works, even in those in which most particularities abound, there is a frequent want of proportion and coherency of parts, so as to prove a deficiency of invention in the grouping and consistency of the events. There must certainly always be some truth, where many particularities respecting time, place, and persons are related, and in which consistency is observable; but where all or most of these are absent, the inference is, that the account or history must necessarily be far from authentic, and, of course, fictitious or a narrative combined of fact and fiction. Writers of avowed fiction, however true to nature, are frequently careless respecting such consistency; but writers, or rather forgers, of what they wish to pass in the world as authentic, because anxious about consistency, are careful to avoid striking particularities, since critical readers might easily find important errors and inconsistencies not obvious to every eye. And further, when it is considered, what an amount of minute knowledge is required in writing history, to furnish particularities—so as to be accurate in giving names of persons, in stating times and describing places and events—it will appear evident, that no mere forger or writer of superficial narrative, to suit a certain base purpose, could create them and make a show of consistency in every part, so as to impose such history upon the intelligent world as genuine and authentic. But, on the other hand, if the writers themselves had been, though in different times and places, concerned in the events narrated, or eye-witnesses of the events as they occurred, or stated clearly, simply, and impartially the stories they had received from truthful testimony, the particularities related would bear the impression of consistency and truth. And, again, if forgers, hazarding the setting forth of such particularities in their narratives, were certain of the fraud being detected by common readers thousands of years after their death, they must, *à fortiori*, have been certain of their fraud being detected and exposed when first published by the persons who, like the forgers themselves, had been concerned in the transactions and witnesses of the events recorded. When, therefore, such witnesses, and these to the number of thousands, concerned in the events, could, when the histories were written and preserved among the archives of their race as of all but infinite importance, detect neither fraud, misstatement nor imposture; and when, moreover, the internal evidence has been, and is such, that no subsequent critics or commentators could, upon comparison of books, or dates, or circumstances, wring one single error or contradiction from their pages, the fact of their authenticity and genuineness becomes still more striking and incontrovertible.

"Apply these criteria to the books of the Old Testament and the result will be demonstrative of their authenticity. Not only do they contain the names of the persons who wrote the various books, known in their own various ages as the authors of them, and recognized as the writers of undoubted truths, but they abound in those particularities with regard to times, places, and events of the most note and importance in relation to the human race, without which no history can be authentic and genuine. Look to the particular account of the creation and the fall,—of the deluge, the building of Babel, the dispersion of mankind, and the short duration of human life after the deluge;—look to the accounts of the successive patriarchs, the interesting history of Joseph in Egypt, the sojourn in that country of the Israelites, and their escape from the tyranny of Pharaoh, and their long journeyings in the wilderness, marked by such marvellous events, before they entered the promised land;—look to the history of the Israelites afterwards, their various offences against God, both in the times of the Judges and the Kings, and their as signal punishment and subsequent captivity in Babylon: and in connection with all these events, look at the accuracy of geographical detail, which no geographer, ancient or modern, from Strabo down to the present day, could prove erroneous; and consider also that the Jewish historians and prophets were not depicting the manners and customs, or chronicling the deeds of Gentile nations, but of their own peculiar people,—and then mark the impartiality of their narratives—the simplicity with which they record their iniquities against God, as well as their obedience to His laws, and the manner in which they state the nature and extent of the awarded punishments;—look to all those features and consider whether any profane histories, such as those of Thucydides or Tacitus in ancient, or of Clarendon or Hume in modern times, all received as genuine, and in most part authentic, show such internal evidences of authenticity, and then say, after all this, whether or not the sacred Scriptures can be forgeries!

"Forgeries are never committed without some particular motive, or without some probability of success. But the sacred writers could not be influenced by any such motives as those of literary vanity, pecuniary gain, or a desire through their histories to perpetuate national glory; and when writing for their own people accounts of themselves, and the events distinguishing them as a people chosen of God for a particular purpose, they must be afflicted with no common blindness, who can imagine them to have written falsehoods. As the characters of all authors are some guarantee for the honesty or otherwise of their productions, it cannot be denied by even the enemies of Scripture, that the books of both the Old and New Testaments are written in the highest style of morality, and that, hence, the writers themselves were men of the highest characters. Otherwise their books would not have been treasured by the people, and been regarded for so many centuries as the archives of their history and of their laws, rites and ceremonies, and revered with a degree of inalienable affection, which persecutions, proscriptions, and massacres could not quench, nor even weaken. And, further, as those writers or books possess such diversity of style, as to prove them the work of no single Jew, or of any one age, and as allusions are frequently made to each other by successive writers, it would inevitably follow, if the books were forgeries, that there must have existed a number of impostors in successive ages from Moses to Malachi, a period of one thousand and fifty-four years, all animated by one spirit, as if the living and dead were in actual collusion, all writing in harmony and having reference, more or less, to one great and absorbing event, seen prophetically in the far distance, and yet all proclaiming the iniquity of their own people, and threatening them with, and warning them of, impending woes and judgments. Now all this is absurd and incredible.

"But when could such forgeries have been written and imposed upon the Jews as genuine and authentic histories and prophecies? Before or after the Babylonish captivity? Not assuredly before it, because the imposition thus practised upon the minds and belief of a whole people would have been detected and exposed; and as assuredly not after it, as the Hebrew then ceased to be a spoken language. And as no Hebrew grammar existed till many ages afterwards, and it is difficult to write in a dead language, even with the help of a grammar, it is next to impossible to write without one. It is therefore plain that all the books of the Old Testament must have been written prior to the Babylonian captivity; and as, from internal evidence, they could not all have been written in the same age, and by one or more authors, some of them must have been written long previous to the others, and hence, if they be not genuine and authentic, we are again led back to a collusion of impostors living centuries apart, all resolved upon deceiving a whole people, who openly and willingly submitted to, and professedly believed in, the inconceivable deception; and who also transmitted it through their successors, amidst trying and singular events, to the present day.

"Admitting that some changes had necessarily taken place in the language during the thousand and fifty-four years between Moses and Malachi, the narrative styles of the various writers still retained the majesty and simplicity suitable for the people for whose more immediate information they wrote, and to the circumstances of the authors themselves. And this simple naturalness is alone sufficient to disprove the assertion of their being forged. The dramatic and sublime parts of Job, and much of the prophetic writings, may be less simple, and more glowing and figurative in style; but still this was natural in looking along the vistas of futurity, and deciphering in figures the threatenings of woe upon peoples and empires, and the promises of grace and peace to the followers of the 'Man of Sorrows;' whereas, a style strained and affected in even the loftiest narrative, proves that the writer is more anxious to display himself than his subject. But the Scripture narratives are models of simplicity and perfection. Nothing is affected—nothing is strained; the majesty of the subject is seen, and great truths are stated, and events narrated, with a force and clearness, often with a beauty and pathos which no other writers ever rivalled, whilst the writers themselves are personally, as authors, hid behind the veil."[1]

It is because they will not stand such tests as the above that the books termed the Apocrypha are by Protestants rejected from the sacred canon. The term Apocrypha is Greek, signifying *hidden* or *concealed*, and is applied to those books whose origin is unknown, or the authority of which is either doubtful or absolutely denied. The books

[1] McBurnie's Prize Essay on Infidelity.

in question were, most of them, the work of Jews in the century before Christ. Some of them, as Tobit, Susannah, and (as it is called by Jerome) the *fable* of Bel and the Dragon, &c., are religious romances. Some of the books contain false doctrine, as praying for the dead, praising suicide, &c.; and some are distinguished by anachronisms. Some of them contain much that is instructive, and have been held in high esteem by not a few of the greatest men in the Christian Church. But it is certain that they have never been considered as on a level with the Hebrew Bible. They never belonged to it. The Jews never acknowledged them as inspired writings. Philo and Josephus never mention them; the New Testament is altogether silent about them—never once quoting them. At length in the sixteenth century, the Council of Trent ventured to decree that they should be regarded as an integral part of the Word of God. By those, however, who do not accept the dogma of Papal infallibility, the judgment of St. Augustine will be regarded as carrying far more weight. "Let us," he says, "lay aside those books which have been called *apocryphal*, because their authors were not known to our fathers, who have by a constant and certain succession transmitted down to us the certainty and truth of the Holy Scriptures. Though some things in these apocryphal books are true, yet as there are in them multitudes of others which are false, they are of no authority."

"It is an important fact," says Dr. Alexander, "that a short time after the canon of the Old Testament was closed, a translation was made of the whole of the books into the Greek language. This translation was made at Alexandria, in Egypt, at the request, it is said, of Ptolemy Philadelphus, king of Egypt, that he might have a copy of these sacred books in the famous library which he was engaged in collecting. It is called The Septuagint, from its being made, according to the accounts which have been handed down, by seventy, or rather seventy-two, men; six from each of the tribes of Israel. So many fabulous things have been reported concerning this version, that it is very difficult to ascertain the precise truth. But it is manifest from internal evidence, that it was not the work of one hand, nor, probably, of one set of translators; for, while some books are rendered with great accuracy, and in a very literal manner, others are translated with little care, and the meaning of the original is very imperfectly given.

"The probability is, that the Pentateuch was first translated, and the other books were added from time to time, by different hands; but when the work was once begun, it is not likely that it would be long before the whole was completed.

"Now this Greek version contains all the books which are found in our canonical Hebrew Bibles. It is a good witness, therefore, to prove that all these books were in the canon when this version was made.

"There is, moreover, a distinct and remarkable testimony to the antiquity of the five books of Moses in the Samaritan Pentateuch, which has existed in a form entirely separate from the Jewish copies, and a character totally different from that in which the Hebrew Bible has been for many ages written. It has also been preserved and handed down to us by a people who have ever been hostile to the Jews. This Pentateuch has, without doubt, been transmitted through a separate channel, ever since the ten tribes of Israel were carried captive. It furnishes authentic testimony to the great antiquity of the books of Moses, and shows how little they have been corrupted, during the lapse of nearly three thousand years."

Overwhelming as is the train of evidences of the authenticity of the books of the Old Testament, the testimony in behalf of those of the New Testament is even yet more cogent and irresistible.

We have, it is true, no precise information as to when the New Testament canon was completed. There does not appear to have been any particular time or place in which the writings were collected and authenticated. From the manner in which they were at first circulated, some of them were necessarily longer of reaching certain places than others. Owing to this circumstance, and to that of a few of the books being addressed to individual believers, or to their not having the name of their writers affixed or the designation of the apostle added, a doubt for a time existed among some respecting the genuineness of the Epistle to the Hebrews, the Epistle of James, the second Epistle of Peter, the second and third Epistles of John, the Epistle of Jude, and the Book of Revelation. These, however, though not universally, were generally acknowledged; while all the other books of the New Testament were without dispute received from the beginning. The hesitation with which the claims of a portion of them were regarded in some places of the Christian world, is of itself a strong presumption that the universal and cordial reception which was given to all the other books of the New Testament, proceeded upon clear, incontestable evidence of their authenticity.

At length these books, which had not at first been admitted, were, like the rest, universally received, not by the votes of a council, as is sometimes asserted, but after deliberate and free inquiry by many separate churches, under the superintending providence of God, in different parts of the world. And it is certain, that though several Apocryphal writings were published under the name of Jesus Christ and His Apostles, most of which have perished, though some are still extant, yet no other books besides those which at present compose the volume of the New Testament, were admitted by the churches.

The arguments which sustain the authenticity of that

volume may be thus briefly summed up. Its several portions are quoted as the productions of the writers whose names they bear, by Christian authors of the first century, several of whom had known and conversed with the Apostles and immediate disciples of Christ. They were uniformly spoken of in terms expressive of the highest respect, as inspired compositions. They were publicly read and expounded in the religious assemblies of the early Christians. They were in very early times collected into a distinct volume, and distinguished by appropriate names and titles of respect. Commentaries were anciently composed upon them, harmonies were formed out of them, and translations of them were made into different languages. They were received, not only by orthodox Christians, but by heretics of various descriptions, and were appealed to as authorities in matters of doctrine and controversy. Even the early adversaries of Christianity, such as Julian and Porphyry, have never questioned the genuineness of the sacred books, but speak of the Gospels as the composition of the Evangelists. And formal catalogues of the Scripture were formed by private individuals and by councils, from which it appears that the same books were then received which are at present acknowledged. In short, no evidence which the subject admits of is found wanting.

The impossibility of the New Testament being a forgery is thus forcibly demonstrated by Bishop Wilson. "The sacred books are either the productions of the Apostles and Evangelists, or they are a direct and bare-faced fabrication, composed by impostors of the apostolic or a succeeding age. Now, I affirm that it is morally impossible, from the circumstances of the case, that they could be false productions imposed upon the Christian Church. For, take what age you please, and tell me when such an attempt could have been made.

"Could it have been made during the lives of the Apostles? What! twenty-seven books, the production of eight distinct authors, palmed upon the very converts of those authors, with whom they were in constant intercourse, during the very period of that intercourse? The supposition refutes itself.

"But, could it have been in a subsequent age? Certainly not after the commencement of the third century, when the books were actually in circulation over the world, were read in the churches, transmitted by versions into new languages, and preserved as the most precious deposit in the Christian archives! Could false books have been imposed, under such circumstances, upon the wakeful minds of Christians, in every part of the world; and imposed on them, not only as inspired writings, but as the works of the Apostles and Evangelists, which had been received by their immediate parents and forefathers, as their sacred books, and had been handed down to them from the Apostles, from age to age? Incredible—absurd—morally impossible! Ten thousand voices would instantly have cried out that they had never heard of such books previous to their production by the supposed impostor.

"Then the only time when a forgery of such magnitude appears even possible, is between the death of the Apostles and the period of the universal diffusion of the books. But St. John lived till quite the close of the first century—his own disciple, Polycarp, till beyond the middle of the second—and Irenæus, the disciple of Polycarp, to the commencement of the third; when Tertullian and a host of witnesses put the supposition of forgery quite out of the question. Can any one imagine, that during this brief period a daring falsification, such as we are considering, could have been made—a falsification which must at least have demanded a long series of ages—much obscurity—many favorable opportunities, to have been attempted even as to a single book out of the twenty-seven, in a single community, out of the thousands which overspread, according to all testimony, the Roman empire, by the beginning of the second century!

"But not only so. Christianity was planted in the midst of enemies and persecutors. Christianity raised its head amidst Judaism and heathen idolatry. Christianity was assaulted for three hundred years by a succession of violent and cruel and unjust persecutions. Christianity was never without some false disciples in its own bosom, watchful to seize every advantage. It was morally impossible that any fraud should have escaped, not only discovery, but that public exposure and disgrace from all parties, which attend on a detected imposition."

Having ascertained to our satisfaction the authenticity of the books of the Old and New Testaments, we proceed to inquire whether they have come down to us with a *genuine* and *uncorrupted text?*

The importance of this inquiry will be readily seen. For although it is proved that the sacred books proceeded at first from the prophets or apostles whose names they bear, it may still be said that they may have been so altered since that time as to convey to us very false information with regard to their contents. Granted that they may have had the infallible guidance of the Spirit of God; yet if we have not the message as it was imparted to them, if in the course of time the Bible has been mutilated by the dropping out of precious words, while others have been interpolated, how can it command our homage or claim our confidence? Like a harp with broken and missing chords, it has lost its power to charm.

Still there is danger of misapprehension and unreasonable expectation upon this subject. It will not do to rest in the presumption that because God has given us a revelation, His providence would necessarily guard it from all injury, and cause it to be transmitted entire and uncorrupted to all coming generations. The analogy of nature does not support this presumption; for the best blessings of Heaven are abused and perverted by the vices and negligences of those upon whom they are bestowed, and the faults, political or moral, of one generation, entail their evil consequences upon generations following. As to the matter in question, it is an undeniable fact that there are numerous various readings both in the Old and New Testaments, which have been occasioned by frequent transcription. The inspired autographs have long ago perished, and the most ancient copies to which we have access exhibit many textual variations. No promise of infallibility was made to transcribers, and no pledge that the copy should be a perfect copy of the original. Hence that has befallen the Bible which is common to other books that have come down from antiquity. Many of the words and letters of the inspired pages are occasion of question and debate.

When the fact of the various readings was first made known in the course of the last century, it was a subject of triumph to the enemies of the Christian faith and a cause of some apprehension to its friends. It led, however, to a most thorough investigation of the state of the sacred text, and the result of the untiring labors of numerous great scholars has vindicated the inspired oracles on this point also. It is now conceded that, though there are numerous various readings, yet they are all of an exceedingly unimportant character. Referring to this subject, it is said by the learned Dr. Adam Clarke " that all the omissions of the ancient manuscripts put together, would not countenance the omission of any essential doctrine of the Gospel, relative to faith and morals, beyond what may be found in the Complutensian or Elzevir editions." The Jews, it is well known, were most scrupulous in preserving entire the works of their inspired writers, and in preventing the intrusion of literal errors into the copies which were from time to time transcribed. Among the means which they adopted to this end, was that of noting and recording the exact number of words, verses, points and accents, in each book. The duty of doing so was the province of the Jewish doctors or learned men, called Masorites. By these acute grammarians, all the verses of each book and of each section were numbered, and the amount placed at the end of each in numerical letters, or in some symbolical word formed out of them; the middle verse of each book was also marked, and even the very letters were numbered; and all this was done to preserve the text from any alteration by either fraud or negligence.

What has been said of the integrity of the text of the Old Testament, applies equally to that of the New. Though it must be admitted that the New Testament text, by being more frequently transcribed than the Old, became liable to a greater proportion of various readings, originating from the mistakes of the transcribers, yet this very circumstance was likewise a sure protection against wilful perversion or corruption; for in proportion as copies were multiplied, the difficulty of effecting a general corruption was increased. No such system as that of the Masorites was ever adopted to preserve the purity of the New Testament text, but there are not wanting ample means for ascertaining the true reading. More than three hundred and fifty ancient manuscript copies of the books of the New Testament, written in different ages and countries, have come down to us. There are numerous ancient translations, some of which were made as early as the second century. And a third source of correction exists in the numberless quotations from the New Testament with which the works of the Christian fathers and other early writers abound. In all these sources of evidence there is a substantial agreement, proving beyond dispute that the words spoken by the Saviour, and those written by the Apostles and Evangelists, have come down to us unchanged.

The arguments for the genuineness and authenticity of the Holy Scriptures require volumes in order fully to do them justice. They have been thus conclusively summed up by Isaac Taylor, in the last chapter of his work on the Transmission of Ancient Books: "In the number and antiquity of manuscripts; in extent of early circulation; in the importance attached to them by their possessors; in the respect paid to them by copyists of later ages; in the various and conflicting sentiments of those who accepted the sacred writings as the rule of faith; in the visible effects of these books from age to age; in the body of references and quotations; in the number of early versions; in the peculiar circumstances connected with the extinction, as vernacular idioms, of the languages in which the originals were written; in the means of comparison with spurious or rival compositions; in the strength of the inference from the genuineness to the credibility of the books; in all these points, the comparative weight of evidence in favor of the records of Christianity, is incontrovertibly and immeasurably greater than that which is allowed, without a scruple, in the instance of the remains of profane antiquity."

THE END.

THE TRIUMPHS OF THE BIBLE,

WITH THE TESTIMONY OF SCIENCE TO ITS TRUTH.

BY REV. HENRY TULLIDGE. 1 vol. 12mo. $1 50.

Extracts from Testimonials, etc.

From the Rt. Rev. ALONZO POTTER, D.D., LL.D., *Bishop of the Diocese of Pennsylvania.*

The Rev. Mr. Tullidge has written a work on *Modern Unbelief* and its objections, with which, from a cursory examination, I have been favorably impressed, and which I think peculiarly calculated to arrest and multiply readers. It is spirited, forcible, and enlivened as well as graced by many quotations from the best writers. It seems to me fitted to command an extensive sale.

Yours truly,

PHILADELPHIA, *Sept. 24th*, 1862. ALONZO POTTER.

From the Rt. Rev. W. H. ODENHEIMER, D.D., *Bishop of the Diocese of New Jersey.*

From an examination of the Rev. Mr. Tullidge's work, I am prepared to express my favorable opinion of its merits and of its adaptation to the wants of Biblical scholars at the present time.

BURLINGTON, N. J., *Jan.* 1863. W. H. ODENHEIMER.

From the Rev. S. H. TYNG, D.D., *Rector of St. George's Church, New York.*

The Rev. Henry Tullidge, long and well known to me, has prepared a very compact and extended work on the Triumphs of the Bible, &c., designed to illustrate the complete vindication of its historic truth from all the discoveries of modern investigations. The scheme is laid out with skill, and from the superficial view I have been able to take of it, connected with my knowledge of the ability of its author, I cannot doubt that the work will prove useful and desirable.

ST. GEORGE'S RECTORY, *Jan. 7th*, 1863. S. H. TYNG.

From the Rev. ISAAC FERRIS, D.D., LL.D., *Chancellor of the University of the City of New York.*

I cheerfully add my commendation of Mr. Tullidge's work to that of Dr. Tyng.

ISAAC FERRIS.

UNIVERSITY OF THE CITY OF NEW YORK, *Jan. 9th*, 1863.

From the Rev. WILLIAM M. ENGLES, D.D., *Editor of the Presbyterian.*

REV. AND DEAR SIR:

I have examined the portion of the MS. which you left with me on the Triumphs of the Bible, &c., and feel free in expressing the opinion, that both in its plan and execution, it is admirably adapted to be a popular and useful work, impressive in its argument and calculated to interest all classes of readers. I remain,

Yours, very truly, WILLIAM M. ENGLES.

From the Rev. Henry A. Boardman, D.D., *Pastor of the Presbyterian Church, Corner of Twelfth and Walnut Streets, Philadelphia.*

On a cursory examination of the Rev. Mr. Tullidge's book on the Evidences of Christianity, I am very favorably impressed both with the plan of the work and the execution of the same. It will be found, I think, a useful aid in dealing with the shifting phases of modern Infidelity.

Philadelphia, *Oct. 31st*, 1862. HENRY A. BOARDMAN.

From the Rev. J. P. Durbin, D.D., *Secretary of Missionary Society of Methodist Episcopal Church.*

I have taken time and pains to examine largely the plan and the execution of "The Triumphs of the Bible, with the Testimony of Science to its Truth, by Rev. Henry Tullidge, A.M," and can commend it strongly. I know of no work that covers the same ground. That part of it on the Testimony of Science to the Authenticity of the Bible, is of great value.

New York, *Jan. 10th*, 1863. J. P. DURBIN.

From the Rev. Richard Newton, D.D., *Rector of the Church of the Epiphany, Philadelphia.*

I have examined with great interest portions of the MS. of the Rev. H. Tullidge's work on the "Triumphs of the Bible," &c., and the perusal of a part of it has given rise to an earnest desire to enjoy the pleasure of reading the whole. It will prove a very valuable addition to our works on the evidences of the divine origin of our holy religion. It will furnish most efficient aid to the lover of the Bible in defending it against the plausible attacks of infidelity in its latest developments. The student will prize it for its sound learning, the general reader will be interested and attracted by the lively and agreeable style in which it discusses the grave and important themes of which it treats. It can hardly fail to prove both a useful and a popular book.

RICHARD NEWTON.

From the Rev. G. Emlen Hare, D.D., *Professor of Biblical Learning in Philadelphia Divinity School.*

The subject of the book is most important. Mr. Tullidge's treatment of his theme bespeaks a man much acquainted with literature, and fluent in the use of the pen. And I am not without hope that the work will attract and benefit many readers.

G. EMLEN HARE.

From the Rev. Edward Lounsberry, *Rector of St. Jude's Church, Philadelphia.*

I fully concur with Dr. Newton in the conviction of the usefulness of Mr. Tullidge's work, and an earnest desire to see it given to the public in a permanent form. The field of inquiry is to some extent comparatively new; the style sufficiently attractive to ensure a reading; and the materials he has industriously collated such as cannot fail to interest and instruct. It is a book adapted to the times and to the general reader.

www.ingramcontent.com/pod-product-compliance
Lightning Source LLC
Chambersburg PA
CBHW030943110726
47900CB00004B/1113

* 9 7 8 3 3 3 7 0 3 5 1 8 1 *